# THE GREAT CHAIN OF BEING

# THE GREAT CHAIN OF BEING

*A Study of the History of an Idea*

THE WILLIAM JAMES LECTURES DELIVERED AT
HARVARD UNIVERSITY, 1933

BY

ARTHUR O. LOVEJOY

CAMBRIDGE · MASSACHUSETTS

HARVARD UNIVERSITY PRESS

ISBN 0-674-36153-9

THE William James Lectures on Philosophy and Psychology were established at Harvard in 1929 from a bequest of the late Edgar Pierce. The purpose of the Lectureship is to honor the memory of William James and at the same time provide public lectures and informal instruction by an eminent scholar not permanently connected with the University. Professor Lovejoy's lectures were given as the second series on this foundation in the second half of the academic year 1932–33.

# PREFACE

THE TITLE of this book, I find, seems to some not unlearned persons odd, and its subject unfamiliar. Yet the phrase which I have taken for the title was long one of the most famous in the vocabulary of Occidental philosophy, science, and reflective poetry; and the conception which in modern times came to be expressed by this or similar phrases has been one of the half-dozen most potent and persistent presuppositions in Western thought. It was, in fact, until not much more than a century ago, probably the most widely familiar conception of the general *scheme* of things, of the constitutive pattern of the universe; and as such it necessarily predetermined current ideas on many other matters.

The real oddity, then, is that its history has not previously been written and its meaning and implications analyzed. In now attempting this I shall be presenting what, I think, ought to be, but apparently are not, historical commonplaces; if they are not, I venture to hope that this book may help to make them such. Many separate parts of the history have, indeed, been told before, and are therefore presumably more or less familiar; it is their relation to a single pervasive complex of ideas — and thereby, often, to one another — that still seems to need to be set forth. That the use of the term "the chain of being" as the descriptive name for the universe was usually a way of predicating of the constitution of the world three specific, pregnant, and very curious characteristics; that these characteristics implied a certain conception of the nature of God; that this conception was for centuries conjoined with another to which it was in latent opposition — an opposition which eventually became overt; that most of the religious thought of the West has thus been profoundly at variance with itself; that with the same assumptions about the constitution of the world was associated an assumption about ultimate value, also in conflict with another and equally prevalent conception of the good — the former manifesting its full consequences only in the Romantic period; that this idea of value, together with the belief that the universe *is* what the term "the chain of being" implied that it is, provided the chief basis for most of the more serious attempts to solve the problem of evil and to show that the scheme of things is an intelligible and rational one; and that the same belief about the structure of nature lay in the background of much early modern science, and therefore influenced the formation of scientific hypotheses in various ways — these are some of the more general historical facts which I have attempted to exhibit and illustrate in some detail. This preliminary intimation of them may at least help the possible reader to judge whether any of the themes of the volume are of interest to him, and to facilitate the task of the reviewer — though, as a prudent author should, I have tried to avoid disclosing in a prefatory summary too much of the plot of the story to be told.

The history of this complex of ideas has seemed to me to suggest, if not to demonstrate, certain philosophical conclusions; and these I have tried to indicate in the "moral" appended to the final lecture. But they are, I realize, very inadequately set forth; to have developed them fully would have inordinately lengthened the volume.

The lectures are for the most part printed as they were orally delivered; but the liberality of the Syndics of the Harvard University Press has made it possible to expand them considerably, chiefly by the addition of more citations of illustrative passages. These last will, I dare say, seem to some readers too abundant. But in my own reading of works of this character I have often been exasperated by finding *précis* or paraphrases where I desiderated the actual language of the authors whose ideas were under consideration; and my rule has therefore been to give the words of relevant texts as fully as was consistent with reasonable brevity. On the other hand, no attempt has been made to include the whole mass of possible illustrations; the volume makes no pretension to be, even approximately, a *corpus* of the texts in which the central and the related ideas dealt with occur.

There is in the nature of the enterprise attempted a certain difficulty for which I hope the benevolent reader will make some allowance. The lectures were not designed for specialists in a single field, but for a mixed academic audience; and it is an essential part of the purpose of the book to pursue the ideas with which it is concerned into a number of distinct provinces of the history of thought. It has in consequence occasionally seemed advisable, when dealing with subjects belonging to one province, to explain certain matters which, to those especially conversant with that province, will need no explanation — but which may not be equally known to specialists in other fields, or to the " general reader."

Most of what is here printed as Lecture VII and some sentences of Lecture X have previously been published in the *Publications of the Modern Language Association of America*, vol. XLII, 1927.

My thanks are due to several colleagues and friends who have generously read in manuscript parts of the book on which their learning made them especially valuable critics and advisers. For such assistance I am particularly indebted to Dr. George Boas, Dr. Harold Cherniss, Dr. Robert L. Patterson, and Dr. Alexander Weinstein, of Johns Hopkins University, and Dr. Marjorie Nicolson of Smith College. I cannot refrain from expressing to the Harvard Department of Philosophy my high appreciation of the honor and privilege of presenting at Harvard, upon a lectureship bearing the name of William James, some slight fruits of the years since, in my philosophical novitiate, I first heard him exemplify in his incomparable way the meaning of "pragmatic openness of mind" and the possibility of fresh and revivifying approaches to man's ancient problems.

ARTHUR O. LOVEJOY

JOHNS HOPKINS UNIVERSITY
    *March, 1936*

# CONTENTS

# THE GREAT CHAIN OF BEING

# I

## INTRODUCTION

## THE STUDY OF THE HISTORY OF IDEAS

THESE lectures are primarily an attempt to offer a contribution to the history of ideas; and since the term is often used in a vaguer sense than that which I have in mind, it seems necessary, before proceeding to the main business in hand, to give some brief account of the province, purpose, and method of the general sort of inquiry for which I should wish to reserve that designation. By the history of ideas I mean something at once more specific and less restricted than the history of philosophy. It is differentiated primarily by the character of the units with which it concerns itself. Though it deals in great part with the same material as the other branches of the history of thought and depends greatly upon their prior labors, it divides that material in a special way, brings the parts of it into new groupings and relations, views it from the standpoint of a distinctive purpose. Its initial procedure may be said — though the parallel has its dangers — to be somewhat analogous to that of analytic chemistry. In dealing with the history of philosophical doctrines, for example, it cuts into the hard-and-fast individual systems and, for its own purposes, breaks them up into their component elements, into what may be called their unit-ideas. The total body of doctrine of any philosopher or school is almost always a complex and heterogeneous aggregate — and often in ways which the philosopher himself does not suspect. It is not only a compound but an unstable compound, though, age after age, each new philosopher usually forgets this melancholy truth. One of the results of the quest of the unit-ideas in such a compound is, I think, bound to be a livelier sense of the fact that most philosophic systems are original or distinctive rather in their patterns than in their components. When the student reviews the vast sequence of arguments and opinions which fill our historical textbooks, he is likely to feel bewildered by the multiplicity and seeming diversity of the matters presented. Even if the array of material is simplified somewhat by the aid of conventional — and largely misleading — classifications of philosophers by schools or -*isms*, it still appears extremely various and complicated; each age seems to evolve new species of reasonings and conclusions, even though upon the same old problems. But the truth is that the number of essentially distinct philosophical ideas or dialectical motives is — as the number of really distinct jokes is said to be — decidedly limited, though, no doubt, the primary ideas are considerably more numerous than the primary jokes. The seeming novelty of many a system is due solely to the novelty of the application or arrangement of the old elements which enter into it. When this is realized, the history as a whole should look a much more manageable thing. I do not, of course, mean to maintain that essentially novel conceptions, new problems and new modes of reasoning about them, do not from time to time emerge in the history of thought. But such increments of absolute novelty seem to me a good deal rarer than is sometimes supposed. It is true that, just as chemical compounds differ in their sensible qualities from the elements composing them, so the elements of philosophical doctrines, in differing logical combinations, are not always readily recognizable; and, prior to analysis, even the same complex may appear to be not the same in its differing expressions, because of the diversity of the philosophers' temperaments and the consequent inequality in the distribution of emphasis among the several parts, or because of the drawing of dissimilar conclusions from partially identical premises. To the common logical or pseudo-logical or affective ingredients behind the surface-dissimilarities the historian of individual ideas will seek to penetrate.

These elements will not always, or usually, correspond to the terms which we are accustomed to use in naming the great historic conceptions of mankind. There are those who have attempted to write histories of the idea of God, and it is well that such histories should be written. But the idea of God is not a unit-idea. By this I do not mean merely the truism that different men have employed the one name to signify superhuman

beings of utterly diverse and incongruous kinds; I mean also
that beneath any *one* of these beliefs you may usually discover
something, or several things, more elemental and more explanatory, if not more significant, than itself. It is true that
the God of Aristotle had almost nothing in common with the
God of the Sermon on the Mount — though, by one of the
strangest and most momentous paradoxes in Western history,
the philosophical theology of Christendom identified them,
and defined the chief end of man as the imitation of both. But
it is also true that Aristotle's conception of the being to whom
he gave the most honorific name he knew was merely one
consequence of a certain more general way of thinking, a
species of dialectic (of which I shall later speak) not peculiar to
him but highly characteristic of the Greek and almost wholly
foreign to the ancient Jewish mind — which has historically
manifested its influence in ethics and aesthetics, and sometimes even in astronomy, as well as in theology. And it would,
in such a case, be to the prior idea, at once more fundamental
and more variously operative, that the historian of ideas would
apply his method of inquiry. It is in the persistent dynamic
factors, the ideas that produce effects in the history of thought,
that he is especially interested. Now a formulated doctrine is
sometimes a relatively inert thing. The conclusion reached by
a process of thought is also not infrequently the conclusion of
the process of thought. The more significant factor in the matter may be, not the dogma which certain persons proclaim —
be that single or manifold in its meaning — but the motives or
reasons which have led them to it. And motives and reasons
partly identical may contribute to the production of very
diverse conclusions, and the same substantive conclusions may,
at different periods or in different minds, be generated by
entirely distinct logical or other motives.

It is not, perhaps, superfluous to remark also that the doctrines or tendencies that are designated by familiar names
ending in *-ism* or *-ity*, though they occasionally may be, usually
are not, units of the sort which the historian of ideas seeks to
discriminate. They commonly constitute, rather, compounds
to which his method of analysis needs to be applied. Idealism,
romanticism, rationalism, transcendentalism, pragmatism —

all these trouble-breeding and usually thought-obscuring terms, which one sometimes wishes to see expunged from the vocabulary of the philosopher and the historian altogether, are names of complexes, not of simples — and of complexes in two senses. They stand, as a rule, not for one doctrine, but for several distinct and often conflicting doctrines held by different individuals or groups to whose way of thinking these appellations have been applied, either by themselves or in the traditional terminology of historians; and each of these doctrines, in turn, is likely to be resolvable into simpler elements, often very strangely combined and derivative from a variety of dissimilar motives and historic influences. The term 'Christianity,' for example, is not the name for any single unit of the type for which the historian of specific ideas looks. I mean by this not merely the notorious fact that persons who have equally professed and called themselves Christians have, in the course of history, held all manner of distinct and conflicting beliefs under the one name, but also that any one of these persons and sects has, as a rule, held under that name a very mixed collection of ideas, the combination of which into a conglomerate bearing a single name and supposed to constitute a real unity was usually the result of historic processes of a highly complicated and curious sort. It is, of course, proper and necessary that ecclesiastical historians should write books on the history of Christianity; but in doing so they are writing of a series of facts which, taken as a whole, have almost nothing in common except the name; the part of the world in which they occurred; the reverence for a certain person, whose nature and teaching, however, have been most variously conceived, so that the unity here too is largely a unity of name; and the identity of a part of their historic antecedents, of certain causes or influences which, diversely combined with other causes, have made each of these systems of belief what it is. In the whole series of creeds and movements going under the one name, and in each of them separately, it is needful to go behind the superficial appearance of singleness and identity, to crack the shell which holds the mass together, if we are to see the real units, the effective working ideas, which, in any given case, are present.

These large movements and tendencies, then, these conventionally labelled -*isms*, are not as a rule the ultimate objects of the interest of the historian of ideas; they are merely the initial materials. Of what sort, then, are the elements, the primary and persistent or recurrent dynamic units, of the history of thought, of which he is in quest? They are rather heterogeneous; I shall not attempt a formal definition, but merely mention some of the principal types.

(1) There are, first, implicit or incompletely explicit *assumptions*, or more or less *unconscious mental habits*, operating in the thought of an individual or a generation. It is the beliefs which are so much a matter of course that they are rather tacitly presupposed than formally expressed and argued for, the ways of thinking which seem so natural and inevitable that they are not scrutinized with the eye of logical self-consciousness, that often are most decisive of the character of a philosopher's doctrine, and still oftener of the dominant intellectual tendencies of an age. These implicit factors may be of various sorts. One sort is a disposition to think in terms of certain categories or of particular types of imagery. There is, for example, a practically very important difference between (we have no English term for them) *esprits simplistes* — minds which habitually tend to assume that simple solutions can be found for the problems they deal with — and those habitually sensible of the general complexity of things, or, in the extreme case, the Hamlet-like natures who are oppressed and terrified by the multiplicity of considerations probably pertinent to any situation with which they are confronted, and the probable intricacy of their interrelations. The representatives of the Enlightenment of the seventeenth and eighteenth centuries, for example, were manifestly characterized to a peculiar degree by the presumption of simplicity. Though there were numerous exceptions, though there were powerful ideas in vogue which worked in the contrary direction, it was nevertheless largely an age of *esprits simplistes*; and the fact had the most momentous practical consequences. The assumption of simplicity was, it is true, combined in some minds with a certain sense of the complexity of the universe and a consequent disparagement of the powers of man's understanding, which might at first seem entirely incongruous with it, but which

in reality was not so. The typical early-eighteenth-century writer was well enough aware that the universe as a whole is physically an extremely large and complicated thing. One of the favorite pieces of edifying rhetoric of the period was Pope's warning against intellectual presumptuousness:

> He who through vast immensity can pierce,
> See worlds on worlds compose one universe,
> Observe how system into system runs,
> What other planets circle other suns,
> What vary'd being peoples every star,
> May tell why Heaven has made us as we are.
> But of this frame, the bearing and the ties,
> The strong connections, nice dependencies,
> Gradations just, has thy pervading soul
> Look'd thro? Or can a part contain the whole?

You may find this sort of thing in abundance in the popular philosophy of that time. This pose of intellectual modesty was, in fact, an almost universally prevalent characteristic of the period, which Locke, perhaps, more than anyone else had brought into fashion. Man must become habitually mindful of the limitations of his mental powers, must be content with that "relative and practical understanding" which is the only organ of knowledge that he possesses. "Men," as Locke puts it in a familiar passage, "may find matter sufficient to busy their heads, and employ their minds with variety, delight and satisfaction, if they will not boldly quarrel with their own constitution, and throw away the blessings their hands are filled with, because they are not big enough to grasp everything." We must not "loose our thoughts into the vast ocean of being, as if all that boundless extent were the natural and undoubted possession of our understandings, wherein is nothing exempt from its decisions or that escapes its comprehension. But we shall not have much reason to complain of the narrowness of our minds, if we will but employ them about what may be of use to us, for of that they are very capable. . . . It will be no excuse to an idle and untoward servant, who would not attend his business by candle-light, to plead that he had not broad sunshine. The candle that is set up in us shines bright enough for all our purposes. The discoveries we can make with this ought to satisfy us, and we shall then use our understandings right, when we entertain all objects in that way and proportion that they are suited to our faculties."

But though this tone of becoming diffidence, this ostentatious modesty in the recognition of the disproportion between man's intellect and the universe, was one of the most prevalent intellectual fashions of a great part of the eighteenth century, it was frequently accompanied by an extreme presumption of the simplicity of the truths that *are* needful for man and within his reach, by a confidence in the possibility of "short and easy methods," not only with the deists, but with pretty much all matters of legitimate human concern. "Simplicity, noblest ornament of truth," wrote John Toland, characteristically; and one can see that to him, and to many of his time and temper, simplicity was in fact, not merely an extrinsic ornament, but almost a necessary attribute of any conception or doctrine which they were willing to accept as true, or even fairly to examine. When Pope, in his most familiar lines, exhorted his contemporaries:

> Know then thyself! Presume not God to scan!
> The proper study of mankind is man,

he implied that the problems of theology and speculative metaphysics are too vast for human thought; but he also implied, to the contemporary ear, that man is a tolerably simple kind of entity, to plumb whose nature was well within the scope of the decidedly limited and simple intellectual powers with which he was endowed. Assuming human nature to be a simple thing, the Enlightenment also, as a rule, assumed political and social problems to be simple, and therefore easy of solution. Rid man's mind of a few ancient errors, purge his beliefs of the artificial complications of metaphysical 'systems' and theological dogmas, restore to his social relations something like the simplicity of the state of nature, and his natural excellence would, it was assumed, be realized, and mankind would live happily ever after. The two tendencies I have been mentioning, in short, may probably be traced to a common root. The limitation of the scope of activity of man's interest and even of the ranging of his imagination was itself a manifestation of a preference for simple schemes of ideas; the temper of intellectual modesty was partly the expression of an aversion for the incomprehensible, the involved, the mysterious. When, on the other hand, you pass on to the Romantic Period, you find the simple becoming an object of suspicion and even detestation, and what Friedrich Schlegel characteristically called *eine romantische Verwirrung* the quality most valued in temperaments, in poems, and in universes.

(2) These endemic assumptions, these intellectual habits, are often of so general and so vague a sort that it is possible for them to influence the course of man's reflections on almost any subject. A class of ideas which is of a kindred type may be termed dialectical motives. You may, namely, find much of the thinking of an individual, a school, or even a generation, dominated and determined by one or another turn of reasoning, trick of logic, methodological assumption, which if explicit would amount to a large and important and perhaps highly debatable proposition in logic or metaphysics. A thing which constantly reappears, for example, is the nominalistic motive — the tendency, almost instinctive with some men, to reduce the meaning of all general notions to an enumeration of the concrete and sensible particulars which fall under those notions. This shows itself in fields quite remote from technical philosophy, and in philosophy it appears as a determinant in many other doctrines besides those customarily labelled nominalism. Much of William James's pragmatism bears witness to the influence upon him of this way of thinking; while in Dewey's pragmatism it plays, I think, a much smaller part. Again, there is the organismic or flower-in-the-crannied-wall motive, the habit of assuming that, where you have a complex of one or another kind, no element in that complex can be understood, or can, indeed, be what it is apart from its relations to all the other components of the system to which it belongs. This, too, you may find operative in some men's characteristic modes of thinking even upon non-philosophical matters; while it, also, shows itself in systems of philosophy other than those which make a formal dogma of the principle of the essentiality of relations.

(3) Another type of factors in the history of ideas may be

described as susceptibilities to diverse kinds of metaphysical pathos. This influential cause in the determination of philosophical fashions and speculative tendencies has been so little considered that I find no recognized name for it, and have been compelled to invent one which is not, perhaps, wholly self-explanatory. 'Metaphysical pathos' is exemplified in any description of the nature of things, any characterization of the world to which one belongs, in terms which, like the words of a poem, awaken through their associations, and through a sort of empathy which they engender, a congenial mood or tone of feeling on the part of the philosopher or his readers. For many people — for most of the laity, I suspect — the reading of a philosophical book is usually nothing but a form of aesthetic experience, even in the case of writings which seem destitute of all outward aesthetic charms; voluminous emotional reverberations, of one or another sort, are aroused in the reader without the intervention of any definite imagery. Now of metaphysical pathos there are a good many kinds; and people differ in their degree of susceptibility to any one kind. There is, in the first place, the pathos of sheer obscurity, the loveliness of the incomprehensible, which has, I fear, stood many a philosopher in good stead with his public, even though he was innocent of intending any such effect. The phrase *omne ignotum pro mirifico* concisely explains a considerable part of the vogue of a number of philosophies, including some which have enjoyed great popular reputation in our own time. The reader doesn't know exactly what they mean, but they have all the more on that account an air of sublimity; an agreeable feeling at once of awe and of exaltation comes over him as he contemplates thoughts of so immeasurable a profundity — their profundity being convincingly evidenced to him by the fact that he can see no bottom to them. Akin to this is the pathos of the esoteric. How exciting and how welcome is the sense of initiation into hidden mysteries! And how effectively have certain philosophers — notably Schelling and Hegel a century ago, and Bergson in our own generation — satisfied the human craving for this experience, by representing the central insight of their philosophy as a thing to be reached, not through a consecutive progress of thought guided by the ordinary logic available to every man, but through a sudden leap whereby one rises to a plane of insight wholly different in its principles from the level of the mere understanding. There are expressions of certain disciples of M. Bergson which admirably illustrate the place which the pathos of the esoteric has in this philosophy, or at least in the response to it. M. Rageot, for example, declares that unless one is in some sense born again one cannot acquire that *intuition philosophique* which is the secret of the new teaching; and M. Le Roy writes: "A veil interposed between the real and ourselves, which falls of a sudden as if an enchantment were dissipated, and leaves open before the mind depths of light hitherto unimagined, wherein is revealed before our very eyes, for the first time, reality itself: such is the feeling which is experienced at every page, with singular intensity, by the reader of M. Bergson."

These two types of pathos, however, inhere not so much in the attributes which a given philosophy ascribes to the universe as in the attributes which it ascribes to itself — or which its votaries ascribe to it. Some examples of metaphysical pathos in the stricter sense ought therefore to be given. A potent variety is the eternalistic pathos — the aesthetic pleasure which the bare abstract idea of immutability gives us. The greater philosophical poets know well how to evoke it. In English poetry it is illustrated by those familiar lines in Shelley's *Adonais* of which we have all at some time felt the magic:

> The One remains, the many change and pass,
> Heaven's light forever shines, earth's shadows fly . . . .

It is not self-evident that remaining forever unchanged should be regarded as an excellence; yet through the associations and the half-formed images which the mere conception of changelessness arouses — for one thing, the feeling of rest which its *innere Nachahmung* induces in us in our tired moods — a philosophy which tells us that at the heart of things there is a reality wherein is no variableness nor shadow that is cast by turning, is sure to find its response in our emotional natures, at all events in certain phases of individual or group experience. Shelley's lines exemplify also another sort of metaphysical pathos, often conjoined with the last — the monistic or pan-

theistic pathos. That it should afford so many people a peculiar satisfaction to say that All is One is, as William James
once remarked, a rather puzzling thing. What is there more
beautiful or more venerable about the numeral *one* than about
any other number? But psychologically the force of the monistic pathos is in some degree intelligible when one considers the
nature of the implicit responses which talk about oneness produces. It affords, for example, a welcome sense of freedom,
arising from a triumph over, or an absolution from, the
troublesome cleavages and disjunctions of things. To recognize that things which we have hitherto kept apart in our
minds are somehow the same thing — that, of itself, is normally an agreeable experience for human beings. (You will
remember James's essay "On Some Hegelisms" and on Mr.
B. P. Blood's book called *The Anaesthetic Revelation*.) So, again,
when a monistic philosophy declares, or suggests, that one is
oneself a part of the universal Oneness, a whole complex of
obscure emotional responses is released. The deliquescence of
the sense — the often so fatiguing sense — of separate personality, for example, which comes in various ways (as in the
so-called mob-spirit), is also capable of excitation, and of
really powerful excitation, too, by a mere metaphysical
theorem. Mr. Santayana's sonnet beginning "I would I
might forget that I am I" almost perfectly expresses the mood
in which conscious individuality, as such, becomes a burden.
Just such escape for our imaginations from the sense of being a
limited, particular self the monistic philosophies sometimes
give us. Distinct from the monistic pathos is the voluntaristic
— though Fichte and others have contrived to unite them.
Here it is the response of our active and volitional nature, perhaps even, as the phrase goes, of our fighting blood, which is
aroused by the character which is ascribed to the total universe with which we feel ourselves consubstantial. Now all this
has nothing to do with philosophy as a science; but it has a
great deal to do with philosophy as a factor in history, for the
reason that it is not chiefly as a science that philosophy has
been a factor in history. The susceptibility to different sorts of
metaphysical pathos plays, I am convinced, a great part, both
in the formation of philosophical systems by subtly guiding

many a philosopher's logic, and in partially causing the vogue and influence of different philosophies among groups or generations which they have affected. And the delicate task of discovering these varying susceptibilities and showing how they help to shape a system or to give an idea plausibility and currency is a part of the work of the historian of ideas.

(4) Another part of his business, if he means to take cognizance of the genuinely operative factors in the larger movements of thought, is an inquiry which may be called philosophical semantics — a study of the sacred words and phrases of a period or a movement, with a view to a clearing up of their ambiguities, a listing of their various shades of meaning, and an examination of the way in which confused associations of ideas arising from these ambiguities have influenced the development of doctrines, or accelerated the insensible transformation of one fashion of thought into another, perhaps its very opposite. It is largely because of their ambiguities that mere words are capable of this independent action as forces in history. A term, a phrase, a formula, which gains currency or acceptance because one of its meanings, or of the thoughts which it suggests, is congenial to the prevalent beliefs, the standards of value, the tastes of a certain age, may help to alter beliefs, standards of value, and tastes, because other meanings or suggested implications, not clearly distinguished by those who employ it, gradually become the dominant elements of its signification. The word 'nature,' it need hardly be said, is the most extraordinary example of this, and the most pregnant subject for the investigations of philosophical semantics.

(5) The type of 'idea' with which we shall be concerned is, however, more definite and explicit, and therefore easier to isolate and identify with confidence, than those of which I have been hitherto speaking. It consists in a single specific proposition or 'principle' expressly enunciated by the most influential of early European philosophers, together with some further propositions which are, or have been supposed to be, its corollaries. This proposition was, as we shall see, an attempted answer to a philosophical question which it was natural for man to ask — which reflective thought could hardly have failed to ask, sooner or later. It proved to have a natural logi-

cal affinity for certain other principles, originally advanced in the course of reflection upon certain quite different questions, which consequently became agglutinated with it. The character of this type of ideas, and of the processes which constitute their history, need not be further described in general terms, since all that follows will illustrate it.

*Second*, any unit-idea which the historian thus isolates he next seeks to trace through more than one — ultimately, indeed, through all — of the provinces of history in which it figures in any important degree, whether those provinces are called philosophy, science, literature, art, religion, or politics. The postulate of such a study is that the working of a given conception, of an explicit or tacit presupposition, of a type of mental habit, or of a specific thesis or argument, needs, if its nature and its historic rôle are to be fully understood, to be traced connectedly through all the phases of men's reflective life in which those workings manifest themselves, or through as many of them as the historian's resources permit. It is inspired by the belief that there *is* a great deal more that is common to more than one of these provinces than is usually recognized, that the same idea often appears, sometimes considerably disguised, in the most diverse regions of the intellectual world. Landscape-gardening, for example, seems a topic fairly remote from philosophy; yet at one point, at least, the history of landscape-gardening becomes a part of any truly philosophical history of modern thought. The vogue of the so-called "English garden," which spread so rapidly in France and Germany after 1730, was, as M. Mornet and others have shown, the thin end of the wedge of Romanticism, or of one kind of Romanticism. That vogue itself — partly, no doubt, the expression of a natural revulsion of taste from an over-dose of the formal gardening of the seventeenth century — was partly also an incident of the general craze for English fashions of all kinds, which Voltaire, Prévost, Diderot, and the Huguenot *journalistes* in Holland had introduced. But this change of taste in gardening was to be the beginning and — I do not, assuredly, say, *the* cause, but the foreshadowing, and one of the joint causes — of a change of taste in all the arts and, indeed, of a change of taste in universes. In one of its aspects that many-sided thing called Romanticism may not inaccurately be described as a conviction that the world is an *englischer Garten* on a grand scale. The God of the seventeenth century, like its gardeners, always geometrized; the God of Romanticism was one in whose universe things grew wild and without trimming and in all the rich diversity of their natural shapes. The preference for irregularity, the aversion from that which is wholly intellectualized, the yearning for *échappées* into misty distances — these, which were eventually to invade the intellectual life of Europe at all points, made their first modern appearance on a grand scale early in the eighteenth century in the form of the new fashion in pleasure-gardens; and it is not impossible to trace the successive phases of their growth and diffusion.[1]

While the history of ideas — in so far as it may be spoken of in the present tense and the indicative mood — is thus an attempt at historical synthesis, this does not mean that it is a mere conglomerate, still less that it aspires to be a comprehensive unification, of other historical disciplines. It is concerned only with a certain group of factors in history, and with these only in so far as they can be seen at work in what are commonly considered separate divisions of the intellectual world; and it is especially interested in the processes by which influences pass over from one province to another. Even the partial realization of such a program would do much, I cannot but think, to give a needed unifying background to many now unconnected and, consequently, poorly understood facts. It would help to put gates through the fences which, in the course of a praiseworthy effort after specialization and division of labor, have come to be set up in most of our universities between departments whose work ought to be constantly correlated. I have in mind especially the departments of philosophy and of the modern literatures. Most teachers of literature would perhaps readily enough admit that it is to be *studied* — I by no means say, can solely be enjoyed — chiefly for its thought-content, and that the interest of the history of literature is largely as a record of the movement of ideas — of the ideas which have affected men's imaginations and emotions and behavior. And the ideas in serious reflective literature are, of course, in great part philosophical ideas in dilution — to change the figure, growths from seed scattered by great philosophic systems which themselves, perhaps, have ceased to be. But, through a lack of adequate training in philosophy, students and even learned historians of literature often, I think, have not recognized such an idea when they met it — have not, at least, known its historic lineage, its logical import and implications, its other appearances in human thought. Happily, this condition is fast altering for the better. On the other hand, those who investigate or teach the history of philosophy sometimes take very little interest in an idea when it does not wear philosophical full dress — or war-paint — and are prone to disregard its ulterior workings in the minds of the non-philosophic world. But the historian of ideas, while he oftenest will seek for the initial emergence of a conception or presupposition in some philosophic or religious system or scientific theory, will seek for its most significant manifestations in art, and above all in literature. For, as Mr. Whitehead has said, "it is in literature that the concrete outlook of humanity receives its expression. Accordingly, it is to literature that we must look, particularly in its more concrete forms, if we hope to discover the inward thoughts of a generation." [2] And, as I think — though there is not time to defend the opinion — it is by first distinguishing and analyzing the major ideas which appear again and again, and by observing each of them as a recurrent unit in many contexts, that the philosophic background of literature can best be illuminated.

*Third*: in common with what is called the study of comparative literature, the history of ideas expresses a protest against the consequences which have often resulted from the conventional division of literary and some other historical studies by nationalities or languages. There are some good, and obvious, reasons why the history of political institutions and movements, since it must in some way be broken up into smaller units, should be divided upon national lines; yet even these branches of historical inquiry have in recent times gained greatly in accuracy and fruitfulness through an increasing realization of the necessity of investigating events or tendencies

or policies in one country in order to understand the real
causes of many events, tendencies, or policies in another. And
it is far from self-evident that in the study of the history of
literature, not to speak of that of philosophy, in which this practice has been generally abandoned, departmentalization by
languages is the best way of recognizing the necessity for specialization. The existing scheme of division is partly a historical accident, a survival of the time when most professors of
foreign literatures were primarily language-masters. As soon
as the historical study of literature is conceived as a thorough
investigation of any causal process — even the comparatively
trivial one of the migration of stories — it must inevitably disregard national and linguistic boundary lines; for nothing is
more certain than that a great proportion of the processes to
be investigated disregard those lines. And if the function of
teachers or the training of advanced students is to be determined by the affinity of certain minds for certain subjects, or
certain types of thought, it is at least dubious whether, instead
of professors of English or French or German literature, we
ought not to have professors of the Renaissance, of the later
Middle Ages, of the Enlightenment, of the Romantic Period,
and the like. For there was doubtless, on the whole, more in
common, in fundamental ideas and tastes and moral temper,
between a typical educated Englishman and a Frenchman or
Italian of the later sixteenth century than between an Englishman of that period and an Englishman of the 1730's or the
1830's or the 1930's — just as there is manifestly more in common between an average New Englander and an Englishman
of 1930 than between a New Englander of 1630 and his present
posterity. If, then, a special capacity for sympathetic understanding of that with which he deals is desirable in the historical specialist, a division of these studies by periods, or groups
within periods, would, it might plausibly be argued, be more
appropriate than a division by countries, races, or languages.
I do not seriously urge such a reorganization of the humanistic
departments of universities; there are obvious practical difficulties in the way. But these difficulties have little to do with
any real cleavages among the facts studied — least of all when
the facts have to do with the history of ruling categories, of

beliefs, of tastes, of intellectual fashions. As Friedrich Schlegel long ago said: "Wenn die regionellen Theile der modernen Poesie, aus ihrem Zusammenhang gerissen, und als einzelne für sich bestehende Ganze betrachtet werden, so sind sie unerklärlich. Sie bekommen erst durch einander Haltung und Bedeutung." [3]

*Fourth*: Another characteristic of the study of the history of ideas, as I should wish to define it, is that it is especially concerned with the manifestations of specific unit-ideas in the collective thought of large groups of persons, not merely in the doctrines or opinions of a small number of profound thinkers or eminent writers. It seeks to investigate the effects of the sort of factors which it has — in the bacteriologist's sense — isolated, in the beliefs, prejudices, pieties, tastes, aspirations, current among the educated classes through, it may be, a whole generation, or many generations. It is, in short, most interested in ideas which attain a wide diffusion, which become a part of the stock of many minds. It is this characteristic of the study of the history of ideas in literature which often puzzles students — even advanced students — in the present-day literature departments in our universities. Some of them, at least, my colleagues in those departments often tell me, are repelled when called upon to study some writer whose work, *as* literature, is now dead — or at best, of extremely slight value, according to our present aesthetic and intellectual standards. Why not stick to the masterpieces, such students exclaim — or at least to these *plus* the minor classics — the things that can be still read with pleasure, or with a feeling of the significance for men of the present age of the ideas or the moods of feeling which they express? This is a natural enough state of mind, if you don't regard the study of literary history as including within its province the study of the ideas and feelings which other men in past times have been moved by, and of the processes by which what may be called literary and philosophical public opinion is formed. But if you *do* think the historian of literature ought to concern himself with these matters, your minor writer may be as important as — he may often, from this point of view, be more important than — the authors of

what are now regarded as the masterpieces. Professor Palmer
has said, with equal truth and felicity: "The tendencies of an
age appear more distinctly in its writers of inferior rank than in
those of commanding genius. These latter tell of past and
future as well as of the age in which they live. They are for all
time. But on the sensitive responsive souls, of less creative
power, current ideals record themselves with clearness." [4]
And it is, of course, in any case true that a historical understanding even of the few great writers of an age is impossible
without an acquaintance with their general background in the
intellectual life and common moral and aesthetic valuations of
that age; and that the character of this background has to be
ascertained by actual historical inquiry into the nature and
interrelations of the ideas then generally prevalent.

Finally, it is a part of the eventual task of the history of ideas
to apply its own distinctive analytic method in the attempt to
understand how *new* beliefs and intellectual fashions are introduced and diffused, to help to elucidate the psychological
character of the processes by which changes in the vogue and
influence of ideas have come about; to make clear, if possible,
how conceptions dominant, or extensively prevalent, in one
generation lose their hold upon men's minds and give place to
others. To this large and difficult and important branch of historical interpretation the method of study of which I am speaking can make only one contribution among many; but it is, I
can't but think, a necessary contribution. For the process can
hardly be made intelligible until the natures of the separate
ideas which enter as factors in it are discriminated and separately observed in their general historic working.

These lectures, then, are intended to exemplify in some small
measure the sort of philosophical-historical inquiry of which I
have been merely sketching the general aims and method. We
shall first discriminate, not, indeed, a single and simple idea,
but three ideas which have, throughout the greater part of the
history of the West, been so closely and constantly associated
that they have often operated as a unit, and have, when thus
taken together, produced a conception — one of the major
conceptions in Occidental thought — which came to be ex-

pressed by a single term: "the Great Chain of Being"; and we shall observe the workings of these both separately and in conjunction. The example will necessarily be inadequate, even as a treatment of the special topic chosen, being restricted not only by limitations of time but by the insufficiency of the lecturer's knowledge. Nevertheless, so far as these limitations permit, we shall try to trace these ideas to their historic sources in the minds of certain philosophers; to observe their fusion; to note some of the most important of their widely ramifying influences in many periods and in diverse fields — metaphysics, religion, certain phases of the history of modern science, the theory of the purpose of art and the criteria of excellence therein, moral valuations, and even, though to a relatively slight extent, in political tendencies; to see how later generations derived from them conclusions undesired and undreamed-of by their originators; to mark some of their effects upon men's emotions and upon the poetic imagination; and in the end, perhaps, to draw a philosophic moral from the tale.

But I ought, I think, to close this preamble with three notes of warning. The first relates to the very program which I have outlined. The study of the history of ideas is full of dangers and pitfalls; it has its characteristic excess. Precisely because it aims at interpretation and unification and seeks to correlate things which often are not on the surface connected, it may easily degenerate into a species of merely imaginative historical generalization; and because the historian of an idea is compelled by the nature of his enterprise to gather material from several fields of knowledge, he is inevitably, in at least some parts of his synthesis, liable to the errors which lie in wait for the non-specialist. I can only say that I am not unmindful of these dangers and have done what I could to avoid them; it would be too sanguine to suppose that I have in all cases succeeded in doing so. In spite of the probability, or perhaps the certainty, of partial failure, the enterprise seems worth attempting.

The other warnings are addressed to my hearers. Our plan of procedure requires that we deal only with a part of the thought of any one philosopher or any one age. The part, therefore, must never be mistaken for the whole. We shall not, indeed, confine our view solely to the three connected ideas which are the theme of the course. For their philosophical significance and historic operation can be understood only by contrast. The story to be told is in great part a story of conflict, at first latent, eventually overt, between these ideas and a series of antagonistic conceptions, some of the antagonists being their own offspring. We must, then, observe them throughout in the light of their antitheses. But nothing that is to be said is to be construed as a comprehensive exposition either of any system of doctrine or of the tendencies of any period. Finally, it is evident that, when one tries to relate in this fashion the biography of even one idea, a heavy demand is made upon the catholicity of the intellectual interests of one's auditors. In tracing the influence of the conceptions which form the subject of this course we shall be obliged, as has been intimated, to take account of episodes in the history of a number of disciplines usually supposed to have little to do with one another, and usually studied in comparative isolation. The history of ideas is therefore no subject for highly departmentalized minds; and it is pursued with some difficulty in an age of departmentalized minds. It presupposes, also, an interest in the workings of human thought in the past even when these are, or seem to many of our generation to be, misguided, confused, or even absurd. The history of philosophy and of all phases of man's reflection *is*, in great part, a history of confusions of ideas; and the chapter of it with which we shall be occupied is no exception to this rule. To some of us it is not less interesting, and little less instructive, on that account. Since man, for better or worse, is by nature, and by the most distinctive impulse of his nature, a reflective and interpretative animal, always seeking *rerum cognoscere causas*, to find in the bare data of experience more than meets the eye, the record of the reactions of his intellect upon the brute facts of his sensible existence constitutes, at the least, an essential part of the natural history of the species, or sub-species, which has somewhat too flatteringly named itself *homo sapiens*; and I have never been able to see why what is distinctive in the natural history of that species should appear — especially to a member of it — a less respectable subject of study than the natural history of the *para-*

*mecium* or the white rat. No doubt man's quest of intelligibility in nature and in himself, and of the kinds of emotional satisfaction which are conditioned by a sense of intelligibility, often, like the caged rat's quest of food, has found no end, in wandering mazes lost. But though the history of ideas is a history of trial-and-error, even the errors illuminate the peculiar nature, the cravings, the endowments, and the limitations of the creature that falls into them, as well as the logic of the problems in reflection upon which they have arisen; and they may further serve to remind us that the ruling modes of thought of our own age, which some among us are prone to regard as clear and coherent and firmly grounded and final, are unlikely to appear in the eyes of posterity to have any of those attributes. The adequate record of even the confusions of our forebears may help, not only to clarify those confusions, but to engender a salutary doubt whether we are wholly immune from different but equally great confusions. For though we have more empirical information at our disposal, we have not different or better minds; and it is, after all, the action of the mind upon facts that makes both philosophy and science — and, indeed, largely makes the 'facts.' Nevertheless, those who do not care for the natural history of man in his most characteristic activity, who have neither curiosity nor patience to follow the workings of other minds proceeding from premises which they do not share, or entangled in what seem to them, and often are, strange confusions, or engaged in speculative enterprises which they may regard as hopeless, ought in fairness to be warned that much of the story which I am to try to tell will be for them without interest. On the other hand, I think it only fair to warn those who, for such reasons, are indifferent to the story here to be told, that without an acquaintance with it no understanding of the movement of thought in the Occident, in most of its major provinces, is possible.

## II

## THE GENESIS OF THE IDEA IN GREEK PHILOSOPHY:
## THE THREE PRINCIPLES

THE most fundamental of the group of ideas of which we are to review the history appears first in Plato; and nearly all that follows might therefore serve as an illustration of a celebrated remark of Professor Whitehead's, that "the safest general characterization of the European philosophical tradition is that it consists in a series of footnotes to Plato." But there are two conflicting major strains in Plato and in the Platonic tradition. With respect to the deepest and farthest-reaching cleavage separating philosophical or religious systems he stood on both sides; and his influence upon later generations worked in two opposite directions. The cleavage to which I refer is that between what I shall call otherworldliness and this-worldliness. By otherworldliness I do not mean a belief in and a preoccupation of the mind with a future life. To be concerned about what will happen to you after death, or to let your thought dwell much upon the joys which you hope will then await you, may obviously be the most extreme form of this-worldliness; and it is essentially such if that life is conceived, not as profoundly different in kind from this, but only as more of much the same sort of thing, a prolongation of the mode of being which we know in the world of change and sense and plurality and social fellowship, with merely the omission of the trivial or painful features of terrestrial existence, the heightening of its finer pleasures, the compensation of some of earth's frustrations. The two most familiar expressions by Victorian poets of the desire for a continuance of personal existence perfectly illustrate this. In nothing was Robert Browning's breezy gusto for the life that now is more manifest than in his hope to "fight on, fare ever, there as here." And when Tennyson's *meditatio mortis* ended with a prayer simply for "the wages of going on, and not to die" he, too, in his less robustious way, was declaring the sufficient worth of the general conditions of existence with which common experience has already acquainted us. Both writers were, indeed, giving utterance to a special form of this feeling which had been somewhat exceptional before the Romantic period — though our present historical survey will show us its earlier emergence — and was highly characteristic of their own age — an identification of the chief value of existence with process and struggle in time, an antipathy to satisfaction and finality, a sense of the "glory of the imperfect," in Professor Palmer's phrase. This is the complete negation of the otherworldliness of which I am speaking. For of that, even in its milder manifestations, a more or less sweeping *contemptus mundi* has been of the essence; it has had no necessary — though in most of its Occidental phases it has had an actual — connection with the craving for a separate personal immortality; and in its more thorough-going forms it has seen in that craving the last enemy to be overcome, the root of all the misery and vanity of existence.

By 'otherworldliness,' then — in the sense in which the term, I suggest, is an indispensable one for distinguishing the primary antithesis in philosophical or religious tendencies — I mean the belief that both the genuinely 'real' and the truly good are radically antithetic in their essential characteristics to anything to be found in man's natural life, in the ordinary course of human experience, however normal, however intelligent, and however fortunate. The world we now and here know — various, mutable, a perpetual flux of states and relations of things, or an ever-shifting phantasmagoria of thoughts and sensations, each of them lapsing into nonentity in the very moment of its birth — seems to the otherworldly mind to have no substance in it; the objects of sense and even of empirical scientific knowledge are unstable, contingent, forever breaking down logically into mere relations to other things which when scrutinized prove equally relative and elusive. Our judgments concerning them have seemed to many philosophers of many races and ages to lead us inevitably into mere quagmires of confusion and contradiction. And — the theme is of the tritest — the joys of the natural life are evanescent and delusive, as age if not youth discovers. But the human will, as conceived by the otherworldly philosophers, not only seeks but is capable of finding some final, fixed, immutable, intrinsic, perfectly satisfying good, as the human reason seeks, and can find, some stable, definitive, coherent, self-contained, and self-explanatory object or objects of contemplation. Not, however, in this world is either to be found, but only in a 'higher' realm of being differing in its essential nature, and not merely in degree and detail, from the lower. That other realm, though to those enmeshed in matter, occupied with things of sense, busy with plans of action, or absorbed in personal affections, it appears cold and tenuous and barren of interest and delight, is (to those who have been emancipated through reflection or emotional disillusionment,) the final goal of the philosophic quest and the sole region in which either the intellect or the heart of man, ceasing, even in this present life, to pursue shadows, can find rest.

Such is the general creed of otherworldly philosophy; it is familiar enough, but we need to have it explicitly before us as the contrasting background for what is to follow. That this is a persistent type, and that it has, in one form or another, been the dominant official philosophy of the larger part of civilized mankind through most of its history, I need not remind you. The greater number of the subtler speculative minds and of the great religious teachers have, in their several fashions and with differing degrees of rigor and thoroughness, been engaged in weaning man's thought or his affections, or both, from his mother Nature — many of them, indeed, in seeking to persuade him that he must in very truth be born again, into a world whose goods are not Nature's goods and whose realities he cannot know through those processes of the mind by which he becomes acquainted with his natural environment and with the laws to which its ever-changing states conform. I have said "official philosophy" because nothing, I suppose, is more evident than that most men, however much they may have professed to accept it, and have even found in the reasonings or the rhetoric of its expositors a congenial and moving sort of metaphysical pathos — which is partly the pathos of the ineffable — have never quite believed it, since they have never been able to deny to the things disclosed by the senses a genuine and imposing and highly important kind of realness, and have never truly desired for themselves the end which otherworldliness held out to them. The great metaphysicians might seek to demonstrate its truth, the saints might in some measure fashion their lives in accordance with it, the mystics might return from their ecstasies and stammeringly report a direct experience of that contact with the absolute reality and the sole satisfying good which it proclaimed; but Nature in the main has been too potent for it. While the plain man might admit the metaphysician's demonstration, might humble himself before the saint, and might credit, without professing to understand, the mystic's report, he has manifestly continued to find something very solid and engrossing in the world in which his own constitution was so deeply rooted and with which it was so intimately interwoven; and even if experience defeated his hopes and in age the savor of life grew somewhat flat and insipid, he has sought comfort in some vision of a better 'this-world' to come, in which no desire should lack fulfilment and his own zest for things should be permanently revitalized. These facts, it is incidentally to be observed, do not mean that the general character and tone of a society in which, at least nominally, an otherworldly philosophy is widely accepted or officially dominant is little affected by that circumstance. The spectacle of medieval Europe, or of India before, and even since, its infection with the Western plague of nationalism, is sufficient evidence to the contrary. Where some form of otherworldliness is generally professed, the socially prevalent scale of values is largely shaped by it and the principal themes and objectives of intellectual effort receive their character from it. The 'worldly' man in such a society commonly reveres — and is usually obliged to support — the minority who have more or less thoroughly and sincerely turned from the pursuit of temporal goods and detached themselves from the hurly-burly of the world in which he is not unpleasurably engrossed; and, by a familiar paradox, exemplified often in medieval Europe as it is in contemporary India, the chief power in the affairs of this world is not unlikely to fall, or to be forced, into the hands of those who have withdrawn from it. The otherworldly philosopher is made the ruler, or the secret ruler of the ruler, the mystic or the saint becomes the most powerful, and sometimes the shrewdest, of politicians. There is perhaps nothing so favorable to success in this world's business as a high degree of emotional detachment from it.

But the social and political effects of otherworldliness, though a rich and interesting theme, do not here concern us, except as a reminder that otherworldliness has always been compelled in practice to make terms with this world and has often been instrumental to ends foreign to its principles. It is of its own nature as a mode of human thought and feeling, and especially of the philosophic motives which provide its grounds or its 'rationalization,' that some further consideration is pertinent to our topic. It manifestly may exist, and historically has existed, in diverse degrees; it may receive partial application in some provinces of thought and not in others; and strains of it may turn up in queer and incongruous contexts. There is a purely metaphysical otherworldliness which is sometimes to be found completely dissociated from any corresponding theory of the nature of the good, and therefore from any otherworldly moral and religious temper. Perhaps the oddest example of this is to be seen in those half-dozen irrelevant chapters about the Unknowable which Herbert Spencer, under the influence of Hamilton and Mansel, prefixed to the Synthetic Philosophy. There are, moreover, as I have intimated, several distinct features or categories of the world of common thought and experience which may give rise to the denial of either its 'reality' or its value. It may be metaphysically condemned merely because of its temporal character and perpetual incompleteness; or because of the seeming relativity of all its component members, the lack in each of them of any self-contained intelligibility in which thought can find its term; or because it seems to be merely a random collection of petty existences, all of them fragmentary, imperfect, and without any obvious and necessary reason for being; or because our apprehension of it is through those deceitful organs, the senses, which neither in themselves nor even in any inferential constructions based upon them and defined in the terms which they provide, can be freed from the suspicion of subjectivity; or because of its mere multiplicity, its recalcitrance to that insatiable craving for unity which besets the speculative reason; or — in the case of certain less ratiocinative minds —simply because of intermittent experiences in which it loses the *feel* of reality —

> Fallings from us, vanishings,
> Blank misgivings of a creature
> Moving about in worlds not realized —

so that the conviction becomes to such minds overpowering that true being, the world in which the soul can feel itself at home, must be *somehow* other than 'all this.' Any one of these motives may give rise to a genuinely otherworldly ontology because each of them fixes upon some one truly distinctive and constitutive character of 'this' world. But when only one or only a few of them are operative, there does not result what may be called an integral otherworldliness in the metaphysical sense; some other characters of the world known to natural experience remain exempt from the impeachment. On the side of value, again, 'this' world may be dismissed as evil or worthless on the ground of any one, or all, of the familiar complaints which fill the pages of the otherworldly moralists and religious teachers: because the world-process, when the attempt is made to conceive it as a whole, presents to the imagination only an incoherent and tedious drama, full of sound and fury but signifying nothing — either a pointless repetition of the same episodes, or a tale of endless change which begins nowhere, has reached no consummation commensurate with the infinite time in which it has been going on, and verges to no intelligible goal; or because all desires that arise in time and are fixed on ends in time have been found by experience to constitute only an endless renewal of dissatisfaction, and can be seen by reflection to share necessarily in the baffling transiency of the process in which they are immersed; or because there is, in not a few men, even in some not themselves capable of the true mystic ecstasy, a recurrent emotional rebellion against the mutual externality of things and against the confining separateness of their own being, a craving to escape from the burden of self-consciousness, to "forget that I am I," and be lost in a unity in which all sense of division and all consciousness of otherness would be transcended. An integral otherworldliness would combine all these motives, and indict this world upon all counts. It is best exemplified in some of the Upanishads, in the system of the Vedânta, in the Vedântist and Buddhist strain — so ironically alien to the actual life and personal temper of Schopenhauer — in *Die Welt als Wille und Vorstellung*; primitive Buddhism, which is a kind of pragmatic otherworldliness, falls short of it only by its negativity, its insistence upon the insubstantiality and worthlessness of this world without any altogether unequivocal assertion of the positive reality and positive value of the alternative. Some modern observers of otherworldliness will perhaps question whether Buddhism has not in this come nearer to disclosing the strange truth that many of the great philosophers and theologians have been occupied with teaching the worship of — nonentity; though of nonentity made to seem more 'real' and emotionally more satisfying by an emphasis upon its freedom from the particular defects and limitations — the relativity, the internal logical conflicts, the lack of finality for thought and desire — which characterize all the concrete objects of which we can think at all. It is not necessary for our purpose to attempt to answer this large question here. What is certain is that such philosophers have always believed themselves to be doing precisely the reverse of this.

But any otherworldliness, whether integral or limited, can, it would seem, make nothing of the fact that there is a 'this world' to be escaped from; least of all can it justify or explain the being of such a world, or that of any particular feature or aspect of empirical existence which it negates. Its natural recourse, therefore, is, as in the Vedânta, to the device of illusionism. But to call the characters of actual experience 'illusion,' blank nonentity, though it is a kind of poetry which has a very potent metaphysical pathos, is, philosophically considered, plainly the extremest kind of nonsense. 'Unreal' those characters may conceivably be in the sense that they have no existence or no counterparts in an objective order outside the consciousness of those who experience them. But to speak of them as absolutely unreal, while experiencing their existence in oneself and assuming it in other men, and while expressly pointing to them as imperfections to be transcended

and evils to be overcome, is obviously to deny and affirm the
same proposition in the same breath. And a self-contradiction
does not cease to be meaningless by seeming sublime. Thus
any otherworldly philosophy which does not resort to this
desperate subterfuge of illusionism seems to have this world,
whatever its ontological deficiencies, on its hands as an unaccountable mystery, a thing unsatisfying, unintelligible, and
evil, which seemingly ought not to be, yet somehow undeniably
*is*. And this embarrassment is as evident in the partial forms
of otherworldliness as in the integral variety. Even though it
be only to the temporality, the successiveness and lapsingness,
of the experiences we know, that you wish to deny the eulogis-
tic epithet of 'real,' it remains the fact that all the experienced
existence that we have is successive and lapsing, and that such
existence is, by initial hypothesis, antithetic to that which is
eternal and forever at the goal.

It is in the light of this primary antithesis of otherworldliness
and this-worldliness that the dual rôle of Plato in Western
thought can best be understood. Unhappily, when one attempts to set forth the essentials of Plato's philosophy today
one is confronted at the outset with radical differences of
opinion among learned specialists concerning two distinct
questions: first, whether the doctrines to be found in many, or
even in any, of the *Dialogues* were held by Plato himself;
second, what these doctrines — to whomever attributable —
actually were. If nothing can be said to be 'known' upon
which there is disagreement among specialists of high repute,
we can hardly be said to know anything of the teaching of
Plato himself about the profounder issues of philosophy.
Plato's characteristics as a writer naturally make the *Dialogues*
an even more fruitful field than the works of other philosophers
for learned controversies. The dramatic form in which the
reasoning is cast; his tendency to introduce avowedly 'mythical' or figurative modes of expression precisely at the crucial
or culminating points of an argument; the pervasive irony in
the Socratic dialogues; the intrinsic logical difficulties of the
problems raised; the apparent irreconcilability of the arguments of some of the dialogues with those of others; the difference between Aristotle's version of some of Plato's theories and

that which might be gathered from his own writings — these all give immense room for diversities of interpretation, and, in particular, make it easy for modern exegetes to find in him the expression, or at least the adumbration, of doctrines to which they themselves incline. I wish, so far as possible, in these lectures to avoid entering upon controverted questions of exegesis, or of the intellectual biography of individual writers. But it would, no doubt, seem an evasion of a relevant issue if, in speaking of Platonism, no account were taken of these differences in the conclusions of scholars who have devoted much of their lives to the study of the Platonic writings. The disputed question to which some brief reference must at this point be made is that concerning the attribution, not of the writings themselves, but of the doctrines (whatever they may be) contained in them. The long current view that, with the exception of some of the earlier dialogues in which the Theory of Ideas does not appear, Plato was propounding a metaphysical doctrine of his own which went far beyond the teaching of Socrates, is still affirmed by the most eminent of German Plato-scholars, Constantin Ritter, who, indeed, in his most recent work, assures his readers that " no one doubts this." [1]  But in fact there has been a marked, though not universal, tendency among recent British students of Plato to attribute the conceptions and arguments which are put into the mouth of Socrates or the other principal interlocutors in the dialogues to these philosophers, rather than to Plato himself. If Burnet's contentions are right, the entire Theory of Ideas must be ascribed to Socrates, of the substance of whose final philosophy Plato, a sort of greater Boswell, was, in the dialogues in which Socrates is the chief speaker, merely giving an objective and historically trustworthy report. It is, according to Burnet, questionable whether Plato ever accepted that theory; it is certain that when he began to set forth his own distinctive and original opinions he had already rejected it, and that the Platonic teaching, properly so called, was concerned, not with the Ideas, but mainly with "two things which hardly play any part in his earlier writings, or at least only in a mythical form, namely, God and the Soul," these being now treated "quite simply and without any touch of mythical imagery." [2]  The anthropomorphic God of the *Timaeus* and the *Laws*, in short, not the Idea of the Good, is the supreme theme of Plato's own philosophy; and the story of the creation in the former dialogue is (it would seem to be implied) to be taken, in the main, literally, and not as a myth expressing in figurative and popular language a far subtler metaphysical conception. And while one great authority thus regards as probably non-Platonic the theory most conspicuous in the dialogues of Plato's middle period, in which Socrates still sustains the burden of the argument, another, Professor A. E. Taylor, deals in a similar manner with the most important of the later ones. Agreeing substantially with Burnet that we "have no right to assume without proof" that, for example, "the doctrine of the *Phaedo* and the *Republic* was ever taught by Plato as his own," Taylor adds that it is equally "a mistake to look in the *Timaeus* for any revelation of distinctively Platonic doctrines." [3] The theories therein expounded are — or were by Plato conceived to be — those of the speaker whose name the dialogue bears, a South-Italian philosopher and medical man of an earlier generation, a contemporary of Empedocles, who sought to amalgamate the biological ideas of that philosopher "with the Pythagorean religion and mathematics." [4] This is "in fact the main thesis" of that work of vast learning which is Taylor's *Commentary on the Timaeus*.[5] If we accept both conclusions, a great part of what has usually been regarded as the philosophy of Plato is taken away from him and assigned to other and earlier thinkers; and most of the dialogues are to be understood mainly as contributions to the history of pre-Platonic speculation. From this it would follow that Plato himself (in his extant writings) must be regarded chiefly as a historian of other men's philosophies rather than as a great original philosopher.

In spite of the admirable learning and force of argument with which these views have been defended, I find it, I confess, difficult to accept them; and the difficulty is especially great with respect to those dialogues which present various aspects of the Theory of Ideas. That Plato should, solely out of piety to his early teacher, have devoted a great part of his mature life as a writer to expounding, with apparent fervor and incomparable eloquence (which was pretty certainly not that of

Socrates himself), a doctrine which he did not desire to inculcate nor believe to be true, seems to me psychologically very improbable. Nor are we without better evidence than psychological probabilities. There are two weighty evidences against Burnet's theory. The first is the testimony of Aristotle, who was extremely unlikely to be ignorant upon the matter and had no conceivable motive for misrepresenting it. And he plainly and repeatedly reports that Socrates occupied himself only with questions of moral philosophy and not at all with "the general nature of things," and that Plato introduced the name and the conception of the " Ideas " — in short, that he was responsible for the transformation of the Socratic ethics and logic of definition into a metaphysics.[6] The other piece of evidence lies in a writing of Plato's which has been singularly neglected. Its authenticity, it is true, has sometimes been disputed; but few recent Plato scholars question it. In the Seventh Epistle, probably written near the end of his life, Plato presents not only a vindication of his political activities but a summary of the fundamentals of his philosophy.[7] There is here no dramatic dialogue to render dubious the ascription of the doctrine set forth, no playful irony, no myth. Plato speaks in his own person and with the utmost earnestness. And the doctrine is essentially that of the *Phaedrus* and the sixth and seventh books of the *Republic*. It is the Theory of Ideas culminating in a frank mysticism. His deepest and "most serious" conviction, Plato declares, is, "by reason of the weakness inherent in language," incapable of adequate expression in words; and he therefore never has attempted, and never will attempt, really to convey it by mere writing or speech to other men. It can be gained only by a sudden illumination, in a soul prepared for it by austerity of life and discipline of the intellect. Nevertheless, "there is a certain true argument" which both leads towards it and makes clear why, in itself, it must remain ineffable. What that argument shows is that the true objects of rational knowledge, the only genuine realities, are the immutable essences of things — of circles and all figures, of all bodies, of all living creatures, of all affections of the soul, of the good and the fair and the just. These essences are never identical with the fleeting objects which are their sensible manifestations, nor even with our thoughts of them; nor can their nature be more than adumbrated in verbal definitions. Thus Plato's philosophic testament is nothing other than a reaffirmation of the doctrine of Ideas in its most unqualified and mystical form — and a declaration that it is this which he has "many times set forth" in his previous writings.[8]

While, for these and other reasons, I find the view that Plato was not the author of Platonism unconvincing, it is incumbent upon any contemporary expositor to recognize that there is a formidable weight of scholarly opinion in favor of it. It may, then, be the case that what I have to say of Plato's part in the history of the ideas that here concern us is true, not of him, but of other men who were before him. But for our purpose the distinction is of minor importance. The Plato with whom we are here concerned is the author of the *Dialogues*, the Plato whose words, whether they expressed his own conceptions or not, have profoundly influenced Western thought through all the subsequent centuries. The Neoplatonists, the Schoolmen, the philosophers and poets of the Renaissance, of the Enlightenment, and of the Romantic period, were, perhaps unfortunately, unacquainted with the theories of recent classical scholars. To them, Platonism was the entire body of conceptions and reasonings contained in the dialogues which they knew; and it was to them a single and, in the main, coherent system of thought — as it still is in the eyes of some not less learned contemporary exegetes.

Now *this* Plato, it need hardly be said, is the main historic source of the indigenous strain of otherworldliness in Occidental philosophy and religion, as distinguished from the imported Oriental varieties. It is through him, as Dean Inge has said, " that the conception of an unseen eternal world, of which the visible world is but a pale copy, gains a permanent foothold in the West. . . . The call, once heard, has never long been forgotten in Europe"; [9] and it is from his writings, it is to be added, that the belief that the highest good for man lies in somehow translocating himself into such a world has been perennially nourished. That the otherworldliness which his successors certainly learned *from* Plato was ever taught *by* him — or is to be found in the *Dialogues* — is, indeed, another matter about which learned opinion differs. It is zealously maintained by Ritter that there is in the Theory of Ideas in general nothing of what he calls "a fantastic view of reality." The fundamental contention of that theory is merely that our judgments, both of fact and of value, when reached by due process of reflection, possess objective validity ("the Platonic Idea is the expression of the simple thought that every rightly formed conception has its solid basis in objective reality"[10]), and that we can therefore attain a knowledge of things as they are independently of our apprehension of them. It is, of course, true that the objective counterparts of true "representations," of which Plato speaks, are universals, corresponding to classnames. But this does not imply a "doctrine of a transcendent realm of Ideas"[11] subsisting by themselves apart from the things of this world in which they are manifested. 'Ideas' are universals because *words* always designate universals; and true knowledge is *of* Ideas chiefly in the sense that "every representation as such has a universal relation, not the individual phenomenon, as its content."[12] A general concept is the result of an act of classification; and a classification is correct if "it is not purely subjective, but has a basis in the objective relations of the things classified," if it presents together a complex of properties which actually occur together in nature, in that particular collection of existing things to which we give a single name, and "is not a combination put together merely by our fancy out of elements which experience, indeed, furnishes separately, but not in such association."[13] No doubt some of "the Platonic myths and the kindred poetic similes of the *Symposium, Republic* and *Phaedrus*" suggest that Plato *did* mean something more than this by "Ideas," but these passages are but *Phantasiegemälde*; they were not meant by their author to be taken seriously, and the modern reader "cannot be too emphatically warned against the common but gross fallacy of treating them as of equal significance with the results methodically reached" by Plato "through scientific inquiry."[14]

But this version of the Platonic teaching — or of what is most emphasized and most characteristic in it — seems to me, despite the great learning of its author, essentially wrong. It rests partly upon the highly improbable assumption that Aristotle's account of the Theory of Ideas is false, not merely in some degree, but in substance and upon the main point. Now Aristotle was not a philosophically unintelligent person; he was for twenty years a pupil and associate of Plato's in the Academy; and when he wrote many other men were still living who could judge, from their own knowledge, of the general correctness of his interpretation. It is true that we have reason to think that he was disposed to make the most of the points of difference between his own philosophy and his master's; this is not uncommon with pupils. But that he completely misrepresented the nature of Plato's central doctrine it is hard to believe. Nor can such a toning-down and simplification of the Platonic doctrine be reconciled without violence with certain of the *Dialogues* themselves; while it conflicts absolutely with the evidence of the Seventh Epistle. It can be held only upon the arbitrary assumption that what seems "fantastic" to a modern philosopher of a certain school cannot possibly have seemed true to a Greek philosopher of the fifth century B. C. It requires us, *inter alia*, to suppose that just those conclusions which Socrates and all the interlocutors in the *Phaedo* agree are logically demonstrable with the highest degree of certainty[15] were for both Socrates and Plato mere flights of poetic fancy; and it requires us also to dismiss as little more than irrelevant rhetorical embellishments nearly all the myths and similitudes in Plato. It is true that he himself warns us that these are not to be taken literally; but this is not equivalent to saying that they are not to be taken seriously, that they are not figurative intimations of theses which Plato regards as both true and important, but difficult to convey "in matter-moulded forms of speech." It is — especially in the *Republic* — precisely when he reaches the height of his argument, the conceptions which for him are plainly the most certain and the most momentous, that he begins to speak in parables. He does so, as he there also explains, because in these ultimate reaches of his thought the terms of common language fail him; the truth can only be shadowed forth through sensible analogues, as in a glass darkly. But that he insisted that philosophy, the highest knowledge, is concerned, not with things that change, not even with the constant general laws of concomitance and succession which hold good of these things and their changes, nor yet solely with the truths of mathematics, but with a transcendent realm of pure noumena of which the natural world is only a dim and distorted shadow — this can be denied only if we are willing to treat as negligible a whole series of Plato's most distinctive and most emphatic utterances. But since this dissent of mine from the opinion of so eminent a specialist as Ritter may well seem both rash and dogmatic, I am happy to be able to support it by the weighty judgment of Professor Shorey: "The hypostatized ideas are Plato's *Ding-an-sich*, deliberately accepted with full perception of the apparent absurdity of the doctrine from the point of view of common sense." [16] "Plato's fearless and consistent realism is so repugnant to 'common sense' that modern critics either take it as a proof of the naïveté, not to say childishness, of his thought, or extenuate the paradox by arguing that he cannot have meant it seriously and must have abandoned or modified the doctrine in his maturer works. All such interpretations spring from a failure to grasp the real character of the metaphysical problem and the historical conditions that made Plato grasp and cling to this solution." [17]

So long, however, as Plato's metaphysics is occupied with a multiplicity of eternal Ideas, corresponding to all the natural variety of things, its otherworldliness is manifestly of a peculiar and partial kind. The sensible world was never for Plato a mere illusion or a mere evil. And the other world, as well as this, was a plurality; and there was also a plurality of individual souls, permanently separate from one another and distinct from the Ideas, even when translated into that higher region. The system in this phase was thus relatively free from the monistic sort of metaphysical pathos, though perhaps richer than any other in the eternalistic. The World of Ideas was rather a glorified, detemporalized replica of this world than a blank negation of it. The 'Idea' of an object of sense, though it be conceived as immutable and not apprehensible through the physical organs of perception, is still only a congealed and inefficacious counterpart of that object — with *some* of its characteristics left indeterminate. Nothing of the rich qualitative diversity of nature is — or, at all events, should be —

left out: simple sensible qualities; the non-temporal relations which subsist between natural objects; the complex groupings of such qualities and relations, which make up the 'what' of the things we experience; and with these, all the moral and aesthetic qualities, justice and temperance and beauty — all are simply projected into another realm of being, where each may be the better enjoyed aesthetically by virtue of its conceived exemption from passage and alteration and of the irrelevance to it, in its eternal fixity, of all human planning and striving. It presents no objects to be achieved; there is nothing to be *done* about it; to contemplate it is, after all, to enjoy, in James's phrase, a "moral holiday." But what is contemplated consists of the ingredients of the world we know viewed *sub quâdam specie aeternitatis* — with perhaps, for Plato at times, some illicit exclusions of the essences which, even when so viewed, are not pleasing matter for contemplation. It is true that Plato himself did not use his World of Ideas as a resort in which to take moral holidays. He was bent upon making it instrumental to terrestrial ends, upon deriving concrete moral and political lessons from it; and he has been reproached for this by Mr. Santayana, who finds him ignorant of the nature of the "spiritual life," for which the disinterested contemplation of the essences is sufficient, which has no preferences and is "disintoxicated" from the values, moral as well as sensual, that engross our lives as temporal and active creatures. "Pure Being is infinite, its essence includes all essences; how then should it issue particular commands, or be an acrimonious moralist?" In this criticism Mr. Santayana has, I think, pointed out a real inconsistency in Plato; though I also think, as apparently Mr. Santayana does not, that it was a happy inconsistency.

It is only when, in the *Republic*, Plato introduces an Idea of Ideas, from which the others seem to be conceived as in some obscure manner derivative, that he plainly appears as the father of otherworldliness in the West—though Parmenides, no doubt, was its *Urgrossvater*. Here, as elsewhere, there is no question as to the nature of Plato's historic influence; the completely 'other' and ineffable 'One,' the Absolute of the Neoplatonists, it is certain, was for those philosophers, and their many later echoers, medieval and modern, Jewish, Moslem, and Christian, an interpretation of Plato's 'Idea of the Good.' But here also, as before, the contemporary specialists in Platonic studies are not agreed that what came out of Plato's doctrine was contained in it. Ritter, in accordance with his general eagerness to free the Theory of Ideas from any strain of " the fantastic or grossly non-natural," finds the " Idea of the Good" synonymous with " the state of good," and holds that both expressions signify only that the concept associated with the word 'good' is "no mere fanciful creation of our own thought, but has an independent, objective reality"; and this proposition, he thinks, can be otherwise expressed by saying that " the world of actuality is really so constituted that we have reason to call it good, to regard good as dominant in it." What, in short, Plato is affirming, in what he says about the Idea of the Good, is " the reign of a rational divine power in all that exists and all that comes to pass in the world" (*das Walten einer vernünftigen göttlichen Macht in allem Weltsein und Weltgeschehen*).[18] This reduces the meaning of the doctrine that the Good is the Idea of Ideas to an optimistic faith in the control of this world's temporal course by a benevolent providence — this faith being at the same time curiously confused with, or regarded as the basis of, the assertion of the objective validity of moral judgments. That Plato held both these beliefs, and that the latter was one of his most persistent and fundamental convictions, cannot be denied. But to suppose that this simple creed was all that Plato meant to convey by his strange and oracular utterances about the Idea of the Good is to leave out of account precisely what is most conspicuous and most distinctive in them. Against all such tendencies (now much in the fashion) to, so to say, naturalize this part of Plato's teaching, his own words too loudly speak.

For there are certain things which the *Republic* surely makes plain enough about Plato's conception of that Idea. First, that it is for him — or for the Platonic Socrates — the most indubitable of all realities. Second, that it *is* an Idea or essence — " Good itself," in distinction from the particular and changing existences which in varying degrees participate in its nature;[19] and that it therefore has the properties common to all the Ideas, of which the most fundamental are eternity and immutability. Third, that it is the polar opposite to 'this' world; to apprehend it, the faculty of knowledge,

along with the whole soul, must be wheeled round from that which is subject to becoming until it is able to endure the contemplation of that which is, and the most resplendent part thereof; and this, we declare, is the Good.[20]

Fourth, that its true nature is therefore ineffable in the forms of ordinary speech; it is "an indescribable beauty," and cannot be literally brought under even the most universal of the categories applicable to other objects of thought; "far from being identical with reality" — i. e., in any sense in which other things have reality — "it actually transcends it in dignity and potency." [21] Fifth, that the Form of the Good is the universal object of desire, that which draws all souls towards itself; and that the chief good for man even in this life is nothing but the contemplation of this absolute or essential Good. It is true that those who have become capable of the contemplative life must be compelled to forgo it in order to become the rulers of the state; but this is for them a temporary sacrifice of their own highest felicity for the sake of others. Those who have caught some vision of the Good "will not willingly busy themselves about the affairs of men, but will ever be eager to occupy themselves with the things that are above." [22] In this world's business they will at first, indeed, be clumsy enough — so different is it from that contemplation of the divine which they once enjoyed. For the genuine knowledge of the Good is for Plato certainly no mere acquaintance with natural laws, and no pragmatic wisdom, even of the highest degree. It is not possessed by those who merely have "the keenest eye for the passing object and remember best all that used to precede and follow and accompany it," and from this "are best able to foresee what is going to happen next." [23]

The interpreters of Plato in both ancient and modern times have endlessly disputed over the question whether this conception of the absolute Good was for him identical with the conception of God. Stated thus simply, the question is meaningless, since the word 'God' is in the last degree ambiguous. But if it be taken as standing for what the Schoolmen called the *ens perfectissimum,* the summit of the hierarchy of being, the ultimate and only completely satisfying object of contemplation and adoration, there can be little doubt that the Idea of the Good *was* the God of Plato; and there can be none that it became the God of Aristotle, and one of the elements or 'aspects' of the God of most of the philosophic theologies of the Middle Ages, and of nearly all the modern Platonizing poets and philosophers. And though in Plato, as in his followers, some vague notion of a sublimated mode of conscious life and blissful feeling probably persisted even in the conception of this otherworldly Absolute,[24] beyond this the attributes of such a God were, in strictness, expressible only in negations of the attributes of this world. You could take, one after another, any quality or relation or kind of object presented in natural experience, and say, with the Sage in the Upanishad: 'The true reality is not like this, it is not like that' — adding only that it is something far better.

It was nevertheless by a peculiar dialectic of his own — quite different, for example, from that which is exemplified in the monism of the Vedânta — that Plato reached this climax of the otherworldly strain in his philosophizing. His Absolute was the Idea of *the Good*; and the term 'good' for him, as in most Greek thought, connoted, above all, a certain definite, though still essentially negative, characteristic. This is manifest in nearly all the Greek schools of moral philosophy which descended from Socrates — in the temper of the ideal Cynic, Diogenes, who needed and wanted nothing that any other man could give him, in the ataraxy of the Epicureans, in the apathy of the Stoics. The essence of 'good,' even in ordinary human experience, lay in self-containment, freedom from all dependence upon that which is external to the individual. And when 'the Good' is hypostatized and made the essence of the supreme reality, the term has the same connotation, except that it is now taken in an absolute and unqualified sense. "The Good," says Plato in the *Philebus,* "differs in its nature from everything else in that the being who possesses it always and in all respects has the most perfect sufficiency and is never in need of any other thing." [25] "The claims of both pleasure and mind to be the Good itself" are, in the argument of the dialogue, "alike set aside" on the ground that "both of them lack self-sufficiency (αὐτάρκεια) and adequacy and completeness." [26] Such is the property in which all particular 'goods' in some degree participate; such in its fullness is the attribute which distinguishes the Absolute Being from all others.

Now there was plainly implicit in this dialectic of the Idea of the Good a strange consequence, which was to dominate the religious thought of the West for more than two thousand years and is, though no longer dominant, still potent in it. If by 'God' you meant — among many other and seemingly incompatible things — the Being who is, or eternally possesses, the good in the highest degree; and if "the good" meant absolute self-sufficiency; and if all imperfect and finite and temporal beings are, as such, not to be identified with the divine essence — then it manifestly followed that *their* existence — that is, the existence of the entire sensible world in time, and of all conscious beings who are not in any sense genuinely self-sufficient — can bring no addition of excellence to reality. The fullness of good is attained once for all in God; and "the creatures" add nothing to it. They have from the divine point of view no value; if they were not, the universe would be none the worse. Plato himself, it is true, does not explicitly draw out this consequence, and the fact that he does not is, no doubt, significant. But it is nevertheless in the clear implication of this part of his doctrine that we must recognize the primary source of that endlessly repeated theorem of the philosophic theologians that God has no need of a world and is indifferent to it and all that goes on in it. This implication of the Platonic Idea of the Good speedily became explicit in the theology of Aristotle. "One who is self-sufficient," he writes in the *Eudemian Ethics*, "can have no need of the service of others, nor of their affection, nor of social life, since he is capable of living alone. This is especially evident in the case of God. Clearly, since he is in need of nothing, God cannot have need of friends, nor will he have any." [27] It is — to cite, by way of anticipation, only one or two out of a thousand later examples — this Platonic as well as Aristotelian strain that Jonathan Edwards may be heard echoing in Colonial America, when he declares: "No notion of God's last end in creation of the world is agreeable to reason which would truly imply or infer any indigence, insufficiency and mutability in God; or any dependence of the Creator on the creature, for any part of his perfection or happiness. Because it is evident, by both Scripture and reason, that God is infinitely, eternally, unchangeably and independently glorious and perfect; that he stands in no need of, cannot be profited by, or receive anything from the creature, or be truly hurt, or be the subject of any suffering or impair of his glory and felicity from any other being." [28] This eternally serene and impassible Absolute is, manifestly, somewhat difficult to recognize in the sadistic deity of the sermon on "Sinners in the Hands of an Angry God"; but Edwards did not differ from most of the great theologians in having many Gods under one name. This element in the Platonic tradition, no doubt, has owed its persistence to the fact that it corresponds to one of the natural varieties of religious experience. There is plainly one type or mood of religious imagination and feeling, and a concomitant kind of theological dialectic, which can be satisfied with nothing less than an assurance of the utter isolation of the supreme object of contemplation from the natural world, and its sublime indifference even to its worshippers. The perennial vitality of this way of thinking may be seen in the expression of it by a writer in many respects extremely 'modern,' in whom one would not have anticipated finding it. "The artistic and intellectual consciousness," Mr. C. E. M. Joad has recently declared, "are exalted, not degraded, by the otherness of their objects. The point applies with even greater force to the religious consciousness. A Deity who, conceived as permanent and perfect, yet enters into relation with a world which is changing and imperfect, with the changing and imperfect human beings that inhabit it, or with the principle of life that animates it, is diminished in respect of the qualities for which he is venerated. Like Goodness and Beauty, Deity, if Deity exists, must be a non-human value, whose significance consists in His very unlikeness to the life that aspires to Him. He may be known by life, and, as life evolves and develops, He may be known increasingly, . . . but God himself is unaffected by such contemplation. . . . He is unaware of the movement of life towards Him. . . . God, it is obvious, if He is to be an

object worthy of our adoration must be kept unspotted from
the world that adores him." [29] That is a contemporary and
quite precise phrasing of a characteristic note of the mode of
otherworldliness which soon developed out of — if it was not
quite unequivocally expressed in — the Platonic doctrine concerning the Idea of the Good.

Now if Plato had stopped here, the subsequent history of
Western thought would, it can hardly be doubted, have been
profoundly different from what it has been. But the most notable — and the less noted — fact about his historic influence
is that he did *not* merely give to European otherworldliness its
characteristic form and phraseology and dialectic, but that he
also gave the characteristic form and phraseology and dialectic
to precisely the contrary tendency — to a peculiarly exuberant
kind of this-worldliness. For his own philosophy no sooner
reaches its climax in what we may call the otherworldly direction than it reverses its course. Having arrived at the conception of an Idea of Ideas which is a pure perfection alien to all
the categories of ordinary thought and in need of nothing external to itself, he forthwith finds in just this transcendent and
absolute Being the necessitating logical ground of the existence
of this world; and he does not stop short of the assertion of the
necessity and worth of the existence of all conceivable kinds of
finite, temporal, imperfect, and corporeal beings. Plato clearly
was dissatisfied with a philosophy in which no ground or
explanation of the existence of mundane things, and of the
number and diversity of their several modes and degrees of
imperfection, was so much as suggested, and in which the flux
was a wholly senseless and supererogatory addition to the
Eternal. And if any reason for the being of the sensible world
was to be found, it must necessarily, for Plato, be found in the
Intellectual World, and in the very nature of the sole Self-
Sufficing Being. The not-so-good, not to say the bad, must be
apprehended as derivative from the Idea of the Good, as involved in the essence of Perfection. The self-same God who
was the Goal of all desire must also be the Source of the creatures that desire it.

This crucial turn in Plato's doctrine first becomes apparent in the same passage of the *Republic* in which the 'otherness' of the Idea of the Good is so insistently declared.[30] The Good is "not only, to all things known [i. e., by us] the cause of their being known, but also of their existence and their reality" — of the sort of reality they possess, which, as we have seen, is so different for Plato from that of "the Good" that he is unwilling to use the same term for both. The transition here is, no doubt, too abrupt and oracular to be intelligible; but its meaning and its grounds in Plato's mind are to be found more fully indicated in a passage of that later dialogue which — though, as Jowett said, it is to most modern readers "the most obscure and repulsive" — nevertheless had for two millennia by far the greatest influence of all the Platonic writings. In the *Timaeus* Plato definitely undertakes the return journey from that higher region of "absolute being" to the lower world which his thought in certain moods, and perhaps in an earlier phase, so eagerly outsoared.[31] It is true that much of this dialogue is expressly mythical, and that it is therefore necessary to disengage its serious philosophic content from the poetic imagery. Where the lines are to be drawn it is not always easy to determine; there has been, apparently from the second generation of the Academy to the present day, disagreement among the learned on the question where the poetry ends and the philosophy begins. Into most of these involved controversies it is, fortunately, not essential that we should enter. Our concern is solely with two closely related conceptions which the dialogue first introduces, so far as we know, into the general stock of Occidental philosophical ideas. The first is an answer to the question: *Why* is there any World of Becoming, in addition to the eternal World of Ideas, or, indeed, to the one supreme Idea? The second is an answer to the question: What principle determines the number of kinds of being that make up the sensible and temporal world? And the answer to the second question is for Plato — or at all events for the philosopher who holds forth in the dialogue — implicit in the answer to the first.

Both of these are questions of a sort which, for the most part, philosophers no longer ask — though some modern physicists, who are perhaps the boldest speculative minds of our time,

have attempted a kind of answer to the second. It was remarked more than half a century ago by T. H. Green that
"every form of the question why the world as a whole should
be what it is, . . . is unanswerable." [32] There is scarcely any
general contrast between the Platonic strain in European
thought down to the late eighteenth century and the philosophy of more recent times which is more significant than this.
For to acknowledge that such questions are necessarily insoluble or meaningless is to imply that, so far as we can judge,
the world is in final analysis non-rational, that its being at all,
and its possessing the extent that it has and the range of diversity which its components exhibit, and its conformity to the
very curious set of primary laws which empirical science discovers — that these are just brute facts for which no intelligible
reason can be given, and which might equally well have been
other than they are. If that is the case, the constitution of the
world is but a whim or an accident. But Plato transmitted to
later Greek and medieval and early modern philosophy the
vast assumption — which was, indeed, more than once challenged — that these questions may and should be asked; and
he provided, for those after him who asked them, the long
accepted answer. The history we are to review is thus, among
other things, a part of the history of Western man's long effort
to make the world he lives in appear to his intellect a rational
one.

The answer to the first question is introduced in a simple and
doubtless figurative phrase, which was to be reiterated by
countless later philosophers and poets. Before beginning the
story of the genesis of the world, "let us," says Timaeus, "state
the cause wherefor he who constructed it did construct Becoming and the universe." The reason is that "he was good, and
in one that is good no envy of anything else ever arises. Being
devoid of envy, then, he desired that everything should be so
far as possible like himself. This, then, we shall be wholly
right in accepting from wise men as being above all the sovereign originating principle of Becoming and of the cosmos." [33]
What did these sentences mean — or at all events, what were
they understood to mean by later Platonists? The being to
whom "goodness" is here ascribed is nominally the anthropo-

morphic Artificer of the world who is the hero of the creation-myth which the dialogue relates. But if we are to assume that the doctrine of this dialogue is at all reconcilable with that of the *Republic* — to which the *Timaeus* is presented as a sort of supplement — the details of the myth, and most of the characteristics and activities ascribed to the Demiurgus, cannot be taken literally; nor have they been so taken by most ancient and modern followers of Plato. In the *Republic* the ground and source of all being, we have seen, is the Idea of the Good itself; and it has therefore been held by many interpreters that the Creator who figures in the *Timaeus* is simply a poetic personification of that Idea, or — as the Neoplatonists construed it — an emanation, or subordinate divinity, through which the world-generating function of the Absolute and Perfect One was exercised. More probable than either is the view that the two originally distinct strains in Plato's thought are here fused, and the resultant conception then given a largely figurative expression. Plato had in his philosophy two classes of supersensible and permanent beings which were in other respects quite different in nature, as the conceptions of them were in their historic origins — 'Ideas' and 'souls.' Ideas were eternal objects of pure thought, souls were everlasting conscious and thinking beings; and since the former were universals or essences, and the latter were individuals, they could not easily be reduced to unity. But it is at least a probable conjecture — which can be supported by specific passages — that Plato in the end conceived of the highest members of both series as somehow identical. If so, the Demiurgus of the *Timaeus*, as "the best soul," may be regarded as possessing fully the attributes of "that which is good in itself" — however figurative we may suppose the greater part of the characterization of it to be. One or another of these three interpretations must be adopted if we are to assume that the Platonic doctrine has any unity and coherency whatever.

In any case, the passage tells us that the supramundane being whose reality accounts for the existence of this world was "good." And we must keep in mind that, for any Platonist, nothing partook in any degree of the nature or essence expressed by the word 'good,' except in so far as it was self-sufficient. In the *Timaeus* itself, the excellence, after its own fashion, even of the created world, is made to consist in a sort of relative and physical self-sufficiency; the material universe was "so designed that all its active and all its passive processes occurred within itself and by its own agency, since he that constructed it deemed that it would be better if it were self-sufficient rather than in need of other things." [34] The "best soul" would clearly, upon *this* Platonic principle, not be the best if it had need, for its own existence or excellence or happiness, of anything other than itself. Yet when he sets about telling us the reason for being of this world, Plato exactly reverses the essential meaning of "good." In part, no doubt, he is taking advantage of the double signification which the word had in Greek as in modern usage. But the metaphor which he employs in making the transition suggests that he was attempting to reconcile the two senses, and, indeed, to derive the one from the other. A self-sufficient being who is eternally at the goal, whose perfection is beyond all possibility of enhancement or diminution, *could* not be "envious" of anything not itself. Its reality could be no impediment to the reality, in their own way, of beings other than it alike in existence and in kind and in excellence; on the contrary, unless it were somehow productive of them, it would lack a positive element of perfection, would not be so complete as its very definition implies that it is. And thus Plato, tacitly making the crucial assumption that the existence of many entities not eternal, not supersensible, and far from perfect, was inherently desirable, finds in his other-worldly Absolute, in the Idea of the Good itself, the reason why that Absolute cannot exist alone. The concept of Self-Sufficing Perfection, by a bold logical inversion, was — without losing any of its original implications — converted into the concept of a Self-Transcending Fecundity. A timeless and incorporeal One became the logical ground as well as the dynamic source of the existence of a temporal and material and extremely multiple and variegated universe. The proposition that — as it was phrased in the Middle Ages — *omne bonum est diffusivum sui* here makes its appearance as an axiom of metaphysics. With this reversal there was introduced into European philosophy and theology the combination of ideas that for centuries was to give rise to many of the most characteristic internal conflicts, the logically and emotionally opposing strains, which mark its history — the conception of (at least) Two-Gods-in-One, of a divine completion which was yet *not* complete in itself, since it could not be itself without the existence of beings other than itself and inherently incomplete; of an Immutability which required, and expressed itself in, Change; of an Absolute which was nevertheless not truly absolute because it was related, at least by way of implication and causation, to entities whose nature was not *its* nature and whose existence and perpetual passage were antithetic to its immutable subsistence. The dialectic by which Plato arrives at this combination may seem to many modern ears unconvincing and essentially verbal, and its outcome no better than a contradiction; but we shall fail to understand a large and important part of the subsequent history of ideas in the West if we ignore the fact that just this dual dialectic dominated the thought of many generations, and even more potently in medieval and modern than in ancient times.

To the second question — *How many* kinds of temporal and imperfect beings must this world contain? — the answer follows by the same dialectic: *all* possible kinds. The "best soul" could begrudge existence to nothing that could conceivably possess it, and "desired that all things should be as like himself as they could be." "All things" here could consistently mean for Plato nothing less than the sensible counterparts of every one of the Ideas; and, as Parmenides in the dialogue bearing his name (130c, e) reminds the young Socrates, there are in the World of Ideas the essences of all manner of things, even things paltry or ridiculous or disgusting. In the *Timaeus*, it is true, Plato speaks chiefly of "living things" or "animals"; but with respect to these, at least, he insists upon the necessarily complete translation of all the ideal possibilities into actuality. It must not, he says, "be thought that the world was made in the likeness of any Idea that is merely partial; for nothing incomplete is beautiful. We must suppose rather that it is the perfect image of the whole of which all animals — both individuals and species — are parts. For the pattern of the universe contains within itself the intelligible forms of all beings just as this world comprehends us and all other visible creatures. For the Deity, wishing to make this world like the fairest and most perfect of intelligible beings, framed one visible living being containing within itself all other living beings of like nature," that is, temporal and sensible. There is a passage in the *Timaeus* which seems to imply that there are in the intelligible world Ideas even of individuals, or at all events of the most nearly particularized universals, those which are, by virtue of the number of their differentiating qualities, as like individuals as may be: of the perfect and eternal model, says Plato, "the other living beings [i. e., their "Forms"], individually and generically, are parts; and to this model the cosmos is of all things most like." [35] It is because the created universe is an exhaustive replica of the World of Ideas that Plato argues that there can be only one creation; it includes the copies "of all other intelligible creatures," and therefore there is, so to say, nothing left over in the model after which a second world might be fashioned. So, in the form of a myth, the story of the successive creation of things is told. After all the grades of immortal beings have been generated, the Demiurgus notes that mortals still remain uncreated. This will not do; if it lack even these the universe will be faulty, "since it will not contain all sorts of living creatures, as it must do if it is to be complete." In order, then, that "the Whole may be really All," the Creator deputed to the lesser divinities who had already been brought into being the task of producing mortal creatures after their kinds. And thus "the universe was filled completely with living beings, mortal and immortal," and thereby became "a sensible God, which is the image of the intelligible — the greatest, the best, the fairest, the most perfect." In short, Plato's Demiurgus acted literally upon the principle in which common speech is wont to express the temper not only of universal tolerance but of comprehensive approbation of diversity — that it takes all kinds to make a world.

Even if Plato had not given this theological form to his answer to the question how many modes of being the universe must contain, he could hardly have failed to reach the same conclusion on other grounds. For the alternative would have been the admission that, out of the whole range of the Ideas, only a limited selection have sensible embodiment. But this, we may be fairly sure, would have seemed to him a strange anomaly. If any eternal essences have temporal counterparts, the presumption was that all do so, that it is of the nature of an Idea to manifest itself in concrete existences. If it were not so, the connection of the two worlds would have seemed unintelligible, the constitution of the cosmos, indeed, of the realm of essence itself, a haphazard and arbitrary thing. And it was wholly contrary to Plato's way of thinking to entertain such a supposition.

It is this strange and pregnant theorem of the 'fullness' of the realization of conceptual possibility in actuality, that, in conjunction with two other ideas usually associated with it and commonly regarded as implied by it, is to be the principal topic of these lectures. It has, so far as I know, never been distinguished by an appropriate name; [36] and for want of this, its identity in varying contexts and in different phrasings seems often to have escaped recognition by historians. I shall call it the principle of plenitude, but shall use the term to cover a wider range of inferences from premises identical with Plato's than he himself draws; i. e., not only the thesis that the universe is a *plenum formarum* in which the range of conceivable diversity of *kinds* of living things is exhaustively exemplified, but also any other deductions from the assumption that no genuine potentiality of being can remain unfulfilled, that the extent and abundance of the creation must be as great as the possibility of existence and commensurate with the productive capacity of a 'perfect' and inexhaustible Source, and that the world is the better, the more things it contains. Before we proceed to survey the later adventures and alliances of this principle, two implications latent in Plato's original enunciation of it ought to be noted.

(1) In the duality of metaphysical tendencies which we have now seen to be characteristic of Platonism was implicit a corresponding reversal of the original Platonic scheme of values — though of this also the full consequences were to be but tardily worked out. The Intellectual World was declared to be deficient without the sensible. Since a God unsupple-

mented by nature in all its diversity would not be "good," it followed that he would not be divine. And with these propositions the simile of the Cave in the *Republic* was implicitly annulled — though Plato himself seems never to have realized this. The world of sense could no longer, except by an inconsistency, be adequately described as an idle flickering of insubstantial shadow-shapes, at two removes from both the good and the real. Not only did the sun itself produce cave, and fire, and moving shapes, and the shadows, and their beholders, but in doing so it manifested a property of its own nature not less essential — and, as might well appear, even more excellent — than that pure radiance upon which no earthly eye could steadfastly gaze. The shadows were as needful to the Sun of the intellectual heavens as the Sun to the shadows; and though opposite to it in kind and separate from it in being, their existence was the very consummation of its perfection. The entire realm of essence, it was implied, lacked what was indispensable to its meaning and worth so long as it lacked embodiment. And it was, logically, no far cry from this to that later conception in which the allegory of the Cave was precisely reversed — the World of Ideas now becoming an insubstantial thing, a *mere* pattern, having, like all patterns, value only when given concrete realization, an order of "possibles" which had but tenuous and meagre being in a sort of antemundane Kingdom of the Shades until the boon of existence was conferred upon them. Why then, it could be asked, should the mind of man busy itself, either for contemplation or for delight, with these bare, abstract, changeless Forms of things, why should it dwell upon the shadows, when it had before it sensible realities in all their full-blooded particularity and was itself a participant in that same richer mode of being? But even where the inversion of the primary Platonic scheme of things was not carried so far as this, it was eventually to prove easy to find in the logic of this passage of the *Timaeus* support for the conviction that the proper business of a Troglodyte is with the shadows in his cave. For if he should seek to leave the dim region assigned him and turn to the sunlit fields without, he would (it could be, and was to be, argued) be counterworking the Universal Cause, leaving vacant a place in that general order in which the principle of plenitude required that every possible place should be filled.

(2) This expansiveness or fecundity of the Good, moreover, as Plato clearly implies, is not the consequence of any free and arbitrary act of choice of the personal Creator in the myth; it is a dialectical necessity. The Idea of the Good is a necessary reality; it cannot be other than what its essence implies; and it therefore must, by virtue of its own nature, necessarily engender finite existents. And the number of kinds of these is equally predetermined logically; the Absolute would not be what it is if it gave rise to anything less than a complete world in which the 'model,' i. e., the totality of ideal Forms, is translated into concrete realities. It follows that every sensible thing that is, is because it — or at all events, its sort — cannot but be, and be precisely what it is. This implication, it is true, is not fully drawn out by Plato himself; but since it is plainly immanent in the *Timaeus*, he thus bequeathed to later metaphysics and theology one of their most persistent, most vexing, and most contention-breeding problems. The principle of plenitude had latent in it a sort of absolute cosmical determinism which attains its final systematic formulation and practical application in the *Ethics* of Spinoza. The perfection of the Absolute Being must be an intrinsic attribute, a property inherent in the Idea of it; and since the being and attributes of all other things are derivative from this perfection because they are logically implicit in it, there is no room for any contingency anywhere in the universe. The goodness of God — in the language of religion — is a constraining goodness; he is not, in Milton's phrase, "free to create or not," nor free to choose some possible kinds of beings as the recipients of the privilege of existence, while denying it to others. And since the characteristics that each of these has are also, upon Platonistic principles, inherent in the eternal Idea of it — in just that distinctive possibility of being of which it is the realization — neither God nor the creatures could conceivably have been or done aught other than what they are and do. But though the fundamental conceptions of the *Timaeus* were to become axiomatic for most medieval and early modern philosophy, against this implication of them, it is notorious, there has been

in the Western mind a perennial recalcitrance. The reasonings in which this recalcitrance manifested itself, and the motives which prompted it, do not as yet concern us.

The reverse process in Platonism finds no place in the system of Aristotle. There is, it is true, much less of the general temper of otherworldliness in him than in Plato. But his God generates nothing. Except for a few lapses into the common fashions of speech, Aristotle adheres consistently to the notion of self-sufficiency as the essential attribute of deity; and he sees that it precludes that sort of dependence upon others which would be implied by an inner necessity of producing them. It is true that this Unmoved Perfection is for Aristotle the cause of all motion and, it would seem (though there is a duality in Aristotle's ideas here), of all the activity of imperfect beings; but it is their final cause only.[37] The bliss which God unchangingly enjoys in his never-ending self-contemplation is the Good after which all other things yearn and, in their various measures and manners, strive. But the Unmoved Mover is no world-ground; his nature and existence do not explain why the other things exist, why there are just so many of them, why the modes and degrees of their declension from the divine perfection are so various. He therefore cannot provide a basis for the principle of plenitude. And that principle is, in fact, formally rejected by Aristotle in the *Metaphysics*: "it is not necessary that everything that is possible should exist in actuality"; and "it is possible for that which has a potency not to realize it."[38]

On the other hand, it is in Aristotle that we find emerging another conception — that of continuity — which was destined to fuse with the Platonistic doctrine of the necessary 'fullness' of the world, and to be regarded as logically implied by it. Aristotle did not, indeed, formulate the law of continuity with any such generality as was afterwards given to it. But he furnished his successors, and especially his late medieval admirers, with a definition of the continuum: "Things are said to be continuous whenever there is one and the same limit of both wherein they overlap and which they possess in common."[39] That all quantities — lines, surfaces, solids, motions, and in general time and space — must be continuous, not

discrete, Aristotle maintained.⁴⁰ That the qualitative differences of things must similarly constitute linear or continuous
series he did not with equal definiteness assert, still less that
they constitute a single continuous series. Nevertheless, he is
responsible for the introduction of the principle of continuity
into natural history. That all organisms can be arranged in
one ascending sequence of forms, he did not, indeed, hold. He
saw clearly — what it required, certainly, no great perspi-
cacity to see — that living beings differ from one another in
many kinds of ways — in habitat, in external form, in anatomical structure, in the presence or absence or degree of development of particular organs and functions, in sensibility and
intelligence; he apparently saw also that there is no regular
correlation between these modes of diversity, that a creature
which may be considered 'superior' to another in respect to
one type of character may be inferior to it in respect to another. He therefore made, it would appear, no attempt to
frame any single exclusive scheme of classification even of
animals. Nevertheless, any division of creatures with reference
to some one determinate attribute manifestly gave rise to *a*
linear series of classes. And such a series, Aristotle observed,
tends to show a shading-off of the properties of one class into
those of the next rather than a sharp-cut distinction between
them. Nature refuses to conform to our craving for clear lines
of demarcation; she loves twilight zones, where forms abide
which, if they are to be classified at all, must be assigned to two
classes at once. And this insensibly minute gradation of differentness is especially evident at precisely those points at
which common speech implies the presence of profound and
well-defined contrasts. Nature, for example,

passes so gradually from the inanimate to the animate that their continuity
renders the boundary between them indistinguishable; and there is a middle
kind that belongs to both orders. For plants come immediately after inanimate things; and plants differ from one another in the degree in which they
appear to participate in life. For the class taken as a whole seems, in comparison with other bodies, to be clearly animate; but compared with animals to be inanimate. And the transition from plants to animals is continuous; for one might question whether some marine forms are animals
or plants, since many of them are attached to the rock and perish if they
are separated from it.⁴¹

The existence of 'zoophytes' continued for centuries to be the favorite, endlessly repeated, illustration of the truth of the principle of continuity in biology. But Aristotle found numerous further examples of such continuity, in classifications based upon other criteria. You may, for example, distinguish animals by their habitat — which to the Middle Ages was to seem a highly significant distinction — into those of the land, the air, and the waters; but you cannot bring all real kinds within the limits of one or another of these divisions. "Seals are in some sense land and water animals in one" and bats are "intermediate between animals that live on the ground and animals that fly, and may therefore be said to belong to both or neither." Of the mammals, again, it cannot be said that all are either quadrupeds or bipeds, the latter class solely represented by man; for "participating in the nature of both man and quadrupeds is the ape," belonging to neither class or to both. [42]

It will be seen that there was an essential opposition between two aspects of Aristotle's influence upon subsequent thought, and especially upon the logical method not merely of science but of everyday reasoning. There are not many differences in mental habit more significant than that between the habit of thinking in discrete, well-defined class-concepts and that of thinking in terms of continuity, of infinitely delicate shadings-off of everything into something else, of the overlapping of essences, so that the whole notion of species comes to seem an artifice of thought not truly applicable to the fluency, the, so to say, universal overlappingness of the real world. Now just as the Platonic writings were the principal sources both of other-worldliness and of its opposite in Western philosophy, so the influence of Aristotle encouraged two diametrically opposed sorts of conscious or unconscious logic. He is oftenest regarded, I suppose, as the great representative of a logic which rests upon the assumption of the possibility of clear divisions and rigorous classification. Speaking of what he terms Aristotle's "doctrine of fixed genera and indivisible species," Mr. W. D. Ross has remarked that this was a conclusion to which he was led mainly by his "close absorption in observed facts." Not only in biological species but in geometrical forms — "in the division of triangles, for example, into equiangular, isosceles, and scalene — he had evidence of rigid classifications in the nature of things." [43] But this is only half the story about Aristotle; and it is questionable whether it is the more important half. For it is equally true that he first suggested the limitations and dangers of classification, and the non-conformity of nature to those sharp divisions which are so indispensable for language and so convenient for our ordinary mental operations. And the very terms and illustrations used by a hundred later writers down to Locke and Leibniz, and beyond, show that they are but repeating Aristotle's expressions of this idea.

From the Platonic principle of plenitude the principle of continuity could be directly deduced. If there is between two given natural species a theoretically possible intermediate type, that type must be realized — and so on *ad indefinitum*; otherwise, there would be gaps in the universe, the creation would not be as "full" as it might be, and this would imply the inadmissible consequence that its Source or Author was not "good," in the sense which that adjective has in the *Timaeus*.

There are in the Platonic dialogues occasional intimations that the Ideas, and therefore their sensible counterparts, are not all of equal metaphysical rank or excellence; but this conception not only of existences but of essences as hierarchically ordered remains in Plato only a vague tendency, not a definitely formulated doctrine. In spite of Aristotle's recognition of the multiplicity of possible systems of natural classification, it was he who chiefly suggested to naturalists and philosophers of later times the idea of arranging (at least) all animals in a single graded *scala naturae* according to their degree of "perfection." For the criterion of rank in this scale he sometimes took the degree of development reached by the offspring at birth; there resulted, he conceived, eleven general grades, with man at the top and the zoophytes at the bottom. [44] In the *De Anima* another hierarchical arrangement of all organisms is suggested, which was destined to a greater influence upon subsequent philosophy and natural history. It is based on the "powers of soul" possessed by them, from the nutritive, to which plants are limited, to the rational, characteristic of man "and possibly another kind superior to his," each higher order possessing all the powers of those below it in the scale, and an additional differentiating one of its own.[45] Either scheme, as carried out by Aristotle himself, provided a series composed of only a small number of large classes, the sub-species of which were not necessarily capable of a similar ranking. But there were in the Aristotelian metaphysics and cosmology certain far less concrete conceptions which could be so applied as to permit an arrangement of all things in a single order of excellence. Everything, except God, has in it some measure of "privation." There are, in the first place, in its generic "nature" or essence, "potentialities" which, in a given state of its existence, are not realized; and there are superior levels of being, which, by virtue of the specific degree of privation characteristic of it, it is constitutionally incapable of attaining. Thus "all individual things may be graded according to the degree to which they are infected with [mere] potentiality." [46] This vague notion of an ontological scale was to be combined with the more intelligible conceptions of zoological and psychological hierarchies which Aristotle had suggested; and in this way what I shall call the principle of unilinear gradation was added to the assumptions of the fullness and the qualitative continuity of the series of forms of natural existence.

The result was the conception of the plan and structure of the world which, through the Middle Ages and down to the late eighteenth century, many philosophers, most men of science, and, indeed, most educated men, were to accept without question — the conception of the universe as a "Great Chain of Being," composed of an immense, or — by the strict but seldom rigorously applied logic of the principle of continuity — of an infinite, number of links ranging in hierarchical order from the meagerest kind of existents, which barely escape non-existence, through "every possible" grade up to the *ens perfectissimum* — or, in a somewhat more orthodox version, to the highest possible kind of creature, between which and the Absolute Being the disparity was assumed to be infinite — every one of them differing from that immediately above and that immediately below it by the "least possible" degree of difference. Again by way of anticipation, let me quote, out of

many, two or three modern poetic phrasings of these conceptions. In the seventeenth century the principles both of plenitude and continuity find expression in the characteristically
bold, and mixed, metaphors of George Herbert:

> The creatures leap not, but expresse a feast
> Where all thy guests sit close, and nothing wants.
> Frogs marry fish and flesh; bats, bird and beast;
> Sponges, non-sense and sense; mines, th' earth and plants.[47]

Pope in the next century in a passage which, I trust, every
schoolboy knows, enunciates the chief premise of his — which
is to say, the usual — argument for optimism, by summing up
the principles of plenitude and continuity in two neat coup-
lets:

> Of systems possible if 'tis confest
> That wisdom infinite must form the best,

then

> . . . all must full or not coherent be,
> And all that rises, rise in due degree.

From the resultant picture of the whole of things Pope deduces
a moral — much cherished by the eighteenth-century mind —
to which we shall have occasion to return.

> Vast chain of being! which from God began,
> Natures aethereal, human, angel, man,
> Beast, bird, fish, insect, what no eye can see,
> No glass can reach; from Infinite to thee,
> From thee to nothing. — On superior pow'rs
> Were we to press, inferior might on ours;
> Or in the full creation leave a void,
> Where, one step broken, the great scale's destroy'd;
> From Nature's chain whatever link you strike,
> Tenth, or ten thousandth, breaks the chain alike. ·

The consequence of any such elimination of even one link in
the series, Pope goes on to observe, would be a general dissolution of the cosmical order; ceasing to be "full," the world
would cease to be in any sense "coherent." I recall here passages so well known chiefly to remind you that the *Essay on
Man* is also, in part, one of the footnotes to Plato. James
Thomson in *The Seasons* was less expansive on the theme:

"Has any seen," he inquires — somewhat redundantly, since every instructed person in that age was supposed to be acquainted with it —

> Has any seen
> The mighty chain of being, lessening down
> From Infinite Perfection to the brink
> Of dreary nothing, desolate abyss!
> From which astonished thought, recoiling, turns?

But the Chain of Being was not, of course, to become merely the occasion for poetic rhapsodies such as these. Not only in technical metaphysics but in the sciences, it — or the group of principles from which it was forged — was to have consequences of great historical moment. Thus, for example, a special student of the history of classificatory science has pointed out the decisive rôle of the principles of gradation and continuity in the biology of the Renaissance:

> By these assertions [of Aristotle] there was established, from the very beginning of natural history, a principle which was long to remain authoritative: that according to which living beings are linked to one another by regularly graduated affinities. . . . Thus from Aristotelian science two ideas — very differently elaborated and, in truth, rather loosely connected with one another — were received as a legacy by natural history in the Renaissance. The one was the idea of a hierarchy of beings; a philosophical dogma which Christian theology, following Neo-Platonism, had often made the theme of an essentially speculative interpretation of the universe. . . . The other was the postulate that between natural things the transitions are insensible and quasi-continuous. The latter, though it may appear to be of less metaphysical significance, had, for the use of naturalists, the great advantage of permitting an at least apparently easy verification through the examination of actual sensible objects. This, moreover, did not make it impossible at the same time to draw from the Scholastic teaching an axiom which seemed to confer upon this principle a rational necessity: viz., that in the orderly arrangement of the world there can be no 'gap' or no 'dispersion' between the 'forms.' [48]

Though the ingredients of this complex of ideas came from Plato and Aristotle, it is in Neoplatonism that they first appear as fully organized into a coherent general scheme of things. The dialectic of the theory of emanation is essentially an elaboration and extension of the passages in the *Timaeus* which have been cited; it is, in short, an attempt at a deduction of the necessary validity of the principle of plenitude, with which the principles of continuity and gradation are definitely fused. In Plotinus still more clearly than in Plato, it is from the properties of a rigorously otherworldly, and a completely self-sufficient, Absolute, that the necessity of the existence of this world, with all its manifoldness and its imperfection, is deduced.

The One is perfect because it seeks for nothing, and possesses nothing, and has need of nothing; and being perfect, it overflows, and thus its superabundance produces an Other.[49] . . . Whenever anything reaches its own perfection, we see that it cannot endure to remain in itself, but generates and produces some other thing. Not only beings having the power of choice, but also those which are by nature incapable of choice, and even inanimate things, send forth as much of themselves as they can: thus fire emits heat and snow cold and drugs act upon other things. . . . How then should the Most Perfect Being and the First Good remain shut up in itself, as though it were jealous or impotent — itself the potency of all things? . . . Something must therefore be begotten of it.[50]

And this generation of the Many from the One cannot come to an end so long as any possible variety of being in the descending series is left unrealized. Each hypostasis will "produce something lower than itself"; to the "ineffable" potency of generation "we cannot impute any halt, any limit of jealous grudging; it must move forever outward, until the ultimate confines of the possible are reached. All things have come to be by reason of the infinity of that power which gives forth from itself to all things and cannot suffer any of them to be disinherited. For there was nothing which prevented any one of them from participating in the nature of the Good, in the measure in which each was capable of doing so." [51]

The first stages of this descending process belong to the Intelligible World, and have nothing to do with time or sense; but the third of the eternal hypostases, the Universal Soul, is the immediate parent of nature; for it, too, is incapable of "remaining in itself," but, "first looking back upon that from which it proceeded, it is thereby filled full" — i. e., is, so to say, impregnated with all the Ideas, which make up the substance of the next preceding hypostasis, or Reason — "and then going forward in the opposite direction, it generates an image of itself," namely, "the sentient and the vegetative natures" (i. e., animals and plants). Thus "the world is a sort of Life stretched out to an immense span, in which each of the parts has its own place in the series, all of them different and yet the whole continuous, and that which precedes never wholly absorbed in that which comes after." [52]

The Scale of Being, then, as implied by the principle of the expansiveness and self-transcendence of "the Good," becomes the essential conception of the Neoplatonic cosmology. When, for example, Macrobius, in the early fifth century, gives, under the guise of a commentary on a work of Cicero's, a Latin abridgment of much of the doctrine of Plotinus, he sums up the conception in a concise passage which was probably one of the chief vehicles through which it was transmitted to medieval writers; and he employs two metaphors — of the chain and of the series of mirrors — which were to recur for centuries as figurative expressions of this conception.

> Since, from the Supreme God Mind arises, and from Mind, Soul, and since this in turn creates all subsequent things and fills them all with life, and since this single radiance illumines all and is reflected in each, as a single face might be reflected in many mirrors placed in a series; and since all things follow in continuous succession, degenerating in sequence to the very bottom of the series, the attentive observer will discover a connection of parts, from the Supreme God down to the last dregs of things, mutually linked together and without a break. And this is Homer's golden chain, which God, he says, bade hang down from heaven to earth. [53]

The generation of the lower grades of being, or of all of them that are 'possible,' directly by the Soul of Nature, and ultimately by the Absolute, is, it will be seen, regarded by the Neoplatonist as a logical necessity. Plotinus, no doubt, is reluctant to apply the term 'necessity,' or, indeed, any other definite term, to the One; of the highest object of thought that predicate must be both affirmed and denied, as must its opposite, freedom or contingency. But, in spite of this characteristic quibbling, the whole tendency of the Neoplatonic dialectic is adverse to that conception of arbitrary volition and capriciously limited selection from among the possibilities of being, which was to play a great part in the history of Christian theology. Neither the Absolute nor the Cosmic Soul would, for our thought, be what, upon the Neoplatonist's most fundamental principles, we must regard them as being, namely, in their respective degrees "good," unless they were also generative, to a degree limited only by the logical character of the system of Ideas eternally contemplated by the second hypostasis, the Universal Reason. "Is it," Plotinus asks, "by the mere will of the being who meted out to all their several lots that inequalities exist among them?" "By no means," he answers; "it was necessary according to the nature of things that it should be so." [54]

In this assumption of the metaphysical necessity and the essential worth of the realization of all the conceivable forms of being, from highest to lowest, there was obviously implicit the basis of a theodicy; and in the writings of Plotinus and Proclus we find already fully expressed the catchwords and the reasonings to which King and Leibniz and Pope and a host of lesser writers were to give fresh currency in the eighteenth century. The optimistic formula itself, in which Voltaire was to find the theme of his irony in *Candide*, was Plotinian; and the reason which Plotinus gives for holding this to be the best possible world is that it is "full" — "the whole earth is full of a diversity of living things, mortal and immortal, and replete with them up to the very heavens." Those who suppose that the world might have been better fashioned do so because they fail to see that the best world must contain all possible evil — that is, all conceivable finite degrees of privation of good, which Plotinus assumes to be the only meaning that can be attached to the term "evil."

> He who finds fault with the nature of the universe does not know what he does, nor whither his arrogance is leading him. The reason is that men know not the successive grades of being, first, second, third and so on continually until the last is reached. . . . We ought not to demand that all shall be good, nor hastily complain because this is not possible.[55]

Difference of kind is treated as necessarily equivalent to difference of excellence, to diversity of rank in a hierarchy.

> How, if there is to be a multiplicity of forms, can one thing be worse unless another is better, or one be better unless another is worse? . . . Those who would eliminate the worse from the universe would eliminate Providence itself. . . .[56]

It is the [cosmic] Reason that in accordance with rationality produces the things that are called evils, since it did not wish all things to be [equally] good. . . . Thus the Reason did not make gods only, but first gods, then spirits, the second nature, and then men, and then animals, in a continuous series — not through envy, but because its rational nature contains an intellectual variety. But we are like men who, knowing little of painting, blame the artist because the colors in his picture are not all beautiful — not seeing that he has given to each part what was appropriate to it. And the cities which have the best governments are not those in which all citizens are equal. Or we are like one who should complain of a tragedy because it includes among its characters, not heroes only, but also slaves and peasants who speak incorrectly. But to eliminate these low characters would be to spoil the beauty of the whole; and it is by means of them that it becomes complete [lit. "full"].[57]

A rational world, then — and the kind of world implied by the nature of the Absolute — must exhibit all degrees of the imperfection which arises from the specification of differences among creatures through distinctive limitations. It is therefore absurd for man to claim more qualities than he has received; it is as if he should demand that since some animals have horns, all should have them.[58] Man simply happens to be the creature that occupies a particular place in the scale, a place which could not conceivably be left vacant.

The same principles chiefly serve Plotinus when he deals with the problem of the suffering of the non-rational (and therefore sinless) animals. He is well aware that there rages "amongst animals and amongst men a perpetual war, without respite and without truce,"[59] but he is serenely sure that this is "necessary" for the good of the Whole, since the good of the Whole consists chiefly in the "variety of its parts." "It is better that one animal should be eaten by another than that it should never have existed at all"; the tacit assumption here that it could have life only upon those terms obviously can relate, not to a necessity pertinent to animals in general, but only to the specific class of logically possible animals whose "nature" it is to be eaten. They are needed to make up the set. The existence of the carnivora and of their victims is indispensable to the abundance of that cosmic Life whose nature it is to "produce all things and to diversify all in the manner of their existence." Conflict in general, adds Plotinus, is only a special case and a necessary implicate of diversity; "difference carried to its maximum *is* opposition." And since to contain and to engender difference, "to produce otherness," is the very essence of the creative World-Soul, "it will necessarily do this in the maximal degree, and therefore produce things opposed to one another, and not merely things different to a degree falling short of opposition. Only so will its perfection be realized." [60]

Yet Plotinus is unwilling to say that the number of temporal beings, or the number which corresponds to them in the Intelligible World, is literally infinite. Like most Greek philosophers, he feels an aesthetic aversion to the notion of infinity, which he is unable to distinguish from the indefinite. To say of the sum of things that it is infinite is equivalent to saying that it has no clear-cut arithmetical character at all. Nothing that is perfect, or fully in possession of its own potential being, can lack determinate limits. The conception of infinite number is, moreover, self-contradictory; it is, Plotinus says, repeating an already trite argument, "contrary to the very nature of number." On the other hand, he cannot admit that the Ideal Number, the archetype of the numerical aspect of the sensible world, is any assignable finite number. For we can always conceive of a number greater than any such number, but "in the Intelligible World it is impossible to conceive of a number greater than that which *is* conceived" by the divine Intellect, for that number is already complete; "no number is wanting or can ever be wanting to it, whereby it might be increased." [61] Thus Plotinus's position is essentially equivocal; the number of beings is at once finite and greater than any finite number can be. It is to precisely the same evasion that we shall see many others resorting. But, finite or not, the world at all events is for Plotinus in his usual, though not quite invariant, teaching so "full" that no possible kind of being is wanting in it.

# III

## THE CHAIN OF BEING AND SOME INTERNAL CONFLICTS IN MEDIEVAL THOUGHT

FROM Neoplatonism the principle of plenitude, with the group of ideas presupposed by it or derivative from it, passed over into that complex of preconceptions which shaped the theology and the cosmology of medieval Christendom. Two men more than any others determined the formula for this new compound of old ingredients — Augustine and the unknown fifth-century author of that strange collection of misattributed writings or pious forgeries which passed for the work of Dionysius, the Athenian disciple of St. Paul. In the theology of both the influence of the principle is manifest. Thus Augustine, finding in it his answer to the old question, "Why, when God made all things, he did not make them all equal," reduces the Plotinian argument on the matter to an epigram of six words: *non essent omnia, si essent aequalia*: "if all things were equal, all things would not be; for the multiplicity of kinds of things of which the universe is constituted — first and second and so on, down to the creatures of the lowest grades — would not exist." The assumption implicit here, once more, is manifestly that literally all — that is, all possible — things *ought* to be. Still more conspicuous is the principle in the writings of the Pseudo-Dionysius. It constitutes the essence of his conception of the divine attribute of "love" or "goodness," anthropomorphic terms which usually mean with him, as they appear frequently to mean in medieval theology, not compassion, nor the alleviation of human suffering, but the immeasurable and inexhaustible productive energy, the fecundity of an Absolute not conceived as truly possessing emotions similar to man's. God's "love," in other words, in medieval writers consists primarily rather in the creative or generative than in the redemptive or providential office of deity: it is the attribute that (in a wholly Neoplatonic phrase which Thomas Aquinas borrowed from the Areopagite) *non permisit manere Deum in seipso sine germine, id est sine productione creaturarum.*[1] It was a love of which the original beneficiaries, so to say, were not actual sentient creatures or already existing moral agents, but Platonic Ideas, conceived figuratively as aspirants for the grace of actual existence.

Love which works good to all things, pre-existing overflowingly in the Good, . . . moved itself to creation, as befits the superabundance by which all things are generated. . . . The Good by being extends its goodness to all things. For as our sun, not by choosing or taking thought but by merely being, enlightens all things, so the Good . . . by its mere existence sends forth upon all things the beams of its goodness.[2]

Here the phraseology of the primitive Christian conception of a loving Father in Heaven has been converted into an expression of the dialectic of emanationism; and it is to be noted that the inner necessity of generating finite beings thus attributed to the Absolute is represented as also necessarily commensurate with the Absolute's own infinite "superabundance," and by implication, therefore, as inevitably extending to all possible things.

Dante, long after, echoes these passages of the Areopagite, as well as that of Macrobius, and repeats, as most of the theologians had done, Plato's phrase in the *Timaeus*: the good cannot be subject to "envy," and therefore must be self-communicative:

> La divina bontà, che da sè sperne
> Ogni livore, ardendo in sè sfavilla,
> Sì che dispiega le bellezze eterne.[3]

It is in his explanation of the existence of the angelic hierarchies that Dante chiefly elaborates the implications of this conception of the necessarily self-diffusive energy of *l'Eterno Valor*. Even of this one order of beings the number created is infinite, or, at all events, greater than any number of which a finite intellect can conceive.

> This nature doth so multiply itself
> In numbers, that there never yet was speech
> Nor mortal fancy that can go so far.
> And if thou notest that which is revealed
> By Daniel, thou wilt see that in his thousands

Number determinate is kept concealed. . . .
The height behold now and the amplitude
Of the eternal power, since it hath made
Itself so many mirrors, where 'tis broken,
One in itself remaining as before.[4]

But, as is elsewhere expressly said, this necessity of production inherent in the divine goodness is not limited to the creation of an infinity of spiritual beings. It extends to things mortal as well as immortal; the emanation of existence from its fount descends by degrees through all the levels of potentiality.

That which can die and that which dieth not
Are nothing but the splendor of that Idea
Which by His love our Lord brings into being.
. . . . . . . . . . That living Light
Through its own goodness reunites its rays
In new subsistences as in a mirror,
Itself eternally remaining One.
Thence it descends to the last potencies,
Downward from act to act becoming such
That only brief contingencies it makes.[5]

This is a fairly unequivocal expression of the principle of plenitude; for if even the *ultime potenze* could not be refused the privilege of existence, still less could any potentialities higher in the scale. And, for the sort of philosophy which Dante followed and is here assuming, the whole series of possibles was logically antecedent to the creation; it was an eternally fixed program for a "full" universe, which God's "goodness" made certain of realization.

Yet in these passages, though they were but poetic versions of what the Areopagite and many another respected, if less authoritative, philosopher had seemed to say, Dante verged upon a heresy; indeed, it was impossible for a medieval writer to make any use of the principle of plenitude without verging upon heresies. For that conception, when taken over into Christianity, had to be accommodated to very different principles, drawn from other sources, which forbade its literal interpretation; to carry it through to what seemed to be its necessary implications was to be sure of falling into one theological pitfall or another. This conflict of ideas did not, indeed,

arise for those extreme anti-rationalists, represented in the
later Middle Ages by the Scotists, William of Ockham, and
others, who held the arbitrary and inscrutable will of the deity
to be the sole ground of all distinctions of value. If you assumed that a thing was *made* good merely by God's willing it,
and evil, or not good, by his not willing it, you were debarred
from reasoning at all about the implications of the attribute of
"goodness." The world contained whatever it had pleased its
Maker to put into it; but what sort of creatures, or how many
of them, this might mean, no man had any means of judging,
except by experience or revelation. But upon those who felt
the need of meaning something when they called God "good,"
and those who, inheriting the Platonic tradition, had an aversion from the creed of the ultimate irrationality of things, the
principle of plenitude inevitably forced itself — only, however,
to encounter opposing assumptions or needs even more potent
than itself. Since the divine "goodness" admittedly meant
creativeness, the conferring of the gift of actuality upon things
possible, it seemed at once irrational and irreligious to say that
the *ens perfectissimum* is not thus "good" by its essence. Yet to
admit this was seemingly to fall into the extreme opposite to
that of the Scotists, and regard all reality as a necessary deduc-
tive consequence of the necessary nature of the primal Idea.
Hence it followed that God's freedom of choice must be maintained by denying what Dante came so perilously near to asserting, viz., that the actual exercise of the creative potency
extends of necessity through the entire range of possibility.

From Augustine on, the internal strain resulting from the
opposition of these two dialectical motives is clearly apparent
in medieval philosophy. In the twelfth century the issue became overt and acute through the attempt made by Abelard
to carry out consistently the consequences of the principles of
sufficient reason and of plenitude, as these were implicit in the
accepted meaning of the doctrine of the "goodness" of deity.
Abelard saw clearly that these premises led to a necessitarian
optimism. The world, if it is the temporal manifestation of a
"good" and rational World-Ground, must be the best possible
world; this means that in it all genuine possibility must be
actualized; and thus none of its characteristics or components

can be contingent, but all things must have been precisely what they are. That this consequence may appear shocking Abelard recognizes, and he at first professes to hesitate to adopt it; but in the end he leaves his reader in no doubt as to his position.

> We must inquire whether it was possible for God to make more things or better things than he has in fact made. . . . Whether we grant this or deny it, we shall fall into many difficulties because of the apparent unsuitability of the conclusions to which either alternative leads us. For if we assume that he could make either more or fewer things than he has, . . . we shall say what is exceedingly derogatory to his supreme goodness. Goodness, it is evident, can produce only what is good; but if there are things good which God fails to produce when he might have done so, or if he refrains from producing some things fit to be produced (*facienda*), who would not infer that he is jealous or unjust — especially since it costs him no labor to make anything? . . . Hence is that most true argument of Plato's, whereby he proves that God could not in any wise have made a better world than he has made. [Quotes *Timaeus* 30c] . . . God neither does nor omits to do anything except for some rational and supremely good reason, even though it be hidden from us; as that other sentence of Plato's says, *Whatever is generated is generated by some necessary cause, for nothing comes into being except there be some due cause and reason antecedent to it.* Hence also is that of Augustine's, where he shows that all things in the world are produced or disposed by divine providence, and nothing by chance, nothing fortuitously. [Quotes *Quaestiones* LXXXIII, 26] To such a degree is God in all that he does mindful of the good, that he is said to be induced to make individual things rather by the value of the good there is in them than by the choice (*libitum*) of his own will. . . . This is in accord with what Jerome says, *For God does not do this because he wills to do so, but he wills to do so because it is good.*

It is not to God, then, that the attitude *hoc volo, sic jubeo, sit pro ratione voluntas* is to be attributed, says Abelard, but only to men who are given over to the capricious desires of their own hearts. From all this — and much more which I omit — it is certain, Abelard concludes, that it is intrinsically impossible for God to do (or make) or to leave undone (or unmade) anything other than the things that he actually does at some time do or omit to do; or to do anything in any other manner or at any other time than that in which it actually is done: *ea solummodo Deum posse facere vel dimittere, quae quandoque facit vel dimittit, et eo modo tantum vel eo tempore quo facit, non alio.*[6]

Thus Abelard had, some five centuries earlier, drawn from

Plato's premise the most characteristic of Spinoza's conclusions; had, in other words, drawn from that premise its true consequence.[7] His doctrinal affinity with the seventeenth-century Jewish philosopher may be still further seen from the character of his reply to an objection which, he says, had been "very recently made," namely,

that no thanks would be due to God for what he has done, since he could not avoid doing it and acts rather by necessity than by will. This objection is wholly frivolous. For here a certain necessity arising out of his nature, or his goodness, is not separate from his will, nor can we speak of a constraint, as if he were forced to do something against his will. . . . Since his goodness is so great, his will so perfect, that he does what ought to be done, not unwillingly, but spontaneously, he is so much the more completely to be loved because of his very nature, and the more to be glorified because this goodness of his belongs to him not by accident but substantially and immutably.

From all this follows the usual argument for optimism of the sort which was to become so universally familiar in the seventeenth and eighteenth centuries: the goodness of this best of possible worlds consists, not in the absence of evils, but rather in their presence — consists, that is, in the actualization of what Abelard calls the *rationabilis varietas* which requires them. In favor of this view he could, as we already know, cite very high authority.

It is not to be doubted that all things, both good and bad, proceed from a most perfectly ordered plan, that they occur and are fitted to one another in such a way that they could not possibly occur more fittingly. Thus Augustine: since God is good, evils would not be, unless it were a good that there should be evils. For by the same reason for which he wills that good things shall exist, namely, because their existence is befitting (*conveniens*), he also wills that evil things should exist, . . . all of which as a whole tends to his greater glory. For as a picture is often more beautiful and worthy of commendation if some colors in themselves ugly are included in it, than it would be if it were uniform and of a single color, so from an admixture of evils the universe is rendered more beautiful and worthy of commendation.[8]

But though the premises of the argument could scarcely be denied by the most orthodox theologian, the conclusion could as little be admitted; Abelard had indiscreetly made manifest both the deterministic and the antinomian implications of principles which nearly everyone accepted. It was one of the heresies charged against Abelard by Bernard of Clairvaux that he taught "that God ought not to prevent evils, since by his beneficence everything that happens does so in the best possible manner." [9] And Peter Lombard, in the *Liber Sententiarum*, the famous compend which was for centuries to be the chief textbook of students of theology, condemned Abelard's reasoning on these points, and offered a curious refutation of it. To maintain that the universe is so good that it could not be better is "to make the creature equal to the Creator," of whom alone perfection may legitimately be asserted; if, however, it is admitted that the world is imperfect, it follows that there are possibilities of being and of good that are unrealized, and that "God could have made other things and better things than he has made." [10] Henceforward it was recognized to be inadmissible to accept a literal optimism, or the principle of plenitude, or the principle of sufficient reason which was the basis of both.

Yet, though the dominant philosophy of the Middle Ages could not do with these principles, it could not do without them; and the conflict between its characteristic presuppositions, which had in the time of Abelard taken the form of open controversy, continued to manifest itself in the form of an inner opposition of tendencies in the minds of individual thinkers. Nothing could better illustrate this than a review of some of the deliverances on these matters of the greatest of the Schoolmen; through it we shall see both the embarrassment which this internal strain in the traditional doctrine caused him, and the ingenious but futile logical shifts to which it compelled him to resort.

Thomas Aquinas seems first of all to affirm the principle of plenitude quite unequivocally and unqualifiedly.

> Everyone desires the perfection of that which for its own sake he wills and loves: for the things we love for their own sakes, we wish . . . to be multiplied as much as possible. But God wills and loves His essence for its own sake. Now that essence is not augmentable or multipliable in itself but can be multiplied only in its likeness, which is shared by many. God therefore wills things to be multiplied, inasmuch as he wills and loves his own perfection. . . . Moreover, God in willing himself wills all the things which are in himself; but all things in a certain manner pre-exist in God by their types (*rationes*). God, therefore, in willing himself wills other things.

. . . Again, the will follows the understanding. But God in primarily understanding himself, understands all other things; therefore, once more, in willing himself primarily, he wills all other things.[11]

Now this, as a recent Roman Catholic commentator on the *Summa contra Gentiles* observes, "taken by itself might seem to argue that God wills the existence of all things that He understands as possible, and that He necessarily wills the existence of things outside himself, and so necessarily creates them." [12] Not only might the passage mean this; it can, in consistency with assumptions which Aquinas elsewhere accepts, mean nothing else. *All* possibles "fall under an infinite understanding," in Spinoza's phrase, and, indeed, belong to its essence; and therefore nothing less than the sum of all genuine possibles could be the object of the divine will, i. e., of the creative act. But Thomas cannot, of course, admit this; he is under the necessity of affirming the freedom of the absolute will; *necesse est dicere voluntatem Dei esse causam rerum, et Deum agere per voluntatem, non per necessitatem naturae, ut quidam existimaverunt.*[13] Consequently the creation must be restricted to a selection from among the Ideas. In order to exclude necessity without excluding "goodness" from the divine act of choice, Thomas first introduces a distinction — which is almost certainly the source of the similar one in Leibniz and Wolff — between absolute and hypothetical necessity: the will of God, though it always chooses the good, nevertheless chooses it "as becoming to its own goodness, not as necessary to its goodness." This is a distinction which will not bear scrutiny; to choose other than the greater good would be, upon Thomistic principles, to contradict both the notion of the divine essence and the notion of volition; and in any case, the argument grants that the greater good, which here implies the greatest sum of possibles, is in fact chosen. Thomas therefore adds a further and highly characteristic piece of reasoning of which the outcome is simply the negation of the conclusion which he had previously expressed.

Since good, understood to be such, is the proper object of the will, the will may fasten on any object conceived by the intellect in which the notion of good is fulfilled. Hence, though the being of anything, as such, is good, and its not-being is evil; still, the very not-being of a thing may become an object to the will, though not of necessity, by reason of some good which is attached to it; for it is good for a thing to be, even at the cost of the non-existence of something else. The only good, then, which the will by its constitution cannot wish not to be is the good whose non-existence would destroy the notion of good altogether. Such a good is none other than God. The will, then, by its constitution can will the non-existence of anything except God. But in God there is will according to the fullness of the power of willing, for in Him all things without exception exist in a perfect manner. He therefore can will the non-existence of any being except himself, and consequently does not of necessity will other things than himself.[14]

Hence, though the divine intellect conceives of an infinity of possible things, the divine will does not choose them all; and the existence of finite things is therefore contingent and the number of their kinds is arbitrary.

But the argument by which the great Schoolman seeks to evade the dangerous consequences of his other, and equally definitely affirmed, premise is plainly at variance with itself as well as with some of the most fundamental principles of his system. It asserts that the existence of anything, in so far as it is possible, is intrinsically a good; that the divine will always chooses the good; and yet that its perfection permits (or requires) it to will the non-existence of some possible, and therefore good, things. It is therefore not surprising that in a later passage Aquinas again reverts to the thesis that the Absolute, if good or rational, must generate variety in a measure proportional to his power — which could only mean, infinitely, though within the restrictions imposed by the logical impossibility of some things. Origen had, in connection with his doctrine of the pre-existence of souls, declared that God's goodness had been shown at the first creation by making all creatures alike spiritual and rational, and that the existing inequalities among them were results of their differing use of their freedom of choice. This opinion Aquinas declares to be manifestly false. "The best thing in creation is the perfection of the universe, which consists in the orderly variety of things. . . . Thus the diversity of creatures does not arise from diversity of merits, but was primarily intended by the prime agent." The proof offered for this is the more striking because of the contrast between its highly scholastic method and the revolutionary implications which were latent in it.

Since every agent intends to induce its own likeness in the effect, so far as the effect can receive it, an agent will do this the more perfectly, the more perfect itself is. But God is the most perfect of agents; therefore it will belong to him to induce His likeness in creation most perfectly, so far as befits created nature. But creatures cannot attain to any perfect likeness of God so long as they are confined to one species of creature; because, since the cause exceeds the effect, what is in the cause simply, and as one thing, is found in the effect in a composite and manifold way. . . . Multiplicity, therefore, and variety, was needful in the creation, to the end that the perfect likeness of God might be found in things according to their measure. . . . [Again], if any agent whose power extends to various effects were to produce only one of those effects, his power would not be so completely reduced to actuality as by making many. But by the reduction of active power to actuality the effect attains to the likeness of the agent. Therefore the likeness of God would not be perfect in the universe if there were only one grade of effect. . . . [Again] the goodness of the species transcends the goodness of the individual, as form transcends matter; therefore the multiplication of species is a greater addition to the good of the universe than the multiplication of individuals of a single species. The perfection of the universe therefore requires not only a multitude of individuals, but also diverse kinds, and therefore diverse grades of things.[15]

It must be patent to the least critical reader of this passage that here, once more, the Angelic Doctor avoids embracing the principle of plenitude in its unqualified form only by an inconsequence, since he, like every orthodox theologian, held that the divine power extends not simply to "various" but to an infinity of effects. The substitution of "many" for "all possible" was a manifest drawing back from the conclusion which the premises not only permitted but required.

Here, then, or in passages of the same sort in other writings of Thomas Aquinas, is probably the proximate source of the arguments later to be employed by King and by Leibniz in their theodicies, and of a species of theory of value which, as taken over by eighteenth-century writers, was to have momentous consequences — the thesis of the inherent and supreme value of variety of existence as such, the assumption that the more essences, regardless of their rank in the scale, there are realized in the universe, the better it is. If the world were not constituted of things good and things evil (in the sense of deficient in good), then, says Thomas:

All possible grades of goodness would not be filled up, nor would any creature be like God in having pre-eminence over another. Thus the supreme beauty (*summus decor*) would be lost to the creation, if there were lacking that order by which things are dissimilar and unequal. . . . If there were a dead level of equality in things, only one kind of created good would exist, which would be a manifest derogation from the perfection of the creation. . . . It is no part of divine providence wholly to exclude from things the possibility of their falling short of good; but what *can* thus fall short, sometimes *will* do so; and the lack of good is evil.

Thus the great Schoolman does not hesitate before the obviously perilous thesis that "a universe in which there was no evil would not be so good as the actual universe." Those reason falsely, he declares, who say that "since an angel is better than a stone, therefore two angels are better than one angel and a stone. . . . Although an angel, considered absolutely, is better than a stone, nevertheless two natures are better than one only; and therefore a universe containing angels and other things is better than one containing angels only; since the perfection of the universe is attained essentially in proportion to the diversity of natures in it, whereby the divers grades of goodness are filled, and not in proportion to the multiplication of individuals of a single nature." [16]

It is evident from all this that one can hardly say, with the author of a recent admirable study of the Thomistic system, that Thomas holds the realization by man of "that supreme good which consists in assimilation to God" to be "the *sole* reason for being of the universe." [17] It is an equally essential part of the teaching of the great Dominican philosopher that the universe is its own reason for being; that is to say, that the "orderly variety of things," the actualization of Ideas, is an end in itself, an end which is not merely instrumental to man's salvation, and is essentially incompatible with the "assimilation" of the creatures to anything, in any sense which would imply a loss of the dissimilarity of things from one another or even from their source.

It is, probably, also here that we find the principal medium of transmission to various eighteenth-century writers of the Neoplatonic justification of the way of the lion with the ass — and of the lion's Maker. *Non conservaretur vita leonis, nisi occideretur asinus.* "It would be inconsistent with the rationality of the divine government not to allow creatures to act according to the mode of their several natures. But by the very fact of creatures so acting there follows destruction and evil in the world, since things, through their mutual contrariety and opposition, are destructive of one another." This evil of conflict and of suffering on the part of those incapable of moral evil was, then, also one which "it did not befit providence altogether to exclude from the things it governs."

All these attempts to explain evil away as necessary manifestly imply optimism; a supposed proof of the logical inevitability of a given "evil" as an element in the best possible universe could have no point unless it were assumed that the universe actually is and must be the best possible. Yet here, once more, Thomas, remembering, no doubt, the fate of Abelard, shifts his ground; and again we witness the painful spectacle of a great intellect endeavoring by spurious or irrelevant distinctions to evade the consequences of its own principles, only to achieve in the end an express self-contradiction. When he comes to confront directly Abelard's question *utrum Deus possit meliora facere ea quae facit*, Thomas first states honestly and vigorously the arguments (on the basis of accepted doctrines or authorities) for the view he is to reject. To answer the question in the affirmative seemed to be plainly equivalent to denying that God does whatever he does *potentissime et sapientissime* — which it was, of course, not permissible to deny; and again we hear one of the endlessly repeated echoes of the argument of the *Timaeus*: "If God could have made things better than he did, and would not, he was envious; but envy is wholly foreign to God." But to these considerations Thomas replies by a series of distinctions. An individual thing of a given kind cannot be better than the "essence" of its kind; thus the square of a number could not be greater than it is, for if it were it would not be the square but some other number. The irrelevance of this to the real issue is obvious. Of greater seeming relevance is the distinction between "better" when used with reference to the manner of action of the agent (*modus ex parte facientis*) and when used with reference to the character of the thing done or produced (*modus ex parte facti*). In the former sense it must be maintained that "God could not do anything in a better manner than he has done"; in the latter sense, the opposite must be asserted: "God could give to the things made by Him a better *modus essendi* than he has, so far as their accidents are concerned." But the distinction, though possible for a Scotist, was incongruous with Thomas's most cherished convictions; it implied that the "goodness" of an act, at all events in the case of deity, was wholly unrelated to the objective character of the thing done or intended. Finally, the ingenuity even of this subtle doctor was insufficient to save him from an argument of three sentences of which the third is the formal negation of the first.

It is to be maintained that, these things being supposed, the universe cannot be better than it is, because of the supremely befitting order which God has assigned to things, wherein the good of the universe consists. If any one of these things were [separately] better, the proportion which constitutes the order of the whole would be vitiated. . . . Nevertheless, God could make other things than he has, or could add others to the things he has made; and this other universe would be better.[18]

With his guarded and wavering but unmistakable approaches to the principle of plenitude Thomas Aquinas joins an entirely definite assertion of the principle of continuity. Albertus Magnus, writing *De animalibus*, had already laid it down that "nature does not make [animal] kinds separate without making something intermediate between them; for nature does not pass from extreme to extreme *nisi per medium*."[19] Thomas accordingly dwells upon the "wonderful linkage of beings (*connexio rerum*)" which nature "reveals to our view. The lowest member of the higher genus is always found to border upon (*contingere*) the highest member of the lower genus." The stock example of the zoophytes, borrowed from Aristotle, is cited; but the principal application which Thomas gives to the conception is to the relation of mind and body. The material, the *genus corporum*, at its highest, namely, in man, passes over into the mental. Man's constitution is "*aequaliter complexionatum*, has in equal degree the characters of both classes, since it attains to the lowest member of the class above bodies, namely, the human soul, which is at the bottom of the series of intellectual beings — and is said, therefore, to be the horizon and boundary line of things corporeal and incorporeal."[20] Thus the pressure of the principle of continuity tended, even in the Middle Ages, to soften, though it did not overcome, the traditional sharp dualism of body and spirit. The emphasis upon that principle is recurrent in later theological writers of the highest reputation — for example, in Nicolaus Cusanus:

> All things, however different, are linked together. There is in the genera of things such a connection between the higher and the lower that they meet in a common point; such an order obtains among species that the highest species of one genus coincides with the lowest of the next higher genus, in order that the universe may be one, perfect, continuous.[21]

The accepted 'philosophical,' as distinct from the dogmatic, argument for the existence of angels rested upon these assumptions of the necessary plenitude and continuity of the chain of beings; there are manifestly possibilities of finite existence above the grade represented by man, and there would consequently be links wanting in the chain if such beings did not actually exist. The reality of the heavenly hosts could thus be known *a priori* by the natural reason, even if a supernatural revelation did not assure us of it.[22] This — to anticipate — continued for many centuries to be the chief reason offered in justification of the belief in "spiritual creatures"; Sir Thomas Browne exclaims in *Religio Medici,* "It is a riddle to me . . . how so many learned heads should so far forget their metaphysics, and destroy the ladder and scale of creatures, as to question the existence of spirits." Even in the middle of the eighteenth century the poet Young finds in the principle of continuity a proof of the immortality of the human soul, as well as of the existence of purely or permanently incorporeal creatures:

> Look Nature through, 'tis neat gradation all.
> By what minute degrees her scale extends!
> Each middle nature join'd at each extreme,
> To that above it, join'd to that beneath.
> . . . . . . . But how preserv'd
> The chain unbroken upwards, to the realms
> Of Incorporeal life? those realms of bliss
> Where death hath no dominion? Grant a make
> Half-mortal, half-immortal; earthy part,
> And part ethereal; grant the soul of Man
> Eternal; or in Man the series ends.

Wide yawns the gap; connection is no more;
Check'd Reason halts; her next step wants support;
Striving to climb, she tumbles from her scheme.[23]

But in Young's time the assumption that there can, in a rational order, be no missing links was mainly to be turned in quite another direction, with very different results. Yet so persistent has been this inference from the principle of plenitude that we find Victor Hugo still rhetorically elaborating it in the eighteen-fifties:

Comme sur le versant d'un mont prodigieux,
Vaste mêlée aux bruits confus, du fond de l'ombre,
Tu vois monter à toi la création sombre.
Le rocher est plus loin, l'animal est plus près.
Comme le faîte altier et vivant, tu parais!
Mais, dis, crois-tu que l'être illogique nous trompe?
L'échelle que tu vois, crois-tu qu'elle se rompe?
Crois-tu, toi dont les sens d'en haut sont éclairés,
Que la création qui, lente et par degrès
S'élève à la lumière, . . .
S'arrête sur l'abîme à l'homme? .

Such a supposition, implying the illogicality of being, is inadmissible; the scale continues through countless stages higher than man:

Peuple le haut, le bas, les bords et le milieu,
Et dans les profondeurs s'évanouit en Dieu![24]

Returning to the author of the *Summa theologica*, his position with respect to the principles of plenitude and continuity may now be summed up. He employs both freely as premises, we have seen, whenever they serve his purpose; but he evades their consequences by means of subtle but spurious or irrelevant distinctions when they seem to be on the point of leading him into the heresy of admitting the complete correspondence of the realms of the possible and the actual, with the cosmic determinism which this implies. And all orthodox medieval philosophy, except the radically anti-rationalistic type, was in the same position. There were only two possible consistent views — that of Duns Scotus, on the one side, that later represented by Bruno and by Spinoza, on the other. The philosophers who rejected the former horn of the dilemma — who, as the only alternative to admitting that the creation was an irrational caprice, asserted the inherent "goodness" of deity, and accepted the principle of plenitude as implied by this — could escape the other horn only by a judicious inattention to the obvious consequences of their own premises.

The sort of reasoning from the principle of plenitude which I have been illustrating from the Christian Schoolmen was, of course, no monopoly of theirs; it has its parallels in the writings of both Moslem and Jewish medieval philosophers. Averroes writes, for example:

> Why did God create more than one sort of vegetative and animal souls? The reason is that the existence of most of these species rests upon the principle of perfection [or completeness]. Some animals and plants can be seen to exist only for the sake of man, or of one another; but of others this cannot be granted, e. g., of the wild animals which are harmful to men.[25]

There was, however, a still more significant, though less frequently explicit, inner conflict in medieval thought, and in Neoplatonism before it, which was likewise due to the association of the principle of plenitude with certain other elements in the accepted group of fundamental assumptions. It was a conflict between two irreconcilable conceptions of the good. The final good for man, as almost all Western philosophers for more than a millennium agreed, consisted in some mode of assimilation or approximation to the divine nature, whether that mode were defined as imitation or contemplation or absorption. The doctrine of the divine attributes was thus also, and far more significantly, a theory of the nature of ultimate value, and the conception of God was at the same time the definition of the objective of human life; the Absolute Being, utterly unlike any creature in nature, was yet the *primum exemplar omnium*. But the God in whom man was thus to find his own fulfilment was, as has been pointed out, not one God but two. He was the Idea of the Good, but he was also the Idea of Goodness; and though the second attribute was nominally deduced dialectically from the first, no two notions could be more antithetic. The one was an apotheosis of unity, self-sufficiency, and quietude, the other of diversity, self-transcendence, and fecundity. The one was, in the words of Peter Ramus, a *Deus omnis laboris, actionis, confectionis non modo fugiens sed fastidiens et despiciens*; the other was the God of the *Timaeus* and of the theory of emanation. The one God was the goal of the 'way up,' of that ascending process by which the finite soul, turning from all created things, took its way back to the immutable Perfection in which alone it could find rest. The other God was the source and the informing energy of that descending process by which being flows through all the levels of possibility down to the very lowest. The merely logical difficulties of reconciling these two conceptions have already been suggested; but logical difficulties, with respect to the ultimate objects of thought, did not greatly trouble the medieval mind. The notion of the *coincidentia oppositorum*, of the meeting of extremes in the Absolute, was an essential part of nearly all medieval theology, as it had been of Neoplatonism; what Dean Inge has delicately termed "the fluidity and interpenetration of concepts in the spiritual world," or in plainer language, the permissibility and even necessity of contradicting oneself when one spoke of God, was a principle commonly enough recognized, though the benefits of it were not usually extended to theological opponents. The slight uneasiness which the application of such a principle left in the mind could be, and by the scholastic theologian usually was, alleviated by the explanation that the seemingly contradictory terms were used in a *sensus eminentior* — that is to say, that they did not have their usual meanings, nor any other meaning which the human mind could understand. But the inner strain in medieval thought which here concerns us was not simply a discrepancy between two speculative ideas held by the same minds; it was also a discrepancy between two practical ideals. It might appear easy to affirm of the divine nature what to us must seem incompatible metaphysical predicates; but it was impossible to reconcile in human practice what to us must seem incompatible notions of value. There was no way in which the flight from the Many to the One, the quest of a perfection defined wholly in terms of contrast with the created world, could be effectually harmonized with the imitation of a Goodness that delights in diversity and manifests itself in the emanation

of the Many out of the One. The one program demanded
a withdrawal from all "attachment to creatures" and cul-
minated in the ecstatic contemplation of the indivisible Divine
Essence; the other, if it had been formulated, would have
summoned men to participate, in some finite measure, in the
creative passion of God, to collaborate consciously in the processes by which the diversity of things, the fullness of the universe, is achieved. It would have found the beatific vision in
the disinterested joy of beholding the splendor of the creation
or of curiously tracing out the detail of its infinite variety; it
would have placed the active life above the contemplative;
and it would, perhaps, have conceived of the activity of the
creative artist, who at once loves, imitates, and augments the
"orderly variousness" of the sensible world, as the mode of
human life most like the divine.

But in the earlier Middle Ages these implications, however
clearly contained in one side of the accepted body of doctrine,
remained for the most part without effect. Since the two
theories of value could not be concretely harmonized, medieval Christian philosophy, like Neoplatonism before it, was
constrained to choose between them, and, of course, chose the
first. It was the Idea of the Good, not the conception of a
self-transcending and generative Goodness, that determined
the ethical teaching of the Church (at least in her counsels of
perfection) and shaped the assumptions concerning man's
chief end which dominated European thought down to the
Renaissance, and in orthodox theology, Protestant as well as
Catholic, beyond it. The 'way up' alone was the direction in
which man was to look for the good, even though the God who
had from all eternity perfectly possessed the good which is the
object of man's quest was held to have found, so to say, his
chief good in the 'way down' — had, in the curious and significant phrase of the Areopagite, been "cozened by goodness
and affection and love, and led down from his eminence above
all and surpassing all, to being in all." The consummation
towards which all finite things yearn, and towards which men
were to strive consciously, was to return to and remain in the
Unity which yet did not, and by its essence could not, remain
within itself.

Hic est cunctis communis amor,
Repetuntque boni fine teneri,
Quia non aliter durare queant
Nisi converso rursus amore
Refluant causae, quae dedit esse; [26]

though this *amor che muove il sole e l'altre stelle* was the negation
or reversal of the Love which manifested itself in engendering
the multiplicity of things in heaven and earth. Sir Thomas
Browne was (as a recent writer has remarked) but repeating
the usual scholastic assumption when he wrote that "things as
they recede from unity, the more they approach to imperfection and deformity, for they behold their perfection in their
simplicities and as the nearest approach unto God." [27]

But though the scheme of values implicit in the principle of
plenitude lay thus, for the most part, undeveloped in medieval
philosophy and religion, it was too essential a part of the received tradition to remain wholly unexpressed; the conflict
between it and the opposite conception of the good sometimes
becomes apparent even in the writings of the most orthodox
theologians. Thus Augustine in a curious chapter *De pulchri-
tudine simulacrorum* observes that "the supreme art of God" is
manifested in the variety of the things that it has fashioned out
of nothing, while the inferiority of human art is shown in its
limited ability to reproduce this diversity, or *numerositas*, of
natural objects, for example, of human bodies. Augustine,
then, seems on the point of deriving a species of aesthetic theory
from the principle of plenitude; the function of art, he suggests,
is to imitate or parallel this diversity of the created world as
nearly exhaustively as possible; and this, the argument manifestly implies, is truly an *imitatio dei*, and therefore *par excellence*
a religious exercise. But here the saint checks himself and reverts violently to the ascetic and otherworldly side of his doctrine: "Not that those who fashion such works [of art] are to
be highly esteemed, nor those who take delight in them; for
when the soul is thus intent upon the lesser things — things
corporeal which it makes by corporeal means — it is the less
fixed upon that supreme Wisdom from which it derives these
very powers." [28] Thus Augustine is involved in the incongruous conclusion that God as creator is *not* to be imitated, that

certain divine powers in which men in a measure participate
are not to be employed by them, and that the creation in which
alone the divine attribute of "goodness" is manifested is not to
be enjoyed. In the efflorescence of the arts in the later Middle
Ages such an attitude, though it could not be officially abandoned, clearly became increasingly uncongenial; and we
already find Dante dwelling, as even an orthodox and mystical
poet of the fourteenth century could hardly fail to do, rather
upon the kinship of the work of the artist with the divine office
of creation. Since, according to Aristotle, art is the imitation
of Nature, and since Nature is the manifestation of the perfection of God, it follows that "your art is as it were a grandchild
of God" (*vostra arte a Dio quasi è Nipote*).[29]  In the Renaissance
this aspect of the medieval conception comes fully into its own.
"Non merita nome di Creatore," said Tasso proudly, "se non
Iddio ed il Poeta"; and Giordano Bruno wrote that "the gods
take pleasure in the multiform representations of multiform
things, in the multiform fruits of all talents; for they have as
great pleasure in all the things that are, and in all representations that are made of them, as in taking care that they be and
giving order and permission that they be made." [30]

In its ethical bearings the conflict between the implications
of the two conceptions of the *imitatio dei* may be plainly dis-
cerned in Thomas Aquinas. He often declares that "the creature approaches more nearly to God's likeness if it is not only
good but can also act for the goodness of other things, than if it
is merely good in itself," since God's goodness "outpours itself." It is for this reason, among others, that it is well that
"there is in the creatures plurality and inequality"; if all were
in all respects equal, none could "act for the advantage of another." [31]  Yet in the end, of course, the true perfection of man
does not consist, for Thomas any more than for Augustine, in
any concern with the creatures to whom one can communicate
good; it consists in the blissful absorption of the whole consciousness of the individual in the contemplation of a God to
whom one can communicate no good.

If we turn to a typical seventeenth-century Platonist, we
may see the same conflict between these two equally Platonic
conceptions of deity, and therefore of the good, still persisting,

and in an even more acute form. John Norris of Bemerton (1657–1711) dwells with almost equal fondness upon the thought of the eternal self-containedness and the perpetual self-diffusiveness implicit in the idea of an Absolute and Perfect Being. God is, on the one hand, "the universal Plenitude, whose happiness is consummated within his own circle, who supports himself upon the basis of his own all-sufficiency and is his own end and center." But on the other hand:

> The nature of God involves, as in notion and conception, so likewise in truth and reality, absolute and infinite perfection; and consequently, includes a beneficent and communicative disposition, this being a perfection. Nor does the superlative eminency of the divine nature only argue him to be communicative but to be the most communicative and self-diffusive of all beings. For as all kinds, so also all degrees of excellency must of necessity be included in a being absolutely and infinitely perfect. . . . This excellent communicativeness of the Divine Nature is typically represented, and mysteriously exemplified by the Porphyrian Scale of Being.

And Norris accordingly, in his *Divine Hymn on the Creation*, embroiders pleasantly and devoutly upon the theme of the *Timaeus*:

> Love, gentle Love, unlockt [God's] fruitful breast,
> And woke the Ideas which there dormant lay.
>   Awak'd their beauties they display;
>   Th' Almighty smil'd to see
>   The comely form of harmony
>   Of His eternal imag'ry;
> He saw 'twas good and fair, and th' infant platform blest:
> Ye seeds of being, in whose fair bosoms dwell
>   The forms of all things possible,
> Arise and your prolific force display.[32]

Norris therefore finds it difficult to see how a universe which is a replica of the world of Ideas enhanced by the additional dignity of existence, a universe which thus manifests the "favorite and darling excellence" of its Author and deserves his praise, can be an unworthy object of delight for man.

> If the beauty and variety of the creature was so considerable as to merit approbation from Him that made it, what is there of our love and complacency that it may not challenge? That which can but *please* God may well be supposed to *satisfy* man; that wherein the Creator delights, the creature, one would think, might fully rest and acquiesce in. By such considerations

as these, when solely attended to, I have been sometimes almost prevailed upon to think that there is good enough in the creation of God, if amassed together and fully enjoyed, to employ the whole activity of my love and fix the entire weight of my soul.

Yet, even here, the otherworldly mood finally prevails; no created thing can satisfy man:

When I consider experience, and compare the aspirations of my nature with the goodness of the creation, I am driven to conclude that, although the creatures of God . . . are all good enough to afford matter for entertainment and praise, yet they cannot detain and give anchorage to the soul of man. . . . Some repast may be found in the creature, but as for complete satisfaction, and termination of desires, *the Sea saith, it is not in me; and the Depth saith, it is not in me.* All that God ever did or ever can make, will prove insufficient for this purpose, and come under that decretory sentence of the wise Preacher, Vanity of Vanities, all is vanity.

Nor does Norris stop with this; he goes on to declare that in finite things not even a part of our good is to be found; the heavenly Beauty should be not only the ultimate but the sole object of man's love.

Whatever portion of our love does not run in this channel must necessarily fix upon disproportionate and unsatisfied objects, and therefore be an instrument of discontent to us. 'Tis necessary, therefore, to the completing of our happiness, that that object should *engross* our affections to itself, which only can satisfy them; . . . [as] the eye does not only love light above other things, but delights in nothing else.

Doubtless, Norris grants, this is a counsel of perfection not always practicable in this life. "It is the privilege and happiness of those confirmed spirits who are so swallowed up in the comprehensions of eternity, and so perpetually ravished with the glories of the Divine Beauty, that they have not the power to turn aside to any other object." But we may even in this world approximate to this absorption in the otherworldly good; and the more nearly we do so, "the fewer disappointments and dissatisfactions we shall meet with." [33]

There was, of course, a familiar device for mediating in some degree between the two elements of the Platonic heritage which in these passages seem to be merely in blank opposition to one another — a device suggested by Plato himself in the *Symposium* (210–212) and by Plotinus, and always dear to those saints and mystics, pagan or Christian, whose other-worldliness was of the less acrid and impatient sort. Even though (according to one side of the traditional assumptions) no true value could be ascribed to any created thing, it might nevertheless be assumed that the approach to the supreme good was normally, or even necessarily, gradual; and the currency of the metaphor of the scale or ladder of being made such a conception seem the more natural. The graded series of creatures down which the divine life in its overflow had descended might be conceived to constitute also the stages of man's ascent to the divine life in its self-contained completeness. Thus, like Adam's angelic schoolmaster in *Paradise Lost*, the philosophers who could not bring themselves wholly to accept "that decretory sentence of the wise Preacher," dwelt upon the necessity of gradualness in the "way up," and

> The scale of nature set
> From center to circumference, whereon
> In contemplation of created things
> By steps we may ascend to God.

For thus at least a provisional and instrumental value might be recognized in things natural, even while all genuine good was declared to lie in a supersensible and supernatural order. Man might legitimately permit his mind to busy itself with the creatures and to find joy in them, so long as he used each of them as a means of passage to what lay above it on the vast slope of being. It was to this conception that appeal was commonly made to justify that worldly employment, the study of natural science. Even in the eulogy of astronomy at the beginning of the *De revolutionibus orbium*, the labors of the man of science are represented as a way of ascending this scale; the final reason for engaging in them is — not, it is to be observed, that they are occupied with the *works* of God as Creator, though that consideration is mentioned — but that "we are drawn on by them, as by a vehicle, to the contemplation of the highest good." [34]

Yet plainly the conception of the creation as a ladder for man's ascent did not really reconcile the implications of the principle of plenitude as a theory of value with the otherworldly side of Platonistic philosophy and Christian theology. For, in the first place, the parallel between the descending and the ascending process was little more than verbal. The scale of being conceived as a ladder by which man might mount to beatitude was not literally composed of the same steps as the scale of being conceived as the series of natural forms. No one, I think, seriously proposed, as the true method of man's salvation, that he should begin by fixing his thought, whether by way of intellectual contemplation or aesthetic enjoyment, upon what Macrobius called "the dregs of being," and should then proceed from these, by minute transitions, through the successively more complex forms of plant life, should pass from these to the "zoophytes," from these in turn to shellfish, from these to fishes, from these to the higher animals, and so on in detail through the hierarchy of nature as medieval natural history conceived it, and finally through the successive grades of angels. The notion of infinitesimal gradation, which was of the essence of the cosmological Chain of Being, was hardly suitable to a program which was, after all, designed to bring man as speedily as possible to his final supersensible felicity, or to as close an approximation to it as the conditions of earthly life permit. If that consummation were the goal, it was not really evident that a gradual approach was the best; at most such gradualness could in consistency be regarded only as a concession to man's weakness — a dangerous concession, to be made only grudgingly and whenever possible to be avoided altogether. And finally, the program of "ascent to God by contemplation of created things" admitted no such inherent worth in the mere existence of imperfect beings in all possible diversity as was implied by the principle of plenitude. Conceived as steps in the stairway up to perfection, the lower grades of being had only the use that belongs to steps, that of things to be spurned and transcended; and such a conception had little in common with the assumption that the existence of each of these grades is a thing so good on its own account that God himself had been, so to say, constrained by his very divinity and rationality to engender every one of them.

A single example must suffice for the illustration of these last observations; I take it from a writing medieval in its philosophy though not in its date — from a famous devotional book of the Counter-Reformation, the work of one who was scarcely the less a mystic for being a most aggressive and redoubtable theological controversialist. Cardinal Bellarmino's (1542–1621) treatise *De ascensione mentis in Deum per scalas creaturarum* is perhaps the most celebrated modern elaboration of this conception, and it shows plainly the usual incongruity between the importance given to the principle of plenitude in the doctrine of the attributes of deity and the exclusion of it from the theory of the chief good of man. At first the creation seems to be represented as the diffracting lens through which alone any vision of God is possible to a finite mind; a multiplicity which does not exclude absolute simplicity is beyond our comprehension, and therefore, if we are to behold at all the perfection of the divine essence, it must be broken up for us into distinct parts.

God willed that man should in some measure know him through his creatures, and because no single created thing could fitly represent the infinite perfection of the Creator, he multiplied creatures, and bestowed on each a certain degree of goodness and perfection, that from these we might form some idea of the goodness and perfection of the Creator, who, in one most simple and perfect essence, contains infinite perfections.

Thus it is in the consideration of the diversity of existent things that we come, says Bellarmino, to realize the infinite variety which (though without detriment to simplicity) is of the essence of the Divine Reason:

Though the mere multitude of created things is itself wonderful, and a proof of the multiform perfection of the one God, still more wonderful is the variety which appears in that multiplication, and it leads us more easily to the knowledge of God; for it is not difficult for one seal to make many impressions exactly alike, but to vary shapes almost infinitely, which is what God has done in creation, this is in truth a divine work, and most worthy of admiration. I pass by genera and species, which every one agrees are exceedingly various and diverse. . . . Raise now, my soul, the eye of thy mind towards God, in whom are the Ideas of all things and from whom, as from an inexhaustible fountain, this well-nigh infinite variety springs: for God could not have impressed those numberless forms on created things unless in a most eminent and exalted mode he had kept their Ideas or patterns in the depths of his own Being.

Yet the conclusion to which all this might seem to tend is not drawn, but rather its opposite: it is not in the further tracing out of the complexity and richness of detail in nature or human nature through scientific inquiry, nor yet in the imitation of that "divine work most worthy of admiration" through the representation in art of its inexhaustible diversity, that man is to busy himself. His concern is still with the One, not with the Many. For all "the various goods which are found distributed among created things are found in altogether a higher way united in God." [35] The great Jesuit controversialist is, indeed, no harsh ascetic of the fashion of Bernard of Clairvaux; nor will he go to the extreme represented by such a mystic of the Counter-Reformation as St. John of the Cross, who bade "the spiritual man aim at complete abstraction and forgetfulness, so that, as much as possible, no knowledge or form of created things — as if they existed not — shall remain in his memory." Bellarmino concedes that "we are not commanded while on this earth to put away from us all consolation from creatures." Yet their chief office is to remind us of their own transiency and insufficiency, or to serve as sensible symbols of supersensible attributes of deity, and thus to show that "all things other than God are vanity and vexation of spirit, which have no existence, but only appear to have, and do not afford solace, but only affliction." "The ascent of the ladder of created things" is, after all, only another name for a progressive *contemptus mundi*.

There is, it will be observed, in the passage of Bellarmino last cited a touch of illusionism, an intimation of the doctrine that all plurality and individuation are mere unreal appearances. The temptation to lapse into the phraseology of illusionism has never been very remote from either Neoplatonic or Catholic metaphysics, partly because the otherworldly or mystical mood naturally expresses itself by treating as mere nonentity the world from which it turns away, partly because such a conception offers a seeming alleviation of that inner logical conflict of which I have been speaking. If one resorts to that easy, if self-contradictory, expedient of denying that the manifold of finite things has any existence, all problems disappear at a stroke; since nothing except the One really exists, there is nothing really to be explained. Yet this was not a way of escape from its difficulties which Christian theology could adopt. It is not, indeed, that the otherworldliness of either Neoplatonic or Catholic philosophy was in itself less extreme in degree than that of the Vedânta or of other Indian systems. When the mind of Plotinus, or of Augustine, or of the Pseudo-Areopagite, or of John the Scot, or even of Thomas Aquinas, is turned solely upon that side of his doctrine, he is not less thorough-going than the sages of the more mystical Upanishads, or than Shankara, in asserting the 'otherness' of the true reality and the only genuine good — its absolute exclusion of all the characteristics of the existence which we now experience or of which our discursive thought can frame any conception.[36] The difference is merely that the Occidental doctrine was essentially dual; it asserted this, but it also asserted the opposite; the second of the two elements was firmly incorporated in its substance as much by its Platonistic as by its Jewish sources. The influence of the *Timaeus* and of the Neoplatonic dialectic, mediated chiefly through the Pseudo-Dionysius, combined with the authority of Genesis to constrain the medieval theologian to affirm a real generation of a real universe of particular existents and to identify deity with self-expansive and creative energy. Consequently the language of acosmism, when it shows itself in a writer, like Bellarmino, well grounded in this tradition, is never to be taken too literally; it is only an extreme statement of one side of this double doctrine, which must be understood to be offset, however inconsistently, by the other side.

The long suppressed conflict between the two strains in the traditional complex of presuppositions developed in some writers of the Renaissance into an overt dualism of two warring principles, one good and one evil, but both necessarily inherent in the divine nature itself, and consequently present also in human nature. And it is significant that in some of these early modern recombinations of ideas derived from Platonistic, Jewish, and Christian sources, the usual medieval preference is reversed; the higher value is given, not to the Unmoved Mover, the state in which the One is undivided and eternally at rest in its own self-sufficiency, but rather to the restless "active principle," which is manifested in becoming, motion, diversification. Thus Robert Fludd (1574–1637), developing a dualism derived partly, apparently, from the philosophy of Bernardino Telesio and partly from Kabbalistic sources, tells us that as, in the divine essence,

the potential or dark principle, is contrary and opposite in his essential property, unto the actual emanation of light beginning, so also have each of them manifested, or brought forth into this world, two offsprings, or essential properties, which are oppugnant in condition, and flat adversaries in their nature unto one another; and the two active virtues are *Cold* and *Heat*. . . . For the property of the dark Nothing, or deformed abyss, is naturally to rest, and not to act or operate; and the reason is, because that its appetite is to be conversant in and about the center, beyond the which there is no motion or action, and not to dilate itself towards the circumference, as the Spirit of light, or God in his volunty, or patent nature, is accustomed to do. For this reason, the dark principle doth challenge unto itself, by a natural instinct, rest and quietness, and this property begetteth or produceth one essential virtue of its own condition, namely, cold, the which, as it is elected as a champion to resist the assaults of her opposite, namely of Heat, whose comparisons are motion or action; . . . so unless it be roused or stirred up by the assaults of Heat, it moveth not, but seemeth to wait upon its drowsy mother, Darkness and privation, whose children are fixation and rest, which sleep in and cleave fast unto the center, and therefore are unwilling to look forth towards the circumference. And in verity, cold is an essential act, proceeding from, and attending on, the divine puissance, which in this property doth contract its beams from the circumference into its self.

It is, then, this property of God's essence, sensibly manifested in cold, which "is the mother of privation, death, vacuity, inanity, deformation," the "only efficient cause of inspissation, contraction, fixation, immobility, ponderosity, rest, obteneration or darkness, of mortification, privation, stupefaction, and such like." [37] Doubtless, Fludd feels constrained to admit, "it is a wondrous thing, and passing all human understanding, that out of one Unity in essence and nature, two branches of such opposite nature should arise and sprout forth, as are Darkness (which is the seat of error, deformity, contention, privation, death) and Light, which is the vehicle of truth, beauty, love, position, and the like." It is not surprising "that the sect of the Manicheans did so stiffly hold that there were two co-eternal principles"; and Fludd, though he cannot, either as Christian or as Platonist, give up the doctrine of the derivation of all being from a single, simple, and perfect essence, nevertheless is uneasily aware that his two divine attributes, or what we are compelled to conceive as such, have in all practical respects much the same rôles as God and the Devil. What concerns us here is that the part of devil-within-the-deity is taken by the attribute of self-sufficiency or self-containment, of which the influence is manifested by the tendency in things to seek the moveless centre of Being; this is that "discording, privative and hateful affection which darkness and deformity doth afford unto the children of light and life, and to all the beauteous offspring thereof." [38] It is when deity goes forth of itself and lives in its "benign emanations" that, so to say, its better nature is manifested. [39] 'Plenitude,' consequently, is one of Fludd's sacred words, while he dilates eagerly upon nature's *horror vacui*:

> Job argueth that Vacuity, Inanity, and Darkness, are one and the same thing; to wit, Vacuity, Inanity, or Voidness, because that all fullness or plenitude is from God in his actual property. . . . The earth that was before the revelation of God's spirit inane and void, is now become full of divine Light, and multiplying Grace. Whereupon it was no more void and empty, that is to say, destitute of essential being, but became fertile and fruitful, being now replenished with divine fire and the incorruptible spirit of God, according unto that of Solomon, *Spiritus disciplinae sanctus implet orbem terrarum*; . . . And the Apostle, *Christus implet omnia*, Christ *filleth all things*. Whereby we may perceive, that all plenitude is from the divine Act, as contrariwise Vacuity is, when that formal life is absent from the waters, and this is the reason that *Vacuum* or *Inane* is held so horrible a thing in Nature. Forasmuch as the utter absence of the eternal emanation, is intolerable to the creature, because that everything desireth fervently to be informed, and that by a natural appetite or affection, and therefore it is abominable unto each natural thing to be utterly deprived of being. [40]

Thus in Fludd the "evil principle" is defined in precisely those terms in which the traditional philosophy was wont to express the nature of the perfection in which all desire finds its consummation:

> Here all thy turns and revolutions cease,
>     Here's all serenity and peace;
> Thou'rt to the Center come, the native seat of rest,
> There's now no further change, nor need there be,
>     When One shall be Variety. [41]

To Fludd the "native seat of rest" was the abode of darkness and death, and the existence which is "conversant in and about the center" is the negation of all good. Yet he was merely carrying out to its logical consequence one of the two tendencies which had been forcibly conjoined in the Platonistic and the Christian tradition.

Another form of this conflict may be noted. The good for any being, according to an accepted principle also inherited from the Greek philosophy of the fifth century B.C., lies in the realization of its specific "nature"; and it was, therefore, customary to formulate the argument even for the most extreme otherworldliness nominally in terms of "conformity to nature" in this sense. But the concrete meaning given to this was derived wholly from that dialectic whereby the good was identified with self-sufficiency. Man, as rational, was declared to be capable of realizing his nature only in the possession of absolute, underivative, and infinite good, that is to say, in a complete union or *assimilatio intellectus speculativi* [42] with the divine perfection and beatitude. But this denaturalization of the notion of specifically human good would have been impossible if the logic of the principle of plenitude had been applied at this point, as in a later age it was to be applied.

Of this long-lasting conjunction of essentially incompatible ideas, three aspects of which we have been examining, the significance may now be expressed in more general terms. The most important and distinctive circumstance in the history of religious and moral philosophy in the Occident is the fact that both later Platonism and the accepted philosophy of the Church combined otherworldliness with a virtual, if not usually a literal or unqualified, optimism. Both were equally committed to the two contradictory theses that 'this' world is an essentially evil thing to be escaped from, and that its existence, with precisely the attributes it has, is a good so great that in the production of it the divinest of all the attributes of deity was manifested. Of the temporal, sensible, divided world from which it would turn men's thoughts and affections away, a consistent otherworldly philosophy may give any one of three accounts. It may, as we have seen, say that the belief that any such world exists is a pure illusion. It may, while not denying the reality of the world, declare that it *ought* never to have been, that the genesis of anything other than the Eternal and Perfect One was an utter and inexplicable disaster. Or it may, with primitive Buddhism, refuse to discuss such merely speculative questions as the origin, *raison d'être*, or metaphysical status of the world, or even the positive nature of the goal to be sought, and devote its whole energy to persuading men that temporal and sentient existence is an unmitigated evil and to showing them a way of escape from it.[43] But to a choice between these three forms of pessimism such a philosophy is limited.[44] There was manifest for a time in Western religious thought — in Manichaeism and in the Gnostic Christian heresies — a strong tendency towards the second of these positions; if this tendency had prevailed none of the incongruities which we have been noting would have arisen. The emergence out of the untroubled peace of the divine life of a groaning and travailing creation, a universe of sundered and temporal and corporeal beings, would have been regarded as the original and essential Fall, and whatever Demiurgus was conceived to be concerned in the business would have been regarded as the original and essential Devil. How much there was in the assumptions accepted both by pagan Platonists and Christian theologians, during the first four centuries, which might have seemed to make inevitable some outcome of this type is evident. The significance of the decision — concretely manifested in the rejection of the temper and doctrines of the Gnostics by Plotinus and, more dramatically, in Augustine's conversion from Manichaeism — in favor of a fruitful inconsistency, was not to become clearly apparent until modern times, nor, indeed, in its entirety, until the eighteenth century. But through the Middle Ages there were at least kept alive, in an age of which the official doctrine was predominantly otherworldly, certain roots of an essentially 'this-worldly' philosophy: the assumption that there is a true and intrinsic multiplicity in the divine nature, that is to say, in the world of Ideas; that, further, "existence is a good," i. e., that the addition of concrete actuality to universals, the translation of supersensible possibilities into sensible realities, means an increase, not a loss, of value; that, indeed, the very essence of the good consists in the maximal actualization of variety; and that the world of temporal and sensible experience is thus good, and the supreme manifestation of the divine.

# IV

## THE PRINCIPLE OF PLENITUDE AND THE
## NEW COSMOGRAPHY

IN BRINGING about the change from the medieval to the modern conception of the scale of magnitude and the general arrangement of the physical world in space, it was not the Copernican hypothesis, nor even the splendid achievements of scientific astronomy during the two following centuries, that played the most significant and decisive part. In the cosmography that by the beginning of the eighteenth century had come to be commonly held among educated men, the features which differentiated the new from the old world-picture most widely, those whereby it most affected the imagination and modified the prevalent conception of man's place in the universe, the traditional religious beliefs, and the mood of religious feeling, — these features owed their introduction and, for the most part, their eventual general acceptance, not to the actual discoveries or the technical reasonings of astronomers, but to the influence of those originally Platonistic metaphysical preconceptions which, as the preceding lecture has shown, had, though potent and persistent, been always repressed and abortive in medieval thought. In order to make this evident it is needful, first of all, to consider what those aspects of the older cosmography were which had, or seemed to the medieval mind to have, religious and moral implications — which helped to determine how far men could feel themselves emotionally at home in their world and after what fashion they should conceive their status and rôle therein.

It is an error to suppose that the medieval world was a small affair, in which the earth bulked relatively large. Though the distances in the Ptolemaic system were trivial beside those hundreds of millions of light-years in which the astronomer of today reckons, they were not trivial in proportion to the terrestrial magnitudes which furnish the scale for the imagination. Ptolemy himself had said that the earth is a mere dot in comparison with the heavens. Maimonides late in the twelfth century wrote in *The Guide of the Perplexed*:

> In order to form a correct estimate of ourselves we must consider the results of the investigations which have been made into the dimensions and distances of the spheres and stars. It has been shown that the distance between the centre of the earth and the summit of the sphere of Saturn is a journey of about eight thousand seven hundred years of 365 days, assuming that one walked forty leagues a day [i. e., the distance, in round numbers, is 125 million miles]. . . . Consider this vast and terrifying distance; it is of it that the Scripture declares: *Is not God in the height of Heaven? and behold the height of the stars, how high they are!* . . . This great distance which has been shown is, however, only a minimum; for the distance from the centre of the earth to the concave side of the sphere of the fixed stars cannot be less, and may be many times greater. . . . As for the sphere of the fixed stars, its thickness must be at least as great as one of the stars contained in it, of which each has a volume exceeding that of the terrestrial globe more than ninety times; and it is possible that the sphere itself is much thicker still. Of the ninth sphere which imparts to all the others their diurnal motion, the measure is not known; for as it contains no stars we have no means of judging of its magnitude. Consider, then, how immense is the size of these bodies, and how numerous they are. And if the earth is thus no bigger than a point relatively to the sphere of the fixed stars, what must be the ratio of the human species to the created universe as a whole? And how then can any of us think that these things exist for his sake, and that they are meant to serve his uses?[1]

Roger Bacon dilated with unwearying enthusiasm upon the *rerum magnitudo*. "The least of the visible stars is greater than the earth; but the least of the stars has, in comparison with the heavens, virtually no size. . . . According to Ptolemy a fixed star, because of the magnitude of the heaven, does not complete its circuit in less than thirty-six thousand years, though it moves with incredible velocity. But it is possible to walk round the earth in less than three years."[2] The theme continued to be a favorite one with the anti-Copernicans in the sixteenth century. Du Bartas, for example, thus labored it (I quote from Sylvester's version of *La Sepmaine*, 1592):

> The least star that we perceive to shine
> Above, disperst in th' arches crystalline,
> (If, at the least, star-clarks be credit worth)
> Is eighteen times bigger then all the earth . . .

Yea, though a king by wile or war had won
All the round earth to his subjection,
Lo, here the guerdon of his glorious pains:
A needle's point, a mote, a mite, he gains,
A nit, a nothing (did he all possess).[3]

But though the medieval world was thus immense, relatively to man and his planet, it was nevertheless definitely limited and fenced about. It was therefore essentially picturable; the perspectives which it presented, however great, were not wholly baffling to the imagination. The men of the fifteenth century still lived in a walled universe as well as in walled towns. And — unlike medieval towns and other medieval things — this cosmical scheme had the essential qualities of a work of classical art; indeed, the most classical thing in the Middle Ages may be said to have been the universe. Men preferred to worship in Gothic churches, but the architecture of the heavens was not a piece of Gothic design — which is not surprising since it was, in fact, a Grecian edifice. The world had a clear intelligible unity of structure, and not only definite shape, but what was deemed at once the simplest and most perfect shape, as had all the bodies composing it. It had no loose ends, no irregularities of outline. The simplicity of its internal plan had, indeed, under the pressure of observed astronomical facts, come to be more and more recognized as less complete than one could wish; but the chief poetic *cicerone* through the universe paid little attention to these troublesome complications of detail, and they probably did not much disturb the non-astronomical mind.

It has often been said that the older picture of the world in space was peculiarly fitted to give man a high sense of his own importance and dignity; and some modern writers have made much of this supposed implication of the pre-Copernican astronomy.[4] Man occupied, we are told, the central place in the universe, and round the planet of his habitation all the vast, unpeopled spheres obsequiously revolved.[5] But the actual tendency of the geocentric system was, for the medieval mind, precisely the opposite. For the centre of the world was not a position of honor; it was rather the place farthest removed from the Empyrean, the bottom of the creation, to which its dregs and baser elements sank. The actual centre, indeed, was Hell; in the spatial sense the medieval world was literally dia-bolocentric. And the whole sublunary region was, of course, incomparably inferior to the resplendent and incorruptible heavens above the moon. Thus Montaigne, still adhering to the older astronomy, could consistently describe man's dwell-ing-place as "the filth and mire of the world, the worst, lowest, most lifeless part of the universe, the bottom story of the house." How, then, he demanded, could a creature native to it and fellow-lodger with "the lowest of the three orders of animals" (i. e., land animals) dare in imagination "to place himself above the circle of the moon, and reduce heaven under his feet"? "By what authority," asks Montaigne, can man assume that "this admirable moving of heaven's vault, the eternal light of these lamps rolling so proudly over his head, . . . were established and continue so many ages for his com-modity and service?" [6] John Wilkins in 1640 mentions, as one of the arguments still advanced against the Copernican system, that drawn

from the vileness of our earth, because it consists of a more sordid and base matter than any other part of the world; and therefore must be situated in the centre, which is the worst place, and at the greatest distance from those purer incorruptible bodies, the heavens.[7]

It is sufficiently evident from such passages that the geocentric cosmography served rather for man's humiliation than for his exaltation, and that Copernicanism was opposed partly on the ground that it assigned too dignified and lofty a position to his dwelling-place.

There were, of course, other elements in the medieval Christian system which *were* adapted to breed in the featherless biped a high sense of his cosmic importance and of the mo-mentousness of his own doings. But these were not connected with the geocentric astronomy; they easily could survive, and were, indeed, little affected by, its abandonment. It was not the position of our planet in space, but the fact that it alone was supposed to have an indigenous population of rational beings whose final destiny was not yet settled, that gave it its unique status in the world and a unique share in the attention of

Heaven. If it was the only region of corruption it was also the only region of generation; here alone new souls were born, immortal destinies still hung in the balance, and, in some sense, the fulfilment of the design of the Creator himself was at stake. If, then, this dim and squalid cellar of the universe was (with one exception) the least respectable place in which any beings could have their abode, it was also the place in which all that was really dramatic and stirring was going on. Thus, with however glaring a contradiction of the doctrines of the divine self-sufficiency and impassibility, the affairs of men were conceived to be objects of immeasurable solicitude on the part of Deity itself; so that a single natural folly of an unsophisticated pair in Mesopotamia could, by its consequences, constrain one of the persons of the Godhead to take on human flesh and live and die upon this globe for man's salvation. Throughout history lesser beings from the upper world had been busy ministrants to man, while rebel spirits had been scarcely less flatteringly engrossed in the enterprise of his destruction. "As I was looking," says a character in one of Zangwill's novels, "at Signorelli's 'Descent into Hell,' I was thinking how vividly our ancestors enjoyed life, how important each individual soul was, to have the ranged battalions of Heaven and Hell fighting for it. What an intense sense of the *significance* of life!" The actual pleasurableness of this conception to the medieval believer may perhaps be doubted; to be the bone of contention between powers so great and each, in its own way, so exacting, was hardly an agreeable position for the average sensual man, even aside from his natural apprehensions concerning the eventual issue of the conflict in his own case. But undeniably it was a position which tended to encourage and justify a certain racial *amour propre*. This was, however, related to the current cosmography only in so far as that implied that this planet alone contained a race of free creatures half-material and half-spiritual — the middle link in the Chain of Being — for whose allegiance the celestial and the infernal powers competed.

What was poetically and religiously significant in the older cosmography was, then, little touched by the Copernican theory. For Copernicus the solar system and the universe remained identical; his world, though not geocentric, was still centred, still spherical in shape, still securely walled in by the outermost sphere, *se ipsam et omnia continens.*[8] So long as the whole sensible universe remained thus limited and boxed-in, and so long as the planet occupied by man, whatever its spatial position, was still assigned a unique biological, moral, and religious status, the aesthetically and practically distinctive characteristics of the medieval cosmical scheme remained. And the one change of this kind implied by the abandonment of the geocentric system was, as is evident from what has already been said, the reverse of that often attributed to the new astronomy; to remove man from the centre of things was to raise him from his low estate. It meant also the denial of the Aristotelian notion that the central position *is* a peculiarly degraded one, and of the whole antithesis between the sublunary world of becoming and the immortal and immutable heavens. But this had already been attacked by several medieval writers. More than a century before Copernicus, for example, Nicolaus Cusanus had rejected the assumption that the earth is the basest part of the universe; we do not know, he declared, that death and corruption are peculiar to this globe, and the division of the heavens into two parts, occupied by essentially different sorts of bodies, is without justification.[9] This incidental implication of Copernicanism, then, was not novel, though it still seemed to some, in the sixteenth century, startling and revolutionary. And the most serious blow to the traditional conception was given, not by the reasonings of Copernicus, but by Tycho Brahe's discovery of *Nova Cassiopeiae* in 1572 —

> A strange new visitant
> To heavens unchangeable, as the world believed,
> Since the creation.

At this time the Copernican theory had made little progress and was, of course, not accepted even by Tycho himself; it cannot, therefore, be credited with the breaking down of the division of the world in space into two regions utterly dissimilar in their properties and dignity.

A non-geocentric arrangement of the heavens could, indeed, plausibly be regarded as more harmonious than the Ptolemaic scheme with the Christian theology; and this consideration did at least as much as any purely astronomical reasons to gain the potent support of Kepler for the new hypothesis — or rather, for a significant modification of it. For though the theory of Copernicus had ascribed the motions which account for "the appearances" to the earth rather than to the spheres of the sun, planets, and fixed stars, it was not, of course, a heliocentric theory; the centre of the world was the centre of the earth's orbit. The sun, though nearest that position, did not occupy it, and the planes of the planetary orbits did not pass through the sun. Thus, as Dreyer has pointed out, Copernicus had still "felt compelled to give the earth quite an exceptional position in his new system" — so that, as Dreyer somewhat misleadingly adds, "the earth was nearly as important a body in the new system as in the old" (the truth being, as we have seen, that its *position* in the old system was *not* one of importance). The heliocentric theory, properly so called, was due to Kepler, not to Copernicus. In spite of Aristotle there doubtless had always been, for the imagination, a certain incongruity between the central position of the idea of God in medieval metaphysics and the peripheral position of the Empyrean in medieval cosmology; and the chief merit of his new system in Kepler's eyes was that it eliminated this incongruity, placing at the heart of the sensible universe the body which could most naturally be regarded as the physical symbol or counterpart of deity, or, more precisely, of the first Person of the Trinity — the orb which was admittedly "the most excellent of all," the source of all light and color and heat, "that which alone we should judge to be worthy of the Most High God if he should be pleased with a material domicile and choose a place in which to dwell with the blessed angels."[10] It is not without pertinency to the general theme with which we are concerned that this theological argument for the heliocentric theory appeals to Kepler especially because he is here thinking of God, not in the Aristotelian manner as a self-contained and unmoved final cause of motion and endeavor in other beings, but chiefly as a generative and self-diffusive energy.[11] And how essentially medieval the cosmography even of Kepler remained may be seen from the way in which he further carried out his astro-

nomico-theological parallelism and from the fact that, precisely by means of the heliocentric system, he was able to find
new reasons for conceiving the world to be as definitely limited
and enclosed as it had been in the system of Ptolemy. If the
sun is the analogue of God the Father, the sphere of the fixed
stars, Kepler finds, is manifestly the sensible counterpart of the
Son, the intermediate region of the planets being assigned to
the Holy Ghost.[12] The function of the outer sphere is to
"throw back and multiply the light of the sun, like an opaque
and illuminated wall." It may also be described as "the skin
or shirt of the universe" (*mundi cutis sive tunica*), keeping the internal heat generated by the sun from being lost through indefinite diffusion; the theological parallel here seems a trifle
strained. As for the distances between the heavenly bodies,
Kepler professed to have shown (with the aid of the heliocentric assumption) that this manifested a harmonious plan such
as previous astronomers had sought but not found. Convinced that the cosmos must conform to aesthetic requirements
and having, like a typically medieval mind, an essentially
classical taste in universes, he was unable to believe that the
intervals between the orbits of the six then known planets failed
to correspond to some exact rule of proportion. While no
simple arithmetical ratios proved applicable, he finally, as he
supposed, reached the triumphant discovery that "God in
creating the universe and laying out the heavens had in view
the five regular solids of geometry, celebrated since the time of
Pythagoras and Plato, and that it was in accordance with their
properties that he fixed the number of the heavens, their proportions, and the ratios of their movements." [13] In this Kepler
too, it will be observed, was in his own fashion relying upon
the principle of sufficient reason; the Creator must, he could
not doubt, have been guided by some non-arbitrary formula in
assigning these ratios and in fixing the number of planets as
six, and therefore of the intervals as five. There *could* be only
five regular solids; and if this necessity in the world of Ideas
could be transferred to the limitation of the number of heavens,
the general plan of things could be regarded as having in some
sort a rational basis as well as an aesthetic orderliness. It was
in the quest of verification for this wholly fanciful hypothesis

that Kepler eventually achieved his discovery of the third law of planetary motion.

The Copernican doctrine, it is true, demanded of the plain man a difficult revision of certain natural habits of the unregenerate intellect — a revision which he has never yet, in his ordinary mental pictures of the motions in the solar system, succeeded in accomplishing fully. The new hypothesis not only appeared to conflict with the testimony of the senses but contained at least a hint of the repellent notion of relativity — i. e., of the purely relational import of the conceptions of place and motion. Yet to the philosophically enlightened there was in this nothing essentially novel or heterodox. The deceitfulness of the senses was a well-worn theme for edifying discourse; and the new astronomy afforded some welcome fresh illustrations for that theme, of which its seventeenth-century advocates did not fail to make use. As for the general idea of the relativity of apparent motion to the observer, that must, after all, have been a commonplace to every astronomer; and Copernicanism implied no more than this. Any implication of a more thorough-going doctrine of the relativity of position and motion — or even of determinable position and motion — could be avoided so long as the now unmoving sphere of the fixed stars remained to serve as an absolute system of reference — in Copernicus's own phrase, as the *universi locus, ad quem motus et positio caeterorum omnium conferatur*.[14]

The chief affront of Copernicanism to theological orthodoxy lay, not in any fundamental discrepancy between it and the more philosophical parts of the traditional scheme of the universe, but in its apparent irreconcilability with certain details of that body of purely historical propositions which Christianity had, to an extent matched in no other religion, incorporated in its creed. The story of the Ascension, for example, was obviously difficult to fit into the topography of a Copernican world; and it was easy for the ecclesiastical adversaries of the new hypothesis to point to numerous passages of Scripture which made it evident that supposedly inspired and infallible writers had, as a matter of course, assumed the motion of the sun about the earth and other postulates of the astronomy of naïve common sense. Yet, with the aid of some ingenuity and some liberality of exegesis, these embarrassments could be, and in time were, got over with a certain degree of plausibility; and in any case, it was not the merely Copernican innovation that raised the more general and deeper-reaching difficulties, even with respect to the historical content of Christian dogma.

The truly revolutionary theses in cosmography which gained ground in the sixteenth and came to be pretty generally accepted before the end of the seventeenth century were five in number, none of them entailed by the purely astronomical systems of Copernicus or Kepler. In any study of the history of the modern conception of the world, and in any account of the position of any individual writer, it is essential to keep these distinctions between issues constantly in view. The five more significant innovations were: (1) the assumption that other planets of our solar system are inhabited by living, sentient, and rational creatures; (2) the shattering of the outer walls of the medieval universe, whether these were identified with the outermost crystalline sphere or with a definite "region" of the fixed stars, and the dispersal of these stars through vast, irregular distances; (3) the conception of the fixed stars as suns similar to ours, all or most of them surrounded by planetary systems of their own; (4) the supposition that the planets in these other worlds also have conscious inhabitants; (5) the assertion of the actual infinity of the physical universe in space and of the number of solar systems contained it it.

The first of these — and, of course, still more the fourth — deprived human life and terrestrial history of the unique importance and momentousness which the medieval scheme of ideas had attributed to them and Copernicanism had left to them. The theory of the plurality of inhabited worlds tended to raise difficulties, not merely about the minor details of the history included in the Christian belief, but about its central dogmas. The entire moving drama of the Incarnation and Redemption had seemed manifestly to presuppose a single inhabited world. If that presupposition were to be given up, how were these dogmas to be construed, if, indeed, they could be retained at all? Were we, as Thomas Paine afterwards asked, "to suppose that every world in the boundless creation

had an Eve, an apple, a serpent, and a Redeemer?" [15] Had
the Second Person of the Trinity been incarnate on innumerable planets in turn, or was ours the only portion of the universe in which moral agents had any need of redemption?
These difficulties were recognized at least by the early seventeenth century, but they do not appear to have been regarded
by the theologians of the time as very serious. Campanella
refers to them in his *Apologia Pro Galilaeo*, 1622, and his views
on the subject were summarized in English by Wilkins in
1638: If the inhabitants of other globes were men,

then he thinks they could not be infected with Adam's sin; yet, perhaps,
they had some of their own, which might make them liable to the same misery with us; out of which, it may be, they were delivered by the same
means as we, the death of Christ.[16]

By the second and third of these theses, the potential importance of which for the imagination it would be difficult to
overestimate, the physical universe ceased to have *any* center;
it was broken up into (at the least) a vast multiplicity of isolated systems distributed upon no recognizably rational plan;
it ceased to be a shape and became a formless aggregate of
worlds scattered irregularly through unimaginable reaches of
space. The change from a geocentric to a heliocentric system
was far less momentous than the change from a heliocentric to
an acentric one. The "first question concerning the Celestial
Bodies," Bacon said, "is *whether there be a system*, that is, whether
the world or universe compose altogether one globe, with a
centre; or whether the particular globes of earth and stars be
scattered dispersedly, each on its own roots, without any system or common centre." [17] When the number and extension
of these worlds were further assumed to be infinite, the universe
tended to seem baffling not only to the imagination but to the
reason itself; for the mathematical antinomies arising from the
application to reality of the notion of numerical or quantitative
infinity now assumed a new pertinence and gravity.

I have said that the Copernican and Keplerian cosmical systems did not necessarily imply these five more striking and
far-reaching novelties, and that the former were held by some
astronomers and other writers of the sixteenth and seventeenth
centuries who did not accept the latter — and *vice versa*. It is

not, however, historically true that the abandonment of the geocentric scheme did not seem to some minds to render some of these more sweeping hypotheses more probable. Thus Bacon, who was an anti-Copernican, though not an altogether unhesitant one, remarked that "if it be granted that the earth moves, it would seem more natural to suppose that there is no system at all, but scattered globes, than to constitute a system of which the sun is the centre." [18] This, however, Bacon seems to urge as one of the "many and great inconveniencies" which "are found in the system of Copernicus"; it is a deduction, and an obviously forced one, made by an adversary of the theory.

It is true, also, that the heliocentric picture of our system could be regarded as lending a certain plausibility to the hypothesis of other inhabited planets in that system. By placing the earth upon the same footing as these other bodies in one respect, it suggested the possibility that the similarity might extend to other particulars, such as the presence of conscious life. The usual argument may be given in the words of Burton (1621):

hoc posito, to grant this their tenet of the earth's motion; if the earth move it is a planet and shines to them in the moon, and to other planetary inhabitants as the moon and they do to us upon the earth; but shine she doth, as Galileo, Kepler, and others prove, and then per consequens, the rest of the planets are inhabited, as well as the moon. . . . Then (I say) the earth and they [Mars, Venus, and the rest] be planets alike, inhabited alike, moved about the sun, the common centre of the world alike, and it may be those two green children which Nubrigensis speaks of in his time, that fell from heaven came from thence.[19]

But such an inference was obviously a loose argument by analogy, and could, of itself, hardly have convinced anyone not already inclined to the conclusion upon other and more cogent grounds. And in fact that conclusion had been reached before Copernicus, and not as a deduction from the heliocentric theory.

Not only were the more pregnant and startling innovations not dependent upon the Copernican theory; they were none of them, before the nineteenth century, supported by any evidence whatever that we should now call scientific; and at least three of them still remain uncertain. The second and part of the third were not, indeed, beyond the possible scope of astronomical verification; but they could not be verified by any methods in use for three centuries after Copernicus. Whether the fixed stars were grouped at approximately equal distances from the sun within a well-defined zone centering about that body, or were diffused at vast intervals through space, could not be determined until the distance of a number of them from the earth could be measured. But no successful measurement of a stellar parallax was accomplished until 1838,[20] and photometric methods of determining distance were unknown. The acceptance of the heliocentric system implied, indeed, that the remoteness of all the stars was far greater than even the Ptolemaic astronomers had supposed; for it was the recognition of the earth's orbital motion that gave a base-line by means of which it seemed that a parallax should be detectable. Since none could be discovered by what were then deemed highly refined methods, it followed that the distance, and presumably therefore the size, of the nearest star must be incalculably great. But on the other hand, the repeated failures to establish a parallax served for more than a century as plausible arguments against the heliocentric system itself.

The more important features of the new conception of the world, then, owed little to any new hypotheses based upon the sort of observational grounds which we should nowadays call 'scientific.' They were chiefly derivative from philosophical and theological premises. They were, in short, manifest corollaries of the principle of plenitude, when that principle was applied, not to the biological question of the number of kinds of living beings, but to the astronomical questions of the magnitude of the stellar universe and of the extent of the diffusion of life and sentiency in space. God, it seemed, *would*, in the phrase of the *Timaeus*, have been "envious" if he had refused the privilege of actual existence to any logically possible being at any place where such existence was possible — if, at least, as was sometimes conveniently, if inconsistently, added, there were not countervailing reasons why their existence would have been attended by a preponderance of detriment to other beings. The creative power was, by hypothesis, infinite, and its

manifestation should therefore be infinite; and there appeared
to be no reason why, wherever there was matter, there should
not be life. Now these premises, we have seen, were current
throughout the Middle Ages, even in the writings of orthodox
theologians who were unwilling to draw from them all their
implications. And the contention that the infinity of worlds
and of inhabited systems was among these implications was
equally familiar, though usually rejected by the orthodox. The
argument that the universe must be infinite because God's
omnipotence requires that he should not *ab opere cessare* is discussed by Augustine in the *De civitate dei* (X, 5), though it is,
of course, opposed by him. In view of the intimate acquaintance of medieval Christian philosophers with the writings of
Augustine, the thesis must have been familiar to all of them.
By the fifteenth century a tendency towards the acceptance of
it is already marked. In the *Or Adonai* of the Jewish philosopher Crescas (1410) there is offered a refutation of the arguments by which Aristotle in the *De Coelo* thought to show that
"there are not any other worlds" — i. e., any other than the
one system of concentric spheres in which the earth is situated:
"Everything said in negation of the possibility of many worlds
is 'vanity and a striving after wind.'" Commenting on this
in his admirable edition of a part of the work of Crescas, Professor H. A. Wolfson [21] observes that Crescas "does not say
definitely how many worlds may exist. He only contends for
the existence of 'many worlds.' But knowing of his rejection of
Aristotle's denial of an infinite number of magnitudes and of
his contention as to the existence of an infinite space, we may
reasonably infer that the number of Crescas' many worlds may
rise to infinity." Later in the same century the same thesis was
adumbrated by a great Christian metaphysician. The Cardinal Nicolaus Cusanus, one of the subtlest though hardly one
of the clearest philosophical minds of the later Middle Ages,
had transferred to the physical universe the paradoxical figure
which theologians had sometimes employed to express the doctrine of the "immensity" of God. The world, Cusanus declared in his *De docta ignorantia* (1440), is a sphere of which the
"centre coincides with the circumference." Less paradoxi-
cally expressed,

The world has no circumference; for it if had a centre and a circumference there would be some space and some thing beyond the world, suppositions which are wholly lacking in truth. Since, therefore, it is impossible that the world should be enclosed within a corporeal centre and a corporeal boundary, it is not within our power to understand the world, whose centre and circumference are God. And though this world cannot be infinite, nevertheless it cannot be conceived as finite, since there are no limits within which it could be confined. The earth, therefore, which cannot be the centre, cannot be wholly without motion. . . . And just as the world has no centre, so neither the sphere of the fixed stars nor any other is its circumference.

The belief in the stationary and central earth is due merely to a failure to recognize the relativity of apparent motion:

It is evident that this earth really moves, though it does not seem to do so, for we apprehend motion only by means of a contrast with some fixed point. If a man on a boat in a stream were unable to see the banks and did not know that the stream was flowing, how would he comprehend that the boat was moving? Thus it is that, whether a man is on the earth or the sun or some other star, it will always seem to him that the position he occupies is the motionless centre and that all other things are in motion.[22]

These passages were frequently cited by seventeenth-century writers as an anticipation of both these theses of later writers, which thus seemed to have the prophetic endorsement of a Cardinal; and taken by themselves they were such an anticipation. The mind of Cusanus, however, was less concerned with astronomical questions than with a species of mystical theology. It is not the sun, but God, whom he would put in the place of the central earth; he alone is "the centre of the world and of the spheres and of the earth who is at the same time the infinite circumference of all things." And the rejection of the notion of a finite universe bounded by the sphere of the fixed stars does not lead Cusanus to an entirely unequivocal assertion of an infinite physical world of other suns and planets beyond those imaginary limits, but only to the conviction of the unintelligibility of the whole conception of a physical and quantitative world and the necessity, once more, of passing from it to the conception of God. While the passages did propound, as a sort of by-product, a new astronomical thesis, their essential object was to illustrate the author's favorite philosophical contention, to vindicate that *docta ignorantia* which consists in knowing that we do not know. Any antinomy which reflection seemed to reveal served his purpose; it was one more welcome instance of the identity of opposites. And it was precisely in order to exemplify the identity of opposites that Cusanus endeavored to show, by whatever arguments came to his hand, that the concepts of 'centre' and 'circumference,' as applied to the universe, have no clear and distinct meaning. Thus, though one can hardly say with Giordano Bruno that Cusanus enunciated his thesis "rather under his breath" (*suppressiore voce*), for his utterance of it was bold enough, it was in the end so elusively interpreted and so subordinated to theses of quite a different type, that it apparently had no great influence towards the abandonment of the Aristotelian and Ptolemaic conception — which, indeed, Cusanus himself, in a later writing, continues to employ; the divine wisdom, he observes, "placed the earth in the middle and caused it to be heavy and to move at the centre of the world." [23] This, however, may perhaps be supposed to refer only to our own system.

More concrete and unequivocal is Cusanus's assertion of the existence of inhabitants on other globes. He well illustrates what we have seen in other instances, the tendency of medieval writers who reject the principles of plenitude and sufficient reason in general terms, to argue unhesitatingly from these premises in particular cases. *Operarum Dei nulla est ratio*, he roundly declares: there is no reason why the earth is the earth, or man, man, except that he who made them so willed.[24] This, of course, logically implied the impossibility of any *a priori* knowledge about what exists. Yet Cusanus confidently argues that it is inconceivable that "so many spaces of the heaven and stars should be vacant" as the common view implied. Not only of the sun and moon, but also *de aliis stellarum regionibus*,

we conjecture that none of them are without inhabitants, but that there are as many particular partial worlds (*partes mundiales*) composing this one universe as there are stars, which are innumerable, unless it be to him who created all things in number.[25]

The same conclusion follows from the assumption that all grades in the Scale of Being have existence somewhere; "since," he writes, "from God natures of differing degrees of nobility proceed, there are inhabitants in every region" of the heavens. "The earth is perhaps inhabited by lesser beings" than dwell in other globes, though it does not seem that anything nobler and more perfect than the intellectual nature, which is to be found here in the earth and its region, can exist. Of the same generic nature, then, "even if of another species of it, are the inhabitants of the other stars." For the rest, "they remain wholly unknown to us" — though Cusanus ventures some conjectures as to their characteristics, drawn from those of the globes they occupy.

The logical grounds of the new astronomy were thus among the many elements of the modern conception of the world which were carried in solution in medieval thought; and they were by the end of the Middle Ages already beginning to show signs of precipitation. By the early sixteenth century the theories of the plurality of solar systems and of inhabited planets, of the infinity of the number of the stars and the infinite extent of the universe in space, were already common topics of discussion. Thus Palingenius, ten years or more before the publication of the *De revolutionibus orbium*, in an immensely popular poem used in many schools as a textbook, recorded that

> Singula nonnulli credunt quoque sidera posse
> Dici orbes,

and himself argued that there must be creatures in the other regions of the heavens immeasurably superior to man, since it is inconceivable that "the infinite power of God" can have exhausted itself with the production of so insignificant and wretched a being. "Is it not blasphemous," asks the poet, "to say that the heavens are a desert and rejoice in no residents, and that God rules only over us and the beasts,

> Tam paucis, et tam miseris animalibus, et tam
> Ridiculis?"

"It is certain that the omnipotent Begetter had the knowledge, the power and the will to create better things than we are, . . . and the more things he makes, and the more noble, the more resplendently shines forth the beauty of the world and the power of deity." [26] With respect to the literal numerical infinity of the stars Palingenius uses the evasion which had been usual since Plotinus in dealing with the number of grades in the Scale of Being:

Plurima sunt numero, ut possit comprendere nemo.[27]

The whole argument is here again an inference from the assumed infinity of the productive potency of the First Cause to the necessary innumerability of the actual effects. Later in the century, as a recent interesting discovery has shown, the English astronomer, Thomas Digges, added to his exposition (largely a free translation) of Copernicus an assertion of the infinity of the "orb" of the fixed stars, "garnished with lights innumerable and reaching up in *Sphaericall altitude* without end." [28] No specific deduction of this conclusion from the Copernican scheme of the solar system is attempted by Digges; the only reason given for it is that this is a suitable way of conceiving of "the glorious court of ye great God, whose unsercheable works invisible we may partly by these his visible conjecture, to whose infinit power and maiesty such an infinit place surmounting all other both in quantity and quality only is conuenient." [29]

Though the elements of the new cosmography had, then, found earlier expression in several quarters, it is Giordano Bruno who must be regarded as the principal representative of the doctrine of the decentralized, infinite, and infinitely populous universe; for he not only preached it throughout Western Europe with the fervor of an evangelist, but also first gave a thorough statement of the grounds on which it was to gain acceptance from the general public. And while he may have owed his interest in the question to the innovation of Copernicus, whose greatness he never tired of celebrating, it is certain that he was not led to his characteristic convictions by reflection upon the implications of the Copernican theory or by any astronomical observations. Those convictions were for him primarily, and almost wholly, a deduction from the principle of plenitude, or from the assumption on which the latter itself rested, the principle of sufficient reason. The *Timaeus*, Plo-

tinus (for Bruno "the prince of philosophers"), and the Schoolmen, not the *De revolutionibus orbium*, were the chief sources of
his theory. He may be regarded as carrying on the philosophy
of Abelard and extending the same reasonings to the field of
astronomy. His premises are at bottom the same as those from
which Dante argued to the virtual infinity of the celestial
hierarchies and the actualization of all the possibilities of
being; but they are brought to bear upon the question of the
number of potential stellar systems to which the Eternal Power
must be supposed to have imparted actual existence. Bruno
is, in short, precisely in those features of his teaching in which
he seems most the herald and champion of a modern conception of the universe, most completely the continuer of a certain
strain in Platonistic metaphysics and in medieval theology.
The "infinity of worlds" was, it is true, well known to have
been a thesis of Democritus and the Epicureans, but this told
against the theory rather than in its favor; it was its deduci-
bility from much more orthodox premises than the Democritic
that assured its triumph in the seventeenth century.

The essential character of Bruno's argument is perhaps most
clearly and concisely shown in a prose passage in the *De Immenso*, written about 1586. He here contends that the infinity
of stellar worlds in space follows directly and obviously from
*principia communia*, premises that everyone admits. For it is
axiomatic that "the divine essence is infinite"; that the measure of its potency (*modus possendi*) corresponds to the measure
of its being (*modus essendi*), and its *modus operandi*, in turn, to its
*modus possendi*; that a *potentia infinita*, such as is thus admittedly
possessed by the World-Ground, cannot exist *nisi sit possibile
infinitum*. Equally undisputed is it that the Absolute Being is
perfectly simple, that "in it being, power, action, volition . . .
are one and the same." The possible and the actual, in short,
identical in God, must be coextensive in the temporal order.
Hence an infinity of beings and of worlds must exist, in all possible modes. "We insult the infinite cause when we say that it
may be the cause of a finite effect; to a finite effect it can have
neither the name nor the relation of an efficient cause."
Hence, more specifically, it is impossible that the quantity of
matter should be finite, or that, beyond the traditional bound-

aries of the heavens, there should be naught but empty space — a yawning chasm of unrealized possibility of being. Of the endlessly numerous worlds thus demonstrated to exist, some, Bruno adds elsewhere, must be even more magnificent than ours, with inhabitants superior to the terrestrial race.[30]

In a passage in which essentially the same reasoning is less formally presented, the sources of it become still more clearly apparent through Bruno's repetition of the stock phrases and metaphors which we have already noted in earlier writers:

> Why should or how can we suppose the divine potency to be idle? Why should we say that the divine goodness, which is capable of communicating itself to an infinity of things and of pouring itself forth without limit, is niggardly? . . . Why should that centre of deity which is able to expand itself (if it may be so expressed) into an infinite sphere, remain barren, as if it were envious? Why should the infinite capacity be frustrated, the possibility of the existence of infinite worlds be cheated, the perfection of the divine image be impaired — that image which ought rather to be reflected back in a mirror as immeasurable as itself? . . . Why should we assert what is so full of absurdities and, while it in no wise promotes religion, faith, morals, or law, is destructive of so many principles of philosophy?[31]

Elsewhere the proof is made to rest more directly and explicitly upon the principle of sufficient reason. If there was, as we must suppose, a reason why the place occupied by our planet should be filled, there was still more reason why all other places equally capable of occupancy should be filled; and there is nothing in the nature of space which restricts the number of such places. In general, "in so far as there is a reason why some finite good, some limited perfection, should be, there is a still greater reason why an infinite good should be; for, while the finite good exists because its existence is suitable and reasonable, the infinite good exists with absolute necessity." True, the notion of "infinite good" can be applied in strictness only to an incorporeal perfection; but "what prevents the infinity that is implicit in the absolutely simple and undivided First Principle from becoming explicit in this its infinite and unbounded simulacrum, capable of containing innumerable worlds?" Not, adds Bruno here, that mere spatial extension or physical magnitude has in itself any "dignity" whereby should be in itself an expression of the perfection of the First Cause. It is really because of the necessity for the realization of the full Scale of Being that there must be an infinity of worlds to afford room for such a complete deployment of the possibles. "The excellence of the natures and corporeal species" could not otherwise be sufficiently manifested; "for it is incomparably better that Infinite Excellence should express itself in innumerable individuals than in some finite number of them. . . . Because of the countless grades of perfection in which the incorporeal divine Excellence must needs manifest itself in a corporeal manner, there must be countless individuals such as are those great living beings of which our divine mother, the Earth, is one." [32]

With this we encounter once more the usual argument for optimism. "That is perfect which consists of many parts, disposed in a fixed sequence and closely joined together." It is therefore "not permissible to carp at the vast edifice of the mighty Architect because there are in nature some things that are not best, or because monsters are to be found in more than one species. For whatever is small, trivial or mean serves to complete the splendor of the whole." There can be no "grade of being which, in its own place in the series, is not good in relation to the whole body." [33]

The deterministic implications of all this are clearly recognized and are drawn out in much the same form as they had been by Abelard more than four centuries before. Since God is immutable, and since in him potency and act are one,

there is no contingency in his operation; but a determinate and certain effect immutably follows from a determinate and certain cause; so that he cannot be other than he is, nor have any possibility other than that which he has, nor will other than what he actually wills, nor do aught other than what he does. For the distinction between the potential and the actual is pertinent only to beings that are subject to change.[34]

In the other aspects of Bruno's philosophy we are not here interested; but it is perhaps well to avert possible misunderstanding by pointing out that it is not solely the strain in medieval thought connected with the principles of plenitude and sufficient reason, or with the idea of the divine "goodness," that is manifest in his doctrine. While this element in the traditional complex is developed freely and consistently, certain other ingredients quite incongruous with it are likewise retained and are equally emphasized. Thus, for example, the Brunonian Absolute, though on the one hand essentially generative, and manifested in the multitudinous abundance of the creation, is also transcendent, self-sufficient, indivisible, timeless, ineffable, and incomprehensible, all its attributes being completely negative to all those of the world we know, and even, to our understandings, self-contradictory. The intrinsically contradictory nature of the general medieval conception of God, which is present but judiciously obscured and minimized in a writer like Thomas Aquinas, is by Bruno ostentatiously paraded; for him, in one very characteristic mood, the greater the paradox, the better the doctrine.

> The one Perfect and Best Being . . . does not include itself, for it is not greater than itself; it is not included by itself, for it is not less than itself. . . . It is a term in such wise that it is not a term; it is form in such wise that it is not form; it is matter in such wise that it is not matter. . . . In its infinite duration the hour does not differ from the day, the day from the year, the year from the century, the century from the moment. . . . Thou canst not more nearly approach to a likeness to the Infinite by being a man than by being an ant; not more nearly by being a star than by being a man; . . . for in the Infinite these distinctions are indifferent — and what I say of these I mean to imply of all the other distinctions whereby things subsist as particular entities (*intendo di tutte l'altre cose di sussistenza particolare*). . . . Since in it centre does not differ from circumference, we may safely affirm that the universe is all centre, or that the centre of the Universe is everywhere and the circumference nowhere, in so far as it differs from the centre; or contrariwise, that the circumference is everywhere and the centre nowhere.[35]

Bruno, too, in short, had, like Plotinus and like the Schoolmen, at least two Gods, whose properties and functions no mind could conceivably reconcile. And at times, when the strain of these contradictions becomes too great even for him, Bruno all but yields to the temptation to acosmism, which, as has been remarked, was never very far from any philosopher of the Platonistic tradition. "All that constitutes diversity, all that consists in generation, corruption, alteration and change, is not entity, is not Being, but is a condition and circumstance of Being, which is one, etc. . . . Whatsoever makes multiplicity in things is not what is, is not the thing itself (*la cosa*), but only the appearance in which it is represented to the sense. . . . All that constitutes difference and number è *puro accidente*, è

*pura figura, è pura complessione.*" [36]  All this, of course, is utterly
contrary to the side of Bruno's doctrine which has occupied us
here — the thesis that there is in the absolute essence a real
necessity of the real existence of all possible things to the maximal possible degree of diversity.  So too in Bruno's ethics, as
illustrated, for example, in the *Eroici furori*, much of the otherworldly or anti-naturalistic strain persists.  He represents, in
short, nearly all aspects of the complex of preconceptions current in medieval philosophy.  But he makes the meaning of
each of these preconceptions, as well as the incongruity of the
whole compound, far clearer than ever before, by developing
each with bold and rigorous logic within its own sphere, and
with a fine indifference to any lack of harmony between it and
any of the others.  And the result, among other things, was a
supposed proof, from strictly traditional and medieval premises, of a conclusion which meant the destruction of the medieval picture of the physical universe — and therewith of
much else that was inseparably associated with it.

The three greatest astronomers of Bruno's own and the succeeding generation — Tycho Brahe, Kepler, Galileo — all,
at least ostensibly, rejected the doctrines both of the infinity
and the "plurality" of worlds; but they all more or less definitely accepted the first of the five new theses — i. e., that of
the plurality of inhabited globes within our solar system.[37]
Galileo in his actual belief, it is fairly certain, inclined to the
Brunonian view; he remarks with emphasis in the *Dialogue on
the Two Principal Systems of the World* that "no one has ever
proved that the world is finite and of a definite shape." [38]
Nevertheless his spokesman in the dialogue formally concedes
to the Aristotelian interlocutor that in fact the universe "is
finite and spherical in form and therefore has a centre." [39]
But when the question is raised whether, assuming that there
are inhabitants on the moon, they are like those upon the
earth or quite dissimilar from them, Galileo clearly betrays the
influence upon his mind of the principle of plenitude.  We
have, he points out, no "sure observations" to decide the matter; and the astronomer as such cannot affirm a thing to exist
merely because it is logically possible (*per una semplice non re-*

*pugnanza*). Yet, Galileo adds, if he is asked what his "primary intuition and pure natural reason tells him as to there being produced upon the moon things similar to or different from those known to us here," he is constrained to answer "that they are entirely different and to us wholly unimaginable"; for this appears to him "to be required by the richness of Nature and the omnipotence of its Creator and Governor." [40]  It was, therefore, not because he rejected in principle all conclusions based upon considerations of this kind that Galileo failed to champion openly the larger theses which Bruno had drawn from the same premises.

But it is to be noted that precisely these more profound innovations in cosmological ideas were well fitted to reinforce certain characteristic strains in the traditional religion.  For example, one of the chief themes of the Christian moralist had always been the virtue of humility.  Pride, the initial sin, first source of all our woes, could never be sufficiently inveighed against.  A medieval or early modern writer, discoursing on this theme, could employ a supposed cosmographical fact (as we have seen Montaigne doing) to point his moral: man's almost central, and therefore all but lowest, place in the entire creation.  This astronomical reason for humility, as has been already remarked, the new astronomy destroyed.  But the doctrine of the incalculable vastness, still more that of the infinity, of the world provided a substitute; if man's position in the universe was no longer peculiarly degraded, his littleness, at all events, was more apparent than ever.  To make man thus sensible of his inexpressible unimportance, in so far as he was regarded merely as a part of nature, might well prepare him to walk humbly with his God; and, as we shall presently see, this adaptability of the more extreme new theses in cosmography to the uses of edification clearly did much to render them more acceptable in comparatively orthodox circles in the seventeenth century than they might have been expected to prove.  Those who held them chiefly, no doubt, on other grounds, did not fail to point out their value for purposes of religious edification.

After the fifth decade of the seventeenth century, not only the Copernican but also the Brunonian theses had the advantage of the support of the most influential philosopher of the age. Mindful of Galileo's condemnation, Descartes, who had no taste for martyrdom, was always careful, in defending the Copernican system, to refer to it as a "fable" or mere "hypothesis," which, indeed, agreed with the known facts better than any other, but need not on that account be regarded as true; but no reader can have been in doubt either as to the logical outcome of the philosopher's arguments or as to his actual opinion.[41] But Descartes showed not even this cautious reserve with respect to what might have seemed greater heresies, but which in fact, as he was careful to note, "the Cardinal of Cusa and several other doctors" had adopted *sans qu'ils aient jamais été repris de l'Église de ce sujet*"[42] — the rejection of the enveloping sphere and the assertion of the infinity of inhabited worlds. For the conclusions that the fixed stars are at varying distances from the sun and that the distance between the nearest of them and the orbit of Saturn is incalculably greater than the diameter of the earth's orbit, Descartes gives ostensibly astronomical reasons, but even these reasons were evidently strengthened in his mind by their congruity with the principle of plenitude; and upon that premise chiefly rested his further assurance of the existence of innumerable other stars and systems invisible to us. It is "much more suitable to believe" this than "to suppose that the power of the Creator is so imperfect that no such stars can exist."[43] In short the presumption from which we must reason, where other evidence is unavailable, is that what, so far as we can judge, is capable of being, is. The production of an infinity of worlds was possible to the Creator; and the principle which we must always accept in such matters is that the possibility has been realized.

> We must ever keep before our eyes the infinity of the power and goodness of God, and not fear to fall into error by imagining his works to be too great, too fair and too perfect; on the contrary, we must take care lest, by supposing limits (of which we have no certain knowledge) to exist [in God's works] we may seem to be insufficiently sensible of the greatness and power of the Creator.[44]

From these doctrines of the new cosmography Descartes drew moral and religious lessons of a sufficiently edifying and by no means novel sort. They furnished him, as the older theory had

furnished Montaigne, with reasons for rejecting the anthropocentric teleology with which many theologians had naïvely
flattered the pride of man. " It is not at all probable that all
things have been made for us in such a way that God had no
other end in view in making them. . . . We cannot doubt that
there is an infinity of things which exist now in the world, or
which formerly existed and have now ceased to be, which have
never been seen by any man or been of use to any." [45]   When
Montaigne had inveighed against " pride," it had hardly been
from otherworldly motives; having a profound temperamental
antipathy to everything stilted, pretentious, affected, and a
penetrating sense of the comedy of human existence, he had
delighted in pricking the bubble of man's vanity and putting
him in his undistinguished but not unsuitable nor, if he will
adapt himself to it, unenjoyable place in nature. Descartes,
however, uses his astronomical conceptions as a corrective of
our self-esteem in quite another spirit; he illustrates the underlying affinity, already pointed out, between the new cosmographical conceptions, especially in their extreme or Brunonian
form, and what was, after all, the fundamental thing in the
traditional religious temper, namely, its otherworldliness.
Writing in 1645 to the Princess Elizabeth, he enumerates four
principles of the understanding which should guide us in the
conduct of life; the third of these is that the universe is infinite.
Meditation upon this teaches us modesty and helps " to de-
tach our affections from the things of this world." " For if a
man imagine that beyond the heavens there exist nothing but
imaginary spaces, and that all the heavens are made solely for
the sake of the earth, and the earth for the benefit of man, the
result is that he comes to think that this earth is our principal
dwelling-place and this life the best that is attainable by us;
and also that, instead of recognizing the perfections which we
really possess, he attributes to other creatures imperfections
which do not belong to them, in order to raise himself above
them." [46]

It was probably to the vogue of Cartesianism rather than to
any direct influence of the writings of Bruno that the rapidly
growing acceptance of the theories of the plurality and infinity
of worlds in the second half of the seventeenth century was

chiefly due. How completely it was possible for even learned authors to forget the pioneers of the new cosmography and to transfer to Descartes the whole credit for it may be seen from Addison's Latin oration on the new astronomy delivered at Oxford in 1693. It was Descartes, said Addison, who "destroyed those orbs of glass which the whims of antiquity had fixed above" and "scorned to be any longer bounded within the straits and crystalline walls of an Aristotelic world." [47]

In England Henry More became for a time the most zealous defender of the infinity of worlds. His adoption of the theory apparently owed something to Descartes' recent example, though More, steeped both in Plotinus and in the Scholastic philosophers, needed no other sources than these to provide the grounds of his argument. How simply and directly the new conception of the physical world could be drawn from familiar and orthodox medieval premises is as clearly illustrated in More's poetic version of the argument as in Bruno's reasonings.

> If God's omnipotent,
> And this omnipotent God be everywhere,
> Where'er he is, then can he eas'ly vent
> His mighty virtue thorough all extent, . . .
> Unless omnipotent power we will impair
> And say that empty space his working can debar . . .
> Wherefore this precious sweet ethereall dew,
> For ought we know, God each where did distil
> And thorough all that hollow voidness threw,
> And the wide gaping drought therewith did fill,
> His endless overflowing goodness spill
> In every place; which streight he did contrive
> Int' infinite severall worlds, as his best skill
> Did him direct and creatures could receive:
> For matter infinite needs infinite worlds must give.
> The centre of each severall world's a sunne
> With shining beams and kindly warming heat,
> About whose radiant crown the planets runne,
> Like reeling moths about a candle light;
> These all together, one world I conceit.
> And that even infinite such worlds there be,
> That inexhausted Good that God is hight,
> A full sufficient reason is to me,
> Who simple Goodnesse make the highest Deity. [48]

More's disciple Glanvill, restating the argument in prose —
perhaps a less appropriate medium — reduces it to a sentence:
"to affirm that goodness is infinite, where what it doth and intends to do is but finite," is simply "a contradiction." But the
same conclusion can be justified on other grounds:

> Yea, the Scripture affirms that which is the very strength of mine argu-
> ment, *viz.*, that God made all things best. . . . It had been far more
> splendid, glorious and magnificent for God to have made the universe com-
> mensurate with his own immensity, and to have produced effects of his
> power and greatness wherever he himself is, *viz.*, in infinite space and dura-
> tion, than to have confined his omnipotence to work only in one little spot
> of an infinite inane capacity, and to begin to act but t'other day. Thus the
> late creation, and finiteness, of the world seem to conflict with the un-
> doubted oracle of truth.[49]

In Pascal we have the curious combination of a refusal to
accept the Copernican hypothesis with an unequivocal assertion of the Brunonian. Between the Ptolemaic, the Copernican, and the Tychonic arrangement of the solar system Pascal
found it impossible to decide. All three agreed with the visible
appearances which they were designed to explain; "who, then,
can, without danger of error, support any one of these theories
to the prejudice of the others?" [50] Yet no man was ever more
obsessed with the thought of the infinite magnitude of the
world than Pascal, and none ever dilated upon it more elo-
quently. He more than rivals Bruno in this, yet (for the most
part) with precisely the opposite motive and temper. In
Bruno the idea of the infinity of things, in extent, in number,
and in diversity, gives rise to an intense aesthetic admiration
and enjoyment; he seems to expand emotionally with the
magnitude of the objects upon which he expatiates. This
passes over into a mood of religious adoration; but it is usually
an essentially cosmical piety, finding its object in the creative
energy manifested in the sensible universe. The same is, in the
main, true of Henry More. But to Pascal's imagination the
vision of the *infini créé* is not exhilarating but oppressive; he,
even more than Descartes, dwells upon it because it belittles
and humiliates man and baffles his understanding. In his
knowledge of nature — such is the burden of that familiar
piece of gloomy eloquence in the *Pensées* — man finds only a

reason for self-abasement; for what it chiefly shows him is "the disproportion between what is and what he is."

Let him look upon that resplendent luminary set like an everlasting lamp to lighten the universe; let him remember that the earth is but a speck in comparison with the vast circuit which this star describes; and let him then consider with amazement that this circuit is itself no wider than a pinpoint beside that which is embraced by the stars that roll in the firmament. But if our sight stops here, let imagination pass beyond; wit will weary of conceiving before nature wearies of providing it with objects to conceive. The whole of this visible world is only an imperceptible fleck in the ample bosom of nature. No idea of ours can approach it. In vain we swell our conceptions beyond all imaginable distances; our minds still give birth but to atoms, in comparison with the reality of things. It is an infinite sphere of which the centre is everywhere and the circumference nowhere. Finally, it is the chief sensible manifestation of the omnipotence of God; let our imagination, then, lose itself in the thought of it. . . . Let man think of himself as one who has strayed into this out-of-the-way corner of nature, and, from this narrow prison in which he finds himself lodged — I mean the universe — let him learn to estimate at their just value the earth, kingdoms, cities, and himself. What is a man, in the midst of infinity?[51]

To bring man thus to think meanly of himself is, it is true, only one side of Pascal's purpose. His simple rule of procedure in dealing with a race whose self-estimates always tend to one excess or to the other, Pascal has told us: "s'il se vante, je l'abaisse; s'il s'abaisse, je le vante; et je contredis toujours, jusqu'à ce qu'il comprenne qu'il est un monstre incompréhensible." [52] Reflection upon the infinity of the physical world is thus, ostensibly, merely a support for one of the opposed theses which make the antinomy of human nature: "misère et grandeur de l'homme." The compensatory consideration is that of the superior dignity of "thought" — even the most transitory and ineffectual thought — over insensible matter, however vast and however potent. "All the bodies that exist, the firmament, the stars, the earth and its kingdoms, are of less value than the least of minds; for it is aware of them, and of itself — while they are aware of nothing." "By virtue of space I am comprehended and engulfed in the universe as a mere point; but by virtue of thought I comprehend it." [53] Yet to stop with this would be, after all, to leave the last word to the more cheerful side of the antinomy, which Pascal has no mind to do. While "all man's dignity lies in thought," and while "thought is in its nature a thing admirable and incomparable," in its actual operation in man it is a fatuous thing: "il fallait qu'elle eût d'étranges défauts pour être méprisable; mais elle en a de tels que rien n'est plus ridicule." [54] And the assumption of the infinity of the universe once more provides a means of abasing man, by showing him the futility of his noblest endowment. The natural office and aspiration of thought is to understand; but a reality that is infinite is necessarily unintelligible. "For want of having contemplated these infinities, men have set forth rashly upon the investigation of nature, as if there were some proportion between it and them." But after they have once truly faced the immensity of even the physical world, they must inevitably be plunged into "an eternal despair of ever knowing either the beginning or the end of things"; they will be certain only that no *assurance et fermeté*, no certain and solid knowledge, is attainable by them through the use of their natural intellectual powers. "This being realized, men will, I think, remain at rest, each in the state in which nature has placed him. This middle position which has fallen to our lot being equally removed from the two extremes [of infinity and nonentity], what matters it that a man should have a little more understanding of things?" It is not merely, for Pascal, that an infinite world is too big to be exhaustively investigated by us — though that of itself, he declares, means that no single part of it can be really understood, since "its parts all are so related and interlinked with one another that it is impossible to know the parts without knowing the whole or the whole without knowing all the parts." [55] The still deeper difficulty is that the very notion of infinite number or magnitude, which we know to be truly predicable of reality, at the same time involves our thought in insoluble antinomies. "We know that there is an infinite and we are ignorant of its nature." Thus, "we know that it is false that numbers are finite, therefore it is true that a numerical infinite exists; but we do not know what it is. It is false that it is odd, it is false that it is even; nevertheless, it is a number, and every number is either odd or even." Plunged thus into mysteries and inconceivabilities in its contemplation of mere nature, the reflective mind will be neither surprised nor rebellious when it encounters them in religion. God is like the physical infinite, a being "of whom it is possible to know *that* he is, without knowing what he is" — except in so far as supernatural means of attaining a certain practical knowledge of him are vouchsafed to us.[56]

Pascal's use of the assumption of the world's infinity is, however, arbitrary, not to say malicious; he employs it when it fits his mood and in so far as it serves his purpose of chastening man's pride, but he characteristically ignores the supposition — common enough in his time and usually regarded as a corollary of the former assumption — that these infinite worlds áre populated. To a Bruno, even to a Kepler with his walled universe, the race that occupies this planet has no lack of company, though it unfortunately possesses no means of communicating with its neighbors on other globes; and thus these and many other writers of the period could look out upon the reaches of stellar space with a cheerful sense of the ubiquity of conscious life and enjoyment. But Pascal seems to conceive of mankind as alone in a dead infinity of matter that travels endlessly upon its barren rounds, without thought or understanding, with naught in it that is akin to man. "L'éternel silence de ces espaces infinis m'effraie." But if he had thought otherwise, had permitted himself to consider seriously the implications of the theory of a plurality of worlds, Pascal would have been faced by difficulties to him more embarrassing than this feeling of solitude in the physical world. For the intellectual basis of the religious convictions in which he found escape from the pessimism and scepticism which the spectacle of mere nature bred, lay (apart from the argument of the wager) almost wholly in the belief in the reality of a supernatural revelation through the history of Judaism and Christianity and the documents in which that history is recorded. That belief would, for reasons already suggested, have been somewhat difficult to adjust to the assumption of the existence throughout the infinity of space of countless other races of rational and presumably sinful beings.

Pascal better than any other writer makes evident a certain ironic aspect of the history of the principle of plenitude. That principle, we have seen, primarily tended towards, and was congenial to, what I have called the this-worldly type of religious feeling and moral temper; for it implied the genuine reality and the metaphysical necessity of the sensible world; it found in the creation of such a world an actual enhancement of the divine perfection; and it served, for century after century, as the chief basis of the arguments for optimism. Yet since it seemed to make the world literally infinite, its consequences could, as has also been pointed out, easily be turned to the service of otherworldliness; and it was upon this possibility of the astronomical application of the conception that Pascal seized. Again, the principle at bottom was, as has already appeared in numerous instances, the manifestation of a kind of rationalism; it expressed the conviction that there is an essential reasonableness in the nature of reality, a sufficient ground in the intelligible world for everything that concretely exists. But when it was construed as implying the real existence of a quantitative or numerical infinite, it seemed rather to make reality essentially alien to man's reason, permeated throughout with paradoxes and contradictions. He who thus followed the principle of sufficient reason to what appeared to be its ultimate consequence, found his conclusion destructive of the assumption from which it had been derived. He might thus be easily converted into such a *pyrrhonien accompli* as made, in Pascal's eyes, the most hopeful material for a *chrétien soumis*.

In the last quarter of the seventeenth century the triumph of the new cosmographical ideas was rapid; and by the first or second decade of the eighteenth century not only the Copernican theory of the solar system but also the belief in other inhabited planets and in the plurality of worlds seems to have been commonly accepted even in highly orthodox circles. The *Entretiens sur la pluralité des mondes* (1686) of Fontenelle no doubt did more than any other single writing to diffuse these ideas among the educated classes generally. Of no book was the levity of the manner ever more incongruous with the magnitude of the theme; to this, no doubt, was in great measure due the success of the *Entretiens* as an *oeuvre de vulgarisation*. Its vogue in England was scarcely less than in France.[57] The first English translation was published within two years, and a dozen other editions of this or other versions appeared in the course of the following century. Fontenelle's arguments for the presence of "inhabitants" (which appears usually to mean intelligent beings) on other bodies of our system, and for the hypothesis that all the fixed stars are centres of systems of inhabited planets, are chiefly four. In part he relies upon a simple argument from analogy, which probably derived its plausibility from its approximation to the inference from (supposed) identity of cause to identity of effects. "You grant" — so he sums up this argument — "that when two things are like one another in all those things that appear to you, it is possible that they may be like one another in those things that are not visible, if you have not some good reason to believe otherwise." Now this, continues Fontenelle, passing somewhat easily from "possible" to "probable," is "the way of reasoning I have made use of. The moon, say I, is inhabited because she is like the earth; and the other planets are inhabited because they are like the moon." [58] About the population of the moon Fontenelle is not, in fact, altogether serious; he recognizes that the absence of a lunar atmosphere renders it doubtful, and finally adopts the theory only to please his Marquise. But with regard to the other planets of our system the contention is seriously advanced, and on the same ground it is maintained that the other suns probably have planets about them, which are the abodes of life. This, of course, is the argument from analogy at its lowest level; it has no real probative force. At times Fontenelle recognizes that this part of his reasoning amounts to little more than asking "Why not?" and so thrusting the burden of proof upon the other side. The second argument is that from the analogy of nature on this planet to probable conditions elsewhere. We see from our own observation and from the recent disclosures of the microscope that nature tends to crowd all matter with life, so that "every grain of sand" sustains millions of living creatures. "Why, then, should nature, which is fruitful to excess here, be so very barren in the rest of the planets?" This, however, should not be assumed to be a mere multiplication of the same models. "Nature hates repetitions," and diversifies her products in each of the inhabited worlds. This dissimilarity increases with the distance, "for whosoever should see an inhabitant of the moon and inhabitant of the earth would soon perceive that they were nearer neighbors than one of the earth and one of Saturn." [59]

But the argument rests much more heavily upon the other two considerations, both already traditional, and both in essence applications of the principle of sufficient reason. The first of these is the argument from the irrational wastefulness, the wanton squandering of opportunities, which we must acribe to the Author of Nature, if we accept the conclusions of astronomy as to the extent of the universe, and then suppose that only a tiny fraction of this extent is occupied by living things. And there is finally the almost conclusive presumption drawn from the theological doctrine of the infinity and goodness (in the sense of fecundity) of the Absolute Being from whom all things proceed. In short, Fontenelle observes in his preface, "l'idée de la diversite infinie que la Nature doit avoir mis dans ses ouvrages, règne dans tout le livre" — an idea which certainly "cannot be disputed by any philosopher." The conclusion drawn is, Fontenelle grants, only a probable one; but it has a probability of approximately the same order as that of the former existence of Alexander. Neither is capable of demonstrative proof; but all that we know is favorable to the supposition, and there is nothing whatever against it.

> You have all the proofs you could desire in a like matter: the entire resemblance of the planets with the earth, which is inhabited, the impossibility of conceiving any other use for which they were created, the fecundity and magnificence of nature, the certain regard she seems to have had to the necessities of their inhabitants, as in giving moons to those planets remote from the sun.

Upon the effect of the belief in the plurality of worlds on the imagination Fontenelle touches playfully. His Marquise protests that the spectacle of the world which the philosopher has disclosed to her is "dreadful." The philosopher is not downhearted.

> Dreadful, Madam, said I; I think it very pleasant. When the heavens were a little blue arch, stuck with stars, methought the universe was too strait and close; I was almost stifled for want of air; but now it is enlarged in height and breadth and a thousand vortexes taken in. I begin to breathe

with more freedom, and I think the universe to be incomparably more magnificent than it was before.[60]

But this, of course, is a purely aesthetic consolation — and that only for those whose taste values bigness and variety more than simplicity and intelligibility and perfection of form. The effect of the enlargement of the world upon man's active nature is, Fontenelle admits, depressing. It affords a justification for doing nothing, since it makes all human achievement seem of infinitesimal consequence. "We must confess," concludes the Marquise, "that we scarce know where we are, in the midst of so many worlds; for my own part, I begin to see the earth so fearfully little, that I believe that from henceforth I shall never be concerned at all for anything. That we so eagerly desire to make ourselves great, that we are always designing, always troubling and harassing ourselves, is certainly because we are ignorant what these vortexes are; but now I hope my new lights will in part justify my laziness, and when anyone reproaches me with carelessness, I will answer, *Ah, did you but know what the fixed stars are!*"

Many Englishmen, and perhaps most English clergymen, of the early eighteenth century derived their general notions of astronomy largely from William Derham's *Astro-Theology, or a Demonstration of the Being and Attributes of God from a Survey of the Heavens* (1715). The book appeared under royal patronage, and its author was a Canon of Windsor and a Boyle Lecturer, as well as a Fellow of the Royal Society. It thus presumably represented a position officially approved by the orthodoxy of the time, theological as well as scientific. Derham unequivocally supports the infinitist cosmography, which, under the name of the "New System," he carefully distinguishes from the Copernican. It

is the same as the Copernican as to the Systeme of the Sun and its Planets. . . . But then whereas the Copernican Hypothesis supposeth the Firmament of the Fixt Stars to be the Bounds of the Universe, and to be placed at an equal Distance from its Center the Sun; The *New Systeme* supposeth that there are many other Systemes of *Suns* and *Planets*, besides that in which we have our residence: namely that every Fixt Star is a Sun, and encompassed with a Systeme of Planets, both Primary and Secondary, as well as ours. . . . In all probability there are many of them [Systemes of the Universe], even as many as there are Fixt Stars, which are without number.

And Derham holds that all the planets (including the moon) in our own system, and all those in the infinity of other solar systems, are "Places, as accommodated for Habitation, so stocked with proper Inhabitants." This "New System" he thinks "far the most rational and probable of any"; and his first and chief reason for this opinion is the usual theological one:

[This System] is far the most magnificent of any; and worthy of an infinite CREATOR: whose *Power* and *Wisdom*, as they are without bounds and measure, so may in all probability exert themselves in the Creation of many Systemes, as well as one. And as Myriads of Systemes are more for the Glory of GOD, and more demonstrate his *Attributes*, than one, so it is no less probable than possible, there may be many besides this which we have the Privilege of living in.[61]

And the moral which is drawn from the "New System" is precisely that which the medieval writers and the early anti-Copernicans had drawn from the Ptolemaic:

From the consideration of the prodigious Magnitude and Multitude of the Heavenly Bodies, and the far more noble Furniture and Retinue which some of them have more than we, we may learn not to overvalue this world, not to set our hearts too much upon it, or upon any of its Riches, Honours, or Pleasures. For what is all our Globe but a Point, a Trifle to the Universe! a Ball not so much as visible among the greatest part of the Heavens, namely the Fixt Stars. And if Magnitude or Retinue may dignify a Planet, *Saturn* or *Jupiter* may claim the preference; or if Proximity to the most magnificent Globe of all the Systeme, to the Fountain of Light and Heat, to the Center, can honour and aggrandize a Planet, then *Mercury* and *Venus* can claim that dignity. If, therefore, our World be one of the inferior parts of our Systeme, why should we inordinately seek and desire it?[62]

Derham, however, adds the pleasant suggestion that among the principal advantages of "the Heavenly State" will be improved facilities for astronomical observation — or exploration.

We are naturally pleased with new things, we take great Pains, undergo dangerous Voyages, to view other countries: with great Delight we hear of new Discoveries in the Heavens, and view these glorious Bodies with great Pleasure through our Glasses. With what pleasure, then, shall departed, happy Souls survey the most distant Regions of the Universe, and view all those glorious Globes thereof, and their noble Appendages, with a nearer View.[63]

Further evidence of the currency of the same hypothesis in the most respectable and orthodox circles by the beginning of the eighteenth century is to be seen in Sir Richard Blackmore's *Creation* (1712). Blackmore is one of the most ridiculed of eighteenth-century poets; he had the ill luck to draw upon himself the animosity of both Dennis and Pope, besides lesser satirists. Yet his *Creation*, which seems to most readers now one of the most tedious of the didactic poems of an age of tedious didactic poetry, was much admired by many of his contemporaries and eighteenth-century successors. Addison said of it (*Spectator*, 339): "It was undertaken with so good an intention, and is executed with so great a mastery, it deserves to be looked upon as one of the most useful and noble productions in our English verse. The reader cannot but be pleased to find the depths of philosophy enlivened with all the charms of poetry, and to see so great a strength of reason, amidst so beautiful a redundancy of the imagination." Even Dennis described the *Creation* as "a philosophical poem which has equalled that of Lucretius in the beauty of its versification, and infinitely surpassed it in the solidity and strength of its reasoning"; and Dr. Johnson compared it with Pope's philosophical poems to the disadvantage of the latter. The *Creation*, then, is, in point of vogue and contemporary reputation, one of the important philosophical poems of the century.

Blackmore on the whole accepts the Copernican theory, though he seems to waver on the question a little. But about the plurality of worlds he has no doubts.

> Yet is this mighty system, which contains
> So many worlds, such vast etherial plains,
> But one of thousands, which compose the whole,
> Perhaps as glorious, and of worlds as full.
>   .     .     .     .     .     .     .
> All these illustrious worlds, and many more
> Which by the tube astronomers explore;
> And millions which the world can ne'er descry
> Lost in the wilds of vast immensity,
> Are suns, are centers, whose superior sway
> Planets of various magnitude obey.[64]

And he finds it — for pretty much the reasons which Milton

forty years before had rejected — impossible to doubt that
these other bodies are inhabited.

> When we on faithful nature's care reflect,
> And her exhaustless energy respect, . . .
> We may pronounce each orb sustains a race
> Of living things adapted to the place. . . .
> Were all the stars, those beauteous realms of light,
> At distance only hung to shine by night,
> And with their twinkling beams to please our sight? . . .
> Are all those glorious empires made in vain?[65]

The "globe terrestrial" is but "a mean part" of the whole;
of some of the others the denizens

> Must this low world's inhabitants excel.
> And since to various planets they agree,
> They from each other must distinguished be
> And own perfections different in degree.

The type of religious thought and feeling which the assumption of the infinity of the world and the multiplicity of inhabited globes probably chiefly tended to produce in the
average orthodox and commonplace mind in the eighteenth
century finds perhaps its best expression in the last book of
Young's *Night Thoughts* (Night IX), 1745. Few poems are
comparable to it in the contrast between its contemporary and
its later vogue and influence. The Ninth Night is an offset to
the other eight; they were entitled *The Conflict*, this *The Consolation*. The Ninth Part consists of Night Thoughts in a different sense from the others. Night had, in the main, been the
time congenial to Young's muse because it is sombre, appropriate to thoughts of death, the grave, and the other world, or
evocative of sorrowful memories. But now night is the time
when the starry heavens are disclosed to us, when the work of
the astronomer begins.   It is night that

> sets to view
> Worlds beyond number; worlds conceal'd by day
> Behind the proud and envious star of noon.

It is, then, of a succession of religious musings upon astronomy
that the poem chiefly consists.

The theory of the infinity of worlds Young accepted, no

doubt, chiefly because most people by this time accepted it; but it also evidently had an especial appeal to him as a poet and as a writer of works of religious edification. It lent itself to that sort of swelling, diffuse, and ejaculatory rhetoric which Young and his readers loved — to the taste which Mr. Saintsbury indicates when he speaks of the *Night Thoughts* as "an enormous soliloquy addressed by an actor of superhuman lung-power to an audience of still more superhuman endurance." And it suited the type of religiosity which seeks to find the sources of awe and reverence and devotion in dwelling upon the physical bigness of the creation. It is somewhat in the vein of the American preacher who devoted a sermon to elaborating the proposition that God is greater than Niagara Falls. Young was not one who expected to find God, not in the thunder and the whirlwind, but in the still, small voice. He seems to have believed that he might bring about the moral reformation of the youthful Lorenzo whom he is constantly apostrophizing — and whose nocturnal employments, he intimates, were neither astronomical observation nor meditations among the tombs — by overwhelming his imagination with the spectacle of the vastness of the world, and by thus making him sensible, sometimes of the littleness of man, sometimes of the possibilities open to him as the being capable of occupying himself with thoughts so vast. He, also, finds a means of abasing the human understanding, and therefore the better preparing it for accepting the "mysteries" of Christian theology, in the thought of the spatial and physical infinite. There is, too, in Young the expression of a distinctly 'Romantic' taste in universes — in one sense of that equivocal term:

> Nothing can satisfy but what confounds,
> Nothing but what astonishes is true.

While these seem to be some of the motives which prompt Young to the acceptance of the infinitist cosmology, he too justifies it argumentatively by the same sort of reasons which had been advanced long before by Bruno, and had now become the stock-proof of the doctrine.

> Where ends this mighty building? Where begin
> The suburbs of creation? Where, the wall

Whose battlements look o'er into the vale
Of non-existence, NOTHING's strange abode!
Say, at what point of space JEHOVAH dropp'd
His slacken'd line, and laid his balance by;
Weigh'd worlds and measur'd infinite, no more?

The question is a hard one, Young grants; but it is "harder still" to admit that the creation has an end in space. To believe in its infinity is the more "just conjecture":

If 'tis an error, 'tis an error sprung
From noble root, high thought of the most high.
But wherefore error? Who can prove it such? —
He that can set OMNIPOTENCE a bound.
Can man conceive beyond what GOD can do? . . .
A thousand worlds? There's space for millions more;
And in what space can his great fiat fail!

There is internal evidence that Young conceived himself to be here offering a direct poetic counterblast to Milton's poetic expressions of finitism.

The existence of countless races of intelligent inhabitants on the other celestial systems seems to Young not less indubitable. The argument is largely from the usual presumption of the plenitude of the creation and the inconceivability that the Author of Nature could have wasted matter by leaving any great portion of it untenantable by human beings (here, again, there is a pretty evident polemic reference to *Paradise Lost*, VIII, 100–106):

Vast concave! ample dome! wast thou designed
A meet apartment for the Deity?
Not so: that thought alone thy state impairs,
Thy lofty sinks, and shallows thy profound,
And straitens thy diffusive; dwarfs the whole,
And makes an universe an orrery . . .
. . . . . . . For who can see
Such pomp of matter, and imagine, mind,
For which alone inanimate was made,
More sparingly dispens'd? . . .
. . . . . . . 'Tis thus the skies
Inform us of superiors numberless,
As much, in excellence, above mankind,
As above earth, in magnitude, the spheres.

There is thus, as a consequence, apparently, of a curious fusion of literary influences and a resultant confusion of ideas, a hint of the fanciful idea, which Kant was to elaborate a decade later, that there is a gradation of the types of beings in proportion to their distance from the centre — or at all events, from the earth. The poet takes an imaginary voyage through space, and at the same time conceives of this as an ascent of the Scale of Being.

> I wake; and waking, climb Night's radiant scale,
> From sphere to sphere; the steps by Nature set
> For man's ascent; at once to tempt and aid;
> To tempt his eye, and aid his tow'ring thought;
> Till it arrives at the great Goal of all.

Even in the middle and late eighteenth century these cosmological doctrines were, it is to be noted, defended, by some of the most eminent minds of the period, not at all upon observational grounds, but upon the familiar Platonistic and Brunonian premises. J. H. Lambert, for example, as a pioneer in the determination of stellar magnitudes and distances by photometric methods, holds a high place in the history of scientific astronomy; yet it was wholly from the principle of plenitude that he confidently concluded (1761) that other worlds must be inhabited.

Could the world be the effect of an infinitely active Creator, unless in every part of it life and activity, thoughts and desires, were found in the creatures? Could I conceive its perfection to consist in a continuous and inexhaustible diversification of similarities, and yet leave in it vacant places where there were no parts of a whole which should be infinitely complete? Such gaps I could not admit; and I had no hesitation in filling every solar system with habitable globes, so far as the admirable order which has been given to their course permits. . . . Those who still doubt or wholly deny this are so limited in their understanding because they recognize no means of verification except their eyes, and therefore will not hear of proofs from general principles and of moral certainty.[66]

Yet even the existence of these limited intelligences, Lambert intimates, is in keeping with the same general plan of the universe; it takes all kinds of people, even stupid ones, to make the world complete. The infinity of the world in space, however, Lambert cannot admit. In time it must be regarded as continuing *in infinitum*, but its spatial infinity seems to him to involve the inadmissible conception of a realized infinite number.

Kant, about the same time, was arguing both for the infinite extension of the physical universe and the infinite plurality of worlds on the usual Platonistic grounds. Since we must "conceive of the creation as proportionate to the power of an Infinite Being, . . . it can have no limits at all. . . . It would be absurd to represent the Deity as bringing into action only an infinitely small part of his creative potency — to think of that reservoir of a true immensity of natures and of worlds as inactive and shut up in an eternal desuetude. Is it not much more reasonable, or, to express it better, is it not necessary, to represent the totality of the creation as it must be in order that it may bear witness to that Power which is beyond all measurement?" [67] And the philosopher who was later to find — as others had done before him — a supposedly clinching proof of metaphysical idealism in the antinomies of the spatial and temporal infinite and continuum, now disposes with a somewhat contemptuous brevity of such objections to the logic of the principle of plenitude. To "the gentlemen who, because of the supposed impossibility of an infinite aggregate, without number and limit, find difficulty in this idea," Kant puts a question which he seems to regard as conclusive. The future is admittedly an infinite series of changes. The conception of it in its entirety must be present all at once to the divine understanding. Such a concept, therefore, cannot be logically impossible, that is, self-contradictory. But if the simultaneous representation of a successive infinity is not inherently impossible — to a sufficiently comprehensive intelligence — how can there be any logical impossibility in the concept of a simultaneous infinity, i. e., of the infinity of the world in space? Since, then, the infinity of the world is possible, it is also necessary.

Kant was here mindful of a logical dilemma which, when he came to set forth the antinomies in the *Kritik der reinen Vernunft*, he seems to have forgotten. Even though future events, like all others, are declared by an idealistic philosophy to be purely mental, their number must be either finite or infinite. If it is infinite, and if an infinite sum of particulars is not merely baffling to the human imagination but "unrepresentable," inherently incapable of being thought together by any mind, it follows that there is no cosmical intelligence which is acquainted with all the facts that make up the total history of the world. Even a so-called divine mind would be incapable of grasping the future in its entirety; time would be too big for it. The alternative to this consequence of Kant's later doctrine of the unthinkableness and absurdity of the numerical infinite would be the conception of the future arrival of a time "when time shall be no more," the cessation, after a certain date, of all change, process, succession, the winding-up of the universe in which things happen. This would mean either an eventual lapse of everything into sheer nonentity, or else — what seems a very odd and difficult conception — the continuance, after that date, of an existence without dates or experienced duration, the contemplation, by one or many timeless minds, of an eternally immutable object of thought. Kant in his later period ought to have been aware that this embarrassing choice between alternative implications confronted him, since he had himself once virtually pointed it out; but in his "solution" of the antinomies he appears wholly oblivious of it.

Yet Kant — to return to his cosmological speculations of the seventeen-fifties — unlike many of his predecessors and contemporaries in this vein, did not feel constrained by the principle of plenitude "to assert that all planets must be inhabited" — though, he hastens to add, "it would be an absurdity to deny this with respect to all or, indeed, to most of them."

In the abundance of Nature, in which worlds and systems are, in comparison with the whole, mere motes, there may well be vacant and uninhabited regions, which are not, strictly speaking, made serviceable to the object of Nature, namely, the contemplation of rational beings. [To question this] would be as if one were to make the wisdom of God a reason for doubting the fact that sandy deserts occupy wide areas of the earth's surface and that there are islands in the seas without human inhabitants; for a planet is a much smaller thing in comparison with the whole creation than a desert or island in comparison with the earth's surface. . . . Would it not be rather a sign of poverty than of superabundance in Nature, if she were so careful to exhibit all her riches at every point in space? [68]

It is, moreover, Kant observes, evident that the laws of nature are such that life can exist only under certain physical conditions; bodies on which these conditions have not yet been evolved will naturally be uninhabited. "The excellence of the creation loses nothing by this, since the infinite is a magnitude which cannot be diminished by the subtraction of any finite part." Here, it will be observed, the paradoxes of the concept of the quantitative infinite are being turned against an argument which for two centuries had been based upon the principle of plenitude. Kant, too, holding that the universe must be infinite, and still implying that the *number* of inhabited worlds must be so, does not find that it follows from this that *all* planets or solar systems must be the abodes of living beings, since an infinite collection does not cease to be such when a finite part is taken away from it.

There has been a somewhat curious paradox in the history of the relations of cosmographical ideas and moral and religious feeling in Western thought. The habit of mind naturally appropriate to a finite and geocentric universe did not much manifest itself in the age when the universe was actually so conceived, but appeared at its maximum long after such a conception had become, for science and philosophy, obsolete. This incongruity has two chief aspects. (1) The infinities, spatial or temporal, which baffle both the understanding and the imagination, and to minds of a certain type, such as Pascal's, make the natural hopes and ambitions and endeavors of men seem petty and futile, tend in themselves to breed otherworldliness; thought and will, seeking some finality to fix themselves upon, and finding none here, look for it elsewhere. The profound otherworldliness of most Indian religious philosophy is perhaps not unrelated to a certain arithmetical grandiosity of that race's imagination, to the tedious interminableness of all the vistas which it confronts — most of all those in time. But in European thought we find the anomaly that a metaphysical and practical otherworldliness coexisted for centuries with a cosmological finitism; and that on the other hand, when the latter began to be theoretically abandoned, the preoccupation of men's minds with supersensible and supratemporal realities also steadily diminished, and religion itself became more and more this-worldly. (2) Aside from this general difference in scale between the medieval and the modern cosmographies, the medieval, however low the place it assigned to man in his unregenerate state, at all events attributed a unique significance to terrestrial history. There were no other stars upon which similar dramas, or more momentous ones, were conceivably being enacted, each in isolation, and without influence upon another's course. The universe was at least not a many-ringed circus. Yet, once more, the temper which might have been expected to result from such a preconception was relatively little characteristic of medieval thought. It was *after* the earth had lost its monopoly that its inhabitants began to find their greatest interest in the general movement of terrestrial events, and presently came to talk of their own actual and potential racial achievements — though the whole of these admittedly constituted but a momentary episode in the endless vicissitudes of time, and had for its scene but a tiny island in an immeasurable and incomprehensible cosmos — as if the general destiny of the universe wholly depended upon them or should reach its consummation in them. It was not in the thirteenth century but in the nineteenth that *homo sapiens* bustled about most self-importantly and self-complacently in his infinitesimal corner of the cosmic stage. The reasons for this paradox are, of course, to be found in the fact that, in the later period as in the earlier, certain associated ideas in large measure counteracted the characteristic tendency of the received cosmographical presuppositions. Into the nature of these counteracting factors we need not here further inquire; it is sufficient to note that certain consequences which might naturally have resulted from the introduction of the new spatio-temporal scale and scheme of things actually manifested themselves tardily and partially, though, as we have seen, with some fluctuation, and that their full repercussion is perhaps still in the future.

# V

## PLENITUDE AND SUFFICIENT REASON IN LEIBNIZ AND SPINOZA

AMONG the great philosophic systems of the seventeenth century, it is in that of Leibniz that the conception of the Chain of Being is most conspicuous, most determinative, and most pervasive. The essential characteristics of the universe are for him plenitude, continuity, and linear gradation. The chain consists of the totality of monads, ranging in hierarchical sequence from God to the lowest grade of sentient life, no two alike, but each differing from those just below and just above it in the scale by the least possible difference. Since the metaphysics of Leibniz is a form of idealism, or, more precisely, of panpsychism, the gradation is defined primarily in psychological rather than morphological terms; it is by the levels of consciousness which severally characterize them, the degrees of adequacy and clarity with which they "mirror" or "represent" the rest of the universe, that the monads are differentiated. Nevertheless, the material world also, as a *phenomenon bene fundatum*, the mode in which these incorporeal entities necessarily manifest themselves to one another, has a derivative and somewhat equivocal, but essential, place in Leibniz's scheme of things; and he habitually employs without hesitation the ordinary language of physical realism, and discusses the problems of physical science as genuine, not as fictitious, problems. And in the material world too the same three laws hold good; and they should be used by the investigator of nature as guiding principles in his empirical researches. The best expression of this is in a letter of Leibniz's, usually omitted in the editions of his collected writings, to the special importance of which several recent students of his philosophy have drawn attention.[1] He writes:

All the different classes of beings which taken together make up the universe are, in the ideas of God who knows distinctly their essential gradations, only so many ordinates of a single curve so closely united that it would be impossible to place others between any two of them, since that would imply disorder and imperfection. Thus men are linked with the animals, these with the plants and these with the fossils, which in turn merge with those bodies which our senses and our imagination represent to us as absolutely inanimate. And, since the law of continuity requires that when the essential attributes of one being approximate those of another all the properties of the one must likewise gradually approximate those of the other, it is necessary that all the orders of natural beings form but a single chain, in which the various classes, like so many rings, are so closely linked one to another that it is impossible for the senses or the imagination to determine precisely the point at which one ends and the next begins — all the species which, so to say, lie near to or upon the borderlands being equivocal, and endowed with characters which might equally well be assigned to either of the neighboring species. Thus there is nothing monstrous in the existence of zoophytes, or plant-animals, as Budaeus calls them; on the contrary, it is wholly in keeping with the order of nature that they should exist. And so great is the force of the principle of continuity, to my thinking, that not only should I not be surprised to hear that such beings had been discovered — creatures which in some of their properties, such as nutrition or reproduction, might pass equally well for animals or for plants, and which thus overturn the current laws based upon the supposition of a perfect and absolute separation of the different orders of coexistent beings which fill the universe; — not only, I say, should I not be surprised to hear that they had been discovered, but, in fact, I am convinced that there must be such creatures, and that natural history will perhaps some day become acquainted with them, when it has further studied that infinity of living things whose small size conceals them from ordinary observation and which are hidden in the bowels of the earth and the depths of the sea.[2]

These, however, are familiar aspects of Leibniz's system. We shall in this lecture be concerned with a more special and somewhat more difficult group of inter-connected questions, about which some differences of interpretation have arisen among those who have studied his doctrine. These questions are: first, the relation of the principle of plenitude to that fundamental theorem in his philosophy which he calls the principle of sufficient reason; second, the scope which he consequently gives to the principle of plenitude; and third — a question involved in both the others — whether he really escapes that absolute logical determinism which is characteristic of the philosophy of Spinoza.

In his formulations of the principle of sufficient reason Leibniz is less precise and consistent than a philosopher ought to be, when he is dealing with a proposition to which he ascribes such immense importance in natural science and in metaphysics. Sometimes it seems to include, if not to reduce to, the ordinary scientific postulate of causal uniformity in nature. More frequently it is expressed in terms which seem to relate to final rather than efficient causation; and it has commonly been construed as an extreme assertion of a teleological view of nature — as equivalent to the thesis that the existence and properties and behavior of things are to be explained ultimately by the values which they serve to realize, and that we can discover factual truths of science by tracing out the implications of the fundamental scheme of values which the universe expresses. Thus Russell in his volume on Leibniz writes that "the law of sufficient reason, applied to actual existents, reduces itself to the assertion of final causes." Hence, "in order to infer actual existence, whether from another existent, or from mere notions, the notion of the good must always be employed" — a doctrine which, as Russell adds, confers upon the concept "good" a relation to real existence such as no other concept possesses.[3] While such a summary of Leibniz's meaning can be supported by fairly numerous citations from his text, it nevertheless fails to express his more fundamental and characteristic view on the matter, and tends to give an inverted conception of the relations in his philosophy of the notions of 'good' and 'existence.' The motive which can be shown to have begotten his faith in the principle of sufficient reason, as a cosmological generalization, was not chiefly a desire to find what is commonly meant by teleology in nature — that is, neat adjustments to such ends as the comfort, convenience, happiness, or edification of man or other conscious beings. Leibniz was less concerned (I do not say he was not at all concerned) to maintain that the reason for a thing is a 'good,' in the common sense of conduciveness to the subjective satisfaction of God or man or animal, than to maintain that the thing at all events has *some* reason, that it is *logically* grounded in something else which is logically ultimate.

For it still seemed to Leibniz, as to others of his time, highly important, and not necessarily impossible, to know whether or not the existence of any world at all and the general constitution of the world that actually exists are anything more than colossal accidents; whether the universe might just as conceivably never have been, or have been of quite another sort, but simply happened by some lucky or unlucky chance to find itself real and possessing the characters it has. To all appearance reality is full, not only in its minor details but also in its more general features, of mere idiosyncrasies, for which no sort of explanation can be given. This is especially evident when we consider the purely numerical and quantitative attributes of the universe. One number in the arithmetical series is no more sacred nor more obviously suited to existence than another. Is it nevertheless true that, out of all the possible numbers of, say, prime-atoms, or planets, or suns, or germ-cells, or minds, some one number, a wholly arbitrary selection, rose fortuitously into actual being? Or again, are what we call the laws of nature themselves mere whimsies of matter, which (for a time at least) happens unaccountably to behave with apparent regularity in one manner, out of a million others that were, logically considered, equally open to it? There was, of course, a familiar element in the philosophic heritage of Leibniz and his age which at once intensified this difficulty and determined the special form in which it presented itself. Most non-materialistic philosophers of the seventeenth and eighteenth centuries still habitually thought in terms of two realms of being. The world of essences, 'natures,' or Platonic Ideas, was to them as indubitably and objectively there to be reckoned with as the world of individual, temporal existents, physical or spiritual. The former, indeed, though it did not 'exist,' was the more fundamental and the more solid reality of the two.[4] It is true that conceptualism rather than strict Platonic realism was the commonly accepted doctrine about the status of the Ideas; Leibniz himself, for example, held that the realm of essences would have no being at all, if it were not eternally contemplated by the mind of God. "Every reality must be based upon something existent; if there were no God there would be no objects of geometry." [5] Yet this did not, of course, mean that, for the mind of man, the essences were any the less independent and substantial; and even in the mind of God every essence (including his own) had, by the prevalent though

not universal opinion, a certain logical priority over the existent or existents corresponding to it.  And in this eternal order
alone was the necessity which is identical with complete rationality to be found; it was the locus of all ultimate reasons,
the region in which the only finally satisfying explanations of
facts were to be sought.  An 'explanation' which simply referred one opaque fact to another — even though the latter
were an event or existent prior in time, or one of those generalized facts which we call empirical laws — never touched
bottom; [6] and to assert that this was, not merely the situation
in which our limited understanding frequently finds itself, but
also the situation of the objective world, was, it seemed, to
proclaim the fundamental fortuitousness of everything.  If, on
the other hand, the existence of an entity, or its properties
and behavior, could be seen to be rooted in "the natures of
things" — i. e., to be implied in the very constitution of some
essence or in the immutable system of relations which obtains
between essences [7] — a further quest for reasons became not
only superfluous but impossible.  The bare fact had been traced
back to a necessity, and was no longer opaque to the understanding; a seeming accident of contingent existence had been
apprehended under its eternal aspect — that is, as consequent
upon some "eternal truth" inherent in the Ideas, the opposite
to which would be a logical absurdity.  In the typical phraseology of an eighteenth-century writer: "When it appears that
an absolute necessity in the nature of things themselves," as,
for example, in geometrical figures, "is the reason and ground
of their being what they are, we must necessarily stop at this
ground and reason; and to ask what is the reason of this reason
which is in the nature of things the last of all reasons, is absurd." [8]

To a philosophy which thus had constantly before it two
planes of reality, in only one of which the reason-seeking intellect of man could come to rest, the need for somehow and
somewhere finding in the realm of Ideas not merely necessary
connections between attributes which might or might not
'exist,' but a determining ground of concrete existence itself,
was naturally acute.  Unless the fact of existence could at some
point be exhibited as a necessity subsisting in the world of

essences, the two worlds remained strangely unrelated; there was no bridge from one to the other; and the whole realm of the existent appeared given over to blank unreason.  Such was the issue in seventeenth- and eighteenth-century philosophy to which Leibniz's principle of sufficient reason was one of several answers.  And that principle was, we shall find, essentially a development and elaboration of the theme sounded in the *Timaeus*.  Leibniz himself, in a letter of 1715, described his own philosophy as in part an attempt to systematize Platonism:

> I have, ever since my youth, been greatly satisfied with the ethics of Plato, and also, in a way, with his metaphysics; these two, moreover, go together, like mathematics and physics.  If someone should reduce Plato to a system, he would render a great service to the human race; and it will be seen that I have made some slight approximation to this.[9]

We shall, however, better understand the meaning and historical significance of Leibniz's answer to the question if we recall the nature of the others which were current in his time. That there must be a sufficient reason why *something* exists rather than nothing — i. e., that somewhere existence is explicable as a necessity arising out of the logical system of essences — was accepted as axiomatic by many who rejected the principle formulated by Leibniz.  Thus Samuel Clarke, who during the first three decades of the eighteenth century passed for the foremost of living English philosophers, declared that it is "an express contradiction" to suppose that "of two equally possible things, *viz.* whether *anything* or *nothing* should from eternity have existed, the one is determined, rather than the other, absolutely by nothing."  Whatever exists, in short, must have some "cause"; and since "to have been produced by some external cause cannot possibly be true of everything," there must be somewhere a being which "exists by an absolute necessity originally in the nature of the thing itself."  And this necessity or internal reason for being

must be antecedent; not, indeed, in time, to the existence of the being itself, because that is Eternal; but it must be antecedent in the natural order of our ideas, to our supposition of its being; that is, this necessity must not barely be *consequent* upon our supposition of the existence of such a being, . . . but it must antecedently force itself upon us, whether we will or no, even when we are endeavoring to suppose that no such being exists. . . .

(For) a necessity . . . absolutely such in its own nature, is nothing else but its being a plain impossibility, or implying a contradiction, to suppose the contrary.[10]

The being whose nature or essence is thus the necessitating — and therefore, for our thought, the explanatory — ground of its existence, is, of course, God: "if any one asks, what sort of Idea the Idea of that being is, the supposition of whose non-existence is thus an express contradiction, I answer: 'Tis the first and simplest idea we can possibly frame, or rather which (unless we forbear thinking at all) we cannot possibly extirpate or remove out of our minds, of *a most Simple Being, absolutely Eternal and Infinite, Original and Independent.*" If there were not in this case a reason determining existence, all sorts of absurdities would be possible; the First Cause would be as likely to be finite as infinite; it might "as possibly in other places without any reason not exist, as it does without any reason, exist, in those places where the phenomena of nature prove that it does exist." [11] Nay, worse; as a disciple of Clarke's argued, unless there is in God's essence a sufficient reason for his existence, we have no rational assurance that he may not some day lapse into nonentity.

It is plain and certain that any alteration of existence of a being may as possibly be affected without a cause or reason, as the existence of that being can either be supposed to be originally determined without any cause or reason, or to continue to exist without any cause or reason. If therefore the first cause existed originally without any cause or reason, it may be mutable or corruptible in its nature, and so may carry within itself the cause, ground, or reason of its ceasing to be.[12]

These were theological ways of saying that the position of a universe in which existence was at no point grounded in necessity would be in the last degree precarious — such a position as Victor Hugo long afterwards described with a more adequate rhetoric: "La fin toujours imminente, aucune transition entre être et ne plus être, la rentrée au creuset, le glissement possible à toute minute, c'est ce précipice-là qui est la création."

In the case of one being, then, Clarke, and a numerous company of other philosophers and theologians of the time, were as averse as Spinoza or Leibniz from admitting that existence has no determining reason. God's existence, at all events, could not be supposed to be an accident. It is true that many of those who affirmed this — and Clarke among them — at the same time raised somewhat quibbling demurrers to Anselm's ontological argument, which involved the same dialectic; yet there were, apparently, only a small minority [13] who were prepared to deny that there is an *ens necessarium*, i. e., an entity of which the essence is such that it would not be what, *quâ* essence, it is, if it did not also exist.

But was it sufficient to recognize only one such instance, and to leave all the rest of the world of existents with no point of support in the World of Ideas — or, what was the theological expression for the same conception, in the divine reason? To this question the philosophy of Spinoza (like that of Abelard and of Bruno before him) had given an emphatic answer in the negative. *Every* fact of existence must be held to have its roots in the eternal order, in the necessities belonging to essences and their relations; and every essence, likewise, must have its flowering among existents. That the necessary actualization of all possibles is affirmed by Spinoza also has not been evident to all of his expositors. With some logical implications of his system, and with a few of his express statements, it seems to conflict. To suppose him to have accepted the principle of plenitude would, it has been suggested, entail the contradiction that all successive entities and events must exist simultaneously. For the necessity of their existence would be a logical necessity; and to it therefore time would be irrelevant. We do not — or the mathematicians of Spinoza's time did not — say merely that, given a plane triangle, it is necessary that its interior angles should some day *become* equal to two right angles. As little could one who maintained that the universe by logical necessity contains all things capable of existence admit that some individual things come into being after others. But individual things do come into existence one after another; and we ought not to impute to Spinoza without clear warrant a doctrine inconsistent with this truism. Again, he sometimes definitely says that we may have "ideas of non-existent modes" i. e., of particular objects which have no being apart from the conceiving intellect.[14] Furthermore, he declares that "no definition involves or expresses any particular multitude or definite number of individuals"; e. g., the definition of a triangle tells us only the "nature" of a triangle and implies nothing as to the number of triangles that exist. Hence it is argued that the actual particulars which at any time make up the universe are for Spinoza a non-necessary, and therefore arbitrary, selection from among the far more numerous things which might have been. But this way of interpreting him is, I think, quite impossible. The principle of sufficient reason, as he lays it down, applies to non-existence as well as to existence: "of everything whatsoever a cause or reason must be assigned, alike for its existence or its non-existence." [15] And it is "the intellect of God, in so far as it is conceived to constitute the divine essence," that "is in reality the cause of all things." [16] Could there be any reason lying in the nature of this fundamental cause why some things that are capable of existence should not exist? Manifestly not; there is nothing that can be conceived, i. e., nothing that is not self-contradictory, which does not "fall under an infinite intellect." Since, then, God can conceive of all essences, since neither he nor the universe would be rational if existence arbitrarily accrued to some finite essences while others lacked it, since "whatever we conceive to be in the power of God necessarily exists," [17] and since this power is unlimited (except by the impossibility of conceiving or producing the self-contradictory), it follows that "from the necessity of the divine nature must follow an infinite number of things in infinite ways — that is, *all* things which can fall within the sphere of an infinite intellect." [18] Indeed, Spinoza in some passages infers the necessary existence of all possible finite modes of each attribute directly from the principle of sufficient reason, without recourse to the argument from the existence of God as cause — his existence being itself, in fact, deduced from the same principle. While the essence "triangle," taken separately, does not of itself imply the existence of any triangles, their existence *does* follow "from the order of the material universe as a whole (*ex ordine universae naturae corporeae*)*; for from this it must follow either that a triangle necessarily exists, or else that it is impossible that it should now exist. This is self-evident. From which it follows that a thing necessarily exists if no cause or reason can be given which prevents its existence." In other words, the class "triangles" is one possible species of material bodies (with respect to shape), one mode of "extension"; and both the species, and any individual of the species, will have actual existence, unless there is a "reason" which renders this impossible; and such a reason would consist solely in the fact that its existence in some manner involved self-contradiction. Similarly, God's necessary existence can be proved simply from the fact that "no cause or reason can be given which prevents him from existing, or which rules out his existence." For it would be "absurd to affirm of an absolutely infinite and supremely perfect being" that his existence involves contradiction.[19] There are thus in Spinoza two distinct arguments for the existence of God. The first is the ontological argument, simply from the definition of *causa sui* as that "whose essence involves existence"; and this argument is applicable solely to God, since there can (it is assumed) be only one such essence. The other is the argument from the necessity of the existence of *anything* whose existence is not precluded by some logical impossibility; and that is applicable to all essences, though the essence "God" has with respect to it one unique advantage, inasmuch as (Spinoza assumes) it is evident that an essence defined as having the properties of "absolute infinity" and "perfection" cannot be debarred from existence by any intrinsic or extrinsic logical impediment. And to these two proofs correspond the two ways of deducing the principle of plenitude: the first indirectly, through the conception of God whose existence is already independently proved by the ontological argument, the second directly, from the same premise by which, in the second proof, God's own existence is established.

It has, however, been suggested by at least one learned commentator that Spinoza affirms the principle of plenitude only in the sense that all conceivable things either have existed or will hereafter exist. But this interpretation not only conflicts with the truism that the logically necessary is no more so at one time than another, but is also expressly repudiated by Spinoza, both in the *Short Treatise* and the *Ethics*. Those, he declares, are in error who contend that, "if God *had* created everything that is in his intellect," so that there would now be nothing more

left for him to create, he could not now be said to be omnipotent. On the contrary, we must, Spinoza says, conceive "that
God's omnipotence has been displayed from all eternity and
will for all eternity remain in the same state of activity." [20] It
would be an absurdity to imagine that at some former time he
created a world different from that which he now creates; for
this would imply that his intellect and will were then different
from what they now are. If his creation had at one time been
incomplete or imperfect, *he* would have been at some time incomplete or imperfect — which would be a contradiction in
terms. In short, there can at no time be any "cause whereby
he could be moved to create one thing rather or more than another." Thus "from the supreme power of God, or from his
infinite nature, an infinity of things in an infinity of modes —
that is, all things — have necessarily flowed forth, or always
follow by the same necessity, just as from the nature of a triangle it follows from all eternity and to all eternity that the
sum of its three angles is equal to two right angles." [21] The
existence of all possible beings at all times is therefore an implicate of the divine nature.

Our principle of plenitude — in what may be called its
static form — is thus inherent in the very substance of Spinoza's doctrine. From the timeless immutability of the
World-Ground he argues directly to the necessary "fullness"
and also the necessary invariability of the temporal world's
contents. But the paradox of that principle is more apparent
in his philosophy than in others; and it is, in part, this fact
which has led certain expositors to the misinterpretation to
which I have referred. From the eternal logical necessity belonging to an essence there is, in truth, *no* valid argument to
any conclusion about existence in time. For time itself is alien
to that necessity; it is an alogical character of nature. Whatever is true of an essence is true of it all at once; but what is
true of the temporal world is not true of it all at once. Becoming and change, as such, simply do not fit into an eternal rational order. The attempt to pass over from that order to one
in which some things have their being at one time, and quite
other things at a later time, is a *non-sequitur*, and worse; but
this was required by the principle of plenitude — was most

clearly of all so required when that principle was regarded as an implicate of the principle of sufficient reason. If a literal realization of all genuine possibles is essential to a reasonable world, everything and everybody should have existed, and every event should have occurred, from all eternity, in a *totum simul*; but nature is not a *totum simul*. What makes this paradox more apparent in Spinoza is the fact that the notion of species plays, as a rule, no such part in his system as it does in many others equally committed to the same principle. As frequently interpreted, the "fullness" of the universe was sufficiently realized if every *kind* of being was always exemplified in the temporal order; species, not individuals, were the units for which Nature cared. But Spinoza usually leaps at once from the divine attributes or the "infinite modes" to individuals existing at one time and not at others, and in differing numbers at different times. That, in this sense, nature is *not* constant, nor constantly "full," was evident; and Spinoza therefore, while asserting the principle of plenitude, was driven into inevitable and glaring inconsistencies in his application of it. An increasing realization of this difficulty we shall find giving rise in writers of the following century to a radical reinterpretation of the principle.

Spinoza had thus expressed the principle of plenitude in its most uncompromising form and had represented it as necessary in the strict logical sense. Everything shared in the same completely sufficient reason for being that the existence of God was by most philosophers conceived to possess. But Spinoza (unlike Bruno) had not made a great deal of the aspect of the principle of plenitude which was to be most fruitful of consequences in the eighteenth century; what most interested him in his own doctrine was not the consideration that everything that logically can be must and will be, but the consideration that everything that is must, by the eternal logical nature of things, have been, and have been precisely as it is. It was this consequence of his dialectic, the sense of the utter inevitability (amounting to the ultimate inconceivability of the opposite) of every characteristic and every vicissitude of human life, that was most congenial to his own moral temper and seemed to him most fitted to free men from the torment of the passions.

This universalization of necessity rendered teleological ways of thinking about things inadmissible; since nothing could conceivably have been otherwise, nothing could be said to manifest purpose or preference, a choice of good where evil, or a lesser good, might have been genuinely possible; hence these very distinctions lost their meaning.

The alternative view, that there is only one point at which a reason for existence can be found in the realm of essence, was represented by a great body of philosophical and theological opinion, both before and after Spinoza. According to this view, while there is, indeed, an *ens necessarium*, the being which necessarily exists is itself a pure Will, a power to choose independently not only of external causes but also of rational motives. To make the divine will subject even to the constraint of reason would be to deny its freedom and its sovereignty over all lesser things. Hence the existence of God involved no necessity that the world of finite beings should exist. The more extreme and consistent form of this doctrine declared that not even a general tendency to create *something*, to share the privilege of existence with other beings, could be held to belong to the essence of deity. This thesis had, indeed, a double historic root. It was primarily a manifestation of that apotheosis of irresponsible will which constituted one side, though only one side, of the orthodox theology of Christendom. It could also be deduced from one of those two conflicting Platonic conceptions of God which were the heritage of what is called Christian theology. If the essence of deity was the same as the Idea of the Good, if the differentiating attribute of the Absolute Reality was self-sufficiency, God, even though he *did* create a world, could have no reason for doing so. Nothing in his essential nature made it necessary or desirable for him to bring a universe of imperfect beings into existence. The creative act must therefore be conceived to be entirely groundless and arbitrary in itself, and therefore in its inclusions and exclusions. As Duns Scotus, or a follower of his, declared, "every creature has a merely accidental relation to the goodness of God, since from them [the creatures] nothing is added to his goodness, any more than the addition of point to a line lengthens the line." [22]

Thus from medieval as well as Greek philosophy it had come

down as an axiom that nothing could be more contradictory of the very notion of deity than to admit that anything in the existence of such a being is dependent upon, or in any degree affected for better or worse by, the existence or action of any being conceived as distinct from it. Perhaps the most extraordinary triumph of self-contradiction, among many such triumphs in the history of human thought, was the fusion of this conception of a self-absorbed and self-contained Perfection — of that Eternal Introvert who is the God of Aristotle — at once with the Jewish conception of a temporal Creator and busy interposing Power making for righteousness through the hurly-burly of history, and with primitive Christianity's conception of a God whose essence is forthgoing love and who shares in all the griefs of his creatures.[23] When applied to the notion of creation — which is the aspect of this syncretism which here concerns us — the doctrine of the self-sufficiency of deity implied, as we have already seen, that from the divine — that is, from the final and absolute — point of view a created world is a *groundless* superfluity. The existence of creatures, as Augustine had said, "is a good which could in no way profit God"; and therefore, he had added, the question why God chose to create is a self-contradictory as well as impious one, since it seeks for a cause for that primary act of sheer will which is the cause of all other things [24] — except certain other acts of sheer will permitted certain of the creatures. For Augustine, and a long line of successors, the Platonic-Aristotelian conception of the self-sufficiency of deity thus became an essential safeguard against the doctrine of universal necessity. If the world-generating act had been determined by any motive, had had any ground even in the divine essence, it would not have been free; but since any action of a being already self-sufficing must be absolutely unmotivated, its freedom could not be doubted. The connection of the two ideas was summed up by Augustine in a neat sorites which played a great part in European thought for many centuries: *ubi nulla indigentia, nulla necessitas; ubi nullus defectus, nulla indigentia; nullus autem defectus in Deo; ergo nulla necessitas.*[25]

Two potent elements in the philosophical tradition, then — the Platonic and Aristotelian apotheosis of self-sufficiency and

the Augustinian insistence upon the primacy of will in the constitution of reality — both alike could be construed as implying that the being which necessarily exists, though it has in
fact generated other beings, did so by an essentially motiveless,
unaccountable, and therefore accidental — and, indeed, incongruous — exercise of its freedom. Upon this theorem the
changes are rung interminably by seventeenth- and eighteenth-
century philosophers and divines. Descartes is especially insistent upon it: God must have been *tout-à-fait indifférent à créer
les choses qu'il a créées.*

> For if some reason, or some appearance of good, had preceded his pre-
> ordination of things, it would without doubt have determined him to create
> what was best; but, on the contrary, because he determined to make the
> things that are actually in the world, for this reason they are, as it is writ-
> ten in Genesis, 'very good'; that is, the reason of their goodness depends
> upon the fact that he willed to make them.[26]

For Descartes this dependence of things upon the Absolute
Will extended, not merely to their existence, but to their essences or 'natures.' There is nothing in the essence 'triangle'
which makes it intrinsically necessary that the sum of the interior angles of such a figure should be equal to two right
angles, nothing in the nature of number which requires that
two and two should make four. What to us appear as "eternal
truths" are in reality "determined solely by the will of God,
who, as sovereign legislator, has ordained and established them
from all eternity." [27]

So far, at least, as existence is concerned this same consequence is deduced from the Platonic premise in the chief classic
of orthodox Anglican divinity. Bishop Pearson's *Exposition of
the Creed* (1659) declares that

> God is in respect of all external actions absolutely free without the least
> necessity. . . . Those creatures which are endued with understanding,
> and consequently with a will, may not only be necessitated in their actions
> by a greater power, *but also as necessarily be determined by the proposal of an in-
> finite good*; whereas *neither* of these necessities can be acknowledged in God's
> actions, without supposing a power beside and above Omnipotency, or a
> real happiness beside and above All-Sufficiency. Indeed, if God were a
> necessary agent in the works of creation, the creatures would be of as neces-
> sary being as he is; whereas the necessity of being is the undoubted prerog-
> ative of the First Cause.[28]

This was equivalent to saying that the only way of escape from such a philosophy as Spinoza's — then still to be published — lay in holding that God had no reason in his creative activity and could not possibly derive any satisfaction from it.

The expressions of this theme in philosophic or religious poetry sometimes sound like echoes of classical passages setting forth the Epicurean conception of the "careless gods"; when Ronsard, for example, hymns the "goddess Eternity" in a strange mixture of pagan and Christian imagery, one is reminded as much of Lucretius as of Aristotle.

> La première des Dieux, où bien loin de souci
> Et de l'humain travail qui nous tourmente ici,
> Par toi-même contente et par toi bienheureuse,
> Tu règnes immortelle en tout bien plantureuse.[29]

But when Drummond of Hawthornden rewrote Ronsard's hymn in English and converted it into a finer and more consistent piece of Christian Platonism, he retained this passage, but elaborated it and gave it further point, by bringing the notion of self-sufficiency into conjunction with that of creation:

> No joy, no, nor perfection to Thee came
> By the contriving of this world's great frame;
> Ere sun, moon, stars, began their restless race,
> Ere paint'd with purple clouds was Heaven's round face,
> Ere air had clouds, ere clouds weept down their showers,
> Ere Sea embracèd Earth, ere Earth bore flowers,
> Thou happy lived; World nought to Thee supplied.
> All in Thy self Thy self Thou satisfied.[30]

The question, disapproved by Augustine, to which such a conception nevertheless perennially gave rise,[31] was pointedly expressed by a late seventeenth-century Platonist, John Norris: since God is

> . . . In himself compendiously blest, . . .
>
> .  .  .  .  .  .  .  .  .
>
> . . . Is one unmov'd self-center'd Point of Rest,
> Why, then, if full of bliss that ne'er could cloy,
> Would he do ought but still enjoy?
> Why not indulge his self-sufficing state,
> Live to Himself at large, calm and secure,
>     A wise eternal Epicure?

> Why six days work, to frame
> A monument of praise and fame
> To him whose bliss is still the same?
> What need the wealthy coin, or he that's blest, create?[32]

Milton in this matter, as in others, is an interesting example of a mind beset by cross-currents; but in the main it was towards the assertion of the arbitrariness of the deity's action that the poet-theologian tended. He rejects at times the extreme nominalistic doctrine of Descartes; the essences of things, and the truths concerning the intrinsic relations of essences, are logically prior to any will, so that not even God could alter them; thus he declared in the *Treatise of Christian Doctrine* that "a certain immutable and internal necessity of acting right, independently of all extraneous influence whatever, may exist in God conjointly with the most perfect liberty, both which principles in the divine nature tend to the same point." Yet this, Milton evidently felt, inclined too much to determinism; for a little later he asserted virtually the opposite: it cannot be "admitted that the actions of God are themselves necessary, but only that he has a necessary existence, for Scripture itself testifies that his decrees and therefore his actions, of what kind soever they be, are perfectly free." [33] And the consideration of the divine self-sufficiency leads Milton to give especial emphasis to the motivelessness of the deity's exercise of his creative power. God is not inherently 'good,' in the theological sense in which goodness consists in the actual conferring of existence upon other beings. His "goodness was free to act or not." [34] "Questionless," we are told in the *Christian Doctrine*,

it was in God's power consistently with the perfection of his own essence not to have begotten the Son, inasmuch as generation does not pertain to the essence of Deity, who stands in no need of propagation;[35]

— an observation repeated in *Paradise Lost*:

> No need that Thou
> Shouldst propagate, already infinite,
> And through all numbers absolute, though One.

The implication of this, that there appeared to be in the nature of things not only no reason why any world of imperfect creatures should exist, but every reason why it should not exist, Adam almost makes explicit, when briefly expounding some points of theology to his Maker:

> Thou in Thyself art perfect and in Thee
> Is no deficience found; . . .
> Thou in Thy secrecy although alone,
> Best with Thyself accompanied, seek'st not
> Social communication.[36]

Though this may seem a somewhat odd thing for Adam to say under the circumstances, it proves to have, in the poem, some dramatic motivation; for this proleptic quotation from Aristotle [37] serves the human interlocutor as a polite opening for a reminder that he is not himself self-sufficient, and therefore needs a companion in Eden. But what is clearest about the passage is that Milton the theologian saw in this juncture of his narrative an opportunity to affirm once again that a self-absorbed and unproductive God would be not less, but, if possible, more divine, and that there is no necessity and, indeed, no reason for the existence of any creature. Milton's zeal for this thesis is the more curious because his theology here seems out of harmony with his ethical creed and moral temper.[38] As recent writers have pointed out, he was no Puritan rigorist, but in many respects a typical mind of the humanistic Renaissance, delighting in the splendor and diversity of the sensible world; and the excellence of man did *not* for him consist in the imitation of God in respect of the most distinctive of the divine attributes. It is not by an attempt to approximate or to become absorbed into the divine sufficiency through ascetic self-discipline, the cultivation of a *contemptus mundi*, or a withdrawal from those

> Relations dear and all the charities
> Of father, son, and brother,

that man attains his good. "Propagation," indeed, was the first of duties imposed upon man by a deity himself represented as only tardily, unessentially, and (relatively to his possibilities) meagrely propagative:

> Our Maker bids increase, who bids abstain
> But our Destroyer, foe to God and man?

> . . . . . Man by number is to manifest
> His single imperfection, and beget
> Like of his like, his image multiplied,
> In unity defective, which requires
> Collateral love and dearest amity.[39]

There were thus in the thought of Milton some significant and instructive internal strains, characteristic not only of the man but of the historic juncture in which he lived. But our present concern is only with one element in this complex of mutually counter-working ideas.

A generation later Fénelon was with equal zeal elaborating upon the same ancient theme — now with Spinoza definitely in mind as the chief representative of the error to be attacked. No doubt, the Archbishop of Cambrai grants, it may be said to be "plus parfait à un être d'être fécond que de ne l'être pas"; but it does not follow that the divine perfection requires "an actual production." The possession of a power is sufficient without the exercise of it — a strange proposition, but one to which Fénelon was driven as the only escape from Spinoza's argument that an omnipotent being must also of necessity be omnificent. This theological paradox was apparently rendered more plausible to Fénelon by the undeniable truth that, though the gift of speech presumably makes human beings "more perfect," their perfection is not necessarily proportional to their use of that faculty: "il arrive même souvent que je sois plus parfait de me taire que de parler." There is, then, nothing on the side of the divine essence which necessitates the generation of everything, or even of anything: "nothing is more false than to say that God was obliged by that order which is himself to produce all that he could that is most perfect." As little can it be said that there is anything on the side of the finite essences which could constitute a reason for their being:

> If God considers the essences of things, he finds therein no determination to existence; he finds only that they are not impossible to his power. . . . Thus it is in his positive will that he finds their existence; for as to their essence, it contains in itself no reason or cause of existing; on the contrary, it necessarily contains in itself non-existence.[40]

Any other view than this would make "the creature essential to the Creator," an indispensable part or aspect of his being. He would "produce eternally and of necessity," and so would have no freedom — and no long ante-mundane sabbath; and the *ens perfectissimum* would be, not a God above the world in his eternal and absolute self-sufficiency, but the total collection of finite beings conceived as the expression of this fundamental generative necessity.[41]

These reasonings of *a priori* theology were doubtless somewhat elusive to many minds even in the seventeenth and the early eighteenth century; but the same conclusion could be defended on more empirical grounds. It could be argued that — whether or not there be any inherent disposition to create in the divine essence — at all events the actual scope and specific contents of the created world give evidence of the arbitrariness of the choice of its Author. Samuel Clarke, for example, develops at some length the contention that the universe is full of facts which cannot be reconciled with Spinoza's doctrine — i. e., which are not 'necessary' in the sense required.

All things in the world appear plainly to be the most arbitrary that can be imagined. . . . Motion itself, and all its quantities and directions, with the laws of gravitation, are entirely arbitrary, and might possibly have been altogether different from what they are now. The number and motion of the heavenly bodies have no manner of necessity in the nature of the things themselves. . . . Everything upon the Earth is still more evidently arbitrary, and plainly the product, not of necessity but will. What absolute necessity for just such a number of species of animals or plants?[42]

In such a doctrine, obviously, the principle of plenitude had no proper place (though sometimes, as by Archbishop King, the two were inconsistently combined). That principle ostensibly gave certain important *a priori* knowledge about the constitution of the world of existents, though it was supposed to be also capable of empirical confirmation. But the anti-rationalistic theology which insisted upon the arbitrariness of the divine decrees had affinities rather with scientific empiricism. Since such matters as the number of species, the continuity or discontinuity of the differences between them, the quantity and original distribution of matter, the existence or non-existence of vacua, are purely arbitrary, the facts respecting them must be ascertained through experience or remain unknown.

It was therefore natural that the philosophic poets who

dwelt with predilection upon the divine absoluteness and freedom from even rational constraint should reject the principle
of plenitude and its implications. Drummond of Hawthornden, for example, is at pains to declare explicitly that there is
an infinite number of Ideas which never are actualized, since
God does not so choose; in the *Hymn to the Fairest Fair* Truth is
pictured as standing before the throne of Heaven holding a
mirror

> Where shineth all that was,
> That is, or shall be; here, ere ought was wrought,
> Thou knew all that Thy pow'r with Time forth-brought,
> And more, things numberless that Thou couldst make,
> That actually shall never being take.

Milton likewise seems to have been as antipathetic to the
principle of plenitude as to that of sufficient reason, and makes
no use of it for his theodicy, either in *Paradise Lost* or in the
*Treatise of Christian Doctrine.* The notion of a hierarchical scale
of nature is, indeed, not lacking, and the law of continuity is
clearly expressed. All things are composed of

> One first matter all,
> Indu'd with various forms, various degrees
> Of substance, and in things that live, of life;
> But more refin'd, more spiritous, and pure,
> As nearer to him plac'd, or nearer tending,
> Each in their several active spheres assign'd,
> Till body up to spirit work in bounds
> Proportion'd to each kind. . . .[43]
> . . . . Flowers and their fruit,
> Man's nourishment, by gradual scale sublimed,
> To vital spirits aspire, to animal,
> To intellectual, give both life and sense,
> Fancy and understanding, whence the soul
> Reason receives.[44]

There are passages in which the poet dilates upon the magnitude and variety of the sensible world; and in the prose treatise
he repeats without qualification the pregnant scholastic maxim
that "entity is good, non-entity not good." [45] But the general
view which he adopted forbade him to suppose that all possible
forms necessarily exist or even tend to exist. On the contrary,
the original act of creation was not merely belated but also ex-

tremely restricted. How little the dialectic of the idea of plenitude determined Milton's scheme of things is most clearly shown by his adoption of the doctrine of Jerome and of Origen — which Thomas Aquinas and Dante had expressly rejected [46] — according to which the creation was at first confined to "heavenly essences," spiritual or ethereal natures. It was only after the disappointing behavior of many of this highest order of possible creatures that the Supreme Being (whose self-sufficiency here seems quite completely forgotten), by second intention, bethought himself of the possibility of "repairing that detriment" by the creation of "another world," including the earth and man and its other inhabitants — in other words, by calling into being a certain number of possibles of a lower order.[47]

In the next generation the principle of plenitude was more explicitly assailed in stodgy verse by Blackmore in his *Creation* (1712):

> Might not other animals arise
> Of diff'rent figure and of diff'rent size?
> In the wide womb of possibility
> Lie many things which ne'er may actual be:
> And more productions of a various kind
> Will cause no contradiction in the mind. . . .
> These shifting scenes, these quick rotations show
> Things from necessity could never flow,
> But must to mind and choice precarious beings owe.[48]

It is, then, chiefly in its connection with these preoccupations of Leibniz's predecessors and contemporaries, and with their conflicting doctrines concerning the relation of the world of finite existents to the logical order of essences constituting the primary object of the divine intellect, that his principle of sufficient reason is historically to be understood. The principle was, first of all, an affirmation of the fundamental proposition common to Spinoza and to most of those who in nearly all other respects were in complete disagreement with that philosopher — the proposition that there is at least one being whose essence necessarily and directly implies existence. The ontological argument, in short, is for Leibniz a part of the law of sufficient reason — a fact well recognized in the eighteenth century. It is because that law is valid that we are entitled to ask, as the first question in metaphysics (in distinction from physical science): "Why does something exist rather than nothing? For 'nothing' is simpler and easier than something."

Now this sufficient reason of the existence of the universe cannot be found in the series of contingent truths. . . . The sufficient reason which has no need of any other reason must be outside the sequence of contingent things, and must be a necessary being, else we should not have a sufficient reason with which we could stop.[49]

Here, then, the "sufficient reason" is nothing less than a logical necessity believed to be inherent in an essence; it is specifically in this sense that Leibniz speaks of God as the *ultima ratio rerum*.

But the principle further means for Leibniz that the existence of all *finite* things must likewise in some manner be grounded in the rational order of Ideas and their implications — in the world of possibles which, as it was commonly phrased, God had present to him "before the creation." Here Leibniz is still at one with Spinoza, who, he observes, was entirely right in opposing those philosophers who "declared that God is indifferent and that he decrees things by an absolute act of will." [50] If there were so much as a single fact in nature which had its cause in a fiat not wholly determined by rational grounds, the world would *eo ipso* be an affair of "blind chance." [51] And chance becomes no more satisfactory to the philosopher as a category for describing the ultimate constitution of reality by being piously called God. The supposition, exemplified in so many of Leibniz's contemporaries, that the number of existents in general, or of the members of any given class of them — of atoms, or of monads, or (what was the purely theological form of the same difficulty) of the elect — constitutes a small selection from among the possibles, is not, to Leibniz, rendered less obnoxious by the supposition of a Selector, if his foible for that particular numeral is assumed to be itself fortuitous, a reasonless eccentricity of Omnipotence.

If the will of God did not have for a rule the principle of the best, it would either tend towards evil, which would be worst of all; or else it would be in some fashion indifferent to good and evil and guided by chance. But a will which always allowed itself to act by chance would scarcely be of more value for the government of the universe than a fortuitous concourse of atoms, with no God at all. And even if God should abandon himself to chance only in some cases and some respects, . . . he would be imperfect, as would the object of his choice; he would not deserve to be wholly trusted; he would act without reason in those cases, and the government of the universe would be like certain games, half a matter of chance, half of reason.[52]

In all this Leibniz was continuing the tradition of Platonistic rationalism in theology which during the previous half-century had been best represented by the Cambridge Platonists, to whose doctrine his own is also in many other points very similar. Henry More, for example, had written in 1647:

> If God do all things simply at his pleasure,
> Because he will, and not because it's good,
> So that his actions will have no set measure,
> Is 't possible it should be understood
> What he intends? . . .
> Nor of well-being, nor of subsistency
> Of our poor souls when they do hence depart,
> Can any be assur'd, if liberty
> We give to such odd thoughts, that thus pervert
> The laws of God, and rashly do assert
> That will rules God, but Good rules not God's will.[53]

Why anyone should think it an enhancement of the dignity of either God or man to act, or even to be capable of acting, without a determining reason, is to Leibniz, as it was to his Platonistic precursors, wholly incomprehensible; "it is a paradox to represent as a perfection the least reasonable thing in all the world, of which the advantage would consist in being privileged against reason." Such a character as Clarke and King had ascribed to the First Cause might perhaps be attributed by a poet to "some imaginary Don Juan," or, conceivably, some "*homme romanesque* might affect the appearance of it and even persuade himself that he actually possesses it; but there never will be found in nature any choice to which one is not brought by an antecedent representation of good and bad, by inclinations or by reasons." [54] The freedom of indifference, in short, "is impossible, but if there were such a thing, it would be harmful."

If we leave for a moment the question of the meaning of this aspect of the principle of sufficient reason for Leibniz, and consider the grounds of his faith in it, they appear, as in the passage last cited, to be chiefly two. Partly, he presents it as a sort of axiomatic proposition in psychology: just as all physical events must have efficient causes, so all conscious choices must have motivating reasons; and these reasons must lie in the apparent values inherent in the objects chosen. This proposition, then, is for Leibniz an "eternal truth"; "a power of determining oneself without any cause, or any source of determination, implies contradiction. . . . It is metaphysically necessary that there be some such cause." [55] But at bottom Leibniz, like More, adopts the principle, it is evident, for reasons which may, in one sense of a highly ambiguous term, be called pragmatic. The conception of the world we live in which would follow from the rejection of the principle was intolerable to such a mind as his. It meant placing Caprice on the throne of the universe — under however venerable a title. It implied that Nature, having no determining reason in it, flouts and baffles the reason that is in man. A world where chance-happening had so much as a foothold would have no stability or trustworthiness; uncertainty would infect the whole; anything (except, perhaps, the self-contradictory) might exist and anything might happen, and no one thing would be in itself even more probable than any other. Such a hypothesis was not one which Leibniz could entertain if any alternative was available; and the principle of sufficient reason would unquestionably have seemed to him a practically indispensable postulate if he had not believed it to be a logically necessary truth. [56]

There was, however, it may be noted in passing, one rather awkward consequence of the proposition that God can do nothing without a reason. This difficulty Samuel Clarke effectively pressed home in his controversy with Leibniz. The celebrated ass of Buridan, being, by hypothesis, a perfectly rational ass, was unable to choose between two equally large and equally appetizing bales of hay equidistant from his nose; having no sufficient reason for preferring one to the other, the sagacious animal starved to death in the midst of plenty. Clarke pointed out, in substance, that Leibniz attributed to his Maker precisely such an irrational excess of rationality. There presumably confront even omnipotence, Clarke suggested, some situations in which it is desirable to choose one *or* the other of two alternatives, though there is no reason why one should be chosen rather than the other. In these situations, then, such a deity as Leibniz had set up would never be able to act at all. Leibniz was unable to deny that, if there are any such situations, this consequence must follow from his premises.

'Tis a thing indifferent to place three bodies, equal and perfectly alike, in any order whatsoever; and consequently they *never will be placed in any order* by Him who does nothing without wisdom.

But Leibniz adds that there cannot be, in any possible world, such a perfect balance of values between any two alternatives.[57] This assertion was manifestly difficult to prove and, on the face of it, highly improbable. Leibniz was involved in this embarrassment by that excessively simple and quasi-mechanical conception of volition, which, as we have seen, was one of the senses which the principle of sufficient reason had for him. Where there was no preponderance of value in one contemplated object rather than another, an intelligent agent would be as powerless to move as a piece of matter in an equilibrium of forces. But this was not the significant essence of the principle. Leibniz might with advantage have limited it to the proposition that where there *is* an actual difference between possibles, that which by its own nature has the greater reason for existing must necessarily be created by God.

Thus far Leibniz's argument seems to place him on the side of Spinoza, as against the critics of that philosopher. The primary being exists by a logical necessity; it is also necessary that all the things derivative from it should have "reasons" for existence lying in its nature and in their own; and this might seem to mean that all things follow *ex necessitate divinae naturae*, and that the existent universe is just such a system as Spinoza had represented — logically inevitable in its least detail, so that no alternative could ever have been so much as conceived by an infinite intellect. From this consequence, however, Leibniz professed to have found a way of escape. Temperamentally wishful, like many other philosophers, to eat his cake and have it too, he conceived that his position was as effectually differentiated from Spinoza's cosmic determinism as from the theory — whether in its theological or in its naturalistic or Epicurean form — of a chance-world; and the original and distinctive thing in his formulation of the principle of sufficient reason seemed to him to consist precisely in its indication of a third possible view opposed to both these extremes.

His attempted differentiation of his position from Spinoza's rested upon two points. (*a*) In Spinoza, the divine reason allowed the divine will no option, and, indeed, there was no distinction between them. Such a view seemed to Leibniz objectionable, partly for reasons similar to those indicated in passages already cited from other writers. He too, at least at times, desired a God who might be said to possess a will, and not merely an intellect consisting in an infinity of automatically self-realizing essences; and to him too Spinoza's metaphysics appeared to exclude the possibility of any moral philosophy. But he had also a special reason of his own for rejecting this feature of Spinozism — a reason which at the same time, as he thought, showed the solution of the difficulty. Spinoza had, Leibniz observes, failed to see that existence must be limited not only to the possible, in the logical sense, but also to the compossible; i. e., that any actual world must be made up of entities which, besides being consistent with themselves, are also compatible with one another. And although, in the world of essences, all simple, positive 'natures' find a place without conflict, when the world of concrete existents is considered not all combinations are possible. Essences, therefore, conceived as materials for translation into existence, come in sets, each set excluding some essences, but including all that form one com-possible group. When this is borne in mind, Leibniz argues, it becomes apparent that there not only may but must have been a selection, namely, of one of those sets, and therewith the ex-clusion of all that did not belong to it, before any world of con-crete existents could arise at all; in theological terms, that the divine Reason before the creation was confronted with a multi-tude — in fact, as Leibniz tells us, with an infinite number — of models of worlds, any one, but only one, of which could con-ceivably be created. An act of choice is thus seen to be a logi-cally necessary implicate of the very idea of an existent world. It seems to follow that the principle of plenitude does not hold for Leibniz in the same absolute sense as for Spinoza: "the question *utrum detur vacuum formarum*, i. e., whether there are species which are possible but nevertheless do not exist" must be answered (subject to a large qualification presently to be noted) in the affirmative; "there necessarily are species which never have existed and never will exist, since they are not compatible with the series of creatures which God has chosen." [58]

In his discovery of this notion of compossibility Leibniz took great pride, but it has no definite meaning until we know what the criterion of compossibility is supposed to be; and about this he has little to say, and that little by no means clear. Once, at least, he admits that no statement of that criterion can be given:

> It is not yet known to men from what the incompossibility of different things arises or how it comes about that different essences are opposed to one another, since all purely positive terms appear to be compatible *inter se*.[59]

Some hints of an explanation, however, are elsewhere discoverable; and there is some, if not altogether conclusive, textual justification for Russell's suggestion that the criterion of compossibility for Leibniz lay in an assumed necessity that any possible world should be subject to uniform laws. If a world, for example, is to contain motion, then there must also be for it invariable laws of motion. In some possible world, the law of inverse squares will be one of these laws; and for that world, though not for other possible ones, any arrangement or movement of matter not in accordance with the Newtonian formula will be incompossible. Thus, in Russell's phrase, "what is called the 'reign of law' is metaphysically necessary in Leibniz's philosophy." [60] Yet if this be Leibniz's meaning, he neither states it unequivocally nor gives it any detailed application or illustration. What, however, seems plain is that compossibility does not differ in principle from possibility, in the traditional philosophical sense of the latter term; it is merely a special case of it. No truths concerning compossibility are contingent, but all inhere in the logical natures of the essences concerned. In short, both the make-up of each world and the limitation of the possibility of actualization to *some* one of them were among the necessities subsisting eternally in the realm of Ideas, antecedently to the choice of a particular one among the worlds to be the recipient of the privilege of existence.

(b) Consequently, Leibniz's introduction of the notion of compossibility did *not* of itself, as he sometimes seems to have supposed, essentially differentiate his principle of sufficient reason from Spinoza's universal necessity. It was merely a refinement or elaboration upon the familiar conception of "possibility," which Spinoza could without inconsistency have accepted.[61] The original question remained, namely, whether anything, and if anything, what, necessitated the choice of the actually existent world from among the possibles. But here Leibniz propounded a further distinction by which he professed to escape decisively from the deadly reproach of Spinozism. In maintaining that the divine will must necessarily be determined by the most sufficient reason, and must therefore infallibly choose the one best out of the many possible worlds, he is not, he explains, asserting the "brutal, metaphysical necessity" of Spinoza, but a "moral necessity." For the opposite, i. e., the choice of one of the other worlds, would not be impossible in the metaphysical sense; it would not imply contradiction. The will, according to the principle of sufficient reason, is "always more *inclined* to the alternative which it takes, but it is not under the necessity of taking it. It is certain that it will take it without its being necessary for it to do so." Thus a residuum of contingency is supposed to be left in the universe and therewith room is found for the freedom of the will of the First Cause.[62]

The distinction which Leibniz here attempts to set up is manifestly without logical substance; the fact is so apparent that it is impossible to believe that a thinker of his powers can have been altogether unaware of it himself. Without abandoning all that is most essential in the principle of sufficient reason he could not possibly admit that a sufficient reason "inclines" the will without necessitating its choice, and least of all in the case of a will supposed to be enlightened by an infinite intelligence. The choice of any world other than the best would, according to propositions which Leibniz frequently and plainly lays down, be as inconsistent with the essence of deity as non-existence would be; as Leibniz admits even in one of the passages in which he is endeavoring to persuade his readers that his universe contains a real margin of contingency, "chez le sage nécessaire et dû sont des choses équivalentes." [63] "The author of the world is free" only in a sense which is perfectly consistent with his "doing all things determinately." When Leibniz says that, upon his principles, the opposite to the actual choice would not involve self-contradiction he confuses two things. The mere *concept* of the existence of any of the inferior and non-existent worlds is, by the hypothesis, free from contradiction, if taken by itself, in abstraction from the principle of sufficient reason; but it was absolutely impossible that it should be *selected* for existence, since this would contradict both the perfection of God and the very notion of voluntary choice, of which the principle of sufficient reason is an expression.

Nor, of course, could it be consistently maintained by Leibniz that, though the divine will was necessitated to choose the best world, the bestness of that world was conferred upon it by some spontaneous preference, some free act of valuation, on the part of the chooser. To no doctrine was Leibniz more bitterly opposed than to this. For him value was purely objective, and valuing a strictly logical process. The existence-justifying good which may be predicable of any essence or collection of essences is one of its inherent properties, known, indeed, by the divine reason, but belonging to the realm of essential or metaphysical necessity which is prior to will and regulative of it. The worth of an object is involved in its Idea in precisely the same way in which divisibility by other whole numbers without a remainder is involved in the Ideas of certain whole numbers. [64] If, then, God had pronounced any other world best, he would have contradicted himself as absolutely as if he had asserted that four is not a multiple of two; in other words, both were equally impossible to him, and therefore the existence of any other scheme of things than the one which actually exists was from all eternity impossible.

An absolute logical determinism, then, is as characteristic of the metaphysics of Leibniz as of that of Spinoza, though the reasons why it is are somewhat more complicated in the former case, and though Leibniz lacked the candor and courage to express the certain, and almost obvious, outcome of his reasonings, in his more popular writings, without obscuring it by misleading if edifying phraseology — especially by the verbal distinction, absolutely meaningless in the light of his other doctrines, between "necessitating" and "infallibly inclining" reasons. The real meaning, in his system, of the principle of sufficient reason thus resolves itself into the proposition that the existence of everything that does exist, and also its attributes, behavior, and relations, are determined by a necessary truth, or a system of such truths. The reasonableness of the universe which the formula affirms is, as with Spinoza, of the same type as the reasonableness of a geometrical system — as geometrical systems were conceived by seventeenth-century logic. This could hardly be more plainly and emphatically declared than it is by Leibniz himself in one of the most important of his shorter writings, *On the Primary Origination of Things* (*De rerum originatione radicali*, 1697).

> In reality we find that all things in the world take place (*fieri*) according to the laws of eternal truths, not only geometrical but also metaphysical, that is, not only according to material but also to formal necessities; and this is true not merely generally, with respect to the reason, already explained, why the world exists rather than does not exist and why it exists thus rather than otherwise; but even when we descend to the details we see that metaphysical laws hold good in a wonderful manner in the entire universe. . . . Thus, then, we have the ultimate reason of the reality both of essences and existences in one being, which is necessarily greater than the world itself, and superior and antecedent to it.[65]

The same cosmical determinism is manifest in a logical thesis of Leibniz most plainly expressed in certain writings of his published only within the past fifty years. This thesis is that all contingent truths are ultimately reducible to *a priori* or necessary truths. We, no doubt, because of the limitations of our human understanding, cannot, in many cases, accomplish this reduction; the distinction between the necessary and the contingent expresses a genuine and persistent difference between the ways in which certain specific truths present themselves to our minds. A judgment which appears to us as contingent could by itself be shown to be necessary — i. e., to be simply the expression of the essential meaning or "nature" of the notions contained in it — only through an analysis of those notions which would proceed *in infinitum* and is therefore impossible to a finite mind. But though we are unable to attain an intuitive apprehension of the necessity, in the specific instance, we can nevertheless be sure that the necessity is there, and is recognized by the mind of God, who sees all the natures and their relations through and through in a single perfect intuition or *scientia visionis*. Unless thus ultimately reducible to necessity no proposition can, according to Leibniz, be true at all; for the truth of a proposition can mean only "the inherence of its predicate in its subject" directly or indirectly, so that the subject would not be itself without that predicate.[66] In other words, no judgment is true unless its opposite is — to a sufficiently analytic and sufficiently comprehensive intelligence — a self-contradiction. And the equivalence of this proposition to the principle of sufficient reason is explicitly stated: the *vérité primitive que rien n'est sans raison* is said to be synonymous with the proposition that "every truth has a proof *a priori* drawn from the notion of its terms, though it is not always in our power to carry through this analysis."[67] Not only by its clear implications, then, but by some of the formal definitions of it, the principle of sufficient reason is with Leibniz equivalent to the Spinozistic doctrine of the eternal, quasi-geometrical necessity of all things.[68]

The fact that Leibniz had failed to establish any essential difference between his "sufficient reason" and Spinoza's "necessity" was by no means unrecognized in the eighteenth century. It was pointed out at length, with perfectly sound arguments, by the Halle theologian Joachim Lange in his *Modesta disquisitio*, 1723, and in numerous other writings against the philosophy of Wolff, the systematizer and popularizer of the Leibnitian doctrines. Both Wolff and Leibniz, Lange observes, "derive creation from the nature of God as light is derived from the sun, and make it strictly essential to him and a part of his nature or necessary." The only way in which, on Leibnitian principles, anything could, without contradiction, be other than what it is, would be as a possibility in some other world which does not exist; in the actual world, which is also, by the hypothesis, the only world which God could conceivably have willed, everything is determined with the same "fatal necessity" as in the system of the Jewish philosopher.[69] A similar observation — not, perhaps, in this case, implying real disapproval — later found a place in the less orthodox pages of the *Encyclopédie*. To the immense reputation which Leibniz had in the middle of the century that work bears conclusive testimony; it remarks that "he alone confers as much honor upon Germany as Plato, Aristotle, and Archimedes together conferred upon Greece." [70] But, it asks:

How can Messieurs Leibnits and Wolf bring their principle of sufficient reason into accord with the contingency of the universe? Contingency implies an equal balance of possibilities. But what is more opposed to such a balance than the principle of sufficient reason? It is, then, necessary to say that the world exists, not contingently, but by virtue of a sufficient reason; and this might lead us to the verge of Spinozism. These philosophers attempt, to be sure, to escape this; . . . but it remains true that the sufficient reason does not leave contingency unimpaired. The more a plan has reasons which require its existence, the less are alternative plans possible — i.e., the less can they set up claims to existence. . . . God is the source of all created monads, which have emanated from him by continual fulgurations. . . . Things cannot be other than they are.[71]

The passage shows clearly that one, and perhaps the principal, tendency of Leibniz's insistence upon his principle of sufficient reason — commonly esteemed in the eighteenth century one of the great achievements of philosophy — was to promote the doctrine of universal necessity and to diminish the horror of that hobgoblin which had so terrified even Leibniz himself, the metaphysics of Spinoza.

But it may perhaps be suggested that, even though logical necessity is as absolute and pervasive in Leibniz's universe as in Spinoza's, there is still an essential difference between the two, in that for Leibniz the thing that is necessary is the realization of value; in other words, that the principle of sufficient reason, though it declares that only one world could ever conceivably *exist*, adds that this one must be the best conceivable — an addition not to be found in Spinoza. If, however, we observe what the "good" is that Leibniz regards as the ground of the existence of any particular thing, or of the actual world as a whole, we shall see that even this difference is both less and other than it at first sight appears to be. We shall at the same time see the principle of sufficient reason in the act of passing over explicitly into the principle of plenitude. There can, Leibniz often says plainly enough, be only one ultimate reason why anything exists, namely, that its essence demands existence, and will inevitably attain it unless interfered with by a similar demand on the part of some other essence; and the superiority of the actual world to all the other abstractly conceivable ones consists in the fact that in it this tendency of essences to exist is realized in a greater measure than in any of the others. An *exigentia existentiae* [72] is inherent in every essence; *nisi in ipsa essentiae natura quaedam ad existendum inclinatio esset, nihil existeret.* A mere "possible" is a thing frustrate, uncompleted; and therefore "every possible is characterized by a striving (*conatus*) towards existence," and "may be said to be destined to exist, provided, that is, it is grounded in a necessary being actually existing." True, as we have seen, not all possibles *do* attain existence, since the requirements of compossibility exclude some of them. But, with this restriction, Leibniz comes very near to applying to every essence the principle of the ontological argument. He comes even nearer than Spinoza to doing so. Spinoza's principal (though not his only) argument, it will be remembered, ran thus: given the Idea of one *directly* necessary being as a *point d'appui*, the existence of beings corresponding to all the other Ideas (within the limits of possibility) is equally necessary. [73] With Leibniz the *point d'appui* seems superfluous. While he is usually careful to speak of the other existents as logically dependent upon the existence of God, his emphasis upon the inherency of the *propensio ad existendum* in each essence separately is frequently so unqualified that it becomes difficult to see wherein the dependence consists. The necessity with which God exists would seem to be merely one instance — though the extreme instance — of this generic attribute of essence. The certainty of the realization of the propension in the case of the divine essence is, perhaps, due only to its exemption from the requirements of compossibility; it is an essence *hors concours*, so to say, and does not need to struggle for a place in the real world. [74] The issue of that struggle in the case of the other essences seems to be determined wholly by *their* properties, not by the attributes of God. Leibniz does not hesitate to represent the emergence of the actual from among the possible worlds as the result of a quasi-mechanical process in which the world carrying the greatest weight of potential being inevitably pushed through to actuality: [75]

> From the conflict of all the possibles demanding existence, this at once follows, that there exists that series of things by which as many of them as possible exist; in other words, the maximal series of possibles. . . . And as we see liquids spontaneously and by their own nature gather into spherical drops, so in the nature of the universe the series which has the greatest capacity (*maxime capax*) exists. [76]

Leibniz wavers, it is true, between two possible ways of taking this notion of "maximal capacity." He necessarily admitted a gradation among the essences, of which the graded scale of monads, with God at the summit of the scale, was the expression. And he not infrequently seems to imply that, because of their differing "degrees of perfection," some essences may have a greater claim, or a more potent tendency, to existence than others. Thus the fullness of the actual world would be rather intensive than extensive; it would be measured by the rank, or degrees of excellence, of its component members, and not merely by their number. The following passage illustrates this way of construing the notion:

> The sufficient reason for God's choice can be found only in the fitness (*convenance*) or in the degrees of perfection that the several worlds possess, since each possible thing has the right to aspire to existence in proportion to the amount of perfection it contains in germ. [77]

But though Leibniz, undeniably, often inclines to this sort of phraseology in the popular writings with which eighteenth-century readers were most familiar, the view it suggests was not logically open to him, and is not in fact carried out in his account of the actual constitution of the world. If it be assumed that the essence man "contained in germ" many times the "amount of perfection" attaching to the essence crocodile, and if it be further assumed (as by Leibniz it is) that the rules of compossibility forbid that two bodies should occupy the same space, then it would seem, according to the passage last

cited, that a world containing only men and no crocodiles
would be better than one containing both, since the crocodiles
would certainly require matter and occupy space which might
be devoted to the uses of human beings. But this is precisely the
conclusion which Leibniz does not draw. As the author of a
theodicy he is concerned to justify crocodiles; he must show
that the principle of sufficient reason requires that — once
more, within the limits of compossibility — these creatures
and all the other possible links in the Chain of Being, down to
the lowest, shall really exist. What may, then, be called his
actual working theory on the subject is that of equal rights
among essences as claimants for existence. "To say that some
essences have an inclination to exist and others do not, is to say
something without reason, since existence seems to be universally related to every essence in the same manner." [78] And
the superiority of the actual world consists in the *number* of different essences — in other words, in the variety of types —
realized in it, not in their metaphysical rank or qualitative
excellence. "Perfection is to be placed in form [i. e., as the
context shows, in *quantity* of forms], or variety; whence it follows that matter is not everywhere uniform, but is diversified
by assuming different forms; otherwise, as much variety as
possible would not be realized. . . . It follows likewise that
that series prevailed through which there could arise the greatest possibility of thinking of things as distinct (*distincta cogita-
bilitas*)." [79] "The actual universe is the collection of the possibles *qui forment le plus riche composé.*" [80] "We must say,"
writes Leibniz to Malebranche, "that God makes the greatest
number of things that he can"; and it is precisely for this reason that the *laws* of nature are as simple as possible; by means
of such laws God was able "to find room for as many things as
it is possible to place together. If God had made use of other
laws, it would be as if one should construct a building of
round stones, which leave more space unoccupied than that
which they fill." [81] Thus even the scientific assumption that
the simplest explanatory hypothesis is always to be preferred
appeared to Leibniz — though the connection is hard to follow — as a corollary of the principle of plenitude.

The "good," then, for the sake of which, and by reason of

which, things exist, is simply existence itself — the actualization of essence; and the world that in the eternal nature of things was necessitated to be, was the world in which "the quantity of existence is as great as possible." [82] Thus the difference between Leibniz's nominal assertion and Spinoza's denial of final causes approaches the vanishing point. There are, of course, in Leibniz plenty of passages dilating in the conventional way upon the evidences of design in nature, the "fitness" of everything to everything else, and to man's advantage, in particular. [83] But his fundamental view, expressed in his most methodical and comprehensive summaries of his doctrine, was that each thing exists, not primarily for the sake of other things, not as an instrument to an ulterior good, but because its essence, like every essence, had its own underivative right to existence. And since this is realized (so far as it is possible) by logical necessity, and since its realization differs from what Spinoza had represented as following *ex necessitate divinae naturae* only by the limitations inherent in the rule of incompossibility, the metaphysical outcome of the two arguments is still essentially the same.

Nevertheless, the difference between the Leibnitian and Spinozistic ways of putting what was, in logical substance, the same fundamental metaphysics, was historically important. Where Spinoza had (ostensibly) asserted that the realization of the principle of plenitude, being necessary, cannot properly be called either good or bad, Leibniz declared that, while necessary, it is also supremely good; he thereby gave to that principle (without qualification) the status of a doctrine about value as well as (with a qualification) that of a doctrine about the constitution of reality. Spinoza, as we have seen, appears more interested in the thought of the necessity of the universe than in the thought of its plenitude. Leibniz was genuinely interested in both aspects of this dialectic; but he was also somewhat afraid of the cosmic determinism to which it led him, while in the notion of the cosmic "fullness" he took, and he tended to impart to his readers, a lively imaginative and emotional satisfaction.

The qualification to which the principle of plenitude was subject when taken as a generalization about reality did not,

in the concrete application of Leibniz's metaphysics to questions lying within the purview of natural science, prove to be
of much consequence. Though he had affirmed the reality of
a *vacuum formarum*, i. e., of the non-existence of some possibles,
it was a vacuum lying wholly outside the particular series of
forms which defines the world that actually exists. Within
this world no gaps of any sort could be admitted; Leibniz had
a *horror vacui* which he was certain that Nature shared. In its
internal structure the universe *is* a *plenum*, and the law of continuity, the assumption that "nature makes no leaps," can
with absolute confidence be applied in all the sciences, from
geometry to biology and psychology. "If one denied it, the
world would contain hiatuses, which would overthrow the
great principle of sufficient reason and compel us to have recourse to miracles or pure chance in the explanation of phenomena." What this means, of course, is that since the general
types of entity actually found in the world must obviously be
possible and compossible, and since (as Leibniz somewhat un-
critically assumes) all species of those types must be equally
possible, then the absence from reality of any such species
would amount to an arbitrary, which is to say a fortuitous,
exclusion of a possible from existence — the inconceivability
of which to Leibniz needs no further exposition.[84]

The principle of plenitude, and that of continuity as a special form of it, involve him in some embarrassment when he
comes to consider the two questions of the existence of matter
and of the possibility of physical vacua, the latter a topic still
much debated among physicists during his lifetime. In some
passages he comes near to deducing from these principles, as
Archbishop King had done, a proof of physical realism.[85]
God *must* have created real matter, since if he had not, there
would be not only an unrealized possibility of existence, but
also a lack of coherency in things: "if there were only minds,
they would be without the necessary connection with one another (*liaison*), without the order of times and places." This
order "demands matter and motion and the laws of motion."
And if there is to be any matter at all, then it must be continuous; there can be no empty spaces where matter might
have been but is not. Leibniz therefore vehemently attacked

the physical vacuists. But on the other hand, he found reasons, which it is not needful to set forth here,[86] for concluding that space is merely the "order of coexistences," a form in which entities not really extended appear sensibly to one another; and with this the material world, as conceived by ordinary physical realism, goes by the board, and material bodies are reduced to the equivocal status already mentioned. The principle of plenitude, in short, here comes into conflict with certain other dialectical motives which played an important part in Leibniz's thought, and, at this particular point, gets the worst of it.[87] When, from this point of view, he still continues to criticize the believers in the vacuum, it is not because they hold that empty spaces exist somewhere, but because they hold that real spaces exist at all.[88] Meanwhile, of the reality of which matter is the manifestation, the denial of the possibility of any vacuum holds good literally; nature is everywhere teeming with life, all of it accompanied with some degree of sentiency. "There is," Leibniz writes in the *Monadology*, "nothing fallow, nothing sterile, nothing dead in the universe"; and again elsewhere: "If there were a vacuum, it is evident that there would be left sterile and fallow places in which, nevertheless, without prejudice to any other things, something might have been produced. But it is not consistent with wisdom that any such places should be left." [89] "In every particle of the universe a world composed of an infinity of creatures is contained."[90]

But, as the metaphysical argument already outlined implies, it is not of mere quantity or numbers that Nature is thus insatiably avid; it is essentially the maximization of diversity that she seeks, the multiplication of species and sub-species and differing individuals to the limit of logical possibility. "Just as there is no vacuum in the varieties of the corporeal world, so there is no less variety among intelligent creatures." [91] Some notable consequences drawn from this aspect of the principle of plenitude in the eighteenth century we shall observe in later lectures.

# VI

## THE CHAIN OF BEING IN EIGHTEENTH–CENTURY THOUGHT, AND MAN'S PLACE AND RÔLE IN NATURE

IT WAS in the eighteenth century that the conception of the universe as a Chain of Being, and the principles which underlay this conception — plenitude, continuity, gradation — attained their widest diffusion and acceptance. This at first seems somewhat strange. That a group of ideas which owed its genesis to Plato and Aristotle and its systematization to the Neoplatonists should have had so belated a fruition may well appear surprising — especially as there was much in the intellectual fashions of (roughly) the first three quarters of the century which seemed inimical to these assumptions. Aristotle's authority had, of course, long since been lost. Scholasticism and its methods were, among those who plumed themselves on their "enlightenment," usually objects of contempt and ridicule. The faith in speculative *a priori* metaphysics was waning, and the Baconian temper (if not precisely the Baconian procedure), the spirit of patient empirical inquiry, continued its triumphant march in science, and was an object of fervent enthusiasm among a large part of the general educated public. And the notion of the Chain of Being, with the assumptions on which it rested, was obviously not a generalization derived from experience, nor was it, in truth, easy to reconcile with the known facts of nature.

Nevertheless there has been no period in which writers of all sorts — men of science and philosophers, poets and popular essayists, deists and orthodox divines — talked so much about the Chain of Being, or accepted more implicitly the general scheme of ideas connected with it, or more boldly drew from these their latent implications, or apparent implications. Addison, King, Bolingbroke, Pope, Haller, Thomson, Akenside, Buffon, Bonnet, Goldsmith, Diderot, Kant, Lambert,

Herder, Schiller — all these and a host of lesser writers not only expatiated upon the theme but drew from it new, or previously evaded, consequences; while Voltaire and Dr. Johnson, a strange pair of companions in arms, led an attack upon the whole conception. Next to the word 'Nature,' 'the Great Chain of Being' was the sacred phrase of the eighteenth century, playing a part somewhat analogous to that of the blessed word 'evolution' in the late nineteenth.

It was, probably, not chiefly to any direct influence of Greek or medieval philosophy that the conception owed its vogue in the eighteenth century. For it had been insisted upon by both of the two philosophers of the late seventeenth whose reputation and influence were greatest in the ensuing fifty years. Locke was not less explicit, though he was less exuberant, than Leibniz in repeating the ancient theses:

In all the visible corporeal world we see no chasms or gaps. All quite down from us the descent is by easy steps, and a continued series that in each remove differ very little one from the other. There are fishes that have wings and are not strangers to the airy region; and there are some birds that are inhabitants of the water, whose blood is as cold as fishes. . . . There are animals so near of kin both to birds and beasts that they are in the middle between both. Amphibious animals link the terrestrial and aquatic together; . . . not to mention what is confidently reported of mermaids or sea-men. There are some brutes that seem to have as much reason and knowledge as some that are called men; and the animal and vegetable kingdoms are so nearly joined, that if you will take the lowest of one and the highest of the other, there will scarce be perceived any great difference between them; and so on until we come to the lowest and the most unorganical parts of matter, we shall find everywhere that the several species are linked together, and differ but in almost insensible degrees. And when we consider the infinite power and wisdom of the Maker, we have reason to think, that it is suitable to the magnificent harmony of the universe, and the great design and infinite goodness of the architect, that the species of creatures should also, by gentle degrees, ascend upwards from us towards his infinite perfection, as we see they gradually descend from us downwards.[1]

Addison made this aspect of the Platonistic metaphysics familiar even to that part of the public which left the works of philosophers and theologians unread, by repeated references to it in the *Spectator* — for example, in No. 519.

Infinite Goodness is of so communicative a Nature, that it seems to delight in the conferring of Existence upon every degree of Perceptive Being.

As this is a Speculation which I have often pursued with great Pleasure to myself, I shall enlarge farther upon it by considering that part of the Scale of Beings which comes within our own Knowledge. There are many other creatures . . . which have no other sense beside that of feeling and taste. . . . It is wonderful to observe, by what a gradual progress the World of Life advances through a prodigious variety of species, before a creature is formed that is compleat in all its Senses. . . . If after this we look into the several inward Perfections of Cunning and Sagacity, or what we generally call Instinct, we find them rising after the same manner, imperceptibly one above another, and receiving additional Improvements, according to the Species in which they are implanted. This progress in Nature is so very gradual, that the most perfect of an Inferior Species comes very near to the most imperfect of that which is immediately above it. . . . Nor is [the] goodness [of the Supream Being] less seen in the Diversity than in the Multitude of living Creatures. Had he made only one Species of Animals, none of the rest would have enjoyed the Happiness of Existence; he has, therefore, *specified* in his Creation every degree of Life, every Capacity of Being. The whole Chasm in Nature, from a Plant to a Man, is filled up with diverse Kinds of Creatures, rising one over another by such a gentle and easie Ascent, that the little Transitions and Deviations from one Species to another, are almost insensible. This intermediate Space is so well husbanded and managed, that there is scarce a degree of Perception which does not appear in some part of the World of Life.[2]

Another writer, the Anglican divine Edmund Law, was not content even with this picture of the 'fullness' of creation, but, after quoting Addison, added that within each species as many individuals as are capable of existing together must have been generated:

From the . . . observation that there is no manner of *chasm* or *void*, no link deficient in this great chain of beings, and the reason of it, it will appear extremely probable that every distinct order, every class or species of them, is as full as the nature of it would admit, or God saw proper. There are perhaps so many in each class as could exist together without some *inconvenience* or *uneasiness* to each other. This we are sure of, that nothing but an *impossibility* in the nature of the thing, or some greater (sic) inconvenience, can restrain the exercise of the power of God, or hinder him from producing still more and more beings capable of felicity. . . . We have the highest reason to conclude that everything is as perfect as possible in its own kind, and that every system is in itself full and complete.[3]

Out of the many special turns given to these general ideas, we shall in the present lecture consider certain of the deductions made from them with respect to man — his status in the scale, his nature, and the ethical consequences to be drawn from these.

A. *The Chain of Being and Man's Place in Nature.* We have already considered the effects of the belief in the infinity of the world and the plurality of inhabited globes — itself chiefly an inference from the principle of plenitude — upon man's conception of his place and consequence in the cosmic system. This belief, we have seen, did less to abate the self-esteem of our race than might have been expected and has often been supposed. But there were four other implications of the notion of the full and infinitesimally graduated Scale of Being which tended definitely to lower man's estimate of his cosmic importance and uniqueness; and these were much dwelt upon by eighteenth-century philosophers and popularizers of philosophical ideas.

1. It was implied by the principle of plenitude that every link in the Chain of Being exists, not merely and not primarily for the benefit of any other link, but for its own sake, or more precisely, for the sake of the completeness of the series of forms, the realization of which was the chief object of God in creating the world. We have already seen that, though essences were conceived to be unequal in dignity, they all had an equal claim to existence, within the limits of rational possibility; and therefore the true *raison d'être* of one species of being was never to be sought in its utility to any other. But this implication was in conflict with an old assumption, highly flattering to man, which still persisted in the seventeenth and eighteenth centuries. The 'physico-theology' so much beloved by the writers of works of edification, deistic as well as orthodox, was in intent a proof of the existence of God; but it was in effect a glorification of man. For it rested in great part upon the supposition that all other created beings exist for man's sake. *Tout est créé pour l'homme* is at once the tacit premise and the triumphant conclusion of that long series of teleological arguments which constitutes so large a fraction of the 'philosophical' output of the eighteenth century — and is one of the most curious monuments of human imbecility. This later age, in this, but repeats a strain heard frequently in the Middle Ages. The principal textbook of Scholastic philosophy had declared:

As man is made for the sake of God, namely, that he may serve him, so is the world made for the sake of man, that it may serve him.[4]

Bacon had elaborated upon the theme:

Man, if we look to final causes, may be regarded as the centre of the world; insomuch that if man were taken away from the world, the rest would seem to be all astray, without aim or purpose, . . . and leading to nothing. For the whole world works together in the service of man; and there is nothing from which he does not derive use and fruit . . . insomuch that all things seem to be going about man's business and not their own.[5]

In a Protestant theological work of the late seventeenth century which was much admired in the eighteenth it is written:

If we consider closely what constitutes the excellence of the fairest parts of the Universe, we shall find that they have value only in their relation to us, only in so far as our soul attaches value to them; that the esteem of men is what constitutes the chief dignity of rocks and metals, that man's use and pleasure gives their value to plants, trees and fruits.[6]

"In nature not only the plants but the animals," says Fénelon, "are made for our use." Predatory animals may seem an exception; but "if all countries were peopled and made subject to law and order as they should be, there would be no animals that would attack man." Yet the wilder beasts also serve man, partly as means to the cultivation of physical address and courage, partly as aids to the preservation of international peace. For Fénelon too had some sense of man's need of a "moral substitute for war"; he proposed to meet it by maintaining preserves of "ferocious animals" in remote regions, to which those men whose fighting propensities needed outlet might repair. And the beneficence of nature was not least shown in thus providing fighting creatures of other species to kill, so that men might be relieved of the necessity of killing one another.[7] The Creator has aimed, said Bernardin de St-Pierre — whose *Études de la Nature*, 1784, was looked upon as one of the masterpieces in this *genre* — "only at the happiness of man. All the laws of nature are designed to serve our needs."[8]

Not only against this assumption that the rest of the creation is instrumental to man's good but — though less obviously — against the premises of the teleological argument in general, the logic of the conception of the Chain of Being worked potently, though the protest against this form of human vanity was prompted also by other considerations. Galileo had written: "We arrogate too much to ourselves if we suppose that the care of us is the adequate work of God, the end beyond which the divine wisdom and power does not extend." [9] Henry More, clearly under the influence of the principle of plenitude, declared that:

We are not to be scandalized . . . that there is such careful provision made for such contemptible vermine as we conceive them [the lower animals] to be. For this only comes out of Pride and Ignorance, or a haughty Presumption, that because we are encouraged to believe that in some Sense all things are made for Man, therefore they are not at all made for themselves. But he that pronounces this is ignorant of the Nature of God, and the Knowledge of things. For if a good Man be merciful to his Beast; then surely a good God is bountiful and benign, and takes Pleasure that all his Creatures enjoy themselves that have Life and Sense, and are capable of any enjoyment. [10]

Descartes was, however, the foremost opponent in the seventeenth century not only of an anthropocentric teleology but of all forms of teleological reasoning in science. Aside from other objections, he found the theory in conflict with obvious facts.

It is not at all probable that all things have been created for us in such a manner that God has no other end in creating them. . . . Such a supposition would, I think, be very inept in reasoning about physical questions; for we cannot doubt that an infinitude of things exist, or did exist though they have now ceased to do so, which have never been beheld or comprehended by man, and have never been of any use to him. [11]

Most, indeed, of the greater philosophers of the seventeenth century repeat the same remark. Leibniz expressly concurs with Spinoza in the theorem *non omnia hominum causa fieri*.[12] It is not surprising, he observes, that "we find in the world things that are not pleasing to us," since "we know that it was not made for us alone." It is, in fact, "absurd," said Archbishop King, to imagine that "the earth was made for the sake of mankind, and not of the universe"; no one "who is not blinded by pride and ignorance" could ever suppose it. The same proposition is the principal burden of Bolingbroke's polemic against all "divines" except King, in the *Fragments, or Minutes of Essays,* from which Pope probably got most of the ideas for the First Epistle of the *Essay on Man.* The agreement of the deist with the orthodox apologist is here complete. Bolingbroke professes, it is true, to scorn all theosophic speculation, all the pretensions of theologians to an acquaintance with the secret counsels of the Most High; and for Plato and his followers, ancient and modern, he has an especially lively contempt. Yet he too, in the end, quietly assumes that he is not entirely ignorant of "the design of the Author of all nature." The completeness of the cosmic scheme as a whole is, Bolingbroke is sure, the true *raison d'être* of the universe. We have no reason to think that "Infinite Wisdom had no other end in making man" — or, indeed, any other link in the chain — "than that of making a happy creature."[13]

> The sensitive inhabitants of our globe, like the *dramatis personae,* have different characters, and are applied to different purposes of action in every scene. The several parts of the material world, like the machines of a theatre, were contrived, not for the actors, but for the action; and the whole order and system of the drama would be disordered and spoiled, if any alteration was made in either.[14]

The universe, in short, was made in order that all possible forms of being might manifest themselves after their kinds. Thus what a writer of our own time has called the *point de vue spectaculaire* — the cosmical piety and the sort of Romantic delight in the world which can arise, not from any belief in its adaptation to man's needs or hopes, but from its infinite richness and diversity as a spectacle, the prodigious sweep of the complex and often tragic drama which it exhibits — was by no means unfamiliar in the early eighteenth century.[15] This favorite thesis of so many eighteenth-century writers was most tersely summed up by Goethe in his poem *Athroismos* (1819): "every animal is an end in itself":

> Zweck sein selbst ist jegliches Tier.

2. A second consequence of the same sort was often drawn from the accepted view as to man's relative position in the Chain of Being. The customary thing to say about this was, as we have seen, that he is the "middle link" in the chain. This did not necessarily or (I think) usually mean that the kinds

above him and below him are equal in number. On the contrary, Locke thought that "we have reason to be persuaded that there are far more species of creatures above us, than there are beneath; we being in degrees of perfection much more remote from the infinite Being of God, than we are from the lowest state of being, and that which approaches nearest to nothing." [16] Addison puts the argument still more sharply; the "space and room" upwards is infinite, and must all be filled; but the number of grades below is finite.[17] Man was thus not midway in the series, but well down towards the lower end of it. He was the "middle link" in the sense that he was at the point of transition from the merely sentient to the intellectual forms of being. Did this suggest a flattering or a humbling view of man? To the poet Young, who construed the notion of the middle position literally, it appeared to permit man to hold a rather high opinion of himself; he is a

> Distinguished link in being's endless chain,
> Midway from nothing to the deity.

But to most of those who reflected upon the position in the universe which the theory assigned to man, it was an added reason for humility. Even though he had been made but a little lower than the angels, he was lower than the lowest of the angels, or other spiritual beings; and the successive hierarchies above him were so numerous that when his mind dwelt upon them a sort of racial inferiority-complex naturally resulted. "The principall use of considering these scales of Creatures," wrote Sir William Petty (1677), "is to lett man see that beneath God there may be millions of creatures superior unto man. Wheras Hee generally taketh himself to be the chiefe and next to God." For it shows him that "there are beings within . . . the orb of the fixed Starrs . . . which do [more] incomparably excell man in the sense of dignity and infirmity then man doth excell the vilest insect." [18] If, wrote a lady of quality in 1710 — the authorship of the passage shows how completely a commonplace this way of thinking then was —

. . . if . . . we farther consider, that there being a Scale of Beings, which reaches from the first Cause to the most imperceptible Effect, from the infinite Creator to the smallest of his Productions, we have reason to believe, that as we see an innumerable Company of Beings below us, and each Species to be less perfect in its Kind, till they end in a Point, an indivisible Solid: so there are almost an infinite Number of Beings above us, who as much exceed us, as we do the minutest Insect, or the smallest Plant, and, in comparison of whom, the most elevated Genius's, the greatest Masters of Reason, the most illuminated and unweary'd Enquirers after Knowledge, are but Children, such as hardly deserve to be of the lowest Form in the School of Wisdom, we cannot but have contemptible Thoughts of our selves, cannot but blush at our own Arrogance, and look back with Shame on the several Instances of our Folly.

Methinks I see those bright Intelligences . . . who by the Dignity of their Nature are raised to sublime Stations, to the most intimate Union that created Minds can have with the Supream Good, viewing us with a scornful Smile, but with a scorn that is mix'd with Pity.[19]

Addison merely condensed this a few years later: "If the notion of a gradual rise in Beings from the meanest to the most High be not a vain imagination, it is not improbable that an Angel looks down upon a Man, as a Man doth upon a Creature which approaches the nearest to the rational Nature." [20] The philosopher Formey reports the similar impression made upon him when he first became acquainted with the conception of the Scale of Being:

How little cause have I to exalt myself above others, and whence can I derive motives for pride? Heretofore I used to conceit myself one of the most excellent of God's creatures, but I now perceive how great my delusion was. I find myself towards the lowest part of the Scale, and all I can boast of is, that I have a small pre-eminence above irrational creatures; and this is not always so, there being many things in which they possess advantages which I have not. On the contrary I see above me a multitude of superior intelligences.[21]

There was, of course, nothing new in this belief in many ranks of "intelligences" superior to man; the passages cited thus far merely illustrate its persistence, its recognized philosophical basis in the general scheme of the Chain of Being, and its effect upon man's conception of himself. But in the eighteenth century the belief began to take on a more naturalistic form. This is illustrated in some passages of Bolingbroke. That there is an unbroken Chain of Being "almost from nonentity up to man" he supposed to be established by observation; and like the Schoolmen whom he ridiculed, he found that, though empirical evidence here fails us, "we have the most probable reasons to persuade us, that it continues up to natures infinitely below the divine, but vastly superior to the human." But these superior natures were not for him the angelic hierarchies, but simply the inhabitants of some of the other globes in this or other solar systems. For this faith in the existence of higher links in the chain he gives an interesting reason, supplementary to the general postulate of plenitude: the fact that man's intellectual powers so obviously fall far short of the maximal possibilities even of finite intelligence.

We cannot doubt that numberless worlds and systems of worlds compose this amazing whole, the universe; and as little, I think, that the planets which roll about the sun, or those which roll about a multitude of others, are inhabited by living creatures, fit to be inhabitants of them. When we have this view before our eyes, can we be stupid or vain or impertinent enough to imagine that we stand alone or foremost among rational created beings? We who must be conscious, unless we are mad, and have lost the use of our reason, of the imperfection of our reason? Shall we not be persuaded rather that as there is a gradation of sense and intelligence here from animal beings imperceptible to us for their minuteness, without the aid of microscopes and even with them, up to man, in whom, though this be their highest stage, [they] remain very imperfect; so there is a gradation from man, through various forms of sense, intelligence, and reason, up to beings who cannot be known by us, because of their distance from us, and whose rank in the intellectual system is above even our conceptions? This system, as well as the corporeal, . . . must have been alike present to the Divine Mind before he made them to exist.[22]

Bolingbroke too, in short, in spite of his ostentation of agnosticism, wanted to have faith in the universe; and this seemed to him impossible without the postulate that nature has somewhere produced better specimens of rationality than *homo sapiens*. But of the defects of his intelligence it is unreasonable in man to complain; only a segment of the scale exists on this planet, and he happens to be the not altogether non-rational yet on the whole very stupid creature who occupies a certain point in the series — a little higher, indeed, than any other on the globe which he inhabits, yet incalculably below the highest. If he, with his limitations, were wanting, the scheme would be incomplete, and therefore imperfect. Pope puts the same disparagement of man into four pungent lines:

> Superior beings when of late they saw
> A mortal man unfold all Nature's law,
> Admir'd such wisdom in an earthly shape,
> And shew'd a NEWTON as we shew an Ape.[23]

The same notion was afterwards more cheerfully elaborated by Kant:

Human nature occupies as it were the middle rung of the Scale of Being, . . . equally removed from the two extremes. If the contemplation of the most sublime classes of rational creatures, which inhabit Jupiter or Saturn, arouses his envy and humiliates him with a sense of his own inferiority, he may again find contentment and satisfaction by turning his gaze upon those lower grades which, in the planets Venus and Mercury, are far below the perfection of human nature.[24]

Kant, however, had discovered, as he supposed, a physical reason for this unequal distribution of degrees of rationality amongst the planets. Mental functions, he did not, in this early phase of his philosophical development, doubt, are conditioned by the constitution of the material bodies with which they are associated. "It is certain that man derives all his concepts and representations from the impressions which the universe makes upon him through his body"; even "the power of comparing and combining" these impressions, "which may be called the faculty of thought, is wholly dependent upon the constitution of the matter with which the Creator has conjoined him." [25] Now the greater the distance of a planet from the sun, the less it receives of the solar heat and energy; and in order that life and intelligence may subsist on the more remote planets, the matter of which living bodies thereon are constituted must be "lighter and finer" and the physiological structure of organisms, both animal and vegetal, must be more delicately and intricately organized. Hence, Kant concludes, there is a law, "of which the degree of probability falls little short of complete certainty," that

the excellence of thinking natures, their quickness of apprehension, the clarity and vividness of their concepts, which come to them from the impressions of the external world, their capacity to combine these concepts, and finally, their practical efficiency, in short the entire extent of their perfection, becomes higher and more complete in proportion to the remoteness of their dwelling-place from the sun.[26]

Thus "the dullness of man's wits," the confusion (*Verwirrung*) of his ideas, his extreme liability to error, and the depravity of his moral nature — of all of which Kant is no less sensible than Bolingbroke — are the necessary consequences of the dependence of his mind upon a "coarse and inert matter." But from these physical obstructions to mental activity the happier inhabitants of the outer planets are comparatively free.

> To what advances in knowledge will the insight of those fortunate beings in the higher celestial spheres not attain! What fair effects will this clarification of their understandings not have upon their moral condition! . . . What a noble imprint of its nature will not divinity itself . . . form in those thinking natures which, like a quiet sea untroubled by the storms of passion, receive and reflect back its image![27]

Comment on this wild but pleasing speculation would be superfluous. But it would be hard to find a better illustration of the hold which the principles of the Platonistic tradition whose history we are examining had upon even the best minds of the eighteenth century. The illustration is the more noteworthy because, as we have seen, Kant was not prepared to maintain that all globes must have conscious inhabitants. He was nevertheless quite certain that, in a reasonably ordered universe, most of them must have, that life and intelligence cannot possibly be confined to one small planet, and that the Scale of Being must extend far above man. He too finds consolation in the thought that so poor a creature as man is far from the best that nature produces. Upon even the most boasted achievements of our kind, on its necessarily inferior globe, the Jovians and Saturnians can but look down with condescending pity; Kant concludes with a paraphrase of Pope's lines: the higher beings of these other spheres must "view a Newton" as we view a Hottentot or an ape.

Bonnet in 1764 similarly derives from the postulate of the completeness of the Chain of Being light upon the inhabitants of other globes. Since it is a law of nature that no two leaves, or animals, or men, are completely alike, the same must be true of planets and solar systems.

> The assortment of beings which is characteristic of our world is probably not to be found in any other. Each globe has its distinctive economy and laws and products. There are perhaps worlds so imperfect relatively to

ours, that there are to be found in them only . . . [inanimate] beings. Other worlds, on the contrary, may be so perfect that there are in them only beings of the superior classes. In these latter worlds, the rocks are organic bodies, the plants have sensation, the animals reason, the men are angels.[28]

3. This, however, was a motive for humility which had long been insisted upon by the traditional theology. The Church had always bidden the individual man walk humbly with his God and be sensible of his inferiority to countless creatures above him in the cosmic hierarchy. But it had often encouraged him to walk proudly among the creatures below him in that scale. Was he not infinitely removed in dignity from even the highest animals by his participation in the intellectual light of the divine Reason? Yet when one began to consider seriously the implications of the principle of continuity — which great theologians of the Church had taught — it seemed to follow that man can be supposed to differ psychologically or physically from the nearest so-called non-human species only infinitesimally. The curious thing is that this consequence was, for the most part, so tardily drawn. Addison, while he finds matter for pride in man's position as the *nexus utriusque mundi*, the link between the animal and the intellectual natures, nevertheless concludes his reflections on the subject thus:

So that he who, in one respect, is associated with angels and archangels, and may look upon a being of Infinite Perfection as his Father, and the highest order of Spirits as his brethren, may, in another respect, say to Corruption, Thou art my Father, and to the worm, Thou art my Sister.

Arguing specifically from the principle of continuity, Bolingbroke also was diligent in the effort to lower man's too high conceit of himself — though he thought that some had gone too far in racial self-disparagement. Man is, indeed, "the principal inhabitant of this planet, a being superior to all the rest." But his superiority is only one of degree, and of a very slight degree.

The whole chorus of theistical philosophers and divines boast it [reason] to be the distinguishing gift of God to man, that which gives him a pre-eminence and a right of command over his fellow creatures. . . . There have been those who have thought, that the human is a portion of the divine soul. Others have been more modest, and have allowed that the former is a created being, . . . but a being of so high an order, that there is none superior, except the Supreme Being. . . .

There is a middle point between these extremes, where the truth lies; and he who seeks it may find it. . . . He will find . . . many such degrees of comparison between the human intelligence and that of various animals. He may be induced, perhaps, to think that intellectual faculties and corporeal senses, of the same and of different kinds, are communicated in some proportion or other to the whole race of animals. . . .[29]

Man is connected by his nature, and therefore, by the design of the Author of all Nature, with the whole tribe of animals, and so closely with some of them, that the distance between his intellectual faculties and theirs, which constitutes as really, though not so sensibly as figure, the difference of species, appears, in many instances, small, and would probably appear still less, if we had the means of knowing their motives, as we have of observing their actions.[30]

Pope, when he translated these reflections into verse, heightened the emphasis on the more edifying aspect of Bolingbroke's *via media*:

> Far as Creation's ample range extends,
> The scale of sensual, mental powers ascends:
> Mark how it mounts to man's imperial race,
> From the green myriads in the peopled grass. . . .
> How instinct varies in the grovelling swine,
> Compar'd, half-reasoning elephant, with thine!
> 'Twixt that, and reason, what a nice barrier,
> Forever sep'rate, yet forever near!
> Remembrance and reflection how ally'd!
> What thin partitions sense from thought divide!
> And middle natures, how they long to join,
> Yet never pass th' insuperable line!
> Without this just gradation could they be
> Subjected, these to those, or all to thee!
> The pow'rs of all subdu'd by thee alone,
> Is not thy reason all these pow'rs in one? [31]

In spite of Pope's reversion to a more conventional strain in these last lines, he elsewhere attributes man's lapse from the "state of Nature," which was "the reign of God," to the sin of pride — not that which caused man's fall in the biblical narrative, but a pride which led him to separate himself unduly from the other animals:

> Pride then was not, nor arts that pride to aid;
> Man walk'd with beast, joint tenant of the shade;

> The same his table, and the same his bed;
> No murder cloath'd him and no murder fed.
> In the same temple, the resounding wood,
> All vocal beings hymn'd their equal God![32]

Soame Jenyns seeks to alleviate this consequence of the principle of continuity by dwelling upon the many degrees of intelligence found *within* the human species; while the psychological difference between the highest animals and the lowest men is scarcely appreciable, between either of these and the most highly endowed of civilized mankind the gradations are many and the distance wide.

> The farther we inquire into the works of our great Creator, the more evident marks we shall discover of his infinite wisdom and power, and perhaps none more remarkable, than in that wonderful chain of beings, with which this terrestrial globe is furnished; rising above each other from the senseless clod, to the brightest genius of human kind, in which, though the chain itself is sufficiently visible, the links, which compose it, are so minute, and so finely wrought, that they are quite imperceptible to our eyes. The various qualities with which these various beings are endued, we perceive without difficulty, but the boundaries of those qualities which form this chain of subordination, are so mixed, that where one ends, and the next begins, we are unable to discover. . . . The manner by which the consummate wisdom of the divine artificer has formed this gradation, so extensive in the whole, and so imperceptible in the parts, is this: — He constantly unites the highest degree of the qualities of each inferior order to the lowest degree of the same qualities belonging to the order next above it; by which means, like the colours of a skilful painter, they are so blended together, and shaded off into each other, that no line of distinction is anywhere to be seen. . . . Animal life rises from this low beginning in the shell-fish, through innumerable species of insects, fishes, birds, and beasts, to the confines of reason, where, in the dog, the monkey, and chimpanzè, it unites so closely with the lowest degree of that quality in man, that they cannot easily be distinguished from each other. From this lowest degree in the brutal Hottentot, reason, with the assistance of learning and science, advances, through the various stages of human understanding, which rise above each other, till in a Bacon or a Newton it attains the summit.[33]

Yet, Jenyns adds,

> The superiority of man to other terrestrial animals is as inconsiderable, in proportion to the immense plan of universal existence, as the difference of climate between the north and south end of the paper I now write upon, with regard to the heat and distance of the sun.[34]

This sort of utterance did not, for its authors or contemporary readers, in the first half of the eighteenth century, usually imply the consanguinity of man and the animals next to him in the scale. But the belief in such consanguinity is significant, for man's evaluation of himself, only in so far as it minimizes the distinctiveness of man's nature and denies the existence of a wide chasm between him and all other terrestrial creatures. And that chasm the principle of continuity had bridged for many eighteenth-century minds by whom the hypothesis of the transformation of species, then already beginning to emerge, was not accepted. Thus one of the effects often attributed to the influence of biological evolutionism had in fact come about long before the establishment and general diffusion of that doctrine, and quite independently of it.

4. But it was not merely that man's separation from the lower orders of living things was thus reduced to an almost inappreciable degree of difference. The definition of him as the "middle link," in the sense usually given to it, especially emphasized the peculiar duality of his constitution and the tragi-comic inner discord in him which results from this. The recognition of the fact that man is a creature not in harmony with himself was not, of course, due primarily to the influence of the notion of the Chain of Being. Other elements of Platonism, and in Christianity the radical Pauline opposition of "flesh" and "spirit," had made this dualistic theory of human nature one of the ruling conceptions in Western thought; and the moral experience of countless generations indoctrinated in it had seemed to give it poignant confirmation. But the place assigned to man in the graded scale which constitutes the universe lent to this conception still greater sharpness and an air of metaphysical necessity. Somewhere in that scale there *must* exist a creature in which the merely animal series terminates and the "intellectual" series has its dim and rudimentary beginning; and man is that creature. He is therefore — not in consequence of any accidental fall from innocence nor of any perverse machinations of evil spirits, but because of the requirements of the universal scheme of things — torn by conflicting desires and propensities; as a member of two orders of being at once, he wavers between both, and is not quite at home

in either.  He thus has, after all, a kind of uniqueness in nature;
but it is an unhappy uniqueness.  He is, in a sense in which no
other link in the chain is, a strange hybrid monster; and if this
gives him a certain pathetic sublimity, it also results in incongruities of feeling, inconsistencies of behavior, and disparities
between his aspirations and his powers, which render him
ridiculous.  It is this aspect of man's status as the link uniting
the two great segments of the scale which Pope presents, in
lines almost too familiar to quote, but too perfectly illustrative
of the conception — and too superb an example of Pope's
poetic style at its best — to leave unquoted.

> Plac'd in this isthmus of a middle state,
> A being darkly wise and rudely great,
> With too much knowledge for the sceptic side,
> With too much weakness for the stoic pride,
> He hangs between; in doubt to act or rest;
> In doubt to deem himself a god or beast;
> In doubt his Mind or Body to prefer;
> Born but to die, and reas'ning but to err; . . .
> Chaos of Thought and Passion all confus'd,
> Still by himself abus'd, or disabus'd;
> Created half to rise, and half to fall,
> Great lord of all things, yet a prey to all;
> Sole judge of Truth, in endless error hurl'd;
> The glory, jest and riddle of the world.[35]

Haller, apostrophizing his kind as "unselig Mittel-Ding
von Engeln und von Vieh," exhibits man as the same cosmic
paradox:

> Du pralst mit der Vernunft, und du gebrauchst sie nie.
> Was helfen dir zuletzt der Weisheit hohe Lehren?
> Zu schwach sie zu verstehn, zu stolz sie zu entbehren.
> Dein schwindelnder Verstand, zum irren abgericht,
> Sieht oft die Wahrheit ein, und wählt sie dennoch nicht . . .
> Du urteilst überall, und weist doch nie warum;
> Der Irrthum ist dein Rath, und du sein Eigenthum.[36]

Yet the Swiss poet adds the two complementary and consoling
reflections upon which we have already seen other writers of
the century dwelling; there are other globes than ours with
happier inhabitants, and in any case the imperfection of man
is indispensable to the fullness of the hierarchy of being:

Perhaps this world of ours, which like a grain of sand
Floats in the vast of heaven, is Evil's fatherland;
While in the stars perhaps dwell spirits far more fair,
Vice reigning ever here, Virtue triumphant there.
And yet this point, this world, whose worth appears so small,
Serves in its place to make complete the mighty All.[37]

There were in the thought of the eighteenth century, especially after the middle of it, other strains, not pertinent to our present subject, which worked against this fashion of racial self-disparagement and prepared the way for those disastrous illusions of man about himself which were to be so characteristic of the century that followed, and against which our own age has, scarcely less disastrously, revolted. But the immense influence of the complex of ideas which was summed up in the cosmological conception of the Chain of Being tended chiefly, in the period with which we are now concerned, to make man not unbecomingly sensible of his littleness in the scheme of things, and to promote a not wholly unsalutary modesty and self-distrust.

B. *Some Ethical and Political Consequences.* From this and from other aspects of the conception diverse practical morals could be, or, at all events, in the eighteenth century were, deduced.

1. In the earlier part of the century, the most significant of these, and the most characteristic, may be described as a counsel of imperfection — an ethics of prudent mediocrity. Since every place in the scale must be filled, and since each is what it is by virtue of the special limitations which differentiate it from any other, man's duty was to keep *his* place, and not to seek to transcend it — which, nevertheless, he was characteristically prone to do. The good for a being of a given grade, it seemed evident, must consist in conformity to its type, in the expression of just that Idea which defines its position, or that of its species, in the series. There must, then, be a specifically human excellence which it is man's vocation to achieve — an excellence as little to be confused with that of angels or of God as with that of the beasts; and to covet the attributes or imitate the characteristic activities of beings above one in the cosmic order is as immoral as to sink to a lower level of it. The method

of such an ethics would consist in taking stock of man's actual
constitution — his distinguishing instincts, desires, and natural
capacities — and in formulating his good in terms of some bal-
anced and practicable fulfilment of these. And since man's
place is not a very high one, since he is a mixture of the animal
and the intellectual elements, and since the latter is present in
him only in a meagre measure and in its lowest, or almost
lowest, form, the beginning of wisdom for him was to remember and to hold fast to his limitations.

Of this ethics of the middle link Pope, again, was the chief,
though not the first, apostle.

> The bliss of man (could pride that blessing find)
> Is not to act or think beyond mankind:
> No pow'rs of body or of soul to share,
> But what his nature and his state can bear.[38]

Rousseau in *Émile* echoes Pope's preaching:

> O Man! confine thine existence within thyself, and thou wilt no longer
> be miserable. Remain in the place which Nature has assigned to thee in
> the chain of beings, and nothing can compel thee to depart from it. . . .
> Man is strong when he contents himself with being what he is; he is weak
> when he desires to raise himself above humanity.

This moral temper oftenest expressed itself in that constant
invective against "pride," so characteristic of Pope and many
another writer of the period.[39]  Pride is the sin "against the
laws of Order," i. e., of gradation; it is an attempt "to counter-
work the Universal Cause," to disturb the very system of the
universe.

> In pride, in reas'ning pride, our error lies;
> All quit their sphere and rush into the skies.
> Pride still is aiming at the blest abodes,
> Men would be angels, angels would be gods.

Man should, accordingly, eschew all the vaster enterprises of
the mind; he was not meant and is not equipped for them.
"Trace Science then with modesty thy guide"; and when all
the vanities, errors, and excrescences of learning are expunged,

> Then see how little the remaining sum,
> Which serv'd the past, and must the times to come!

Here the conception of the Chain of Being — and of man as its "middle link" — resulted in a species of rationalistic anti-intellectualism. But it also — when made the basis of an ethics — led to a disparagement of all the more pretentious and exacting moral ideals — for example, of that of Stoicism. Above all, the same conception led to the open and unqualified rejection of that otherworldliness which had always been characteristic of the Christian and the Platonic tradition. "Go, wondrous creature!" writes Pope contemptuously,

> Go soar with Plato to the empyreal sphere,
> To the first good, first perfect, and first fair,
> Or tread the mazy round his follow'rs trod,
> And quitting sense call imitating God;
> As Eastern priests in giddy circles run,
> And turn their heads to imitate the sun.

Here the two strains in Platonism, which we distinguished at the outset of these lectures, have become completely sundered; and one of them has overcome the other. The idea of the "way up," of the *ascensio mentis ad Deum per scalas creaturarum*, has been abandoned. Yet the main philosophic reason, if not, perhaps, the most potent motive, for its abandonment lay in the principle of plenitude, which had always been equally characteristic of the Platonic tradition. And this deduction from the principle was, as I have already intimated, at the least a consistent and plausible one. If all the possible links in the chain must be perpetually represented in the universe, and if this consideration was to be turned from a cosmological generalization into a moral imperative, it naturally seemed to follow that the *imitatio dei* could be no business of man's, and that any effort to ascend the scale must be an act of rebellion against the divine purpose — a crime against Nature. The doubt which might well have occurred — but apparently did not occur — to those who reasoned in this manner was whether the completeness of the world might not be presumed to be sufficiently assured by the Eternal Cause — whether, if it is necessary in the nature of things that the world should be an unbroken chain of being, it was likely that any link in the chain *could* leave its place, and thereby

in the full creation leave a void,
Where, one step broken, the great scale's destroyed.

2. The assumption of the mediocrity of man's position in the universe, when thus applied to his mental endowments, contained, or might plausibly be construed as containing, a further implication which some of the gloomier or more tough-minded spirits of the age did not fail to see: that a creature so limited and so near to the other animals, in kind if not in kinship, must necessarily be incapable of attaining any very high level of political wisdom or virtue, and that consequently no great improvement in men's political behavior or in the organization of society could be hoped for. There are, said Soame Jenyns, "numberless imperfections inherent in all human governments," and these are "imputable only to the inferiority of man's station in the universe, which necessarily exposes him to natural and moral evils, and must, for the same reason, to political and religious; which are indeed but the consequences of the other. Superior beings may probably form to themselves, or receive from their Creator, government without tyranny and corruption; . . . but man cannot: God indeed may remove him into so exalted a Society, but whilst he continues to be man, he must be subject to innumerable evils" — such as "those grievous burdens of tyranny and oppression, of violence and corruption, of war and desolation, under which all nations have ever groaned on account of government; . . . but which are so woven into the very essence of all human governments from the depravity of man, that without them none can be either established, maintained or administered, nor consequently can they be prevented without changing that depravity into perfection; that is, without a complete alteration of human nature." [40] Hence, Jenyns concludes, there never has been and never will be *any* good form of government. Some, doubtless, are less bad than others; but those who bitterly indict the existing order and dream of radically transforming it forget this fundamental truth — that "all these evils arise from the nature of things and the nature of man, and not from the weakness or wickedness of particular men, or their accidental ascendency in particular govern-

ments: the degrees of them may indeed be owing to these, but their existence is immutable." [41]

An analogous inference from the conception of the Chain of Being, and of man's place therein, was drawn by the same writer with respect to religion. Neither by the light of nature nor by revelation can man expect to attain much clarity or certainty in religious knowledge:

> God cannot impart knowledge to creatures, of which he himself has made them incapable by their nature and formation: he cannot instruct a mole in astronomy or an oyster in music, because he has not given them members or faculties necessary for the acquisition of those sciences: . . . a religion therefore from God can never be such as we might expect from infinite Power, Wisdom and Goodness, but must condescend to the ignorance and infirmities of man: was the wisest Legislator in the world to compose laws for a nursery they must be childish laws: so was God to reveal a religion to mankind, tho' the Revealer was divine the Religion must be human, . . . and therefore liable to numberless imperfections. [42]

The principles of plenitude and gradation could, in this way, among their many uses, be made to serve the purposes of a species of pessimistic and backhanded apologetic both for the political *status quo* and for the accepted religion. They provided a damper for the zeal of the reformer. Since men are not and were not meant to be angels, let us cease to expect them to behave as if they were; and let us avoid the error of imagining that by an alteration of the form or mechanism of government we shall put an end to those limitations of human nature which are essentially unalterable, because they are inherent in the scheme of the universe which required just such a creature, as well as all other kinds, to make it "complete."

One of Jenyns's critics, however, without denying the premises, detected, as he thought, a *non sequitur* in the conclusion; the argument, he declared, was "a mere quibble upon terms." Doubtless man could not expect "a government or religion calculated for the first order of created beings"; and in that sense any human government or religion must be imperfect. But there was no reason why man should not attain a *relative* perfection in these respects — "such a government and religion as shall be most expedient for the purposes of that set of beings for whose use they were instituted." [43]

The critic unwittingly put his finger here upon a significant tacit assumption in this and certain other applications of the principle. It is the peculiarity of man, these arguments implied, that while his powers and achievements are limited by the position which he occupies in the Scale of Being, he is capable of seeing beyond them and — for better or worse — of feeling dissatisfaction with them and therefore with himself. He is constitutionally discontented with his own nature and his place in the universal nature; and of this the saint, the mystic, the Platonic or the Stoic moralist, and the reformer, in their several ways gave evidence. But here again the principle of plenitude was subtly at war with itself. This perpetual discontent of man with his present constitution and status must after all be one of the differentiae of his species, a characteristic appropriate to his place in the scale. If it were not required by that place, how could he have come to possess it? But if it were required, it could not in consistency be condemned; and its existence at just this point in the best of possible worlds might even be taken as an indication that man, at least, was not intended to occupy forever the *same* place, that the scale is literally a ladder to be ascended, not only by the imagination but in fact. We shall presently see the argument taking this turn. But the less cheerful interpreter of the principle of plenitude could, no doubt, have replied that the specific and defining defect of man consists precisely in his being the creature whose destiny it is to have visions of perfections which he cannot possess and of virtues which he is nevertheless constitutionally incapable of attaining. For this too is one of the possible kinds of creature; must not, then, a full universe contain even this tragic breed of Icarus? Is not this, indeed, the natural and immutable consequence of just that middle place which was traditionally assigned him — a being at once of flesh and spirit, an intermediate species between the purely animal and the rational kind?

3. There was more than one way, however, in which the principles embodied in the cosmological conception of the Chain of Being could be used as weapons against social discontent and especially against all equalitarian movements. The universe, it was assumed, is the best of systems; any other system is good

only in so far as it is constructed upon the same principles; and the object of the Infinite Wisdom which had fashioned it was to attain the maximum of variety by means of inequality. Clearly, then, human society is well constituted only if, within its own limits, it tends to the realization of the same desiderata. This was, of course, the point of the famous dictum of Pope's which has so often been misapplied for the annoyance of little boys and girls:

> Order is Heav'n's first law; and this confest,
> Some are, and must be, greater than the rest,
> More rich, more wise.[44]

This was no casual piece of Toryism on Pope's part; that "Order," that is, hierarchic gradation, is everywhere required by the divine Reason, is a fundamental premise of the argument for optimism in the *Essay on Man*. The doctrine of the Chain of Being thus gave a metaphysical sanction to the injunction of the Anglican catechism: each should labor truly "to do his duty in that state of life" — whether in the cosmical or the social scale — "to which it shall please God to call him." To seek to leave one's place in society is also "to invert the laws of Order." "Cease, then, nor Order imperfection name." Any demand for equality, in short, is "contrary to nature."

Nor was Pope at all original in suggesting this politico-social moral. Leibniz had similarly pointed out the parallel between the best of possible worlds and the best of possible societies:

> Inequality of conditions is not to be counted among evils (*désordres*), and M. Jacquelot rightly asks those who would have all things equally perfect, why rocks are not crowned with leaves or why ants are not peacocks. If equality were everywhere requisite, the poor man would set up his claim to it against the rich man, the valet against his master.[45]

The argument could, it is true, be worked from either end; to those who needed no persuasion to believe that there must be higher and lower ranks in society, this premise could be invoked to justify to man God's plan in the creation. It was in this latter way that Edmund Law reasoned:

> 'Tis impossible all should be rulers and none subjects. From this example we see how the relations which creatures have to one another may put a restraint even on infinite Power, so that it will be a contradiction for them,

while they keep the nature which they have at present, to be in some respects otherwise disposed than they are now, nor can all of the same order be gratified with the same conveniences.[46]

The analogy between the macrocosm and the social microcosm was put still more fully and naïvely by Soame Jenyns:

> The universe resembles a large and well-regulated family, in which all the officers and servants, and even the domestic animals, are subservient to each other in a proper subordination; each enjoys the privileges and perquisites peculiar to his place, and at the same time contributes, by that just subordination, to the magnificence and happiness of the whole.[47]

While this analogy thus served to justify the complacency of those to whom the existing order of society was a very comfortable one, it was, doubtless, a relatively small factor in political thought in the eighteenth century. And it is to be remembered that there was another implication of the accepted scheme of the universe which qualified, though it did not contradict, this mode of conservative apologetics. Subordination, indeed, was essential; but it was a subordination without subservience. No creature's existence, as we have seen, was merely instrumental to the well-being of those above it in the scale. Each had its own independent reason for being; in the final account, none was more important than any other; and each, therefore, had its own claim to respect and consideration from its superiors, its own right to live its own life and to possess all that might be needful to enable it to fulfill the functions and enjoy "the privileges and perquisites" of its station. This dual aspect of the conception — which still, it must be confessed, remained more gratifying to the higher than consoling to the lower ranks — was duly set forth in verse of an appropriate quality:

> Wise Providence
> Does various parts for various minds dispense;
> The meanest slaves or they who hedge and ditch,
> Are useful, by their sweat, to feed the rich;
> The rich, in due return, impart their store,
> Which comfortably feeds the lab'ring poor.
> Nor let the rich the lowest slave disdain,
> He's equally a link of nature's chain;
> Labours to the same end, joins in one view,
> And both alike the will divine pursue.[48]

# VII

## THE PRINCIPLE OF PLENITUDE AND EIGHTEENTH-CENTURY OPTIMISM

The common thesis of eighteenth-century optimists was, as is notorious, the proposition that this is the best of possible worlds; and this fact, together with the connotation which the term "optimism" has come to assume in popular usage, has given rise to the belief that the adherents of this doctrine must have been exuberantly cheerful persons, fatuously blind to the realities of human experience and of human nature, or insensible to all the pain and frustration and conflict which are manifest through the entire range of sentient life. Yet there was in fact nothing in the optimist's creed which logically required him either to blink or to belittle the facts which we ordinarily call evil. So far from asserting the unreality of evils, the philosophical optimist in the eighteenth century was chiefly occupied in demonstrating their necessity. To assert that this is the best of possible worlds implies nothing as to the absolute goodness of this world; it implies only that any other world which is metaphysically capable of existence would be worse. The reasoning of the optimist was directed less to showing how much of what men commonly reckon good there is in the world of reality than to showing how little of it there is in the world of possibility — in that eternal logical order which contains the Ideas of all things possible and compossible, which the mind of God was conceived to have contemplated "before the creation," and by the necessities of which, ineluctable even by Omnipotence, his creative power was restricted.

At bottom, indeed, optimism had much in common with that Manichaean dualism, against Bayle's defence of which so many of the theodicies were directed. Optimism too, as Leibniz acknowledged, had its two antagonistic "principles." The rôle of the "evil principle" was simply assigned to the divine reason, which imposed singular impediments upon the benevolent intentions of the divine will.  The very ills which Bayle had argued must be attributed to the interference of a species of extraneous Anti-God, for whose existence and hostility to the good no rational explanation could be given, were by the optimist attributed to a necessity inhering in the nature of things; and it was questionable whether this was not the less cheerful view of the two.  For it was possible to hope that in the fullness of time the Devil might be put under foot, and believers in revealed religion were assured that he would be; but logical necessities are eternal, and the evils which arise from them must therefore be perpetual.  Thus eighteenth-century optimism not only had affinities with the dualism to which it was supposed to be antithetic, but the arguments of its advocates at times sounded strangely like those of the pessimist — a type by no means unknown in the period.[1]  The moral was different, but the view of the concrete facts of experience was sometimes very much the same; since it was the optimist's contention that evil — and a great deal of it — is involved in the general constitution of things, he found it to his purpose to dilate, on occasion, upon the magnitude of the sum of evil and upon the depth and breadth of its penetration into life.  It is thus, for example, that Soame Jenyns, in one of the typical theodicies of the middle of the century, seeks to persuade us of the admirable rationality of the cosmic plan:

> I am persuaded that there is something in the abstract nature of pain conducive to pleasure; that the sufferings of individuals are absolutely necessary to universal happiness. . . .  Scarce one instance, I believe, can be produced of the acquisition of pleasure or convenience by any creatures, which is not purchased by the previous or consequential sufferings of themselves or others.  Over what mountains of slain is every mighty empire rolled up to the summit of prosperity and luxury, and what new scenes of desolation attend its fall?  To what infinite toil of men, and other animals, is every flourishing city indebted for all the conveniences and enjoyments of life, and what vice and misery do those very equipments introduce? . . .  The pleasures annexed to the preservation of ourselves are both preceded and followed by numberless sufferings; preceded by massacres and tortures of various animals preparatory to a feast, and followed by as many diseases lying wait in every dish to pour forth vengeance on their destroyers.[2]

This gloomy rhetoric was perfectly consistent in principle with optimism, and it manifested at least one natural tendency of the champions of that doctrine; for the more numerous and monstrous the evils to be explained, the greater was the triumph when the author of a theodicy explained them.

The argument, indeed, in some of its more naïve expressions tends to beget in the reader a certain pity for an embarrassed Creator, infinitely well-meaning, but tragically hampered by "necessities in the nature of things" in his efforts to make a good world. What could be more pathetic than the position in which — as Soame Jenyns authoritatively informs us — Omnipotence found itself when contemplating the creation of mankind?

> Our difficulties arise from our forgetting how many difficulties Omnipotence has to contend with: in the present instance it is obliged either to afflict innocence or be the cause of wickedness; it has plainly no other option.[3]

In short the writings of the optimists afforded abundant ground for Voltaire's exclamation:

> Vous criez "Tout est bien" d'une voix lamentable!

Voltaire's chief complaint of these philosophers in the *Poem on the Lisbon Disaster* was not, as has often been supposed, that they were too indecently cheerful, that their view of the reality of evil was superficial; his complaint was that they were too depressing, that they made the actual evils we experience appear yet worse by representing them as inevitable and inherent in the permanent structure of the universe.

> Non, ne présentez plus à mon coeur agité
> Ces immuables lois de la nécessité!

An evil unexplained seemed to Voltaire more endurable than the same evil explained, when the explanation consisted in showing that from all eternity the avoidance of just that evil had been, and through all eternity the avoidance of others like it would be, logically inconceivable.[4] In this his own feeling, and his assumption about the psychology of the emotions in other men, were precisely opposite to Spinoza's, who believed that everything becomes endurable to us when we once see clearly that it never could have been otherwise: *quatenus mens res omnes ut necessarias intelligit, eatenus minus ab affectibus patitur.*[5] Though most of the optimistic writers of the eighteenth century were less thorough-going or less frank in their cosmical determinism than Spinoza, such philosophic consolation as they offered was at bottom the same as his. It was an essentially intellectual consolation; the mood that it was usually designed to produce was that of reasoned acquiescence in the inevitable, based upon a conviction that its inevitableness was absolute and due to no arbitrary caprice; or, at a higher pitch, a devout willingness to be damned — that is, to be as much damned as one was — for the better demonstration of the reasonableness of the general scheme of things. Whether confronted with physical or with moral evils, wrote Pope, "to reason well is to submit"; and again:

> Know thy own point; this kind, this due degree,
> Of blindness, weakness, Heaven bestows on thee.
> Submit!

It is, of course, true that the optimistic writers were eager to show that good comes out of evil; but what it was indispensable for them to establish was that it could come in no other way. It is true, also, that they were wont, when they reached the height of their argument, to discourse with eloquence on the perfection of the Universal System as a whole; but that perfection in no way implied either the happiness or the excellence of the finite parts of the system. On the contrary, the fundamental and characteristic premise of the usual proof of optimism was the proposition that the perfection of the whole depends upon, indeed consists in, the existence of every possible degree of imperfection in the parts. Voltaire, once more, summarized the argument not altogether unjustly when he wrote:

> Vous composerez dans ce chaos fatal
> Des malheurs de chaque être un bonheur général.

The essence of the optimist's enterprise was to find the evidence of the "goodness" of the universe not in the paucity but rather in the multiplicity of what to the unphilosophic mind appeared to be evils.

All this can best be shown by an analysis of the argument in its logical sequence, as it is set forth in the earliest and, perhaps, when both its direct and indirect influence are considered, the most influential, of eighteenth-century theodicies — the *De origine mali* (1702) of William King, then Bishop of Derry, afterwards Archbishop of Dublin. The original Latin work does not appear to have had wide currency; but in 1731 an English version appeared,[6] with copious additions, partly extracts from King's posthumous papers, partly original notes "tending to vindicate the author's principles against the objections of Bayle, Leibnitz, the author of a Philosophical Inquiry concerning Human Liberty, and others," by the translator, Edmund Law, subsequently Bishop of Carlisle. The translation went through five editions during Law's lifetime;[7] and it seems to have been much read and discussed. Law was a figure of importance in his day, being the spokesman of "the most latitudinarian position" in the Anglican theology of the time; and his academic dignities as Master of Peterhouse and Knightbridge Professor of Moral Philosophy at Cambridge in the 1750's and 60's doubtless increased the range of his influence.[8] There can hardly be much doubt that it was largely from the original work of King that Pope derived, directly or through Bolingbroke, the conceptions which, rearranged with curious incoherency, served for his vindication of optimism in the First Epistle of the *Essay on Man*;[9] for it is unlikely that Pope derived them from their fountain-head, the *Enneads* of Plotinus.

It can by no means be said that King begins his reflection on the subject by putting on rose-tinted spectacles. He recognizes from the outset all the facts which seem most incompatible with an optimistic view: the "perpetual war between the elements, between animals, between men"; "the errors, miseries and vices" which are "the constant companions of human life from its infancy"; the prosperity of the wicked and the suffering of the righteous. There are "troops of miseries marching through human life." And King is innocent of the amazing superficiality of Milton's theodicy; while he, too, assumes the freedom of the will, he sees clearly that this assumption can touch only a fraction of the problem. Not all evils are "external, or acquired by our choice"; many of them proceed from the constitution of Nature itself.[10]    The dualistic doctrine of

Bayle, while it, too, has the advantage of "acquitting God of all manner of blame," is philosophically an "absurd hypothesis." King, in short, is to attribute evil, not — at least not primarily nor chiefly — either to the mysterious perversity of man's will or to the machinations of the Devil; he is to show its necessity from a consideration of the nature of deity itself. His undertaking is nothing less than that of facing all the evils of existence and showing them to be "not only consistent with infinite wisdom, goodness and power, but necessarily resulting from them." [11]

The traditional division of evils into three classes — evils of limitation or imperfection, "natural" evils, and moral evils — provides the general scheme of the argument, which is, in brief, that there could not conceivably have been any creation at all without the first sort of evil; and that all of the second sort, at least, follow with strict logical necessity from the first. Even Omnipotence could not create its own double; if any beings other than God were to exist they must in the nature of the case be differentiated from him through the "evil of defect" — and, as is assumed, be differentiated from one another by the diversity of their defects. Evil, in short, is primarily privation; and privation is involved in the very concept of all beings except one. This Law puts in the terms of Aristotelian and Scholastic philosophy in his summary of King's "scheme":

All creatures are necessarily imperfect, and at infinite distance from the perfection of the Deity, and if a negative principle were admitted, such as the Privation of the Peripatetics, it might be said that every created being consists of existence and non-existence; for it is nothing in respect both of those perfections which it wants, and of those which others have. And this . . . mixture of non-entity in the constitution of created beings is the necessary principle of all natural evils, and of a possibility of moral ones.[12]

In other words, in King's own phrase, "a creature is descended from God, a most perfect Father; but from Nothing as its Mother, which is Imperfection." And the virtually dualistic character of this conception is shown by the fact that the inferior parent, in spite of the purely negative rôle which appeared to be implied by her name, was conceived to be responsible for many seemingly highly positive peculiarities of the offspring. This, however, was felt to be an unobjectionable dualism, partly because the second or evil principle was *called* "Nothing," and partly because its existence as a factor in the world, and the effects of it, could be regarded as logically necessary and not as a mysterious accident.

But the significant issue did not lie in this simple, almost tautological piece of reasoning. Doubtless, if the Absolute Being was not to remain forever in the solitude of his own perfection, the prime evil of limitation or imperfection must characterize whatever other beings he brought forth. But that evil was not thereby justified unless it were shown, or assumed, that the creation of such other, necessarily defective beings is itself a good. This crucial Plotinian assumption King unhesitatingly makes, as well as a further assumption which seems far from self-evident. Even if it were granted that it is good that *some* beings other than God, some finite and imperfect natures, should exist, would it not (some might ask) have been less irrational that only the highest grade of imperfection should be generated — as had, indeed, been originally the case, according to an account of the creation supported by a considerable weight of authority in the theological tradition of Christianity, and comparatively recently revived by Milton?[13] If God could be supposed to need company — which it seemed philosophically a paradox and was theologically a heresy to admit — should it not at least have been good company, a *civitas dei* composed wholly of pure spirits? King saw no way of achieving a satisfactory theodicy unless this latter question were answered (again with the support of many ancient and medieval writers) in the negative. It was requisite to show that not only imperfection in general, but every one of the observable concrete imperfections of the actual world, ought to have been created; and this could not be shown unless it were laid down as a premise that it is inherently and absolutely good that *every* kind of thing (however far down in the scale of possibles) should actually be, so far as its existence is logically conceivable, i. e., involves no contradiction.

This proposition then — expressed in theological terminology — was the essential thesis in the argument for optimism propounded by King and Law. There is inherent in the divine essence, as an element in God's perfection, a special attribute of "goodness," which makes it necessary that all other and less excellent essences down to the very lowest — so far as they are severally and jointly possible — shall have actual existence after their kind.

God might, indeed, have refrained from creating, and continued alone, self-sufficient and perfect to all eternity; but his infinite Goodness would by no means allow it; this obliged him to produce external things; which things, since they could not possibly be perfect, the Divine Goodness preferred imperfect ones to none at all. Imperfection, then, arose from the infinity of Divine Goodness.[14]

And, thus committed by his own nature to the impartation of actual being to some imperfect essences, God could not refuse the boon of existence to any:

If you say, God might have omitted the more imperfect beings, I grant it, and if that had been best, he would undoubtedly have done it. But it is the part of infinite Goodness to choose the very best; from thence it proceeds, therefore, that the more imperfect beings have existence; for it was agreeable to that, not to omit the very least good that could be produced. Finite goodness might possibly have been exhausted in creating the greater beings, but infinite extends to all. . . . There must then be many, perhaps infinite, degrees of perfection in the divine works. . . . It was better not to give some so great a degree of happiness as their natures might receive, than that a whole species of being should be wanting to the world.[15]

Not only must all possible species enjoy existence, but, adds King's editor, "from the observation that there is no manner of chasm or void, no link deficient in this great Chain of Being, and the reason of it, it will appear extremely probable also that every distinct order, every class or species, is as full as the nature of it would permit, or [Law devoutly but, upon his own principles, tautologically adds] as God saw proper."

The foundation, then, of the usual eighteenth-century argument for optimism was the principle of plenitude. Since the principle had received expression from hundreds of writers before King, and had been the basis of both the Neoplatonic and the Scholastic theodicy, its utilization by later optimists is no evidence that they derived it from him. Nevertheless, for reasons already indicated, the probability remains that it was because of the reiteration and elaboration of the principle in the

*De origine mali* that Pope gave the fundamental place, in his own argument for the thesis that whatever is is right, to the premise that, in the "best of systems possible,"

> All must full or not coherent be,
> And all that rises, rise in due degree.

For the purposes of a theodicy, the principle of plenitude served most directly and obviously as an "explanation" of the "evil of defect." The limitations of each species of creature, which define its place in the scale, are indispensable to that infinite differentiation of things in which the "fullness" of the universe consists, and are therefore necessary to the realization of the greatest of goods. Man, therefore, cannot rationally complain because he lacks many endowments and means of enjoyment which might conceivably have been granted him. In Law's words:

> From the supposition of a Scale of Beings, gradually descending from perfection to nonentity, and complete in every intermediate rank and degree, we shall soon see the absurdity of such questions as these, Why was not man made more perfect? Why are not his faculties equal to those of angels? Since this is only asking why he was not placed in a different class of beings, when at the same time all other classes are supposed to be full.[16]

It was, in short, "necessary that the creature should fill the station wherein it was, or none at all." If he were anywhere else, he would not be the same entity; and if he did not exist at all, there would be a gap in the series, and the perfection of the creation would thereby be destroyed. Undeniably these distinguishing deficiencies "bring many inconveniences on the persons whose lot it is to fill that part of the universe which requires a creature of such an imperfect nature." For example, a man has no wings, a perfection granted to birds.

> 'Tis plain that in his present circumstances he cannot have them, and that the use of them would be very mischievous to society; and yet the want of them necessarily exposes us to many inconveniences. . . . A thousand instances may be given where the evil of imperfection necessarily subjects us to disappointment of appetite, and several other natural evils, which yet are all necessary for the common good.[17]

To this particular form of purely logical consolation Pope recurs repeatedly, with fairly evident dependence upon King.

In a "full" system "there must be, somewhere, such a rank as Man"; and the occupant of that rank cannot rationally desire the distinctive attributes of those below or those above him in the scale.[18]

> Why has not man a microscopic eye?
> For this plain reason, man is not a fly.

And (to repeat lines already quoted):

> On superior powers
> Were we to press, inferior might on ours;
> Or in the full creation leave a void,
> Where, one step broken, the great scale's destroyed.[19]

But if the principle of plenitude had been applicable only for the explanation of the "metaphysical" evil of limitation or particularity, it would not have carried the optimist far towards his goal. Most of the things we call evil hardly appear to be adequately describable as mere deficiencies. Even a Platonistic philosopher with a toothache will probably find it difficult to persuade himself that his pain is a wholly negative thing, a metaphysical vacuum consisting merely in the absence of some conceivable positive good. King was therefore forced to use some ingenuity — or rather, to utilize the ingenuity of his many precursors — in order to exhibit the numerous train of "natural" evils as equally necessary implications of the same fundamental principle. He seeks to do this, in the first place, on the ground that in a really "full" universe there must be opposition. Creatures necessarily crowd upon, restrict, and therefore come into conflict with, one another. This necessity appears in its primary form in the motion of matter. It was theoretically possible for God to have so disposed matter that it would move "uniformly and all together, either in a direct line or in a circle, and the contrariety of motions by that means be prevented." But a material system so simple and harmonious must also, we are assured, have been barren and useless.

Such a motion therefore was to be excited in it as would separate it into parts, make it fluid, and render it an habitation for animals. But that could not be without contrariety of motion, as any one that thinks of it at all will perceive. And if this be once admitted in matter, there necessarily follows a division and disparity of parts, clashing and opposition, comminution, concretion and repulsion, and all those evils which we behold in generation and corruption. . . . . The mutual clashing of these concretions could therefore not be avoided, and as they strike upon one another a concussion of the parts and a separation from each other would be necessarily produced, . . . [i. e.] corruption.[20]

And since man's place in the Scale of Being is that of a creature partly material, partly spiritual, he is necessarily involved in, and unhappily affected by, these collisions of matter. The preoccupation of the optimists with the notion of the "fullness" of the organic world sometimes led them (by a natural confusion of ideas) to draw an almost Darwinian or Malthusian picture of a Nature overcrowded with aspirants for life and consequently given over to a ubiquitous struggle for existence. King assures us that there is something like a housing problem even in Heaven.

If you ask why God does not immediately transplant men into heaven, since 'tis plain they are capable of that happier state; or why he confines them so long . . . on the earth as in a darksome prison, . . . I answer, Because the Heavens are already furnished with inhabitants, and cannot with convenience admit of new ones, till some of the present possessors depart to a better state, or make room some other way for these to change their condition.[21]

Into the further naïve reasonings by which King seeks to deduce the genesis of "pain, uneasiness and dread of death," and indirectly of the other emotions by which man is tormented, we need not enter. It suffices to quote the concise genealogy of woes in which he sums up his reasons for holding this to be the best of possible worlds:

Behold how evils spring from and multiply upon each other, while infinite Goodness still urges the Deity to do the very best. This moved him to give existence to creatures, which cannot exist without imperfections and inequality. This excited him to create matter, and to put it in motion, which is necessarily attended with separation and dissolution, generation and corruption. This persuaded him to couple souls with bodies, and to give them mutual affections, whence proceeded pain and sorrow, hatred and fear, with the rest of the passions, yet all of them . . . are necessary.[22]

Such an argument for optimism closely resembles, and might easily be substituted for, some of the formulas in which primitive Buddhism summed up the creed of pessimism.

The author of the most popular English theodicy of the mid-
nineteenth century found, as everyone remembers, peculiar
difficulty in the spectacle of "Nature red in tooth and claw
with ravin" — in the universal conflict, the daily and hourly
cruelties and little, dumb tragedies which are hidden behind
the surface beauty of every field and wood. But to the typical
eighteenth-century writer of a theodicy, even these aspects of
Nature gave little trouble. He was no more blind to them than
Tennyson; but his universal solvent, the principle of plenitude,
served him here as elsewhere. Doubtless, King granted, God
could have made a world free from these horrors, simply by
refraining from creating carnivorous and predacious animals.
But this, again, would have meant a world less full of life.

A being that has life is (*caeteris paribus*) preferable to one that has not;
God, therefore, animated that machine which furnishes out provision for
the more perfect animals; which was both graciously and providently
done: for by this means he gained so much life to the world as there is in
those animals which are food for others; for by this means they themselves
enjoy some kind of life, and are of service also to the rest. . . . Matter
which is fit for the nourishment of man, is also capable of life; if therefore
God had denied it life, he had omitted a degree of good which might have
been produced without any impediment to his principal design, which does
not seem very agreeable to infinite goodness. 'Tis better, therefore, that
it should be endowed with life for a time, though 'tis to be devoured afterwards, than to continue totally stupid and unactive. . . . Let us not be
surprised, then, at the universal war as it were among animals, or that the
stronger devour the weaker.[23]

The application of this to the special case of domesticated animals reared for slaughter, which furnished Pope with the
theme for some characteristic and detestable lines, was also
made by King. Man

> Feasts the animal he dooms his feast,
> And, till he ends the being, makes it blest.

Undeniably the carnivora were among the antecedently
possible kinds of creatures; and if the excellence of Nature or
its Author consists quite simply in having as many kinds as
possible, nothing more need be said in justification of the existence of such animals; in the words of another contemporary
divine, quoted with admiration by Law, "it is evident that by
this means there is room for more whole species of creatures

than there otherwise would be, and that the variety of the creation is thereby very much enlarged and the goodness of its Author displayed." [24] The tendency of the theodicies to promote belief in the blessedness of sheer multitude, the all-importance of having an abundance of "different natures" in the world, at whatever cost, could hardly be better illustrated.

But even if the criterion of the goodness of the universe were assumed to consist, not solely in the diversity of creatures, but in the quantity of the *joie de vivre* it contains, the creation of beasts of prey could still, according to a further argument of King's, be justified. "Animals are of such a nature as to delight in action, or in the exercise of their faculties, nor can we have any other notion of happiness even in God himself." But among the pleasurable activities conceivable before the creation were those which might attach to the procuring of food by predatory creatures. Why, then, should these intense and positive pleasures be lacking, merely that feebler kinds might be spared the transitory pains of being pursued and eaten? Clearly, since "the infinite Power of God was able to produce animals of such capacities," his "infinite Goodness" may "be conceived to have almost compelled him not to refuse or envy (them) the benefit of life." "If you insist," says the archbishop genially to a supposititious critic, "that a lion might have been made without teeth or claws, a viper without venom; I grant it, as a knife without an edge; but then they would have been of quite another species [i. e., there would have been a missing link in the Chain of Being], and have had neither the nature, nor use, nor genius, which they now enjoy." As for the lion's victim, if it were a rational animal it doubtless would, or at all events should, rejoice as does its Maker in the thought of the agreeable exercise which it is affording the "genius" of the lion. If the victim be not endowed with reason, or be too mean-spirited to take a large philosophical view of the matter, the consoling insight into the higher meaning of its sufferings is still, through the happy ordering of things, left to be enjoyed vicariously by optimistic archbishops. [25]

Plainly this amiable and devout ecclesiastic had, in the course of his endeavor to justify God's ways to men, been

driven not only to a conception of God but also to a conception of ultimate values which came somewhat strangely from a
Christian teacher. Though King would, of course, have said
that his God was a God of love, the term must necessarily have
had for him an unusual sense. The God of the *De origine mali*
loved abundance and variety of life more than he loved peace
and concord among his creatures and more than he desired
their exemption from pain. He loved lions, in short, as well as
lambs; and loving lions, he wished them to behave in accordance with the "nature," or Platonic Idea, of a lion, which implies devouring lambs and not lying down with them. And in
these preferences the "goodness" of God was assumed to be
most clearly manifested — "goodness" thus meaning chiefly a
delight in fullness and diversity of finite being, rather than in
harmony and happiness. King and his editor seem only occasionally and confusedly aware how deeply their argument has
involved them in such a radical transvaluation of values; they
waver between this and the more conventional conception of
"divine goodness," and for the most part touch but lightly
upon the more paradoxical implications of their premises.
Yet they at times betray some uneasy feeling of the incongruity between these premises and certain traditional elements
of Christian belief. It was, for example, a part of that belief
that in the earthly paradise before the Fall, and also in the
celestial paradise which awaits the elect, most of the evils
which these theologians were zealously proving to be "necessary," because required by the "divine goodness," were in fact
absent. It seemed, therefore, difficult to avoid the awkward
dilemma that either the paradisaical state is not good, or else a
good "system" does not, after all, require quite so much evil
and so many degrees of imperfection as the authors of the
theodicies conceived. King meets this difficulty but lamely;
he is, in fact, driven to suggest that the felicity of our first
parents in Eden has probably been somewhat exaggerated:
"it doth not appear that Adam in Paradise was altogether
without pain or passion," but rather "that he was only secured
from such pains as might cause his death, and that for a time,
till removed to a better place." [26]

The outcome of King's reasoning (so far as it was consistently carried through) is not, of course, surprising. He who attempts a theodicy without first shutting his eyes to a large range of the facts of experience, must necessarily take for the object of his piety the God of Things as They Are; and since things as they are include the whole countless troop of natural ills, it became necessary so to transform the conception of good as to make it possible to argue that these ills are — not, indeed, goods, considered by themselves, but implicates of some supreme good, in the realization of which the essential nature of deity is most truly manifested. The principle of plenitude, taken as a species of value-theory, was a natural, if not the necessary, result of this enforced revision of the notion of good. Certainly that which the author of Nature as it is chiefly values could not, on empirical grounds, be supposed to be identical with those things which men have commonly set their hearts upon and have pictured to themselves in their dreams of paradise. Stated in its most general terms, the paradox underlying all these singular implications of the optimist's reasoning is the assumption which is of the essence of the principle of plenitude itself — that *the desirability of a thing's existence bears no relation to its excellence.*

King's further reflections upon the problem of evil do not concern us here, since the conception of the Chain of Being does not much figure in them. It might, indeed, and with more consistency, have done so. For the sort of evil not dealt with by King upon the principles already indicated, namely, moral evil, might naturally have been regarded as a special case of the "evil of defect." A creature having the specific degree of blindness and weakness appropriate to man's place in the scale, and at the same time subject to the passions which King had represented as necessarily inseparable from our psychophysical constitution, could hardly fail, it would seem, to make frequent "wrong elections."* So much, indeed, King is constrained to admit; there are many errors of conduct which are due to our ignorance and necessary imperfection, and these are to be classed among the "natural evils" and explained in the same manner as others of that class. But there remains a residuum of "moral evil" not so explicable, but due to a "depraved will." On this theme King for the most part repeats the familiar arguments. Bolingbroke did not follow the archbishop in this, but derived the necessity of moral evil directly from the principle of plenitude. If men had been so constituted as to follow always the ethical "law of nature, . . . the moral state of mankind would have been paradisaical, but it would not have been human. We should not have been the creatures we were designed to be, and a gap would have been left in the order of created intelligences." [27] In this application of the principle, the antinomian implications of which are sufficiently obvious, Bolingbroke had been anticipated by so saintly a philosopher as Spinoza:

> To those who ask, Why has not God created all men such as to be directed solely by the guidance of reason, I reply only that it is because he had no lack of material wherewith to create all things, from the very highest to the very lowest grade of perfection, or, more properly speaking, because the laws of his nature were so ample as to suffice for the production of everything that can be conceived by an infinite intellect.[28]

This was carrying a step farther the argument which Pope was to versify: since the best of systems must be as "full" as possible,

> Then in the scale of reasoning life, 'tis plain,
> There must be somewhere such a rank as —

not man only, but also, among men, the fool and the evil-doer.

The theodicy of Leibniz was in most essentials the same as that of his English precursor; [29] and in summarizing with approval the main argument of the archbishop's *bel ouvrage*, *plein de savoir et d'élégance*, Leibniz significantly accentuated the theological paradox contained in it:

> Why, someone asks, did not God refrain from creating things altogether? The author well replies that the abundance of God's goodness is the reason. He wished to communicate himself, even at the expense of that delicacy which our imaginations ascribe to him, when we assume that imperfections shock him. Thus he preferred that the imperfect should exist, rather than nothing.[30]

In this emphasis upon the implication that the Creator of the actual world cannot be supposed to be a "delicate" or squeamish God, caring only for perfection — and that, in fact, he would, if more nicely selective in his act of creation, have thereby shown himself the less divine — the consequence latent from the first in the principle of plenitude is put with unusual vividness and candor; and in general, the German philosopher, in developing the theory of value thus implicit in optimism, is franker, more ardent, and more cheerful than the Anglican theologian. Some analogies in human life to the standards of valuation which the optimists had applied in explaining the supposed purpose of the deity in the creation are not obscurely suggested by Leibniz.

Wisdom requires variety (*la sagesse doit varier*). To multiply exclusively the same thing, however noble it be, would be a superfluity; it would be a kind of poverty. To have a thousand well-bound copies of Vergil in your library; to sing only airs from the opera of Cadmus and Hermione; to break all your porcelain in order to have only golden cups; to have all your buttons made of diamonds; to eat only partridges and to drink only the wine of Hungary or of Shiraz — could any one call this reasonable?[31]

Something very similar to this had, in point of fact, been regarded as the essence of reasonableness both by neo-classical aesthetic theorists and by a multitude of influential moralists. It would scarcely have seemed evident to the former that two copies of Vergil are of less value than one copy *plus* a copy of the worst epic ever written — still less that a reading of the first followed by a reading of the second is preferable to two readings of Vergil. And the apparent object of the endeavor of most ethical teaching had been to produce a close approach to uniformity in human character and behavior, and in men's political and social institutions. The desire for variety — or for change, the temporal form of it — had rather commonly been conceived to be a non-rational, indeed a pathological, idiosyncrasy of human creatures. But Leibniz not only gave it a sort of cosmic dignity by attributing it to God himself, but also represented it as the very summit of rationality.

The ethically significant consequence which is most plainly drawn from this by Leibniz is that neither what is commonly called moral goodness, nor pleasure, is the most important thing in the world. Both hedonism, in short, and an abstract moralism (such, for example, as Kant and Fichte were afterwards to express) were equally contrary to the value-theory implicit in the principle of plenitude. Virtue and happiness both, of course, have their place in the scale of values; but if it were the highest place, it is inconceivable that God would have made the kind of world he has made.

The moral or physical good or evil of rational creatures does not infinitely transcend the good or evil which is purely metaphysical, that is to say, the good which consists in the perfection of the other creatures. . . . No substance is either absolutely precious or absolutely contemptible in the sight of God. It is certain that God attaches more importance to a man than to a lion, but I do not know that we can be sure that he prefers one man to the entire species of lions.[32]

To this thesis Leibniz reverts again and again in the *Théodicée*:

[It is] a false maxim that the happiness of rational creatures is the sole purpose of God. If that had been so, there would, perhaps, have been neither sin nor unhappiness, not even as concomitants. God would have chosen a set of possibles from which all evils were excluded. But he would in that case have fallen short of what is due to the universe, that is, what is due to himself. . . . It is true that one can imagine possible worlds without sin and without suffering, just as one can invent romances about Utopias or about the Sévarambes; but these worlds would be much inferior to ours. I cannot show this in detail; you must infer it, as I do, *ab effectu*, since this world, as it is, is the world God chose. . . . Virtue is the noblest quality of created things, but it is not the only good quality of creatures. There is an infinite variety of others that attract the inclination of God; it is from all these inclinations taken together that the greatest possible sum of good results; and there would be less good than there is if there were nothing but virtue, if only rational creatures existed. . . . Midas was less rich when he possessed only gold.[33]

Leibniz adds the trite aesthetic argument for the indispensability of contrasts in the production of beauty in a work of art, and, indeed, in the mere physical pleasure of the gustatory sense:

Sweet things become insipid if we eat nothing else; sharp, tart and even bitter things must be combined with them so as to stimulate the taste. He who has not tasted bitter things does not deserve sweet, and, indeed, will not appreciate them.

Thus these subtle philosophers and grave divines, and the poets like Pope and Haller who popularized their reasonings, rested their assertion of the goodness of the universe ultimately upon the same ground as Stevenson's child in the nursery:

> The world is so full of a number of things.

This did not, it is true, necessarily make them "as happy as kings." That was a matter of individual temperament; and in point of fact most of them had not the child's robust delight in the sheer diversity and multiplicity of things. They were often men whose natural taste or training would have inclined them rather to prefer a somewhat thin, simple, and exclusive universe. The philosophers of optimism were not, in short, as a rule of a Romantic disposition; and what they were desirous of proving was that reality is rational through and through, that every fact of existence, however unpleasant, is grounded in some reason as clear and evident as an axiom of mathematics. But in the exigencies of their argument to this ambitious conclusion, they found themselves constrained to attribute to the Divine Reason a conception of the good extremely different from that which had been most current among men, and frequently among philosophers; and they were thus led, often against their original temper and intention, to impress upon the minds of their generation a revolutionary and paradoxical theory of the criterion of all value, which may be summed up in the words of a highly Romantic and optimistic lover of paradox in our own day:

> One thing alone is needful: Everything.
> The rest is vanity of vanities.

The results did not become fully apparent until the closing decade of the century.[34] Before we turn to them, we must note certain other new developments which had been taking place in the meantime in the history of our three principles.

# VIII

## THE CHAIN OF BEING AND SOME ASPECTS OF EIGHTEENTH-CENTURY BIOLOGY

No HISTORY of the biological sciences in the eighteenth century can be adequate which fails to keep in view the fact that, for most men of science throughout that period, the theorems implicit in the conception of the Chain of Being continued to constitute essential presuppositions in the framing of scientific hypotheses. But in those sciences, as in other provinces of thought, certain implications which had always been latent in these ancient assumptions now came to be more clearly recognized and more rigorously applied. In the present lecture we shall briefly note three aspects of eighteenth-century biological theory in which it was either affected by the general acceptance of the principles of continuity and plenitude, or in its turn tended to bring about a new interpretation of those principles. A still more important connection between the two will come before us in the following lecture.[1]

1. We have seen that there were present in the logic and the natural history of Aristotle, and therefore of the later Middle Ages, two opposite modes of thought. The first made for sharp divisions, clear-cut differentiations, among natural objects, and especially among living beings. To range animals and plants in well-defined species, presumably (since the Platonic dualism of realms of being was also still influential) corresponding to the distinctness of the Eternal Ideas, was the first business of the student of the organic world. The other tended to make the whole notion of species appear a convenient but artificial setting-up of divisions having no counterpart in nature. It was, on the whole, the former tendency that prevailed in early modern biology. In spite of the violent reaction of the astronomy, physics, and metaphysics of the Renaissance against the Aristotelian influence, in biology the doctrine of natural species continued to be potent — largely, no doubt, because it

seemed to be supported by observation. "It is principally from Aristotle," observes Daudin, "that are derived the traditional notions to which natural history was to give application, beginning with the Renaissance. . . . Thus it was that from the end of the sixteenth to the end of the eighteenth century, the project of distributing all living beings, animal or vegetable, into a hierarchy of collective units enclosed one within another, gained such a hold upon naturalists, that it finally seemed to them the formulation of their scientific task." The first of the great modern systematists, Cesalpino, was a sixteenth-century enthusiast for the Peripatetic philosophy, and it seems to have been largely a fresh study of Aristotle's logical and scientific writings that set him upon the undertaking which he executed in his *De Plantis* (1583). It is true that most of the elaborate "systems" (as they were called) which were the most monumental products of biological science in the seventeenth and early eighteenth centuries, were avowedly, in great part, "artificial" classifications. But the assumption that there really are "natural species, established by the Author of Nature" continued to be generally held; and natural species were, of course, fixed species. And even the artificial systems tended to give the notion of species a peculiar prominence in scientific thought, to encourage the habit of thinking of organisms, and of other natural objects, as falling into well-differentiated classes, rather than as members of a qualitative continuum.

There were, nevertheless, at work in the thought of both these centuries two ideas which tended increasingly to discredit the whole notion of species. The first, which is less closely related to our general subject, was the semi-nominalistic strain in the philosophy of Locke. In the Sixth Chapter of Book III of the *Essay concerning Human Understanding* he had granted that there are "real essences" — by which he chiefly meant "natures" or attributes of which the "ideas" imply the ideas of other attributes necessarily and *a priori*, so that one such "nature" is intrinsically incapable of separation from another. In so far as this is the case, there arise class-concepts of which the definitions are inherent in the nature of things, not arbitrary and contingent.[2] With these real essences Locke believed that the Creator certainly must be, and the angels possibly may be, acquainted; but to us mortals knowledge of them has (with the exception of the essences of mathematical figures and perhaps of moral properties) not been imparted; and our conceptions of species are therefore merely "nominal essences," combinations of ideas of attributes put together by the mind and corresponding to no fixed objective and inherent division between natural things. "Our distinguishing substances into species by names is not at all founded on their real essences; nor can we pretend to range and determine them exactly into species, according to essential internal differences." [3] "I do not deny," says Locke, "but nature, in the constant production of particular beings, makes them not always new and various, but very much alike and of kin to one another; but I think it nevertheless true that the boundaries of species, whereby men sort them, are made by men." And thus biological classifications are but verbal, and relative to varying considerations of convenience in the use of language. Locke is unable to see "why a shock [a breed of shaggy dog] and a hound are not as distinct species as a spaniel and an elephant," . . . "so uncertain are the boundaries of species of animals to us." [4] Even the nominal essence "man" is a term of vague and fluctuating import, which cannot be supposed to correspond to "precise and unmovable boundaries set by nature." It is, in fact, "plain that there is no such thing made by nature, and established by her amongst men." [5] It is, then, only by virtue of some arbitrary definition framed by us "that we can say: This is a man, this is a drill," [6] i. e., a baboon; "and in this, I think, consists the whole business of *genus* and *species*."

But it is evident from much that has been already said that the principle of continuity tended equally directly to the same conclusion; and it did so even more potently because it had a still greater body of tradition behind it, and because both of the philosophers who exercised most influence in the early and middle eighteenth century, Leibniz and Locke, had made so much of it. The result was a rejection of the concept of species by some of the greatest naturalists of that age. Buffon in the opening discourse of the *Histoire Naturelle* (1749) attacked the entire enterprise of the systematists. There is, he declared, "an error in metaphysics" underlying all attempts to find a "natural" definition of species and thereby to arrive at a "natural" system of classification. "The error consists in a failure to understand nature's processes (*marche*), which always take place by gradations (*nuances*). . . . It is possible to descend by almost insensible degrees from the most perfect creature to the most formless matter. . . . These imperceptible shadings are the great work of nature; they are to be found not only in the sizes and the forms, but also in the movements, the generations and the successions of every species. . . . [Thus] nature, proceeding by unknown gradations, cannot wholly lend herself to these divisions [into genera and species]. . . . There will be found a great number of intermediate species, and of objects belonging half in one class and half in another. Objects of this sort, to which it is impossible to assign a place, necessarily render vain the attempt at a universal system." The notion of species, then, Buffon concludes, is an artificial and for the biologist a mischievous one:

> In general, the more one increases the number of one's divisions, in the case of the products of nature, the nearer one comes to the truth; since in reality individuals alone exist in nature.[7]

Buffon, it is true, soon abandoned this position. In the infertility of hybrids he imagined that he had found a proof that species are objective and fundamental realities — are, indeed, "*les seuls êtres de la Nature,* as ancient and as permanent as Nature herself," while "an individual, of whatever species, is nothing in the universe." A species is "a whole independent of number, independent of time; a whole always living, always the same; a whole which was counted as one among the works of the creation, and therefore constitutes a single unit in the creation." [8] Though he subsequently wavered somewhat on this matter, his supposed discovery of a scientific test of difference of "real" species did much for a time to counteract the tendency to which he had at first given his powerful support.[9] But Bonnet took up the strain which Buffon had abandoned. Repeating the customary phraseology about the continuity of the chain, Bonnet unequivocally draws the consequence that there are no such things as species:

If there are no cleavages in nature, it is evident that our classifications are not hers. Those which we form are purely nominal, and we should regard them as means relative to our needs and to the limitations of our knowledge. Intelligences higher than ours perhaps recognize between two individuals which we place in the same species more varieties than we discover between two individuals of widely separate genera. Thus these intelligences see in the scale of our world as many steps as there are individuals.[10]

Goldsmith, who, it will be remembered, was the author of a popular compendium of natural history, adopted and helped to diffuse this doctrine of the scientific inadmissibility of the concept of species: all "divisions" among the objects of nature "are perfectly arbitrary. The gradation from one order of beings to another, is so imperceptible, that it is impossible to lay the line that shall distinctly mark the boundaries of each. All such divisions as are made among the inhabitants of this globe, like the circles drawn by astronomers on its surface, are the work, not of nature, but of ourselves." [11] Numerous other illustrations might be given, but it would be tedious to multiply them.

Thus the general habit of thinking in terms of species, as well as the sense of the separation of man from the rest of the animal creation, was beginning to break down in the eighteenth century. In an age in which, more than in any preceding period, the principle of continuity was reckoned among the first and fundamental truths, it could not have been otherwise. And the change was a pregnant one for science and for other provinces of thought.

2. Even for those biologists who did not explicitly reject the belief in natural species, the principle of continuity was not barren of significant consequences. It set naturalists to looking for forms which would fill up the apparently "missing links" in the chain. Critics of the biological form of this assumption attacked it largely on the ground that many links which the hypothesis required *were* missing. But the more accepted view was that these gaps are only apparent; they were due, as Leibniz had declared, only to the incompleteness of the knowledge of nature then attained, or to the minute size of many of the — presumably lower — members of the series. The metaphysical assumption thus furnished a program for

scientific research. It was therefore highly stimulating to the work of the zoologist and the botanist, and especially to that of the microscopist, in the eighteenth century. Every discovery of a new form could be regarded, not as the disclosure of an additional unrelated fact in nature, but as a step towards the completion of a systematic structure of which the general plan was known in advance, an additional bit of empirical evidence of the truth of the generally accepted and cherished scheme of things. Thus the theory of the Chain of Being, purely speculative and traditional though it was, had upon natural history in this period an effect somewhat similar to that which the table of the elements and their atomic weights has had upon chemical research in the past half-century. The general program of the Royal Society, wrote its first historian (1667), in an interesting passage in which Platonistic and Baconian motives are conjoined, was to discover unknown facts of nature in order to range them properly in their places in the Chain of Being, and at the same time to make this knowledge useful to man.

Such is the dependence amongst all the orders of creatures; the animate, the sensitive, the rational, the natural, the artificial; that the apprehension of one of them, is a good step towards the understanding of the rest. And this is the highest pitch of humane reason: to follow all the links of this chain, till all their secrets are open to our minds; and their works advanc'd or imitated by our hands. This is truly to command the world; to rank all the varieties and degrees of things so orderly upon one another; that standing on the top of them, we may perfectly behold all that are below, and make them all serviceable to the quiet and peace and plenty of Man's life. And to this happiness there can be nothing else added: but that we make a second advantage of this rising ground, thereby to look the nearer into heaven. . . .[12]

The *Encyclopédie* in the middle of the eighteenth century also, though in a less devout tone, dwelt upon this as the program of the advancement of knowledge: Since "everything in nature is linked together," since "beings are connected with one another by a chain of which we perceive some parts as continuous, though in the greater number of points the continuity escapes us," the "art of the philosopher consists in adding new links to the separated parts, in order to reduce the distance between them as much as possible. But we must not flatter ourselves that gaps will not still remain in many places." [13]    It was, in the eyes of the eighteenth century, a great moment in the history of science when Trembley in 1739 rediscovered the fresh-water polyp *Hydra* (it had already been observed by Leeuwenhoek), this creature being at once hailed as the long-sought missing link between plants and animals — for which Aristotle's vague zoophytes were no longer considered quite sufficient. This and similar discoveries in turn served to strengthen the faith in plenitude and continuity as *a priori* rational laws of nature; and the greater credit, it was some-times remarked, was due to those who, not having seen, yet had believed in these principles. The chief glory, said a Ger-man popularizer of science, à *propos* of Trembley's work, is that "of the German Plato [Leibniz], who did not live to know of the actual observation" of this organism, "yet through his just confidence in the fundamental principles which he had learned from nature herself, had predicted it before his death." [14]

The quest of organisms not yet actually observed which would fill these lacunae was prosecuted with especial zeal at two points in the scale: near the bottom of it, and in the interval between man and the higher apes. "Nature," remarked Bon-net, "seems to make a great leap in passing from the vegetable to the fossil [i. e., rock]; there are no bonds, no links known to us, which unite the vegetable and the mineral kingdoms. But shall we judge of the chain of beings by our present knowl-edge? Because we discover some interruptions, some gaps in it here and there, shall we conclude that these gaps are real? . . . The gap that we find between the vegetable and the mineral will apparently some day be filled up. There was a similar gap between the animal and the vegetable; the polyp has come to fill it and to demonstrate the admirable gradation there is between all beings."

But the program of discovering the hitherto unobserved links in the chain played a part of especial importance in the beginnings of the science of anthropology. The close simi-larity in skeletal structure between the apes and man had early been made familiar; yet careful zoologists recognized apparent solutions of continuity, anatomical as well as psychological, in this region of the series. Leibniz and Locke had asserted a greater degree of continuity than could yet be actually exhibited at this important point. It therefore became the task of science at least to increase the *rapprochement* of man and ape. "In the first phase of this quest," as a German historian of eighteenth-century anthropology has pointed out, "the missing link was sought at the lower limits of humanity itself. It was held to be not impossible that among the more remote peoples semi-human beings might be found such as had now and then been described in traveller's narratives. Some voyagers testified to having seen with their own eyes men with tails; others had encountered tribes incapable of speech." [15] Linnaeus mentions a *homo troglodytes* concerning whom it was not established with certainty whether he was more nearly related to the pygmy or the orang-outang; and a writing of his, not published until long after his death, is entitled *The Cousins of Man* and speaks of the apes as the "nearest relations of the human race." [16] This preoccupation with the question of man's relation to the anthropoids gave an especial "philosophical" interest to the rather numerous descriptions of the Hottentots by late seventeenth- and early eighteenth-century voyagers. They were probably the "lowest" savage races thus far known; and more than one writer of the period saw in them a connecting link between the anthropoids and *homo sapiens*. An English essayist of 1713, observing, in the usual fashion, how "surprising and delightful it is" to trace "the scale or gradual ascent from minerals to man," adds:

'Tis easy to distinguish these Kinds, till you come to the highest one, and the lowest of that next above it; and then the Difference is so nice, that the Limits and Boundaries of their Species seem left unsettled by Nature to perplex the curious, and to humble the proud Philosopher. . . . The Ape or the Monkey that bears the greatest Similitude to Man, is the next Order of Animals below him. Nor is the Disagreement between the basest Individuals of our species and the Ape or Monkey so great, but that, were the latter endow'd with the Faculty of Speech, they might perhaps as justly claim the Rank and Dignity of the human Race, as the savage *Hotentot*, or stupid native of Nova Zembla. . . . The most perfect of this Order of Beings, the *Orang-Outang*, as he is called by the natives of *Angola*, that is the Wild Man, or the Man of the Woods, has the Honour of Bearing the greatest Resemblance to Human Nature. Tho' all that Species have some Agreement with us in our Features, many instances being found of Men of Monkey Faces; yet this has the greatest Likeness, not only in his Countenance, but in the Structure of his Body, his Ability to walk upright, as well as on all fours, his Organs of Speech, his ready Apprehension, and his gentle and tender Passions, which are not found in any of the Ape Kind, and in various other respects. [17]

Later Rousseau (1753) and after him Lord Monboddo (1770) took the further step of asserting that man and the higher apes (the orang-outang or chimpanzee) are of the same species, language being not originally "natural to man," but an art which one variety of this species has gradually developed.[18] Thus at this point, at least, the continuity of the series was already being construed genetically. Bonnet, too, though a devout theologian as well as a great naturalist, did not hesitate to intimate a doubt whether man and ape are distinct species.

The wide interval which separates man from the true quadrupeds is filled by the apes and the animals which most nearly approximate them, of which the species are minutely graduated (*très-nuancées*). . . . We ascend as it were by so many steps to a superior or principal species which so closely resembles man that he has received the name of *orang-outang*, or savage man. It is here above all that it is impossible to fail to recognize the graduated progression of beings; it is here above all that is verified the famous axiom of the German Plato, *Nature makes no leaps*. . . . The contemplator of Nature arrives with surprise at a being resembling man so nearly, that the characters which distinguish them seem less the characters of species than of mere varieties.

For, as Bonnet goes on to observe, the orang-outang has the size, the members, the carriage, the upright posture of man; he is "entirely destitute of a tail," but has "a regular face," *un vrai visage*; is intelligent enough to use sticks and stones as weapons; is even "susceptible of education, to the point of acquitting himself creditably of the functions of a *valet de chambre*"; and can acquire many other modes of behavior — including even a sort of politeness — which have been supposed to be peculiar to man. Whether, in short, we compare his mind or his body with ours, "we are astonished to see how slight and how few are the differences, and how manifold and how marked are the resemblances." [19]

By 1760 the triumphs of the missing-link hunters were being celebrated in verse:

Tous les corps sont liés dans la chaîne de l'être.
La Nature partout se précède et se suit . . .
Dans un ordre constant ses pas développés
Ne s'emportent jamais à des bonds escarpés.
De l'homme aux animaux rapprochant la distance,
Voyez l'Homme des Bois lier leur existence.
Du corail incertain, né plante et minéral,
Revenez au Polype, insecte végétal.[20]

From at least the middle of the eighteenth century to the time of Darwin this hunt for missing links continued to engage not only the interest of specialists in natural history but also the curiosity of the general public. On the last point a piece of conclusive evidence may be cited. No one was ever a better judge of what the public wanted than that eminent practical psychologist, P. T. Barnum; and it appears that one of the things that the public wanted in the early eighteen-forties — that is, nearly two decades before the publication of *The Origin of Species* — was missing links. For we are told that the great showman in 1842 advertised among the attractions of his Museum, in addition to the "preserved body of a Feejee Mermaid," other scientific specimens, such as "the Ornithorhincus, or the connecting link between the seal and the duck; two distinct species of flying fish, which undoubtedly connect the bird and the fish; the Siren, or Mud Iguana, a connecting link between the reptiles and fish, . . . with other animals forming connecting links in the great chain of Animated Nature." [21] We may be pretty sure that if Aristotle had been permitted to return to the sublunary scene in the eighteen-forties, he would have made haste to visit Barnum's Museum.

3. We must now turn back to the beginning of that great advance in observational science which began with the invention of efficient microscopes. With the history of the development of this device we are not concerned; for our purpose it suffices to recall that the microscope began to figure as an important instrument of biological discovery in the second half of the seventeenth century, above all through the work of Antony van Leeuwenhoek. The story of his achievements has often been told,[22] and its details need not be repeated here. What, however, we must not forget is that these disclosures of microbiology — like the earlier discoveries of the non-biologi-

cal microscopists — seemed at once to give fresh empirical corroboration to the principles of plenitude and continuity, and in turn — for minds with whom these still passed as virtually axiomatic — received theoretical confirmation from them. The world of micro-organisms was after all nothing more than might have been expected, if those principles were valid; it might have been deduced *a priori* even though it had never become sensibly observable. The existence of units of matter, both organic and inorganic, far more minute than the microscope had yet revealed had, in fact, been conjectured *a priori* before Leeuwenhoek. In a scientific treatise of 1664 the writer, Henry Power, observes:

> It hath often seem'd to me beyond an ordinary probability, and something more than fancy, (however paradoxical the conjecture may seem) to think that the least bodies we are able to see with our naked eyes, are but middle proportionals (as it were) 'twixt the greatest and smallest bodies in nature, which two extremes lye equally beyond the reach of humane sensation: For as on the one side they are but narrow souls, and not worthy the name of Philosophers, that think any Body can be too great or too vast in its dimensions; so likewise are they as inapprehensive, and of the same litter as the former, that on the other side think the particles of matter may be too little, and that nature is stinted at an Atom, and must have a *non-ultra* of her subdivisions. Such, I am sure, our Modern Engine (the Microscope) will ocularly evince and unlearn them their opinions again: for herein you may see what a subtil divider of matter Nature is.

Thus, "if the Dioptricks further prevail," its past achievements will be vastly surpassed; and though the author, in the sequel, deals chiefly with inanimate bodies, his inference seems clearly to imply a parallel extension of the world of organisms into the region of the infinitely small, in which the "incomparable Stenography of Providence" has produced "the Insectile Automata (those Living-exiguities)." [23]

The same logic required this extension of the realm of life downwards which required the hypotheses of the "infinity of worlds" and of inhabited globes within those worlds. The "two infinites" — the infinitely great and the infinitely little — both were implicates of the same premises. We have seen Fontenelle in the *Entretiens sur la pluralité des mondes* arguing from already known facts of microbiology to the conclusion —

itself not susceptible of observational proof — which he was seeking to establish. Every drop of water is crowded with "petits poissons ou petits serpents que l'on n'aurait jamais soupçonnés d'y habiter," etc. Since, then, "Nature has so liberally disseminated animals upon the earth," is it to be believed that "after having pushed her fecundity here to excess, she has, in the other planets, been so sterile as to produce upon them no living things?"[24] And to those who found edification in the common premises of both conclusions, any concrete evidence which tended to confirm either was a welcome verification of supposed metaphysical truths. Observational science, however, played a much greater part in making the general public sensible of this biological implication of the principle of plenitude than it did in persuading them of the truth of the new cosmography.

This second enlargement of nature had two conflicting effects upon men's imaginations and their feeling about the world they lived in. On the one hand, there was something highly sinister about it; it presented the ghastly spectacle of a universal parasitism, of life everywhere preying upon life, and of the human body itself as infested with myriads of tiny predatory creatures which made of it their food and sometimes — as soon began to be conjectured — their eventual victim.[25] On the other hand, it seemed to afford additional and very striking illustrations of the prodigious fecundity of Nature and at the same time of her admirable thrift. Life, it seemed, was ubiquitous. No bit of matter was so small that it could not afford lodging and nutriment for living beings still smaller; and animate matter itself was everywhere turned to use to sustain yet more animate matter, and this in turn yet more, and so on without ascertainable limit. The microbiologist merely confirmed and illustrated Pope's description of Nature's most impressive characteristic:

> See, thro' this air, this ocean, and this earth,
> All matter quick, and bursting into birth.
> Above, how high, progressive life may go!
> Around, how wide! How deep extend below!

It was upon the unpleasant side of the picture that the gloomier minds preferred to dwell. It served well Pascal's pur-

pose of "lowering" and terrifying man, of making him vividly
sensible of his small place in the cosmic scheme and the limitations of his powers of understanding. Swift's lines on the supposed infinite regress of parasitism are too familiar to quote.
This peculiarity of nature was to his mind, no doubt, an illustration of that general nastiness of things on which he was
prone to dwell. It was, in the main, on the alarming aspect
of the conception of "the two infinites" that Écouchard-Le
Brun poetically dilated:

> Entre deux infinis l'Homme en naissant placé,
> Se voit de tous les deux également pressé. . . .
> Pour confondre ses yeux qu'effraya l'Éléphant,
> Le Ciron l'attendait aux confins du Néant.[26]

But the other imaginative reaction was apparently much more
common in eighteenth-century philosophy and literature.
The discoveries of the microscopists, and the assumed existence of micro-organisms far smaller and more numerous than
had actually been discovered, provided delightful new evidence of that insatiable generativeness in which the "goodness of God" had, in all the Platonistic philosophies, been held
peculiarly to consist; and there was thus furnished a new in-
citement to those types of cosmic emotion and piety which had
always been associated with the principle of plenitude. The
following, for example, which might be supposed to have been
written by a late nineteenth- or a twentieth-century bacteriologist in a rhetorical moment, is in fact to be found in one of
Addison's *Spectators* (No. 519):

> Every part of Matter is peopled; every green Leaf swarms with Inhab-
> itants. There is scarce a single Humour in the Body of a Man, or of any
> other Animal, in which our Glasses do not discover Myriads of living Crea-
> tures. The Surface of Animals is also covered with other Animals, which
> are in the same manner the Basis of other animals that live upon it; nay,
> we find in the most solid Bodies, as in Marble itself, innumerable Cells and
> Cavities that are crouded with such imperceptible inhabitants, as are too
> little for the naked eye to discover.

And all of this, for Addison, was a part of that "wonderful and
surprising contemplation" which is afforded by the spectacle
of the Chain of Being, and a further evidence of "the exuberant and overflowing goodness of the Supream Being, whose

Mercy extends to all his Works." Addison even finds in the microbes an argument for the existence of angels or other beings above man in the scale, "since there is an infinitely greater Space and Room for different Degrees of Perfection between the Supreme Being and Man, than between Man and the most despicable Insect." James Thomson's emotions were more mixed. On the one hand — referring as usual to "the mighty chain of beings" — he is sure that micro-organisms have their necessary and "useful" place in the scheme of things, and he rhapsodizes over the way in which, as the existence of such creatures shows, "full Nature swarms with life." For him, too, this is a reason to praise

> that Power
> Whose wisdom shines as lovely on our minds,
> As on our smiling eyes his servant Sun.

On the other hand, the poet cannot but think it fortunate that most of the minuter animals,

> conceal'd
> By the kind art of forming Heaven, escape
> The grosser eye of man; for if the worlds
> On worlds enclosed should on his senses burst,
> From cates ambrosial, and the nectar'd bowl,
> He would abhorrent turn; and in dead night,
> When silence sleeps o'er all, be stunn'd with noise.[27]

Thus, even in those who accepted the premise of the optimists that the rationality and excellence of nature consist in its "fullness," there sometimes broke through a feeling that it would be pleasanter if it were not quite so full.

Even at the end of the century the principle of plenitude and especially that of continuity are still recognized by Kant in the *Kritik der reinen Vernunft* as sound guiding principles for the biological and other sciences, though with the special and important qualifications which followed from the impossibility, implied by the Critical Philosophy, of the detailed completion by our understanding of any such comprehensive synthesis. The former principle is called "the law of specification . . . which requires manifoldness and diversity in things" and "might be expressed by *entium varietates non temere esse minuendas*"; the latter is "the principle of the affinity of all concepts, which requires a continuous transition from every species to every other species by a gradual increase of diversity." From it "springs its immediate consequence *datur continuum formarum*: that is, that the diversities of species touch each other and admit of no transition from one to another *per saltum*." This, however, does not "rest upon empirical grounds," and "no object corresponding to it can be pointed out in experience," since such a continuum would be infinite, and since the principle does not tell us the "criterion of degrees of affinity" between adjacent species, but "only that we ought to seek for them." Kant's conclusion, then, concerning "the famous law of the *continuous scale* of created beings," which he ignorantly supposes to have been "brought into vogue by Leibniz," is that, while "neither observation nor insight into the constitution of nature could ever establish it as an objective affirmation," nevertheless "the method of looking for order in nature according to such a principle, and the maxim of admitting such order (though it may be uncertain just where and how far) as existing in nature, certainly constitute a legitimate and excellent regulative principle of reason." It "points the way which leads towards a systematic unity of knowledge." It follows, in short, from the Kantian analysis of the general conditions of the possibility of knowledge that the conception of the Chain of Being, in its fullness and strict continuity, is a controlling "ideal of the reason" which can never be actually satisfied, though science may hope, and should seek, in its gradual advance to exhibit more and more the empirical evidence of its approximate truth. [28]

# IX

## THE TEMPORALIZING OF THE CHAIN OF BEING

WHEN the principle of plenitude was construed either religiously, as an expression of the faith in the divine goodness, or philosophically, as an implicate of the principle of sufficient reason, it was, as usually understood, inconsistent with any belief in progress, or, indeed, in any sort of significant change in the universe as a whole. The Chain of Being, in so far as its continuity and completeness were affirmed on the customary grounds, was a perfect example of an absolutely rigid and static scheme of things. Rationality has nothing to do with dates. If the non-existence of one of the links in the chain would be proof of the arbitrariness of the constitution of the world today, it would have been so yesterday, and would be so tomorrow. As an early eighteenth-century English philosopher put the point:

[God] always acts upon some ground or Reason, and from thence it follows that he had some Reason for Creation, otherwise he never would have created at all. If then he had any Reason, that Reason certainly was the same from all Eternity that it was at any particular time: For instance, suppose Goodness was the Ground of his Creation, it follows that if it was good at any particular time, it was equally so from all Eternity.[1]

This, a contemporary pointed out, if true, must be true not only of the creation in general, but of every *kind* of being: it implies that, "not only *Angels* and *Men*, but *every other species of creatures*, every *Planet* with *all its Inhabitants*, were eternal," and, what is more, "that God *cannot hereafter* create any new Species of Beings; because, whatever it is good for him to create in time, it was equally good from all Eternity." [2]

The same implication of optimism was remarked by the poet Henry Brooke, in a prose note to *The Universal Beauty* (1735):

Either there is a present absolute fitness in things; or a fitness *in futuro*, that is, in prospect and tendency, and only relative here to what must be absolute hereafter. But if there were an absolute fitness in the present state of things, there could then be no change in anything; since what is best can never change to better.

To many eighteenth-century minds this conception of a world in which, from the beginning, no emergence of novelty had been or would hereafter be possible seems to have been wholly satisfying. The Abbé Pluche, for example, in a widely read popularization of the astronomical knowledge of the time, described the essential immutability of nature as one of the definitive conclusions of philosophy; and he apparently regarded it as an eminently edifying conclusion. No doubt, he grants, the work of creation was in a sense progressive until man was produced. But with him the consummation to which all the earlier phases had been preparatory was reached.

> Nothing more, therefore, will be produced in all the ages to follow. All the philosophers have deliberated and come to agreement upon this point. Consult the evidence of experience; elements always the same, species that never vary, seeds and germs prepared in advance for the perpetuation of everything, . . . so that one can say, *Nothing new under the sun*, no new production, no species which has not been since the beginning.[3]

This assumption sometimes was used early in the century against the then incipient science of paleontology. The view that fossils are the remains of actual organisms now extinct was combated on the ground that, in a well-conducted universe, every species must be constantly represented; so wrote the great English botanist John Ray in 1703:

> It would follow, That many species of Shell-Fish are lost out of the World, which Philosophers hitherto have been unwilling to admit, esteeming the Destruction of any one Species a dismembring of the Universe, and rendring it imperfect; whereas they think the Divine Providence is especially concerned to secure and preserve the Works of the Creation.[4]

This conclusion was both supported and extended by the reigning embryological theory of preformation or *emboîtement* which declared that not only all species but all individual organisms have existed from the beginning. The individuals, no doubt, unlike the species, seem to increase in numbers and to undergo change, but in reality this is a mere expansion or 'unfolding' (*evolutio*) of structures and characters that were already pre-delineated, on a minute scale of magnitude, in the primeval germs which lay encased one within another like a nest of boxes. As Brooke poetically phrased it, the Creative Omnipotence

> could infinitude confine,
> And dwell *Immense* within the minim shrine:
> The eternal species in an instant mould
> And endless worlds in seeming atoms hold,
> Plant within plant, and seed enfolding seed.[5]

Thus an important group of the ruling ideas of the early eighteenth century — the conception of the Chain of Being, the principles of plenitude and continuity on which it rested, the optimism which it served to justify, the generally accepted biology — all were in accord with the supposedly Solomonic dictum, which many others besides Pluche were wont to cite as an inspired confirmation of the conclusions of philosophy and science. There not only is not, but there never will be, anything new under the sun. The process of time brings no enrichment of the world's diversity; in a world which is the manifestation of eternal rationality, it could not conceivably do so. Yet it was in precisely the period when this implication of the old conceptions became most apparent that there began a reaction against it.

For one of the principal happenings in eighteenth-century thought was the temporalizing of the Chain of Being. The *plenum formarum* came to be conceived by some, not as the inventory but as the program of nature, which is being carried out gradually and exceedingly slowly in the cosmic history. While all the possibles demand realization, they are not accorded it all at once. Some have attained it in the past and have apparently since lost it; many are embodied in the kind of creatures which now exist; doubtless infinitely many more are destined to receive the gift of actual existence in the ages that are to come. It is only of the universe in its entire temporal span that the principle of plenitude holds good. The Demiurgus is not in a hurry; and his goodness is sufficiently exhibited if, soon or late, every Idea finds its manifestation in the sensible order.

The causes of this change were of several sorts; but the one which is most pertinent to our subject lay in the difficulties to which the principle of plenitude itself, as it had traditionally been interpreted, gave rise, when its implications were fully drawn out and seriously considered. Those implications were, on the one hand, intolerable to the religious feelings of many minds; and, on the other hand, it became increasingly apparent that they were hard to reconcile with the facts known about nature. The static and permanently complete Chain of Being broke down largely from its own weight.

Let us note the religious and moral difficulties first. The fatal defect of optimism — and of the principle of plenitude upon which its dialectic chiefly depended — was that which we have seen Voltaire pointing out: it left no room for hope, at least for the world in general or for mankind as a whole. If all partial evils are required by the universal good, and if the universe is and always has been perfectly good, we cannot expect that any of the partial evils will disappear. Logically thorough-going optimism is equivalent to the doctrine of the Conservation of Evil, metaphysical, moral, and physical; the sum of imperfection in the parts must remain constant, since it is in the realization of just that sum that the perfection of the whole consists. But to minds whose sense of the reality of the concrete evils of existence was too profound to be alleviated by a syllogism, this optimistic paradox was a grotesque mockery. It was better to admit the world to be not at present entirely rational, and retain some hope of its amendment, than to conceive of it as perfectly rational — and utterly hopeless.

For the individual, it is true, the principle of plenitude did not necessarily exclude a prospect of attaining a higher state of being in another life. Though the permanent structure of the world consisted of a fixed set of ideal pigeon-holes, and though every hole must be occupied, it was not impossible for the inmate of one hole to transfer to a better one. But to this possibility there was attached — according to the interpretation given the principle by some of its most approved expositors — a strange condition. Those of "the inferior orders" in the universe, Edmund Law pointed out, "could not aspire to a higher station without detriment to the superior which possesses that station; for he must quit his place before another can ascend to it." Hence, though a man by the right exercise of his moral freedom might "become fit and qualified for a superior state," he could not be promoted to it until a vacancy occurred through the "degradation" of one of those above him, as a consequence of wrong-doing. This was a strictly consistent deduction from the theory, if it was assumed that each degree of possible difference can have only one representative at a time; and this assumption was required by the principle of the identity of indiscernibles. Two creatures occupying precisely the same place in the scale would be the same creature. But the consequence that no one can ever rise in the world except at the cost of another's fall was, it is evident, a morally monstrous one. The optimist's proof of the rationality of the general constitution of things turned out to be a proof of its essential immorality.

A revolt against these two implications of the scheme, then, was inevitable, as soon as they became fully apparent. The Chain of Being must perforce be reinterpreted so as to admit of progress in general, and of a progress of the individual not counterbalanced by deterioration elsewhere. And on the other hand, the traditional conception, when so reinterpreted, suggested a new eschatology, or rather the revival of an old one. Since the scale was still assumed to be minutely graduated, since nature makes no leaps, the future life must be conceived to be — at least for those who use their freedom rightly — a gradual ascent, stage after stage, through all the levels above that reached by man here; and since the number of these levels between man and the one Perfect Being must be infinite, that ascent can have no final term. The conception of the destiny of man as an unending progress thus emerges as a consequence of reflection upon the principles of plenitude and continuity.

This revision of the traditional eschatology had been foreshadowed in the previous century by Henry More. Inasmuch as *natura non facit saltus*, the dead, he inferred, do not leap immediately from their terrestrial imperfection to celestial beatitude; nor need the plenitude of being be supposed to be realized simultaneously.

A Musician strikes not all strings at once; neither is it to be expected that everything in Nature at every time should act; but when it is its turn, then touched upon it will give the sound; in the interim it lies silent.[6]

Addison, whom we have already found descanting with a kind of poetic rapture upon the notion of the Chain of Being, was led by it to reject even more sharply than More the orthodox Protestant conception of life after death as an eternal fixation in changeless bliss or changeless misery. He wrote in the *Spectator* in 1711:

Among . . . other excellent arguments for the immortality of the soul, there is one drawn from the perpetual progress of the soul to its perfection, without a possibility of ever arriving at it; which is a hint that I do not remember to have seen opened and improved by others who have written on this subject, though it seems to me to carry a great weight with it.[7]

We must believe, Addison declares,

that the several generations of rational creatures, which rise up and disappear in such quick successions, are only to receive their first rudiments of existence here, and afterwards to be transplanted into a more friendly climate, where they may spread and flourish to all eternity. There is not, in my opinion, a more pleasing and triumphant consideration in religion than this of the perpetual progress which the soul makes towards the perfection of its nature, without ever arriving at a period in it. To look upon the soul as going on from strength to strength, to consider that she is to shine forever with new accessions of glory, and brighten to all eternity, that she will be still adding virtue to virtue and knowledge to knowledge; carries with it something that is wonderfully agreeable to that ambition which is natural to the mind of man. Nay, it must be a prospect pleasing to God himself, to see his Creation ever beautifying in his eyes, and drawing nearer to him, by greater degrees of resemblance.

This conception of an endless prospect of bettering one's position in the universe, a prospect equally open to all rational beings, evidently attracted Addison partly because it rid the picture of the Scale of Being of that look of irremediable inequality which it had in its usual form.

Methinks this single consideration, of the progress of a finite spirit to perfection, will be sufficient to extinguish all envy in inferior natures, and all contempt in superior. That Cherubim, which now appears as a God to a human soul, knows very well that the period will come about in eternity, when the human soul shall be as perfect as he himself now is; nay, when she shall look down upon that degree of perfection as much as she now falls short of it.

The Scale of Being thus becomes literally a ladder, with an infinite number of rungs, up which individual souls forever climb. In so far as all do so at an equal pace, the hierarchical order remains and the relative positions do not alter:

> It is true, the higher nature still advances, and by that means preserves his distance and superiority in the Scale of Being; but he knows that how high soever the position is of which he stands possess'd at present, the inferior nature will at length mount up to it and shine forth in the same degree of glory.

Leibniz, a few years later, concludes his *Principles of Nature and of Grace* (1718) with the assurance that no man is destined ever fully to attain the beatific vision:

> Our happiness will never consist, and ought not to consist, in a full enjoyment, in which there is nothing more to desire, and which would make our mind dull, but in a perpetual progress to new pleasures and new perfections.[8]

This reconstruction of the doctrine of immortality is manifest also in the same writing in which the melancholy consequences of the argument for optimism had been so frankly deduced. Edmund Law, a divine sufficiently orthodox to attain a bishopric in his own subsequent ascent of the Scale of Being, finds himself unable to accept the conclusion which Archbishop King's logic and his own required. For he appends to the seemingly triumphant conclusion of the argument — namely, that "the present state of the world is the very best that could be" — a footnote, in which he raises the question "whether God may be supposed to have placed any order of beings in such a fixed, unalterable condition as not to admit of advancement; to have made any creatures as perfect at first as the nature of a created being is capable of." The answer, Law thinks, is not altogether "easy to be determined." Those who answer the question in the affirmative "argue from our notion of infinite or absolute goodness, which must excite the Deity always to communicate all manner of happiness in the very highest degree for the same reason that it prompts him to communicate it ever in any degree. But this, they say, he had not done, except he at first endowed some creatures with all the perfection a creature could possibly receive and gave to every subordinate class of beings the utmost happiness their several natures were capable of." Law himself, however, inclines to the contrary view: "though it may appear something like a paradox," he thinks it "will perhaps upon further consideration, be judged not improbable."

For a creature . . . to meet with a perpetual accession of new, unknown pleasure, . . . and to be always approaching nearer and nearer to perfection — this must certainly advance the sum of its happiness even above that of others whose condition is supposed to have begun and to have ended in that degree of perfection where this will end (if there be any end in either), and which never knew defect, variety, or increase. A finite being fixed in the same state, however excellent, must according to all our conceptions (if we be allowed to judge from our present faculties, and we can judge from nothing else) contract a kind of indolence or insensibility . . . which nothing but alteration and variety can cure. It does not, therefore, seem probable that God has actually fixed any created beings whatsoever in the very highest degree of perfection next to himself. Nay, it is impossible to conceive of such a highest degree, and the supposition is absurd, since that which admits of a continual addibility can have no highest. . . . [God will, then,] we believe never produce any beings in such a state as shall not have room enough for them to be still growing in felicity and forever acquiring new happiness, together with new perfection.[9]

This change in the form of the belief in a future life was closely associated — as the last citation illustrates — with a psychological observation, a generalization about human nature, which was a favorite one with just those philosophers who loved most to dilate upon the principle of plenitude. Man, it was remarked, is capable of happiness only through perpetual alteration. At the opening of Bruno's *Spaccio della bestia trionfante*, which had been englished in 1713 and was much read and admired in the eighteenth century, "Wisdom" appears and utters these words:

If there was no change in bodies, no variety in matter, and no vicissitude in beings, there would be nothing agreeable, nothing good, nothing pleasant. . . . Pleasure and satisfaction consists in nothing else but a certain passage, progress, or motion from one state to another. . . . We can have no delight in anything present till we have been first weary of what is past. . . . The change from one extreme to another, with all the intervals, moving from one contrary to another by all the intermediate spaces, is sure to bring satisfaction.[10]

The same psychological remark occurs repeatedly in Leibniz; e. g., "This is the very law of enjoyment, that pleasure does not have an even tenor, for this begets loathing, and makes us dull, not happy." [11]

The principal historical significance of all this lies in the fact that it exhibits the emergence and diffusion of a way of thinking about the nature of the good which was to unite with that which we have already seen resulting from the logic of optimism. The new eschatology was the manifestation of a second new conception of value. The Platonic identification of the consummate good with αὐτάρκεια and cessation of desire — "he who possesses it has always the most perfect sufficiency and is never in need of anything else" — was giving place to its opposite: *no* finality, no ultimate perfection, no arrest of the outreach of the will. Such passages as those which I have quoted from Leibniz and Addison and Law were plainly foreshadowings of the Faust-ideal. Man is by nature insatiable, and it is the will of his Maker that he should be so; to no moment of his experience can he, if true to his nature and his vocation, ever say: "Verweile doch, du bist so schön!" The tendency to substitute the ideal of a *Streben nach dem Unendlichen*, an interminable pursuit of an unattainable goal, for that of a final rest of the soul in the contemplation of Perfection, an assimilation to "the peace which makes quiet the centre" of heaven in Dante's vision of the Celestial Paradise — this tendency has usually been post-dated by historians. It was no invention of Goethe, nor of the German Romanticists, nor even of Lessing, but had been expressed repeatedly throughout the century, both by eminent philosophers and universally read men of letters; and it was closely associated in their minds with the accepted idea of the Scale of Being, which had long been more vaguely described by theologians of unimpeachable orthodoxy as the course of the mind's ascent to God.

In Lenz's essay on the *First Principles of Morals* (1772) may be heard sounded again, somewhat mildly, this prelude to the Romantic strain, then soon to burst forth in full volume. He has been defining the nature of the "urge towards completeness" (*Volkommenheit*), which he declares to be one of the fundamental impulses in human nature. This completeness consists in the full development of all "the powers and capacities which Nature has implanted in us." But two qualifications, both of them connected in Lenz's mind with the principles of plenitude and continuity, are attached to this ethical ideal of self-realization. (1) "We have learned in our Age of Enlightenment that among our faculties some are superior — those of the mind — and that to these so-called higher faculties of the soul the others should be subordinated. In this proportionality, therefore, should we seek to cultivate and develop them. But since all of them stand in an inseparable, infinitely minute connection with one another,[12] the others [i. e., the 'lower'] are no more to be neglected than the higher — and this in accord with the different tendencies of each individual." (2) But for both the race and the individual the same principle demands a perpetual rejection of the *status quo*, an endless ascent of the Scale of Being.

Take heed that I am speaking here of a *human* perfection. I hope that the reproach will not here be brought against me that, since God created the first men good, they must, on my view, have required no morality, i. e., conscious moral effort. 'Good,' in the case of the earliest men, meant *perfectible*, not perfect, for otherwise there would have been no fall. All creatures from the worm to the seraph must be capable of perfecting themselves, else they would cease to be finite creatures, and would lose themselves, in accordance with the Platonic conception, in the infinite and perfect Being.[13]

This is one of the numerous eighteenth-century anticipations of Emerson's familiar couplet:

> Striving to be man, the worm
> Mounts through all the spires of form.

While, in an age in which many men of science were also theologians, this change in the religious and ethical application of the conception tended, of itself, to promote a kindred change in scientific ideas, the latter was enforced also by reasons of a less speculative kind. One of these was the difficulty, not to say the impossibility, of seeing in extant organic types the degree of continuity which the theory required. Nature as now observable did *not* appear to present even a segment of the chain which was complete and unbroken. This objection was made much of by those few writers who were bold enough to attack the whole assumption of the plenitude of the creation. In the second half of the century Voltaire and Dr. Johnson and the pioneer anthropologist Blumenbach were the most notable of these critics. Voltaire had once, indeed, he tells us, been fascinated by the idea of the Scale of Being.

When I first read Plato and came upon this gradation of beings which rises from the lightest atom to the Supreme Being, I was struck with admiration. But when I looked at it closely, the great phantom vanished, as in former times all apparitions were wont to vanish at cock-crow. At first the imagination takes a pleasure in seeing the imperceptible transition from inanimate to organic matter, from plants to zoophytes, from these to animals, from these to *genii*, from these *genii* endued with a small aerial body to immaterial substances; and finally angels, and different orders of such substances, ascending in beauties and perfections up to God himself. This hierarchy pleases those good folk who fancy they see in it the Pope and his cardinals followed by archbishops and bishops; after whom come the curates, the vicars, the simple priests, the deacons, the subdeacons; then the monks appear, and the line is ended by the Capuchins.[14]

But Voltaire argues on three grounds that the continuous series is non-existent in the organic world. First, some species which once existed have disappeared; others are in process of extinction; and yet others might be or may yet be destroyed by man, if he should so desire. "If the rest of the world had imitated the English there would be no more wolves on the Earth." It is probable also that there have been races of men which have vanished. Secondly, the obvious fact that we can conceive of imaginary species intermediate between the actual ones shows at once that the sequence of forms is broken:

Is there not visibly a gap between the ape and man? Is it not easy to imagine a featherless biped possessing intelligence but having neither speech nor the human shape, who would answer to our gestures and serve us? And between this new species and that of man can we not imagine others?

Finally, the supposition of the completeness of the chain requires the existence of a vast hierarchy of immaterial beings above man. Doubtless a Christian will believe in some of these beings, *parce que la foi nous l'enseigne*. But what reason is there apart from revelation for believing in them — in other words, what reason had Plato to do so? As for the inanimate world, there is plainly no gradation in its component members — for example, in the magnitudes of the planets or of their orbits. In sum, then, Voltaire's criticism is that any man who will give

the slightest attention to the known facts will see at once the
falsity of the supposition that "nature makes no leaps." He
concludes, then, with an apostrophe to Plato, source, as Voltaire supposes, of the entire delusion:

> O Plato, so much admired! I fear that you have told us only fables, and
> have never spoken except in sophisms. O Plato! you have done more harm
> than you know. — How so? I shall be asked; but I shall not answer.[15]

Voltaire also argued elsewhere, though with no too meticu-
lous consistency, against the *a priori* assumptions upon which
the principle of the cosmic plenum rested. "Why should, and
how can, existence be infinite? Newton demonstrated the
reality of a vacuum. If in nature there can be a void beyond
nature, wherein lies the necessity that entities should extend
to infinity? What would an infinite extension be? It could no
more exist than an infinite number." Yet in the same para-
graph in which he denies the infinity of the world in space
Voltaire asserts its infinity in time, and therefore attacks the
traditional doctrine of creation on grounds equally traditional. "The great principle *nothing comes from nothing* is as
true as that two and two make four." The universe, therefore, must be "eternal."

> It is an absurd contradiction to say that the Active Being passed an eter-
> nity without acting, that the Creative Being existed through infinite time
> without creating anything, that the Necessary Being was through an eternity
> a useless being.[16]

Dr. Johnson's attack upon the theory was based upon
similar grounds; but, of the two, it was, somewhat surprisingly,
the more profound and more dialectical.[17] Not only did the
principle of plenitude contradict observable facts; it also
seemed to him to contradict itself. The Chain of Being must be
a genuine continuum, if that principle has any validity at all;
but in a continuum there must be an infinity of intermediate
members between any two members, however "near" to one
another. Johnson thus applied to the accepted conception of
the universe some of the reasonings which, as applied to the
line, were as old as Zeno of Elea.

> The Scale of Existence from Infinity to Nothing cannot possibly have
> Being. The highest Being not infinite must be, as has been often observed,

at an infinite Distance below Infinity. . . . And in this Distance between finite and infinite, there will be Room for ever for an infinite Series of indefinable Existence. Between the lowest positive existence and Nothing, wherever we suppose positive Existence to cease, is another chasm infinitely deep; where there is Room again for endless Orders of subordinate Nature, continued for ever and for ever, and yet infinitely superior to Non-Existence. . . . Nor is this all. In the Scale, wherever it begins or ends, are infinite Vacuities. At whatever Distance we suppose the next Order of Beings to be above Man, there is room for an intermediate Order of Beings between them; and if for one order, then for infinite Orders; since every Thing that admits of more or less, and consequently all the Parts of that which admits them, may be infinitely divided. So that, as far as we can judge, there may be Room in the Vacuity between any two Steps of the Scale, or between any two Points of the cone of Being, for infinite Exertion of Infinite Power.

The principle of plenitude, moreover, Johnson observes, has implications which should be susceptible of empirical verification but are in fact false.

Every Reason which can be brought to prove, that there are Beings of every possible sort, will prove that there is the greatest Number possible of every Sort of beings; but this, with respect to Man we know, if we know anything, not to be true.

In short, Johnson concludes, "this Scale of Being I have demonstrated to be raised by presumptuous Imagination, to rest on Nothing at the Bottom, to lean on Nothing at the Top, and to have Vacuities from step to step through which any Order of Being may sink into Nihility without any Inconvenience, so far as we can Judge, to the next Rank above or below it." Thus

it appears how little Reason those who repose their Reason upon the Scale of Being have to triumph over them who recur to any other Expedient of Solution, and what difficulties arise on every Side to repress the Rebellions of presumptuous Decision. *Qui pauca considerat, facile pronunciat.*[18]

Johnson's criticism reached very nearly to the root of the matter. If it had been duly considered by his contemporaries, the late eighteenth century might have been marked by the breakdown of the principle of continuity and of the traditional argument for optimism, which he also vigorously assailed in the same writing. But it does not appear that either his or Voltaire's criticisms produced much effect. Throughout the century the assumptions of plenitude, continuity, and gradation continued, as we have seen, to operate powerfully upon men's minds, especially in the biological sciences.

Nevertheless, it was becoming increasingly evident — as it had, indeed, been to some medieval writers — that something had to be done to fit the postulate of the necessary complete realization of all the possibles with the fact that the concrete world *is* temporal. The assumed necessity was an *eternal* necessity; but its execution, so to say, manifestly was *not* eternal. If individuals are the links in the chain, they plainly do not exist all at once; and even if the links — by a departure from the rigor of the principle of continuity — were assumed to be species, the simple factual difficulty of the occurrence of gaps in the known organic series had long troubled the believers in the "fullness" and continuity of the creation. One device for meeting this embarrassment, to which so great a mind as Leibniz at times resorted, consisted, as we have seen, in assigning members of the series consecutive in kind to spatially distributed planets or solar systems. To find the links missing here you might need to fly to Mars or the Pleiades.[19] Maupertuis, who ranked as a great man of science in his time, proposed another equally far-fetched conjecture to save the doctrine of the original completeness of the sequence of forms. Many species once existing must, he suggested, have been eliminated by some accident, such as the approach of a comet. Nature as we now see it is like a once regular edifice after it has been struck by lightning: "it presents to our eyes only ruins in which we can no longer discern the symmetry of the parts nor the design of the architect." [20] But to those whose faith in the plenitude and continuity of the universe was tenacious a less unsatisfactory and less arbitrary hypothesis naturally suggested itself: that the Chain of Being, though not observably complete now, would be seen to be so, or to be tending to become ever more nearly so, if we could know the entire sequence of forms in time, past, present, and future.

It has been maintained by several recent writers on Leibniz that this solution was not adopted by him, that he still adhered to the conception of a static universe. A number of passages tending to support this interpretation can be cited; but

the evidence is, on the whole, against it.[21]  There is a famous
letter, probably of 1707, part of which I have already cited, in
which he expatiates with even more than his usual enthusiasm
upon the scientific importance of the principle of continuity;
it concludes as follows: that principle

is therefore to me beyond the reach of doubt; and it might serve to establish a number of important matters in veritable philosophy, which, rising
above the senses and the imagination, seeks the origin of phenomena in the
intellectual regions. I flatter myself that I have some ideas of these truths;
but this age is not prepared to receive them.

What, then, were these further implications of the principle,
so strange that Leibniz hesitated to make them explicit?
There is reason to think that one of them, at least, was the conclusion that the world is as yet incomplete, that the Chain of
Being must be construed as a process in which all forms are
gradually realized in the order of time.  In the *Protogaea* (1693)
Leibniz points out that many species of organisms which
existed in earlier periods of geological time have now become
extinct and that many known to us were then apparently non-
existent, and adds that it is a hypothesis "worthy of belief that
in the course of the vast changes" which have taken place in
the condition of the earth's crust "even the species of animals
have many times been transformed." [22]  "It is possible," he
writes again, that at some previous time "many species which
have in them something of the cat, such as the lion, the tiger,
the lynx, may have been of the same race, and may now be regarded as new sub-varieties of the original cat-species." [23]  In
another writing (1710) he suggests that it is probable that the
earliest animals were marine forms, and that the amphibia
and land-animals are descended from these.[24]  And elsewhere
Leibniz on metaphysical grounds extends this conception of
gradual development to the entire universe.  The *significance* of
time and change, he declares, the reason why *le changement est à
propos*, is that there may thereby "be more species or forms of
perfection, even though they may be equal in degree." [25]
There are, he elsewhere observes, two possible hypotheses on
this matter: "first, that nature is always equally perfect,
second, that it is always increasing in perfection, . . . supposing that it was not possible to give it its full perfection all at

once." If the latter is true, the fact might be explained in either of two ways: "either that there was no beginning, and the moments or states of the world have been increasing in perfection from all eternity, or that there was a beginning of the process." [26] And in one of the most interesting of his shorter writings he pronounces with all possible definiteness in favor of the hypothesis of continual advance. The plenum of possibility is now, and will forever be, like a partially tilled field, out of which new and finer growths must spring without end, since a continuum can never be exhausted.

A cumulative increase of the beauty and universal perfection of the works of God, a perpetual and unrestricted progress of the universe as a whole must be recognized, such that it advances to a higher state of cultivation, just as a great part of our earth is already subject to cultivation and will hereafter be so more and more. . . . As for the objection which may be raised, that if this is true the world will at some time already have become paradise, the answer is not far to seek: even though many substances shall have attained to a great degree of perfection, there will always, on account of the infinite divisibility of the continuum, remain over in the abyss of things parts hitherto dormant, to be aroused and raised to a greater and higher condition and, so to say, to a better cultivation. And for this reason progress will never come to an end.[27]

This general thesis of the creative advance of nature, and also the occasional more concrete assertions of the transformation of species, Leibniz was under the necessity of reconciling with certain other features of his system with which they might at first sight have appeared incongruous. Both his theory of monads and his preformationist embryology affirmed that, in a certain sense, every being which ever exists in nature has always existed in it. The number of individual "substances" i. e., monads, is constant. It can (he wrote in 1715) be declared with certainty, not only that "the soul of every animal has pre-existed" since the creation, but also that it has pre-existed "in an organic body" of its own. "Every birth of an animal is only the transformation of an animal already alive." [28] An individual organism living today existed as an animalcule in the germ-plasm of a primeval ancestor. But this, for Leibniz, did not necessarily mean that the ancestor was morphologically similar to the descendant, a creature of the same species (in the usual sense of the term); nor that the "preformed" body of the present organism was a precise "predelineation" of its present, or its foetal, form; nor yet, apparently, that, throughout the intervening time, the soul of the organism has always been of the same "grade" and its body of the same type. It is through a vast series of "changes, evolutions and involutions," [29] that is, of new developments and (in some cases) of retrogressions, that the original animalcule "has become the present animal." In particular, at the conception of an individual a radical change may take place. "Not only the organic body, but also a soul in this body, and, in a word, the animal itself, was already there before conception; and by means of conception the animal was merely prepared for a great transformation, in order to become an animal of another species. Even apart from generation we may see something approximating this when worms become flies and caterpillars become butterflies." [30] This elevation of the individual germ to a higher species is, Leibniz in this passage observes, the exception rather than the rule; "most of the spermatic animals remain in their own species," and "there is only a small number of the elect that pass on to a greater theatre." [31] But the pre-existent souls of men were not, Leibniz thinks, strictly speaking, human souls.

I should suppose that souls which will some day become human have, like those of the other species, been in the seeds, and in the ancestors, up to Adam, and have consequently existed since the beginning of things, always in a sort of organized body. . . . But it seems proper, for several reasons, that they should have existed then only as sensitive or animal souls . . , and that they should remain in that state until the time of the generation of the man to whom they were to belong, but that they then received reason — whether there be a natural method of elevating a sensitive soul to the grade of a reasonable soul (which I have difficulty in believing) or whether God gave reason to this soul by a special operation, or (if you will) by a kind of transcreation.[32]

Once generated, rational souls not only are exempt from relapse to a lower grade, but (according to Leibniz's progressivist eschatology already set forth), "they advance and ripen continually, like the world itself, of which they are but images." [33] Though the souls of other individual animals are also indestructible "so long as the world endures," they are not, Leibniz at times, and apparently usually, supposed, thus assured of indefinite and continuous progress to higher grades of being; their bodies are subject to "involutions" as well as "evolutions," and, the status of a soul corresponding to that of its body, the former may, through various natural vicissitudes, sink in the scale.[34] Yet he also pronounces it "a certain truth that every substance must arrive at all the perfection of which it is capable, and which is already found in it, though in an undeveloped form (comme enveloppée)"; [35] and he sometimes intimates that the possibility of an unlimited advance lies before all monads: "The eternity which is reserved in the future for all souls, or rather for all animate beings, is a vast field, designed to give, though by degrees, the greatest perfection to the universe." [36] Since Leibniz held that this belief was confirmed by "the gradual progress of physical observation," he probably had in mind, inter alia, such paleontological and other evidences as were then available of organic evolution — evidences which he had himself cited in the Protogaea and other writings already mentioned.   Phylogenetic advance was for him, in consequence of his preformationist embryology, always the manifestation of ontogenetic advance; and any observable fact which pointed to the probability of the one pointed also to the probability of the other.  Thus with the increase of empirical knowledge "we attain to the most sublime and most important truths of metaphysics and of natural theology" — the truth here in question being that of the general progressiveness of the universe.  But the "physical observations" which could be invoked in support of such a theory were, it need hardly be said, in the early eighteenth century very scanty; the considerations which led Leibniz and a number of his contemporaries and immediate successors to adopt such a theory must have chiefly consisted in those arguments "of metaphysics and natural theology" already indicated which, intelligibly enough, were converting the once immutable Chain of Being into the program of an endless Becoming.

Yet this introduction of the doctrine of universal progress, at once an individual, biological, and cosmical evolution, into the philosophy of Leibniz split his system — as the historians of philosophy have seldom, if ever, observed — completely in two.  It conflicted, in the first place, with the principle of sufficient reason, which he had so often declared to be the first and fundamental truth of metaphysics. That principle, as we have seen in an earlier lecture, required the actualization in the created world of all the ideal 'possibles' in so far as they are compossible. But if, as we have also seen, it required this at one time, it required it at all times; a 'necessary and eternal truth' cannot be in process of gradually becoming approximately true. And — another aspect of the same consequence — the evolutionistic version of the system played havoc with the logic of the principle of plenitude itself and with the theory of monads. It was an essential part of that theory that the whole of reality always consists of the same individuals in a fixed number. The number is fixed by the number of degrees of difference which the Eternal Reason recognizes as possibly subsisting between monads with respect to the function which is characteristic of them — that of "mirroring" or representing the universe with greater or less clarity and distinctness. There will be one thinking substance corresponding to each of these *nuances*; if it were not so, the universe would be an utterly haphazard thing, having *no* reason determining its numerical range. The idea of monads as advancing to higher grades did not, as has been shown, formally contradict the assumption of the constancy of their *number*; but it did conflict by implication with the doctrine of the immutable identity of the "substances" making up that number. For — by virtue of the principle of the identity of indiscernibles — what defines the individuality of a monad is the unique degree in which it realizes this function, its place in the Scale of Being — which, in final analysis, consists for Leibniz simply of the continuous series of monads thus minutely differentiated from one another. But if a monad changes its place in the scale by becoming capable of a more adequate representation of the rest of the universe, it loses its identity. In the case of rational souls endowed with memory it was possible for Leibniz to escape this difficulty by resorting to another way of defining the *principium individuationis*: a being which recalls its past experiences *as* its own experience has a continuing sense of personal identity which may persist through any number of changes of any degree. But there are "sensitive" and "animal" souls as well as rational, and to these this psychological basis of individuality is not attributed; nor, indeed, do human minds remember much of their past. We are not able to identify ourselves as having once been animalcules of such and such a kind on the first morning of creation. Consequently, the progress of all monads of lower grades, and of the monads which are now human souls, during the earlier phases of their existence, implied that the universe is not at all times composed of the same individuals; and the constancy of the number could be maintained only if it were assumed that the advance of some, or all, of the monads left gaps somewhere in the scale. If they all advanced, the lower rungs of the ladder would be left vacant. But this was irreconcilable with the principle of plenitude — and consequently with the principle of sufficient reason. Either the number of existing monads was increased with the course of time, or else there was — what Leibniz virtually denied — a *vacuum formarum*, and the Creator, by failing to fill up the grades which the progressive monads had vacated, was guilty of *at some time* denying to some possible and compossible essences in the series the grace of existence, the satisfaction of their *exigentia existendi*. Finally, Leibniz's doctrine of universal and perpetual progress was obviously an abandonment of optimism (in the proper philosophical sense of the term) in favor of meliorism. This world is *not* now, and, indeed, never will be, "the best of possible worlds"; it is only a world which is in process of growing better. It is true, however, that, for Leibniz, a world thus forever falling short of perfection was better than the optimist's "best," because a finite good incapable of being transcended lacks the first essential of value.

There are, then, two Leibnitian systems of philosophy, quite irreconcilable with one another — though their author was seemingly unaware of the fact. If we are, as Professor Montague has suggested, to classify philosophers by their characteristic "visions" of the universe, Leibniz had two visions: one of them that outlined in Lecture V, the other that which we have just seen. The first is the vision of a world which is through and through rational, fashioned completely, so far as the nature of a created world permits, after the model of the eternal order of the Ideas in the Divine Reason. It was, therefore, in its essential structure, an immutable world. Temporal change, it could not be denied, is characteristic of it, but it is not a significant characteristic; in such a vision — so close akin to Spinoza's — time is not "taken seriously." In the other vision, the time-process, conceived as a continuous augmentation of realized values, is the *most* significant aspect of reality — and change is the most indispensable mark of excellence.[37]

From the labyrinth of the Leibnitian metaphysics, cosmology, and embryology I turn to two poetic expressions of evolutionism in the first half of the century. Young in the *Night Thoughts* (1742–44) gives it an astronomical application. Each planet, or rather each solar system, Young supposes, has passed through a long gradual series of stages of what we should now call stellar evolution; has risen

> From obscure to bright,
> By due gradation, nature's sacred law.
> . . . . . . . . . . . . . All the stars,
> Those bright temptations to idolatry,
> From darkness and confusion took their birth;
> Sons of deformity: from fluid dregs
> Tartarean, first they rose to masses rude;
> And then, to spheres opaque; then dimly shone;
> Then brightened; then blazed out in perfect day.
> Nature delights in progress; in advance
> From worse to better.[38]

Young was presumably constructing this account of the normal history of a star chiefly from his imagination. It happens to be not so widely divergent from some recent astronomical hypotheses as might be expected; but that, of course, was mainly a lucky chance. What is of interest in the passage is, once more, the illustration which it affords of the fact that the appearance of the general notion of our own and other stellar systems as the scenes of an evolutionary advance long antedated the discovery of most of the scientific evidence for that hypothesis; that it was becoming familiar in very widely read writings before the middle of the eighteenth century; and that the development of it seems to have been chiefly due to the influence of the principles of plenitude and continuity, conceived as expressed in a succession and not in a ready-made cosmical order. Young characteristically turns this conception also to the uses of moral edification. His youthful Lorenzo is bidden to imitate the stars. But it is not the usual sort of moral teaching drawn by so many other edifying writers from the contemplation of the heavens. It is not in the regularity or changelessness of behavior of the stars in their courses that man is to find a model for his own conduct, but in their progressiveness, their continuous passage from "low to lofty, from obscure to bright." The moral imitation of nature in this case consists in a conscious and deliberate effort at perpetual self-improvement.

> When minds ascend,
> Progress, in part, depends upon themselves . . .
> O be a man! and thou shalt be a god!
> And half self-made! Ambition how divine!

This, it will be noted, was precisely opposite to the moral which Pope had, shortly before, drawn from the conception of the static Chain of Being.

At almost the same time another and a better English poet was elaborating the theme much more fully, and — naturally, since he was also a physician — with an emphasis upon its biological rather than its astronomical bearings. Akenside's *Pleasures of the Imagination* was, as an authority on the poetry of this period has remarked, " aside from the *Essay on Man* and the *Night Thoughts*, the greatest and most admired philosophical poem of the century"; [39] and its most striking passages are a vaguely evolutionistic version, in an eighteenth-century poetic style, of the cosmogony of the *Timaeus*. Akenside was acquainted with Leibniz's *Theodicy* and with some of his other then published writings; but the chief inspiration of his poem is clearly Platonic. He too begins with the World of Ideas; before Nature was formed,

> The Almighty One, then deep retir'd
> In his unfathom'd essence, view'd the forms,
> The forms eternal of created things.
> . . . . . . . From the first
> Of days, on them his love divine he fix'd,
> His admiration: till in time complete

What he admir'd and lov'd, his vital smile
Unfolded into being.  Hence the breath
Of life informing each organic frame,
Hence the green earth, and wild resounding waves;
Hence light and shade alternate; warmth and cold;
And clear autumnal skies and vernal showers,
And all the fair variety of things.[40]

.    .    .    .    .    .    .    .    .    .

   The Sovereign Spirit of the world,
Though, self-collected from eternal time,
Within his own deep essence he beheld
The bounds of true felicity complete;
Yet by immense benignity inclin'd
To spread around him that primeval joy
Which fill'd himself, he raised his plastic arm,
And sounded through the hollow depths of space
The strong creative mandate.[41]

Thus "from the wide complex of coexistent orders" there arose
one temporal world, "all involving and entire." But here the
poet departs from his Platonic original. He cannot believe
that the process of time brings no enrichment to reality, that
the world was as perfect and complete at its birth as it will
ever be.  No: its Author

         beholding in the sacred light
Of his essential reason, all the shapes
Of swift contingence, all successive ties
Of action propagated through the sum
Of possible existence, he at once,
Down the long series of eventful time,
So fix'd the dates of being, so dispos'd
To every living soul of every kind
The field of motion and the hour of rest,
That all conspir'd to his supreme design,
To universal good: with full accord
Answering the mighty model he had chose,
The best and fairest of unnumber'd worlds,
That lay from everlasting in the store
Of his divine conceptions.  Not content
By one exertion of creative power
His goodness to reveal to every age,
Through every moment up the tract of time
His parent hand with ever new increase
Of happiness and virtue has adorn'd
The vast harmonious frame: his parent hand,

> From the mute shell-fish gasping on the shore,
> To men, to angels, to celestial minds,
> Forever leads the generations on
> To higher scenes of being . . .
> So all things which have life aspire to God,
> The sun of being, boundless, unimpair'd
> Centre of souls!

Each creature receives from Nature the means of participating in this universal progress, so that

> in their stations all may persevere
> To climb the ascent of being, and approach
> For ever nearer to the life divine.[42]

Yet Akenside, it is interesting to observe, is apparently still influenced by the assumption that the series of possible forms, if it is to be rational, must be kept "full"; for he assures us that as this progress goes on,

> Inferior orders in succession rise
> To fill the void below.

On the other hand, in a later revision of the poem, while still retaining these lines, Akenside declares that not even in an infinite time will all the Ideas be realized in the created world: the Forms of being, eternally "plac'd in the essential Reason" of the Deity, constitute

> That vast ideal host which all his works
> Through endless ages never will reveal.[43]

That Kant in the following decade propounded a theory of cosmic evolution is well known; what is less familiar is the fact that in doing so he too was simply giving a temporalized version of the principle of plenitude. That this principle was for him a fundamental maxim of philosophical cosmology we have already seen. The creative potentiality of the world-ground is infinite; and "the number and excellence of the systems of worlds" which swarm in the infinity of space must be "commensurate with the immensity of their Creator." [44] "The fruitfulness of Nature is without limits, since it is nothing but the exercise of the divine omnipotence." [45] But this conversion of an infinite ideal possibility into concrete actuality does not take place all at once. The universe began its history in a state of relative simplicity; it has grown increasingly larger, more various, more complex, with the lapse of ages; and the inexhaustibility of its source is the ground of our assurance that it must continue to do so in the future.

In the application of these postulates in the *Allgemeine Naturgeschichte* Kant is concerned chiefly with pre-organic evolution — the formation of stellar systems and systems of systems. His cosmogony is an attempt to combine the implications of the principle of plenitude with the astronomical knowledge of his time; the details he professes to work out upon purely mechanical principles, but these are in fact constantly supplemented by the metaphysical assumptions with which we are familiar. The existence of matter is presupposed. In the "original condition of nature" all the material of which the future stellar systems were to be composed existed in the form of particles diffused through infinite space. But even in determining the presumable character of this initial phase of cosmical history Kant is influenced by a combination of the principle of plenitude with mechanical considerations. "Even in the essential properties of the elements" that constituted this primeval chaos, "there could be traced the mark of that completeness [*Vollkommenheit*] which they derive from their origin, inasmuch as their nature is but a consequence of the eternal Idea of the divine Intelligence. The matter which appears to be merely passive and without form and arrangement has even in its simplest state an urge [*Bestrebung*] to fashion itself by a natural evolution into a more perfect constitution." [46] What Kant means by this, in concrete terms, is that the elementary particles were not all alike; "the kinds of this primary matter" were "without doubt infinitely diverse, in accordance with the immensity which nature manifests on all sides." This is not, however, to be taken literally. The differences in question are not definitely declared to be qualitative, nor are the laws of the behavior of the original bits of matter various; Kant did not anticipate Peirce's tychism. But the prime particles at least differed "as much as possible" in specific density and "attractive force," and — in consequence of this — they were unequally diffused through space. Kant apparently reasoned that if this were not the case no sort of mechanical explanation of the beginning of the process which he is to describe could be given: the totality of matter, without such initial inequalities in density and distribution, would have remained in an eternal equilibrium. But, given these, there must have taken place a condensation of the heaviest particles at a certain point. From this centre the diffusion progressively thinned out in proportion to the levity of the particles.[47] But the "primary activation" of nature which was due to this local condensation led to the formation there of a "world," that is, of a system of planets and satellites revolving around a central mass. Kant attributes this, in general, to the action of gravitational and inertial forces, but the mechanics of it remains, if I am not mistaken, somewhat obscure. From this nucleus "the creation, or rather the development (*Ausbildung*), of Nature spreads by degrees . . . with a continuous advance to an ever greater breadth, in order that, in the process of eternity, the infinity of space may be filled with worlds and systems of worlds." Since the formation of a solar system requires many millions of years, different stages of stellar evolution are always simultaneously represented, verging from the highest stage thus far reached, which is of course at the centre, to the bare beginnings in the outlying regions — beyond which cosmical frontiers, in his view, lies matter in a merely "confused and chaotic condition," the raw material of worlds yet to be born. Though this process had a beginning, it will never end; *die Schöpfung ist niemals vollendet.* "It is forever busy achieving new ascents of nature, bringing into existence new things and new worlds." [48]

No doubt each of these separate worlds, and congeries of worlds, after it has at the end of vast aeons reached "the maturity of its development," will be subject to a reverse process of dissolution and eventual destruction; but the infinite fecundity of Nature warrants us in believing that the losses sustained by the universe in one region will be compensated, and more than compensated, by the production of new worlds elsewhere.[49] Between the law which dooms every part in its turn to final dissolution and the law that the universe as a whole makes incessantly for greater fullness and variety of being there is no conflict; on the contrary, Kant finds that the one is a corollary of the other. "Nothing is more congruous with the abundance (*Reichtum*) of Nature" than the transiency of all that it produces. "For if a system has, in the long period of its existence, exhausted all the diversity of which its constitution is capable, and has thus become a superfluous member of the Chain of Beings, nothing is more fitting than that it should then play its final rôle in the cosmic spectacle of ever-lapsing change — the rôle which becomes every finite thing, that of paying its tribute to mortality."

Thus to Kant at this time continuous development and progressive diversification is the supreme law of nature, not only for the universe as a whole but for every component of it, from solar systems to individual living beings. But in any part the latent potentialities of development have a fixed limit; and when all the "manifoldness" of which it is capable has been realized, it no longer fits into the cosmic scheme. Nature has no more use for that which has ceased to grow, and, sometimes slowly, sometimes speedily and catastrophically, eliminates it. Not only is the Chain of Being as a whole perpetually self-expansive, but it will tolerate no links which do not conform to the same law.

Yet Kant thinks it reasonable to assume that even the lacunae caused by the death of worlds will not be permitted by Nature to remain unfilled; this is "an idea which is as probable as it is conformable to the general plan of the divine works." [50] When a solar system, through the slowing down of the motions of its component parts, collapses and the planets fall into the central mass, the whole process starts over again, and so on *in saecula saeculorum*.

In, roughly, the third quarter of the century theories which may, in a broad sense, be called evolutionistic multiplied. The general hypothesis of the derivation of all present species from a small number, or perhaps a single pair, of original ancestors was propounded by the President of the Berlin Academy of Sciences, Maupertuis, in 1745 and 1751, and by the principal editor of the *Encyclopédie*, Diderot, in 1749 and 1754.[51] The assumption of continuity played some part in Diderot's argument in his suggestion of this theory in the *Pensées sur l'interprétation de la Nature* (1754); but in the main these two expressions of transformism were independent of the group of ideas which concern us here. The evolutionist tendency was manifesting itself in diverse quarters, and under the influence of differing considerations. Yet, even when the principles of plenitude and continuity, and the difficulties in maintaining the conception of the immutable Chain of Being, were not important factors in promoting this tendency, the result was, nevertheless, to increase the pressure towards the transformation of those principles into what I have called their temporalized form. In some cases the growth of the philosophy of change led, by a natural consequence, to the explicit rejection of the assumption that all species must always exist — as in a passage of d'Holbach's *Système de la Nature* (1770):

> Of those who ask, why does not nature produce new beings, we inquire in turn how they know that she does not do so. What authorizes them to believe this sterility in nature? Do they know whether, in the combinations she is at every instant forming, nature is not occupied in producing new beings without the cognizance of these observers? Who told them whether nature be not now assembling in her vast laboratory the elements fitted to give rise to wholly new generations, that will have nothing in common with the species at present existing. What absurdity, then, would there be in supposing that man, the horse, the fish, the bird, will be no more? Are these animals so indispensable to Nature that without them she cannot continue her eternal course? Does not all change around us? Do we not ourselves change? . . . Nature contains no constant forms.[52]

But the most interesting and curious example of the transformation which the Chain of Being was undergoing in this period is to be found in the writings, late in the third quarter of the century, of the French *philosophe* J. B. Robinet. He did not, it is true, have a high repute in his own time, and the historians of eighteenth-century thought have usually done him something less than justice. This has been chiefly due to the fact that, in his excursions into the field of natural history, he fell into some absurdities by which he became better known to posterity than by his more creditable performances. Yet even in these absurdities he is illustrative of certain aspects of the historic phenomenon which we are concerned with. The consequences of the pressure upon Occidental thought of the principles of plenitude and continuity range, as you have already had opportunity to judge, from the sublime to the ridiculous; and if in Robinet we find, among other things, some of the chapters of comedy in this history, an examination of his ideas is hardly on that account the less to our purpose. And on the other hand, he sometimes shows a good deal of philosophical acumen as well as originality in penetrating to new implications, or possible new interpretations, of old assumptions. His merit lay in the characteristic which Grimm found to be his principal defect; he had in a high degree the *esprit de système*, and insisted on carrying out to what he conceived, sometimes rightly, to be their full consequences premises which his predecessors had left undeveloped. And he was, in any case, an early representative of conceptions which were to be taken up by certain more eminent writers, poets, and philosophers of the following decades, were to enjoy in the Romantic period great vogue and influence, and were to be revived in our own.

In the earlier volumes of his *magnum opus, De la Nature* [53] (1761–68) Robinet dwells rather upon the static than the temporalized form of the conception of the Chain of Being. The third volume was in the main an especially full and methodical restatement and defence of the principle of plenitude and of all the familiar deductions which had, for the most part separately, been drawn from it by various earlier writers — the temporal infinity of the creation, both in past and future, its spatial infinity, the numberlessness of inhabited worlds, and the fullness of the series of beings.

> The activity of the Sole Cause is complete; in the product of this activity is everything that could exist. . . . The work of the Creator would have been incomplete if aught could be added to it. . . . He has filled the fossil kingdom with all possible combinations — earths and salts and oils and rock-forming substances and metals. He has made all vegetable species which could exist. All the minute gradations of animality are filled with as many beings as they can contain. The animal mind exists under all the forms fitted to receive it. [54]

And since the same logic which requires us to suppose that the Infinite Cause was never inactive also requires us to suppose that its activity has always been exercised to the full, it follows that there have always been present in the universe as many kinds of creature as there are now. "Can God, then, no more make anything new?" asks Robinet, and answers flatly that he cannot, "for he has already made everything — all possible extension, all possible matter, all possible intelligences, all possible beings." [55] It may not seem so to us; but "we must be very careful not to judge of the system of the world by the small sample of it with which we are acquainted." Besides the innumerable multitude of organisms which we can see, "how many more are hidden in the depths of the sea, on the summits of mountains, and in deserts! How many others . . . elude the powers of even our best instruments!" And those kinds that are missing here are doubtless to be found on other globes; "and who can count the number of globes that form the total system? . . . But we are sure that there are as many of them as can be, and that each possesses all that it can in all possible respects, in such wise that the Creator could not have made more in any class. Otherwise, he would have acted with partiality, would have exercised but a portion of his power; and this cannot be supposed without contradiction." [56]

Unfortunately for his reputation, Robinet pushed his faith in the fullness of nature to somewhat startling lengths. He is perhaps best known to fame, not for his place in the history of biological evolutionism, nor for his frequently acute and sceptical philosophical reasonings, but for his belief in the reality of *l'homme marin*. "There is," he writes, "so much authentic testimony to the existence of fish-men and fish-women (human with respect to the upper part of their bodies) that it would be obstinacy to doubt it." For example, "several persons worthy of credence" had, as recorded by Thomas Bartholin, testified that "in 1669 a siren appeared in the port of Copenhagen." Though the witnesses were unhappily not in accord as to the color of her hair, "all agreed that she had the visage of a beardless man and a forked tail." The *Histoire générale des voyages* had told how in 1560 some Cingalese fishermen had caught as many as seven mermen in their net. A living female of the species had even been exhibited in Paris in 1758, doubtless by some ingenious precursor of Mr. Barnum. Again, one could read in the *Délices de la Hollande* of a *femme marine* stranded in that country after an inundation, who was taken to Edam, "permitted herself to be clothed," and was taught to sew, but could never learn to speak, "and always retained an instinct which led her towards the water." Nor were these interesting creatures peculiar to the Old World; a ship's captain who, oddly, was *nommé Schmidt*, though *Anglais de nation*, "saw in 1614 in New England a siren of great beauty, in no respect inferior to the most beautiful women." Robinet cites more than a score of other witnesses who had enjoyed similar privileges; and the fifth volume of his *De la Nature* is embellished with several agreeable representations of these less familiar links in the Chain of Being. This sort of credulity is not to be set down wholly to the personal discredit of Robinet. It was a sufficiently natural result of the belief that nature is *capable de tout*; even so sober a mind as Locke had, it will be remembered, included "what is confidently reported of mermaids or sea-men" among the possible examples of the infinite variety and the continuity of the series of natural forms.[57] Given the principle of plenitude, which most well-instructed persons then accepted in theory, it followed that the existence of aquatic anthropoids was more probable than their non-existence. As Robinet himself put it — very much as Descartes had done — "I have formed so vast an idea of the work of the Creator that from the fact that a thing can exist I infer readily enough that it does exist." There was thus no reason for an attitude of harsh scepticism towards the worthy seafaring men and others who had reported having actually seen such animals. As Lord Monboddo observed in 1774 (*à propos* of stories of "tailed men"): "A modest inquirer into nature will set no other bound to the variety of her productions, than that which Aristotle has set, in that famous maxim of his, adopted, I see, by Mr. Buffon, *quicquid fieri potest, fit*, and everything can exist that does not imply a contradiction. We ought, therefore, to listen to credible evidence concerning the existence of any animal, however strange, unless we can take upon us to pronounce decisively, that it is impossible by nature that such an animal should exist."[58] The notion of the Chain of Being, in short, though favorable to certain new hypotheses which were destined to play a part of the utmost importance in the scientific thought of the subsequent century, was certainly not conducive to the cautious and sceptical temper requisite in the verification of hypotheses.

Even in his first volume Robinet adopted Turgot's and

Rousseau's notion of perfectibility and applied it to all living beings, though with the assumption of limits fixed by the pre-ordained potentialities of each species. "Every being cherishes its own existence and seeks to expand it, and little by little attains the perfection of its species." [59] Thus from the outset Robinet was an opponent of the still influential primitivism.

The human mind must be subject to the general law. We cannot see what could arrest the progress of its knowledge, or oppose its development, or stifle the activity of this spirit, all of fire as it is, which has certainly a destiny, since nothing has been made in vain. Its destiny can be nothing other than to exercise imagination, to invent, and to perfect. No; men were not made to wander in the forests after the manner of bears and tigers. [60]

"The true State of Nature is," then, "not that in which beings find themselves at their birth, apart from the additions which they are able to give to themselves by virtue of an internal energy or to receive from the action of external objects upon them." "Society, therefore, is the work of Nature, since it is a natural product of human perfectibility, equally fertile of evil and of good. Arts and sciences, laws, the diversity of the forms of government, war and commerce — everything, in short, is only a development. The seeds of all were latent in Nature; they have unfolded, each in its own time. Perhaps she still retains in her womb other germs, of slower growth, of which future races will reap the fruits. Then genius will expand and take on a still greater form. The tree of science will acquire new branches. As the catalogue of the arts is extended, their scope will become more ample. Thus new vices and other virtues will manifest themselves." But let it not be supposed that any creatures "have the power to transcend their natural state; they are held within it by bonds not to be broken. If some have the power to modify their existence, this liberty does not pass beyond the limits of their species." [61]

Robinet, however, at this point, characteristically, becomes sensible of a difficulty. If perfectibility is an attribute of man, why has so great a part of the species failed to manifest it? Why do many races remain in the state of savagery? The explanation Robinet, amusingly enough, finds in the universal solvent — the principle of plenitude: "it is because the productive cause must necessarily fill, with a magnificent profusion, all the classes of animality — must make both domesticable animals and animals incapable of being tamed, savage man and men capable of social life." [62] In short, a full universe must contain unprogressive as well as progressive creatures.

But perfectibility is soon extended by Robinet from a tendency to progress within the limits of specific characters to a universal cosmical law. Doubtless, as Leibniz and Bonnet had maintained, the "germs" of all things have always existed; but these all contain within themselves an internal principle of development which drives them on through a vast series of metamorphoses through which they ascend the "universal scale." And, as in Leibniz, the assurance of the infinite progress of the whole universe is curiously connected with the mathematical principle of the infinite divisibility of the continuum.

All germs have individual differences; that is to say, their life, organization, animality, have *nuances* which distinguish each of them from all the others. There are no elements except the germs; all the elements are therefore heterogeneous. These elements are not simple beings; simplicity is not an attribute compatible with matter. Elements are composed of other elements; or germs are composed of other germs. There is no natural nor artificial process which can bring an element, or germ, to the last degree of possible division. Germs, as germs, are indestructible. They can be dissolved into other germs only after the completion or the beginning of their development; in the state of germ they admit of no division. In the resolution of a developed germ into a multiplicity of other germs, there is no matter that dies. All of it remains alive; only its form and combinations change. The germs considered as forms or moulds pass; considered as organized and living matter, they do not pass. This is to say that there is no destruction of anything in nature, but a continuous transformation. The idea of succession enters necessarily into the definition of Nature. Nature is the successive sum of phenomena which result from the development of the germs. . . . The series [of germs] is inexhaustible, whether read backward into the past or forward into the future. A germ which has begun to develop and has encountered an insurmountable obstacle to the continuance of this development, does not retrogress to its original state. It struggles against this obstacle until its useless efforts bring about its dissolution, as its complete development would also naturally have done. [63]

Robinet accordingly makes his own a proposition which had been suggested by Diderot some two decades earlier. [64]

The existence of Nature is necessarily successive. . . . A state of permanence does not befit it. Germs created all together do not all develop together. The law of their generations, or manifestations, brings about these developments one after another. . . . In this continual vicissitude, there are no two points in the existence of Nature precisely similar in whole or in part. Though always the same, it is always different. I answer, therefore, that it is true that Nature never has been, and will never again be, precisely what she is at the moment at which I am speaking. . . . I doubt not that there was a time when there were not yet either minerals or any of the beings that we call animals; that is to say, a time when all these individuals existed only in germ, and not one of them had come to birth. . . . At least it appears certain that Nature has never been, is not, and never will be stationary, or in a state of permanence; its form is necessarily transitory. . . . Nature is always at work, always in travail, in the sense that she is always fashioning new developments, new generations.[65]

Both before and after this apparently evolutionistic transformation of the principle of plenitude, Robinet is equally zealous in developing and illustrating the implications of the *loi de continuité*. That principle itself, he observed, needs no defence; it is one which " the philosophers have long affirmed and reiterated." It is " the first axiom of natural philosophy" that

the Scale of Beings constitutes a whole infinitely graduated, with no real lines of separation; that there are only individuals, and no kingdoms or classes or genera or species. . . . This great and important truth, the key to the universal system, and the basis of all true philosophy, will day by day become more evident, as we progress in the study of Nature.[66]

Yet Robinet complains that some naturalists "whom its imperious force had constrained to render homage to it" in general terms, nevertheless failed to carry out this law rigorously. Thus Bonnet, "grand amateur de la loi de continuité" though he was, had still thought it possible to "divide the different orders which constitute the scale of being into four general classes: (1) inorganic, (2) organic but inanimate (i. e., plants), (3) organic and animate, but without reason, (4) organic, animate, and rational." Such a classification, Robinet contends, is a plain denial of continuity, because it credits some classes of beings with the possession of certain positive attributes which others absolutely lack. "The negative is always at an infinite distance from the positive," hence distinctions between members of the series should always be in terms, not of positive and negative, but of more and less of some common character. And when this consideration is borne in mind, the principle of continuity is seen to have sweeping philosophical consequences usually overlooked. Every purely *qualitative* difference between two things — whatever be true of differences of position, quantity, or degree — is necessarily a discontinuity. The only way to save the principle, therefore, is by supposing all things to have some degree or measure of any quality which is possessed by anything. Thus to the lowest orders of being must be ascribed some rudiments of the attributes conspicuous in the highest, and to the highest some vestiges of the characteristics of the lowest.

What continuity can there be between the organic and the inorganic, between the animate and the inanimate, between the rational and the nonrational? It is evident that there is no mean between the positive and the negative, and consequently, that there are no intermediate beings which link the two together. If there were such beings, it would be necessary that their constitution should simultaneously participate in two mutually exclusive contraries; . . . e. g., that the passage from inorganic to organic should be filled up by a middle sort of beings which are both organic and inorganic. But such beings are self-contradictory (*répugnent*). If we wish to leave the law of continuity standing, . . . if we wish to allow Nature to pass insensibly from one of her productions to another, without compelling her to make leaps, we must not admit the existence of any inorganic beings, or any inanimate, or any non-rational. . . . Where there is a single essential quality (an *essential* one, I say) characteristic of a certain number of beings to the exclusion of others, . . . the chain is broken, the law of continuity becomes a chimera, and the idea of a whole an absurdity.[67]

This was an acute and important observation upon the concept of the qualitative continuum. It made explicit, and generalized, the logic which was to be more vaguely and less consistently followed by many later philosophers. One of the principal motives, for example, of panpsychism in the philosophy of our own time is the desire to avoid the discontinuity which is manifestly implied by the supposition that consciousness or sentiency is an "emergent" property or function, which abruptly supervenes at a certain level of the integration of matter, and at a certain stage in planetary evolution. Underlying all such reasoning is the assumption of the necessity of what may be called the "retrotensive method"[68] — the rule that whatever is empirically found in or associated with the more complex and highly evolved natural entities must inferentially be read back into the simpler and earlier ones. But where later writers have, as a rule, applied this method only spasmodically and without full realization of its general import, Robinet saw that it must either be applied universally or be admitted to have no cogency at all. The result, it will perhaps seem to the judicious reader, was simply a *reductio ad absurdum* of the principle of continuity. But to Robinet it was the establishment, by a single stroke of logic, of a whole group of important philosophical conclusions — among them, hylozoism, panpsychism, and a peculiar sort of panlogism, a doctrine of the ubiquity of the rudiments of rationality in all natural things.

> For myself I would rather give even intelligence to the least atom of matter — provided it were in a degree and of a quality suitable to it — than refuse organization to the fossils and make of them isolated beings, having no connection with others. It is to no purpose to tell me that this is a bizarre opinion, and that it is not possible that a stone thinks. I should deem it a sufficient reply to say that I am not responsible for consequences correctly deduced, that I have not measured the extent of what is possible, and that, if the law of continuity is admitted, we ought likewise to admit all that follows from it; while it is inexcusable to abandon so general a principle without a sufficient reason.[69]

Though the non-existence of mere "brute matter" is thus inferrible from the principle of continuity alone, Robinet does not fail to offer further argument for the conclusion, with a prolixity which I shall not emulate. But a further (for him) important consequence of the same observation upon the logical meaning of the *lex continui* must be noted; for it involves a restriction by that principle of the scope of the principle of plenitude, of which it was nevertheless conceived to be a corollary. Since there is no continuous series unless *all* members of the series have something in common, though in differing degrees, it follows, Robinet finds, that there must be a single anatomical type-form common to all living things — which is to say, to all things. And this must, of course, be a particular form, distinct from all other possible forms; so that the "fullness" of nature is limited to the realization of all possible variations upon a single "prototype."

There was only one possible plan of organic or animal existence, but this plan could be, and must be, varied in an infinity of ways. The unity of model or plan maintained in the prodigious diversity of its forms is the basis of the continuity or graduated sequence of beings. All differ from one another, but all these differences are natural variations of the prototype, which must be regarded as the element generative of all beings. . . . When I compare the stone with the plant, the plant with the insect, the insect with the reptile, the reptile with the quadruped, I perceive, through all the differences which characterize each of them, relations of analogy which persuade me that they have all been conceived and formed in accordance with a single model (*dessein*), of which they are variations graduated *ad infinitum*. They exhibit all the salient traits . . . of this original exemplar, which in realizing itself has taken on successively the infinitely numerous and diverse forms under which Being manifests itself to our eyes.[70]

But a pattern exemplified equally in so great a variety of shapes must, it is evident, be itself simple and meagre in the last degree. The prototype is nothing more than an "elongated tube or hollow cylinder, naturally active." But in asserting that this is the "model" of which all organic forms are variants, Robinet often seems really to mean that it is the unit of which all organic structures are integrations; in other words, his "prototype," in the concrete, is equivalent to what he calls an "organe," which is in turn equivalent to a protoplasmic cell. [71] His quest of continuity here, in short, has led him to the conclusion that all living things are built up of ultimate units of the same general shape and homogeneous in their properties. But why they should unite into structures so various in form, the law of continuity can hardly be invoked to explain; nor is it evident that the grosser structures are a continuous series in the sense required. Robinet thus seems to have escaped some of the difficulties of his thesis here by conveniently confusing the idea of a community of form between gross structures with the idea of a community of form (and function) between the component units of gross structures.

Here too Robinet was merely elaborating and extending a suggestion of Diderot's, similarly connected with the postulates of plenitude and continuity. Diderot had written in 1754:

It seems that Nature has taken pleasure in varying the same mechanism in an infinity of different ways. She abandons one type (*genre*) of products only after having multiplied individuals in all possible modes. When one considers the animal kingdom, and observes that, among the quadrupeds, there is not one of which the functions and the parts, above all the internal parts, are not entirely similar to those of another quadruped, would not one readily believe that Nature has done no more than lengthen, shorten, transform, multiply, or obliterate, certain organs? Imagine the fingers of the hand united, and the substance of the nails so abundant that, swelling and spreading, it envelops the whole, and instead of the hand of a man you have the foot of a horse. When one sees the successive metamorphoses of the envelope of the prototype, whatever it may have been, approximate one another, from one to another kingdom, by insensible degrees, and people the confines of the two regions (if it is permissible to speak of confines where there is no real division) with beings of uncertain and ambiguous kinds, divested in great part of the forms, qualities, functions of the one, and endowed with the forms, qualities and functions of the other — who would not feel persuaded to believe that there has never been but one primary being, prototype of all beings? But whether this philosophic conjecture be admitted with Doctor Baumann [Maupertuis] or rejected with M. de Buffon, it will not be denied that it is necessary to adopt it as a hypothesis essential to the progress of experimental physical science, to the discovery and the explanation of those phenomena which depend upon organization.[72]

By "prototype" Robinet usually meant, however, not simply a primordial germ of all organisms, but an ideal model or pattern embodied in countless differing particulars: *le prototype est un principe intellectuel qui ne s'altère qu'en se réalisant dans la matière*.[73] It is thus a model which represents the living being "reduced to its lowest terms; it is an inexhaustible ground of variations. Each variation realized constitutes a being, and may be called a metamorphosis of the prototype, or rather of its original envelope, which was its first realization." A great number of accumulated variations "may so disguise the original that it escapes us"; yet we may be sure that in every case the underlying unity is there. If Robinet had limited the application of this notion to the vertebrates he would have been expressing a definite scientific fact, already abundantly established by the anatomical knowledge of his time; but the principle of continuity, as construed by him, compelled him to postulate a single model for all animate and even inanimate natural individuals.[74] Thus Robinet, though not the originator, was (so far as I know) the first elaborator and enthusiastic champion of that notion of an *Urbild*, upon which all organic and perhaps all natural forms are variations, which was to be taken up by Herder [75] and to become almost an obsession of Goethe at one period.

> Alle Glieder bilden sich aus nach ew'gen Gesetzen,
> Und die seltenste Form bewahrt im geheimen das Urbild.[76]

Robinet wavers, however, between two ways of conceiving of what Nature is about in her incessant travail. Sometimes he sees in it merely an illustration of what, in our terminology, we have called the temporalized form of the principle of plenitude: it is an effort to multiply variety to the greatest possible degree.

If the march of Nature seems to us sometimes uncertain and ill-assured, if she seems sometimes to operate in a fumbling, devious, equivocal manner, it is a false appearance, due only to our ignorance and our prejudices. We forget that she should not and cannot let any *nuance*, any variation, go unrealized; we fail to see the too subtle differences of contiguous forms. . . . Nature does nothing useless, her course is minutely graded (*nuancée*), and each *nuance* is necessary in the total plan.    The forms which we so ineptly take for irregularities, redundancies, inutilities, belong to the infinite order of beings and fill a place which would be empty without them.[77]

But in other passages Robinet, under the influence of the idea of the universal prototype, sees in the past history of the formation of new species something more than an urge towards promiscuous variation; a movement of Nature in one general direction is discernible, a striving towards a particular goal — though the movement is stumbling and full of deviations, a progress, as we should now say, by trial-and-error. Thus the multiplicity of forms is, in part, a consequence of Nature's tending towards a consummation not clearly foreseen. Her workshop contains many unsuccessful and discarded models.

In the prodigiously varied sequence of the animals below man, I see Nature in labor advancing fumblingly towards that excellent being who crowns her work. However imperceptible the progress which she makes in one step, that is, in each new production, in each variation upon the original design which she achieves, nevertheless the advance becomes clearly sensible after a certain number of metamorphoses. . . . All the varieties intermediate between the prototype and man I regard as so many essays of Nature, aiming at the most perfect, yet unable to attain it except through this innumerable sequence of sketches. I think we may call the collection of the preliminary studies the apprenticeship of Nature in learning to make a man.[78]

When man is thus viewed as the objective of the slow processes of creation, up to its present phase, the unity and specificity which is the characteristic of the successive series of forms can — Robinet now suggests — be better recognized by considering the goal rather than the start; i. e., by seeing in the other forms adumbrations of man's, rather than in man or other relatively high types variations upon a primitive simple model. This is the theme of the *Parallèle*, in which (if it is his own) his zeal again got the better of his discretion:

> Envisaging the sequence of individuals as so many steps in the progress of being towards humanity, we shall compare each of these with man, first with respect to his higher faculties, that is, his reason. This new way of contemplating Nature and her productions, which refers them all to a single idea generative of the world, is founded upon the law of continuity which links together all the parts of this great whole. Each [organic] mechanism tends immediately and of itself to produce only that which we see it in fact engendering; but the sum of these mechanisms tends towards the final outcome; and we here take man as the final outcome, in order to limit ourselves to terrestrial beings, which alone are within our knowledge.

In the quest of these adumbrations of the human form in the lower orders of creation, Robinet was unhappily led to find similitudes of faces, as well as of arms and legs, in the radish and other plants, and to publish drawings of these vegetable anthropoids.[79]

But the curiously mixed historic rôle of Robinet may be further seen in the fact that the type of biological evolutionism which he adopted was developed by him into a general philosophy of nature of an essentially 'Romantic' sort; it anticipated some of the most characteristic conceptions both of the *Naturphilosophie* of Schelling and of Bergson's in our own time.[80] Robinet was one of the earlier prophets of the *élan vital*. The fundamental reality in nature for him is not matter but *l'activité*; and the pageant of evolution is the manifestation of the expansive, self-differentiating energy, the creative urge, of this *puissance active*. Yet (as his final volume admits) inert matter, in some sense, also must be recognized; and between it and the active principle there is an age-long struggle. At the beginning, and in the lower grades of the Scale of Being, brute matter is dominant; the tendency to spontaneous action is wholly clogged by it; but little by little the force that makes for life gains strength, and finally, in man, establishes its dominance so completely that matter becomes less an obstacle than the instrument whereby that force achieves its ends. (The principle of continuity seems here to have disappeared.)

In the inferior beings, such as minerals and vegetables, we refer all the phenomena that occur to matter, as the principal constituent (*le fond principal*) of these beings. . . . A little higher in the scale, we begin to doubt; we are undecided. We remark a spontaneity of movements and operations which discloses an active principle which we cannot but attribute to them. Nevertheless, this activity may still be seen to be dragged along and invincibly determined by matter, so that, in such systems, matter and activity appear to dominate by turns, being alternately principal and accessory, according to circumstances. The active power seems to be making efforts to raise itself above the extended, solid, impenetrable mass to which it is chained, but of which it is often compelled to submit to the yoke. In man, on the contrary, it is evident that matter is only the organ through which the active principle brings its faculties into play. The former is an envelope which modifies the action of the latter, one without which it would perhaps act more freely, but also without which, perhaps, it could not act at all, and without which it assuredly could not render its activities sensible. Does it not, once more, seem that the active power grows and perfects itself in being, in proportion as it raises itself above matter? . . . Such, according to this hypothesis, would be the progression of the active force inherent in matter. At first it would be but the smallest portion of being. By a multiplication of efforts and progressive developments, it would succeed in becoming the principal part. I am strongly inclined to believe that this force is the most essential and the most universal attribute of being (*le fond de l'être*) — and that matter is the organ whereby this force manifests its operations. If I am asked to define my conception of such a force, I shall answer, with a number of philosophers, that I represent it to myself as a tendency to change for the better; since every change is the proximate predisposition to another and better one.[81]

And the end of the process is not yet, Robinet adds:

La progression n'est pas finie. There may be forms more subtle, potencies more active, than those which compose man. The force may, indeed, be able to rid itself insensibly of all materiality, and so to begin a new world — but we must not let ourselves go astray in the boundless regions of the possible.[82]

Here, manifestly, is a philosophy of *l'évolution créatrice* in outline; and its resemblance to its twentieth-century counterpart is heightened by the fact that it too is, in the end, puzzlingly combined with a species of phenomenalism; the matter which hampers the active principle is nevertheless its product and exists only as an appearance, while the active principle is in itself non-spatial.

Accustomed as we are to judge of the reality of things by the appearances which strike our senses, we are unwilling to admit that anything exists in the world except matter, since we see only matter. And, to borrow the words of a modern author, since all the modifications which our senses observe in Nature consist simply in the variation of the limits of extension, as soon as we are compelled to give up this extension we seem to be confronted with mere nothingness; we come to a stop as if there is naught beyond. We do not give heed to the fact that the material or visible world is an assemblage of phenomena and nothing more — that there must necessarily be an invisible world, which is the foundation, the subject, of the visible world, and into which we ought to resolve all that is real and substantial in Nature. This invisible world is the collection of all the forces which tend to ameliorate themselves, and which do so in fact, by incessantly extending and perfecting their activity, in the proportion suitable to each of them. There is a gradation of forces in the invisible world as there is a progression of forms in the extended or visible world.[83]

Bonnet, in his *Palingénésie philosophique, ou Idées sur l'état passé et sur l'état futur des êtres vivans* (1770) presented one of the most extraordinary speculative compounds to be found in the history of either science or philosophy — an interweaving, even more elaborate than Leibniz's, of geology, embryology, psychology, eschatology, and metaphysics into a general view of the history, past and to come, of our planet and the living beings thereon — a history which may be presumed to have its counterpart on other globes. It was another attempt, differing in some details, to work out in somewhat concrete terms, and with the utilization of the scientific knowledge or generally accepted hypotheses of the time, the Leibnitian conception of a universe essentially and infinitely self-differentiating and progressive. Whether it can properly be called a form of 'evolutionism' is a question of terminology.

Bonnet, following Leibniz, is not prepared to abandon formally the traditional implication of the principle of plenitude that everything was created at the outset. "All the component parts (*pièces*) of the universe are contemporary. The Efficacious Will created by a single act all that could be created." [84] But on the other hand, the fact of the universal mutability of nature is too evident to need argument; and the indications of a progressive differentiation and augmentation of the forms of life on our globe appear to Bonnet to be conclusive. But how can this be reconciled with the doctrine of the completeness of the original creation? Obviously the latter cannot be taken literally. The sense in which it is to be taken is to be found in the embryologico-metaphysical theory of which Bonnet takes over the fundamentals from Leibniz. All the *individuals* making up the universe are as old as it is, and are indestructible. These individuals are primarily "souls." Every organism has a soul; it has also, adds Bonnet, a body, a "germ" or *petit corps organique*, equally indestructible, and permanently associated with that individual soul. But at any given time the body of an individual organism is made up of a number of these minute organic corpuscles, which have as yet to develop organized bodies of their own, capable of the functions of assimilation, growth, and reproduction. The dissolution of the organized body may permit the contained corpuscles to set up in business, so to say, on their own. Since the "soul" of, for example, a polyp is "indivisible, this soul is not broken up into parts when the polyp is broken up; but by this means opportunity is given for certain germs" — i. e., subsidiary and repressed germs previously contained within the creature's body — "to develop; and the soul which I have supposed to be resident in these germs will then begin to experience sensations related to the conservation of the individual. There will thus be formed so many new *persons*, new egos." [85] During most of their existence, therefore, many, or most, of the souls are merely potentialities of sensibility, rather than actually sentient; and their germs remain small unchanged units of animate matter, until the appropriate hour for the beginning of their active life as individuals arrives. Nevertheless Bonnet ascribes to each soul a sort of organic or subconscious memory, of which the germ is the material vehicle, carrying along a permanent record of the effects of its past experiences.

Now it is clear from the evidence of geology and astronomy, says Bonnet, that our globe has passed through a long series of epochs, each terminated by a "revolution," i. e., a cataclysm in which all the then existing organic structures were destroyed

— but not the germs nor, of course, their associated souls. But as the external conditions of each epoch differ materially from those in the preceding eras, and the form, organs, and senses of any species must be adapted to the physical conditions of the epoch in which it lives, the kind of gross body which a given germ takes on when it comes to life again in a new epoch will differ from its preceding embodiments. All these later transformations had been provided for — whether literally predelineated or not — in the constitution of the germ at the creation: "I conceive," says Bonnet, "that the germs of all organized beings were originally constructed or calculated with a determinate correlation with the diverse revolutions which our globe was to undergo." [86] Thus the first morning of creation, after all, in some sense wrote what all later dawns should disclose — but wrote only in a kind of prophetic shorthand.

Bonnet, on scientific, not to speak of religious, grounds, is sure that the sequence of epochs, and accordingly of organic types, constitutes a progress from lower to higher. The embryological stages of ontogenesis show the forms through which the animal has successively passed in the previous epochs of the globe. (This is one of the early foreshadowings of the recapitulation theory.) The "revolutions of the globe," however, cannot be supposed to have an end. In the future, therefore, as in the past, every germ will reappear in a succession of ever higher embodiments. Our present species will somehow unfold into forms "as different from their present ones as the state of our globe will be different from its present state. If it were permitted us to contemplate the scene of this ravishing metamorphosis, we should probably not be able to recognize any of the species of animals with which we are now most familiar. ... We should behold a world completely new, a system of things of which we have now no idea." [87] This progression of types, however, does not seem to be, for Bonnet, a progress from generation to generation. The "perfectibility" of the oyster does not mean that oysters will be gradually transformed in the course of heredity, in the present epoch, until their remote posterity become elephants or men or cherubim; it means that the *corps organique* of each individual oyster will, after its death, be conserved without alteration until the right state of the globe supervenes to call forth its next and higher unfolding. In the case of the germs which actually developed into full-fledged individual animals in this or a preceding age of the world, there will also be a conservation of a sort of personal identity through memory; of those germs that did not come to birth "in the present economy of our world," there will also be a resurrection, but without memory. "The same gradation which we observe today between the different orders of organized beings will doubtless be found also in the future state of our globe [i. e., the series will still be continuous]; but it will follow proportions which will be determined by the degree of perfectibility of each species. Man — who will then have been transported to another dwelling-place, more suitable to the superiority of his faculties — will leave to the monkey or the elephant that primacy which he, at present, holds among the animals of our planet. In this universal restoration of animals, there may be found a Leibniz or a Newton among the monkeys or the elephants, a Perrault or a Vauban among the beavers." [88] Every present species, to be sure, will, as Bonnet conceived, progress towards "perfection"; but only because every individual of it will rise again in improved form, through the future "revolutions of the globe." It would seem, therefore, that it is only in a rather dubious sense that Bonnet can be called, as he sometimes has been called, a "forerunner of evolutionism." The progressive sequence of organic forms which he asserted was not conceived as resulting by the ordinary processes of generation within our present, or any single, world-epoch; it consisted in extreme and discontinuous mutations occurring, apparently, only at vast intervals of time, and after great cataclysms in which, with the exception of the indestructible and imperceptible "germs" of individual animals, the entire organic life of the globe is destroyed. As compared with the evolutionary hypotheses which had already been put forward by Maupertuis, Diderot, and Robinet, these speculations of Bonnet's were obviously crude and retrogressive.

We have now, in the roughly chronological order of our review of the history of an idea, already reached the beginning of that profound and momentous, but complex and confused, change in preconceptions and valuations which is commonly, though somewhat unfortunately, called Romanticism. With the relation to our general theme of two of the most characteristic and significant tendencies of thought in the Romantic period the following lectures will deal.

# X

## ROMANTICISM AND THE PRINCIPLE OF PLENITUDE

It is one of the instructive ironies of the history of ideas that a principle introduced by one generation in the service of a tendency or philosophic mood congenial to it often proves to contain, unsuspected, the germ of a contrary tendency — to be, by virtue of its hidden implications, the destroyer of that *Zeitgeist* to which it was meant to minister. There are few more striking examples of this irony than that which may be found in the history of the principles of plenitude and continuity. As we have seen, they were invoked in the seventeenth and early eighteenth century primarily as a support for the doctrine of the essential logicality of the world. They were designed to justify the belief in the rationality, the perfection, the static completeness, the orderliness and coherency of reality. Yet they were at heart ideas profoundly antipathetic to the simple rationalism of the Enlightenment; the ultimate effect of their vogue was to introduce subtly and gradually into the European mind several of those tastes and those philosophical presuppositions which at the end of the century took form in a conscious and aggressive revolutionary movement in thought, that to which the name of Romanticism is commonly applied. The conception of the complete and continuous Scale of Being came into the circle of accredited eighteenth-century ideas with a letter of recommendation from that venerated figure, the Principle of Sufficient Reason; it ended by helping to make intellectual outcasts of not a few of that circle, including its own sponsor.

For in nearly all the provinces of thought in the Enlightenment the ruling assumption was that Reason — usually conceived as summed up in the knowledge of a few simple and self-evident truths — is the same in all men and equally possessed by all; that this common reason should be the guide of life; and therefore that universal and equal intelligibility, uni-

versal acceptability, and even universal familiarity, to all normal members of the human species, regardless of differences of
time, place, race, and individual propensities and endowments,
constitute the decisive criterion of validity or of worth in all
matters of vital human concernment; that (the German words
sum it up rather more neatly) *Gültigkeit* means *Allgemeingültig-
keit* and is, indeed, to be tested by actual (or supposed) *Gemein-
heit*. Let the individual, when a creed is presented for his
belief or a work of art for his admiration and enjoyment, consider whether there be anything in it which he cannot suppose
to be accessible and obvious to every rational mind through the
"unaided light of nature" or through those modes of experience which are everywhere the same. If such a non-univer-
salizable element be found in it, let him reject it as a false
religion or as unsound ethics or as bad art, as the case may be.
Thus the deist objected to revealed religion chiefly because, in
two ways, it lacked universality: (*a*) it was "historical" and
therefore its doctrines could not be known to those who lived
before its disclosure or to whom convincing historical evidences of it had not come; (*b*)it was, as embodied in the creeds,
complicated and "mysterious," and therefore not the sort of
thing that all men, savage and civilized, simple and learned,
could instantaneously understand and intuitively perceive to
be true. "La religion naturelle," to recall one of Voltaire's
definitions of it, can include only "les principes de morale
communs au genre humain." [1] That truculent defender of
orthodoxy, Dr. Samuel Clarke, declared truly enough that
"all the deniers of revelation" agreed in the premise that
"what is not universally made known to all men is not needful for any." As Swift satirically but not altogether unfairly
put it, the assumption was that unless a proposition "can be
presently comprehended by the weakest noddle, it is no part of
religion."

The same connotation of universality, obviousness to every
rational mind as such, and uniformity of content, was oftenest
carried by the protean term "nature" in its ethical application
— i. e., in the conception of the "law of nature" in moral and
political philosophy. Cicero had already set up a formal equa-
tion of "the universally accepted" with the *lex naturae*; [2] and

the Roman jurists had similarly identified *jus naturale* with *jus gentium* — with those principles of right *quae apud omnes gentes peraeque servantur, divina quadam providentia constituta, semper firma atque immutabilia permanent.*[3] And this was the one thing upon which most schools of eighteenth-century moralists were agreed and upon which they were never weary of discoursing. "The tables of natural law," said Bolingbroke, "are so obvious that no man who is able to read the plainest character can mistake them, and therefore no political society ever framed a system of law in direct and avowed contradiction of them." "The law of nature is too obvious and too important not to have been always the law of laws."[4] It was to this same universal and unvarying code — exceedingly simple in its provisions — that Voltaire reduced the whole duty of man:

> La morale uniforme en tout temps, en tout lieu. . . .
> C'est la loi de Platon, de Socrate, et la vôtre.
> De ce culte éternel la Nature est l apôtre.
> Cette loi souveraine en Europe, au Japon,
> Inspira Zoroastre, illumina Solon.

But the same assumption was manifestly the root from which grew most of the principles of neo-classical criticism. Here, too, high ancient authority could be (and was) cited: Longinus had written:

> You may pronounce that sublime, beautiful, and genuine which always pleases and takes equally with all sorts of men. For when persons of different humours, ages, professions, and inclinations, agree in the same joint approbation of any performance, this combination of so many different judgments, stamps a high and indisputable value on that performance, which meets with such general applause.[5]

The principal eighteenth-century examples of this limitation of aesthetic value to that which makes a universal appeal scarcely need to be recalled: e. g., the familiar passage in Pope's *Essay on Criticism* in which the word "nature" is virtually synonymous with the obvious — i. e., with "what oft was thought":

> Something whose truth convinced at sight we find,
> That gives us back the image of our mind.[6]

Dr. Johnson's expressions of this universalism and uniformitarianism in aesthetic theory are equally familiar; but it is worth while to observe how he brings out the logical connection between the demand for universality of appeal in a work of art and the neo-classical requirement that art shall restrict its "imitation of nature" to generic types and avoid the portrayal of the individual — with the consequent deliberate exclusion of local color and the deliberate preference in poetry for the conventional and generalized epithet. The precise reason, it will be remembered, why it was held to be "a general rule of poetry that all appropriated terms of art should be sunk in general expressions" was that "poetry is to speak a universal language." [7] It will also be recalled how preposterously Dr. Johnson, under the influence of this principle, mispraised Shakespeare, on the ground that his Romans are not particularly Roman nor his kings especially kinglike — that, in short, "his characters are not modified by the peculiarities of studies or professions which can operate upon but small numbers," but exhibit only the traits of "common humanity, such as the world will always supply, and observation will always find." Dr. Johnson detested the deists; but in his famous dictum in *Rasselas* about the streaks of the tulip he demanded in the poetic description of a flower or a landscape precisely what the deist demanded in a religion — and did so, in the last analysis, under the influence of the same preconception. [8] Aesthetic orthodoxy and religious heterodoxy in that age grew from a common root. The classic exposition of all this in English, however, is to be found in Reynolds's *Discourses*; of these there is neither time nor need to speak here. I content myself with recalling a single example of the effect of Reynolds's influence. When Thomas Warton in 1782 recanted his youthful deviation into a taste for Gothic architecture, he exclaimed, apostrophizing Reynolds:

> Thy powerful hand has broke the Gothic chain,
> And brought my bosom back to truth again.
> To truth, by no peculiar taste confined,
> Whose universal pattern strikes mankind.

This aesthetic conversion was, according to the poet, brought about merely by gazing upon Sir Joshua's painted window in the chapel of New College, Oxford; but we may be tolerably sure that that example of supposedly "classic" qualities in art would have had no such effect unassisted by the reasonings of the *Discourses*.

As for the doctrine of the superiority of the ancients and of that art which followed the example of the ancients, it was obviously a corollary of the same universalism. For the ancients alone had, so to say, had time for the test of (supposed) universal acceptance to be applied to them. As a minor but typical writer put it:

> It is not because Aristotle and Horace have given us the rules of criticism that we submit to their authority, but because those rules have been derived from works that have been distinguished by the uninterrupted admiration of all the more improved part of mankind from their earliest appearance to the present hour. For whatsoever, through long ages, has been universally esteemed beautiful, cannot but be conformable to our just and natural ideas of beauty.[9]

The scales were thus heavily weighted against any modern innovator, since in the nature of the case he could not claim to have been "universally esteemed through long ages." Moreover, no quality, no effect, essentially foreign to ancient art could be permitted, since it *eo ipso* must lack universality. Aesthetic or other universalism, so far as it was consistently carried out, had thus an obvious affinity for a kind of primitivism — inasmuch as anything which was not within the reach of the earliest men, or at least of the earliest practitioners of a given art, plainly was not common to the race. By a similar logic the deists were obliged to declare their creed "as old as the creation."

Thus for two centuries the efforts made for improvement and correction in beliefs, in institutions, and in art had been, in the main, controlled by the assumption that, in each phase of his activity, man should conform as nearly as possible to a standard conceived as universal, uncomplicated, immutable, uniform for every rational being. The Enlightenment was, in short, an age devoted, at least in its dominant tendency, to the simplification and the standardization of thought and life — to their standardization by means of their simplification. Spinoza summed it up in a remark reported by one of his early biographers: "The purpose of Nature is to make men uniform, as children of a common mother." [10] The struggle to realize this supposed purpose of nature, the general attack upon the *differentness* of men and their opinions and valuations and institutions — this, with the resistances to it and the eventual revulsion against it, was the central and dominating fact in the intellectual history of Europe from the late sixteenth to the late eighteenth century.[11]

There have, in the entire history of thought, been few changes in standards of value more profound and more momentous than that which took place when the contrary principle began widely to prevail — when it came to be believed not only that in many, or in all, phases of human life there are diverse excellences, but that diversity itself is of the essence of excellence; and that of art, in particular, the objective is neither the attainment of some single ideal perfection of form in a small number of fixed *genres* nor the gratification of that least common denominator of aesthetic susceptibility which is shared by all mankind in all ages, but rather the fullest possible expression of the abundance of differentness that there is, actually or potentially, in nature and human nature, and — for the function of the artist in relation to his public — the evocation of capacities for understanding, sympathy, enjoyment, which are as yet latent in most men, and perhaps never capable of universalization. And these assumptions, though assuredly not the only important, are the one *common*, factor in a number of otherwise diverse tendencies which, by one or another critic or historian, have been termed "Romantic": the immense multiplication of genres and of verse-forms; the admission of the aesthetic legitimacy of the *genre mixte*; the *goût de la nuance*; the naturalization in art of the "grotesque"; the quest for local color; the endeavor to reconstruct in imagination the distinctive inner life of peoples remote in time or space or in cultural condition; the *étalage du moi*; the demand for particularized fidelity in landscape-description; the revulsion against simplicity; the distrust of universal formulas in politics; the aesthetic antipathy to standardization; the identification of the Absolute with the "concrete universal" in metaphysics; the feeling of "the glory of the imperfect"; the cultivation of individual, national, and racial peculiarities; the depreciation of the obvious and the general high valuation (wholly foreign to most earlier periods) of originality, and the usually futile and absurd self-conscious pursuit of that attribute. It is, however, of no great consequence whether or not we apply to this transformation of current assumptions about value the name of "Romanticism"; what it is essential to remember is that the transformation has taken place and that it, perhaps, more than any other *one* thing has distinguished, both for better and worse, the prevailing assumptions of the mind of the nineteenth and of our own century from those of the preceding period in the intellectual history of the West. That change, in short, has consisted in the substitution of what may be called diversitarianism for uniformitarianism as the ruling preconception in most of the normative provinces of thought.

Now the relation of this change to the ideas of which we are reviewing the historic influence and vicissitudes is what I chiefly wish to point out in this lecture. *La nature est partout la même* was the premise from which, explicitly or implicitly, the neo-classic aesthetic theorists had deduced the consequence that art should be the same among all peoples and at all times; [12] but the writers on the Chain of Being — who were in many cases the same writers — had endlessly reiterated the contrary of this premise: that "Nature diversifies its art in as many ways as possible." [13] The rationality of the World-Ground, according to the philosophy of Leibniz, had, as we have seen, manifested itself in the maximal differentiation of the creatures. Every monad mirrors the world from its own unique point of view and therefore in its own unique way, and it is by this means that the fullness of diversity which constitutes the perfection of the universe is attained: "the glory of God is multiplied by so many wholly different representations of his world." [14]

As a city viewed from various sides appears wholly different, and receives as it were a perspective multiplication, in like manner, through the infinite multiplicity of the simple substances [monads], there is a corresponding multiplicity of different universes, which, nevertheless, are only the perspectives of one and the same universe according to the different points of view of each monad. And this is the means whereby the greatest variety possible is obtained, that is to say, the means whereby is obtained the greatest possible perfection.[15]

Any endeavor by man to diminish this differentness would therefore be contrary to the cosmic plan. We have already seen Addison finding the "goodness of God" not less "in the diversity than in the multitude of living creatures"; in the fact that "he has *specified* in his creation every degree of life, every capacity of being," and filled "the whole chasm of nature, from a plant to a man, with diverse kinds of creatures, rising one above another. . . . The intermediate space is so well husbanded and managed, that there is scarce a degree of perception which does not appear in some part of the world of life." [16] Haller had explicitly drawn the moral for man: "Das Glück der Sterblichen will die Verschiedenheit." These are but a few examples out of a long series of early eighteenth-century expressions of this creed; and back of these was the whole continuous tradition from Plato through the Neoplatonists, the Schoolmen, Bruno, and other writers of the Renaissance. And it is to be remembered that it was equally a part of the orthodox tradition in religion and morals that man is to imitate God, to seek, so far as he may, even in this life, to reflect the divine attributes; and that it was not less a part of the classical tradition in aesthetics that art should imitate nature, not merely in the sense of copying natural objects or portraying faithfully the characters of men, but also in the sense of conforming to the general characteristics of nature and to the ways of working of its Author. The human artist must copy not only the products but, in so far as he can, the methods of the Master Craftsman. The vocation of the sculptor, the musician, the painter, said Akenside, is "to strive to display to all the world, by forms, or sounds, or colors," the whole range of the essences present to the divine mind,

> Even as in Nature's frame (if such a word,
> If such a word, so bold, may from the lips
> Of man proceed) as in this outward frame
> Of things, the great Artificer portrays
> His own immense idea . . . .
> . . . . . . . . . . But the chief
> Are poets; eloquent men, who dwell on earth
> To clothe whate'er the soul admires or loves
> With language and with numbers. Hence to these
> A field is open'd wide as Nature's sphere;

Nay, wider: various as the sudden acts
Of human wit, and vast as the demands
Of human will.  The bard nor length, nor depth,
Nor place, nor form controls.[17]

And by the late eighteenth century, we must also recall, the cosmical order was coming to be conceived not as an infinite static diversity, but as a process of increasing diversification. The Chain of Being having been temporalized, the God whose attributes it disclosed had been declared by not a few great writers to be one who manifests himself through change and becoming; nature's incessant tendency was to the production of new kinds; and the destiny of the individual was to mount through all the spires of form, in a continual self-transcendence.  Since the strain in Western thought summed up in the doctrine of the Chain of Being thus consisted in an increasing emphasis upon the conception of God as insatiably creative, it followed that the man who, as moral agent or as artist, would imitate God, must do so by being himself "creative." The word, which through much repetition has in our own day become a sort of tiresome cant, could still in the late eighteenth century express a very exciting, and for the arts a very stimulating, idea.  Man's high calling was to add something of his own to the creation, to enrich the sum of things, and thus, in his finite fashion, consciously to collaborate in the fulfilment of the Universal Design.

Not only diversity and perpetual innovation, but sometimes also a measure of discord and especially of conflict, had been found by the most esteemed philosophers of the early eighteenth century to be implicit in the nature of the good, when the good was construed in conformity with the principle of plenitude.  And in this also they were but repeating what Plotinus and the Schoolmen and the Renaissance Platonists and the theologians and metaphysicians of the seventeenth century had said before them.  The traditional argument for optimism in all ages, as has been made sufficiently evident, represented the Cosmic Artist as cramming his canvas with diversified detail to the last infinitesimal fraction of an inch; as caring far more for fullness and variety of content than for simplicity and perfection of form; and as seeking this richness of coloring and abundance of contrast even at the cost of disharmony, irregularity, and what to us appears confusion. For there is much truth, said Leibniz, in "the fine principle of St. Bernard: *ordinatissimum est, minus interdum ordinate fieri aliquid.*" As Blackmore, in one of the most conventional of early eighteenth-century poems, had said, when speaking not of the human artist but of the Creator:

> If all perfection were in all things shown,
> All beauty, all variety, were gone.

If, then, we recognize in the shift from the uniformitarian to the diversitarian preconception the most significant and distinctive single feature of the Romantic revolution, it is evident that there had always been present in the Platonic tradition a principle tending towards Romanticism, and that this had been enunciated with especial clarity and insistence by the philosophers and moralists and philosophic poets of the so-called Age of Reason. And in the ideas of these philosophers and poets the young men, especially in Germany, who were, in the later decades of the eighteenth century, to be the leaders of that revolution had been reared. By Leibniz and Locke and Kant, by Buffon and Bonnet, by Addison and Pope and Akenside and Haller, and by a hundred minor writers, they had been taught that the best of possible worlds is the most variegated, that it was the divine purpose that no possibility of being should be left unrealized. Most of all had these diversitarian preconceptions been impressed upon the eighteenth-century mind by the controversy over optimism, in which so great a part of the intellectual energy of that age had been engrossed. These presuppositions had, it is true, usually been associated with other conceptions with which they were fundamentally inconsistent and with a temper with which they were not in accord; their full implications could become apparent only when they were more sharply disengaged from these other ideas which had tended to counteract and partially neutralize them. But in the minds of a new generation they came into their own. It is to be remembered, also, that a revival of the direct influence of Neoplatonism was one of the conspicuous phenomena in German thought of the nineties. A special student of this period has gone so far as to declare that

> if we are to speak of a 'key' to early Romanticism, it is to be found in one of the thinkers of antiquity, Plotinus. For this Neoplatonic philosopher not only inspired the entire system of Novalis, scattered through innumerable fragments, and many of the ideas of Schelling in his middle period; his arm reached farther: through Novalis and Schelling he exercised an influence, though an indirect one, upon both the Schlegels, and without a knowledge of this fact many a passage in the 'Dialogue concerning Poetry' and in the Berlin lectures [of Wilhelm Schlegel] remains an enigma.[18]

There were, indeed, several other powerful forces at work upon these minds which helped to produce a fresh intellectual ferment and tended, in some degree, to suggest the same conclusions. But the pressure of the principle of plenitude can be shown to be a major factor in the great change in presuppositions which becomes most clearly manifest in the religious ideas and the moral and aesthetic ideals and enthusiasms of the generation of German writers who came to maturity between the seventies and the nineties, and which were (chiefly) by them to be communicated to the rest of the world. It may, indeed, be suggested, with some plausibility, that these ideas are but the expression of some constant propensities of human nature, which became, for some reason, peculiarly potent at this time, and that the invocation of these ancient principles was but a device for "rationalizing" desires and aesthetic susceptibilities previously restrained. The general psychological issue raised by such a suggestion — the question how far men's philosophies are generated, not by the logical, or supposedly logical, working out of accepted premises, but by emotional cravings, by idiosyncrasies of personal temperament, or by the social and other practical problems of a particular historic juncture — I shall not attempt to discuss here. It remains the fact that, throughout the Enlightenment, the uniformitarian creed *had* in practice been effectively dominant — while the theoretical premises of diversitarianism had, in the same period, been constantly and with increasing frequency dilated upon, and that their practical implications did eventually find acceptance and application. It also, I think, remains the fact that, even though it be assumed — as I am not prepared to assume without a good deal of qualification — that the reasons which men give for their beliefs, their standards, and their tastes are but the "rationalization" of their desires and their spontaneous likings and dislikes, the possibility of giving reasons, or what appear to be such, is not less indispensable. And it was in the principle of plenitude that the protagonists of the revolution with which we are here concerned found one of the two most fundamental and, for their generation, most effective of their reasons.

In the youthful philosophy of Schiller, set forth in the *Philosophische Briefe*, these anti-rationalistic and diversitarian consequences of that principle are deduced with the utmost boldness. From Platonic and Leibnitian premises emerges a justification of the temper of the *Sturm und Drang*.

Every kind of perfection must attain existence in the fullness of the world. . . . Every offspring of the brain, everything that wit can fashion, has an unchallengeable right of citizenship in this larger understanding of the creation. In the infinite chasm of nature no activity could be omitted, no grade of enjoyment be wanting in the universal happiness. . . .

That great Householder of his world who suffers not even a straw to fall to the ground uselessly, who leaves no crevice uninhabited where life may be enjoyed, who hospitably grants even that little flowering of pleasure which finds its root in madness, . . . this great Inventor could not permit even error to remain unutilized in his great design, could not allow this wide region of thought to lie empty and joyless in the mind of man. . . . It is a genuine gain for the completeness of the universe, it is a provision of the supreme wisdom, that erring reason should people even the chaotic land of dreams and should cultivate even the barren ground of contradiction.[19]

From all which the young philosopher-poet romantically concludes that neither he, nor the friend to whom he imparts his musings, need be greatly concerned lest he have sometimes "mistaken the ebullitions of his blood, the hopes and desires of his heart, for sober wisdom." Perhaps the entire structure of his conclusions is but the baseless fabric of a dream; no matter; the world is the richer for the illusion, and the purposes of the Creator are the more fully realized.

In the work of the Divine Artist, the unique value of each part is respected, and the sustaining gaze with which he honors every spark of energy in even the lowliest creature manifests his glory not less than the harmony of the immeasurable whole. *Life* and *liberty* to the greatest possible extent are the glory of the divine creation; nowhere is it more sublime than where it seems to have departed most widely from its ideal.

The aesthetic implication also is evident, and is not left by Schiller unexpressed. The human artist must, like the divine, make fullness in the expression of all possible modes of being and of experience the purpose of his activity. For him, indeed, this can only be a program to be realized grad ally, as the content of art is progressively enriched and diversified through generation after generation.

This higher completeness cannot be grasped by us, with our present limitations. Our vision covers too small a part of the universe; and the harmonious fusion of the vast multiplicity of discords cannot reach our ears. Every step which we mount in the Scale of Being makes us more capable of this aesthetic enjoyment; but such enjoyment has value, certainly, only in so far as it rouses us to a similar activity. To wonder idly at a greatness not our own can never highly profit us. To the man of noble character there is lacking neither matter to act upon nor the power to be, in his own sphere, himself a creator.[20]

And the human artist who takes this for his program is bidden to remember that he will not be following the cosmic model in his small creative efforts if he allows too much concern for "form" to lead him to sacrifice richness of content: *der Fleiss in den Formen kann zuweilen die, massive Wahrheit des Stoffes vergessen lassen.* Here, plainly, the fundamental principles of neo-classical criticism are undergoing reversal.

In the same writing the young theologian formally rejects the notion of the divine self-sufficiency, the Aristotelian principle that a God "can have no need of friends." The pious Klopstock, not long before, had once more apostrophized the deity with the ancient question:

Warum, da allein du dir genug warst, Erster, schaffst du? . . .
Wurdest dadurch du Seliger, dass du Seligkeit gabst?[21]

But the Absolute gave no reply. The mystery Klopstock pronounced insoluble; the finite mind here reaches its limit. Schiller answers the question in terms which would have scandalized most of the great speculative theologians since Aristotle:

Freundlos war der grosse Weltenmeister,
Fühlte Mangel, darum schuf er Geister,
Sel'ge Spiegel seiner Seligkeit.
Fand das höchste Wesen schon keine Gleiches,
Aus dem Kelch des ganzen Wesenreiches
Schäumt ihm die Unendlichkeit.

The direct relation of the thought here to that of the *Timaeus* is evident; these famous lines, too, are a sort of commentary on that dialogue, and a highly pertinent one, though Schiller himself may have been unaware of the connection. For we here see the definite separation of those two conceptions of deity which had been joined together in hopeless discord throughout most of the history of European religious thought. The Platonic Demiurgus has been recognized to be inconsistent with the Platonic Absolute, the God identified with the Idea of the Good as perfection or self-sufficiency; and the latter has been sacrificed in order that the former may be retained. A God who creates a world of finite spirits must be a God who is *not* sufficient unto himself.

In consequence, chiefly, of the belated wave of classicism which swept over the younger German generation in the late seventeen-eighties and early nineties, these exuberances of Schiller's youth presently came to seem to him, not, indeed, false, but one-sided. His attempt to provide the needed complement to them still took the form of a new synthesis of the two strains in the Platonistic tradition — the synthesis being facilitated for him by some conceptions which he had lately learned from Kant and Fichte. The result is set forth in his *Letters on the Aesthetic Education of Mankind* (1795), which have a wider bearing than their title suggests. The constructive part of them begins with an analogy between the two fundamental attributes of the Platonic, or Neoplatonic, Absolute, and two corresponding elements in the constitution of man. On the one hand, "a divine being cannot be subject to becoming," since it is, by its essence, "infinite," i. e., it is eternally complete, and can gain no increment through any process in time. But on the other hand,

a tendency ought to be named divine which has for its infinite program the most distinctive attribute of the divinity — the absolute manifestation of potency, the actuality of all that is possible — and the absolute unity of the manifestation — the necessity of all that is actual.[22]

Schiller thus brings back again the two Gods of Plato — the immutable and self-contained Perfection and the Creative Urge which makes for the unlimited realization in time of all the possibles. In these two characteristics of the divine nature man shares; and there are therefore two forever conflicting tendencies in him, the "two fundamental laws" of a being which is at once rational and sensuous — which has, in Kantian terms, both a noumenal and a temporal Ego. The one is the demand for pure unity, for "form" in the abstract — the *Formtrieb*, as Schiller calls it; and since it is alien to time, it is adverse to change. "It can never exact at one time anything but what it exacts and requires forever." The other, the *Stofftrieb*, is the demand for diversity, for fullness of concrete, particularized content; and it necessarily manifests itself in the life of an incomplete and temporal being as a perpetual impulsion towards change, towards the enrichment of experience through innovation. The object of this "sensuous impulse" (as Schiller also, less adequately, names it), of that which makes man a part of the natural world of becoming, is "*life*, in the widest sense of the term, in which it embraces all material existence and all that is immediately present to the senses." [23]

Since the *world* is spread out in time, since it is change, the complete realization of that potentiality which relates man to the world must consist in the greatest possible variability and extension. Since the *person* is that which is permanent through change, the complete realization of that potentiality which is antithetic to change must consist in the greatest possible self-sufficiency and intension.[24]

Though these two elements in man are forever at war, they are equally indispensable to the attainment of excellence, in character and in art. Beauty, the objective of art, requires always definiteness of form (*Bestimmtheit*); but those aestheticians and critics who dwell upon this truth are prone to forget that that objective is to be attained, not "through the exclusion of certain realities," but through "the absolute inclusion of all." [25]

Thus the temporalized principle of plenitude and the opposite idea of the restriction of content by the imposition of immutable rules of formal perfection are made by Schiller the joint dictators of the program of life and of art. Since they are essentially antithetic, in any actual juncture in experience one of them must in some degree be sacrificed to the other. Between them Schiller himself constantly wavers; sometimes the primacy seems to be given to the one, sometimes to its opposite. Yet he conceived that he had discovered in a third tendency of man, the *Spieltrieb* or play-impulse, the harmonious union of both. Into this confused effort of Schiller to reconcile the ultimately irreconcilable we need not enter. In the end he himself admits that no definitive reconciliation can be achieved. The "equilibrium of form and of content remains always an idea" that reality can never completely reach. "In reality there will always remain a preponderance of one of these elements over the other; and the highest point to which experience can attain consists in an oscillation between two principles," in which now the one and now the other will be preponderant.[26] Thus there must be, in the life of the individual, the development of the race, and the history of art, an unending alternation of contrary phases. Now the insatiable quest of more "life," of greater variety and fullness of content, will break down the forms which have been imposed upon art or upon other modes of man's self-expression; and now the demand for "form," for fixed "principles" and stable order, will arrest the expansive process of life. Thus humanity in all of its activities will — and should — forever swing between opposite exaggerations. But on the whole — it is implied, though not acknowledged, by Schiller — the principle of plenitude has the last word. Since he holds that every unification must be incomplete, every aesthetic form or moral code prove in the end too narrow to contain the potentialities of humanity, it follows that the tendency to increasing diversification through perennial change will be, and should be, the dominant force in man's existence.

In the writings (after 1796) of the German poets, critics, and moralists who adapted the word "romantic" to their own uses and introduced it into the vocabulary of literary history and of philosophy, the diversitarian assumption is pervasively present; and here too it is closely connected with the conception that the artist's task is to imitate, not simply Nature's works, but her way of working, to enter into the spirit of the universe by aiming, as it does, at fullness and variety without end. "All the sacred play of art," said Friedrich Schlegel, "is only a distant copying of the infinite play of the world, that work of art which is eternally fashioning itself." [27] A special student of the German *Romantiker* has recently observed that "just as God's purpose in 'the things that are made' is nothing less than to reveal 'the invisible things of him, . . . even his eternal power and Godhead,' thus Schlegel thought it was the purpose of the romantic poet likewise to show in his equally objective creation his own artistic power, glory, wisdom, and love for the product of his literary genius"; and the same writer has pointed out how crucial in the history of the development of the younger Schlegel's aesthetic ideas was the suggestion which "came to him from the field of religion," that "as God is to his creation, so is the artist to his own." [28] But the most significant element for the young Romanticist in this ancient parallel was that the God whose artistic practice was to be both imitated and complemented by the human artist was a God who valued diversity above all else.

But there was a radical and perilous ambiguity in this assumption when it was applied as a rule of art or of conduct. It could be construed in two ways; and they tended in practice to be antithetic ways, though they were not wholly so in essence. On the one hand, it suggested, as both an aesthetic and a moral aim for the individual, the effort to enter as fully as possible into the immensely various range of thought and feeling in other men. It thus made for the cultivation, not merely of tolerance, but of imaginative insight into the points of view, the valuations, the tastes, the subjective experiences, of others; and this not only as a means to the enrichment of one's own inner life, but also as a recognition of the objective validity of diversities of valuation. The Romantic imperative, so construed, was: 'Respect and delight in — not merely, as with Kant, the universal reason in which all men uniformly participate — but the qualities by which men, and all creatures, are unlike one another and, in particular, are unlike yourself.' "I almost believe" — wrote Friedrich Schlegel — "that a wise self-limitation and moderation of the mind is not more necessary to man than the inward, ever restless, almost voracious, participation in all life, and a certain feeling of the sanctity (*Heiligkeit*) of an abounding fullness." [29] And his own usual tendency, and that of the school whose ideas he so largely formulated, was to regard it as more necessary. The earlier Romantic writers accordingly became zealous preachers of catholicity in aesthetic appreciation.

It is thus that Wackenroder praises *Allgemeinheit, Toleranz und Menschenliebe in der Kunst*:

> The Eternal Spirit knows that each man speaks the language which He has provided for him, that everyone expresses what is within him as he can and should. . . . [God] looks with satisfaction upon each and all, and rejoices in the variety of the mixture. . . . To him the Gothic church is as well-pleasing as the Grecian temple; and the rude war-music of the savage is a sound as dear to him as religious anthems and choruses composed with richest art. Yet when I turn my gaze back from Him, the Infinite, to earth, and look about upon my brothers — ah! how loudly must I lament that they so little strive to become like their great model in Heaven. [Men] always think of the point at which they stand as the centre of gravity of the universe; and similarly they regard their own feeling as the centre of all that is beautiful in art, pronouncing, as from the judge's seat, the final verdict upon all things, without remembering that no one has appointed them to be judges. . . . Why do you not condemn the Indian because he speaks his own language and not ours? And yet you would condemn the Middle Ages because they did not build the same kind of temples as Greece. . . . If you are unable to enter directly into the feelings of so many beings different from yourself and, by penetrating to their hearts, *feel* their works, strive at least, by using the intellect as a connecting bond, to attain to such an understanding of them indirectly.[30]

A. W. Schlegel, more than a decade later, was inculcating the same exacting and salutary aesthetic self-discipline.

> One cannot become a connoisseur without universality of mind, that is, without the flexibility which enables us, through the renunciation of personal likings and blind preference for what we are accustomed to, to transpose ourselves into that which is peculiar to other peoples and times, and, so to say, to *feel* this from its centre outwards. Thus the despotism of good taste, by which [some critics] seek to enforce certain perhaps wholly arbitrary rules which they have set up, is always an unwarranted presumption.

And, recalling the disparagement both of Gothic architecture and of Shakespeare in the preceding period, Schlegel based upon this principle a condemnation of the narrowness of neoclassicism:

The Pantheon is not more different from Westminster Abbey than the structure of a tragedy of Sophocles from that of a play of Shakespeare. . . . But does admiration for one of these really require of us depreciation of the other? Can we not grant that each is in its own way great and admirable, even though the one is utterly unlike the other? . . . The world is wide, and many things can coexist in it side by side.[31]

For the artist, as distinct from the appreciator of art, this ideal led to the program expressed in Friedrich Schlegel's famous definition of Romantic poetry: "die romantische Poesie ist eine progressive Universalpoesie." It must be universal, not in the restrictive sense of seeking uniformity of norms and universality of appeal, but in the expansive sense of aiming at the apprehension and expression of every mode of human experience. Nothing should be too strange or too remote, nothing too lofty or too low, to be included in its scope; no *nuance* of character or emotion can be so delicate and elusive, or so peculiar, that the poet or novelist ought not to attempt to seize it and to convey its unique *quale* to his readers. "From the romantic point of view," wrote Schlegel, "the abnormal species (*Abarten*) of literature also have their value — even the eccentric and monstrous — as materials and preparatory exercises for universality — provided only that there is *something* in them, that they are really original." [32]

It was this strain in Romanticism which was the more harmonious with that note in it of which we observed some illustrations in a previous lecture — the demand for a perpetual transcendence of the already-attained, for unceasing expansion. Romantic art must be progressive as well as universal because the universality of comprehension at which it aimed was assumed to be never fully attainable by any individual or any generation. The *Fülle des Lebens* was inexhaustible; however much of it might have been at any given time expressed through the medium of one or another art, there was always more beyond. The early Romanticists did not suffer from that fear which obsessed the young John Stuart Mill, during his phase of somewhat belated adolescent melancholy — itself a fear which derived its poignancy from the same Romantic preconception — the fear lest all the possible modes and combinations in, for example, music had already been realized, that there could be nothing really new in this art to look forward to. (This was, it need hardly be recalled incidentally, a rather comic cause for alarm in the third decade of the nineteenth century.) Nature and man, for the Romanticist, were various enough to afford the artist ever new material; and his task was indefatigably to appropriate and to embody it in equally various and changing aesthetic forms. And the moral consequence was the same; the good man, for the Romantic as for Goethe's God, was the man *der immer strebend sich bemüht.*

But the idealization of diversity, the program of consciously emulating and even adding to the plenitude of nature, could, as I have said, be quite otherwise interpreted. And this alternative interpretation is apparent in the same group of writers, and even in the same individuals. If the world is the better the more variety it contains, the more adequately it manifests the possibilities of differentness in human nature, the duty of the individual, it would seem, was to cherish and intensify his own differentness from other men. Diversitarianism thus led also to a conscious pursuit of idiosyncrasy, personal, racial, national, and, so to say, chronological. "It is precisely individuality," wrote Friedrich Schlegel in the *Athenaeum*,[33] "that is the original and eternal thing in men. . . . The cultivation and development of this individuality, as one's highest vocation, would be a divine egoism." "The more personal, local, peculiar (*eigentümlicher*), of its own time (*temporeller*), a poem is, the nearer it stands to the centre of poetry," declared Novalis.[34] This, obviously, was the polar opposite of the fundamental principle of the neo-classic aesthetic doctrine. This interpretation of the Romantic ideal suggested that the first and great commandment is: 'Be yourself, which is to say, be unique!'

Both of these highly dissimilar morals drawn from the principle of plenitude are especially well illustrated by Schleiermacher, in two of the chief manifestos of early German Romanticism, his *Reden* (1799) and *Monologen* (1800). The *Reden* may be called the first serious and deliberate attempt to formulate a distinctively "Romantic" ethics, to carry over into moral philosophy the same principle which had been given aesthetic application in the writings of the Schlegels,

especially in their contributions to the *Athenaeum*. Schleiermacher was obviously merely repeating the deduction from
the principles of plenitude and continuity — as these had been
expressed in the argument for optimism — which we have
already, in a previous lecture, seen drawn by Leibniz:

> What would the uniform repetition of even the highest ideal be? Man-
> kind — time and external circumstances excepted — would be every-
> where identical. They would be the same formula with a different co-
> efficient. What would this be in comparison with the endless variety which
> humanity *does* manifest? Take any element of humanity and you will find
> it in almost every possible condition. You will not find it quite isolated, . . .
> nor quite combined with all other elements, . . . but you will find all possible
> mixtures between, in every odd and unusual combination. And if you
> could think of combinations you do not see, this gap would be a negative
> revelation of the universe, an indication that in the present temperature
> of the world this mixture is not possible.[35]

Schleiermacher does not find this assumption overthrown by
"the often bewailed superfluity of the commonest forms of
humanity, ever returning unchanged in a thousand copies."
The explanation is found in the principle of continuity: "the
Eternal Mind commands that the forms in which individuality
is most difficult to discern should stand closest together." Yet
it is still true that "each has something of its own and no two
are identical."

From this, then, both in the *Reden* and the *Monologen*,
Schleiermacher draws the ethical corollary that "uniformity"
in thought and character is the evil which it is man's first duty
to avoid.

> Why, in the province of morals, does this pitiable uniformity prevail,
> which seeks to bring the highest human life within the compass of a single
> lifeless formula? How can this ever have come into vogue, except in conse-
> quence of a radical lack of feeling for the fundamental characteristic of
> living Nature, which everywhere aims at diversity and individuality (*Man-
> nigfaltigkeit und Eigentümlichkeit*)?[36]

But here again the moral takes on two shapes: the first, that
the aim of the individual should be an all-comprehending
understanding and sympathy, an increasing absorption into
oneself, through the imagination, of the full range of diversity
in nature, and especially of the modes of experience and the

types of character and of culture to be found among mankind in all periods of history and in all branches of the race.

How can I help but rejoice in novelty and variety, which but confirms in new and ever different ways the truth of which I am possessed? . . . Am I so complete as not to welcome joy and sorrow alike, indeed whatever the world calls weal or woe, seeing that everything in its own way serves this purpose and further reveals to me the relationships of my own nature? If but this be accomplished, of what importance is it that I be happy? . . . My powers have long been striving to draw nearer to the All; when shall I embrace it in action and in contemplation, and achieve an inner union with the All which is within me? There are sciences without the knowledge of which my outlook on the world will never be complete. There are still many forms of humanity, ages and peoples, which I know no better than the average man does — ages and peoples into whose nature and manner of thought my imagination has not in its own way entered, which occupy no definite place of their own in my picture of the development of the race. Many activities which have no place in my own nature I do not comprehend, and I often lack an understanding of my own of their relations to that All which shows its greatness and beauty in humanity as a whole. Of that whole I shall, part by part and part *with* part, gain possession; the fairest of prospects spreads before me. How many noble natures, wholly different from mine, which humanity has fashioned as elements of itself, do I see close at hand! how many men rich in knowledge who generously or proudly hold out to me in noble vessels the golden fruits of their lives, and how many growths of distant times and regions have been transplanted to the fatherland through their faithful efforts! Can fate so enchain me that I shall not be able to draw nearer to this goal of mine? Can it refuse the means of self-development, withhold from me easy entrance into a fellowship with the activity of mankind as it is at present, and with the monuments of the past — cast me out of the fair world in which I live into those barren wastes where it is vain to seek acquaintance with the rest of mankind, where what is merely common in Nature surrounds me on all sides with everlasting uniformity, and nothing fine, nothing distinctive, stands out in the thick and sodden atmosphere?[37] . . . For me imagination supplies what reality withholds; through it I can put myself in any situation in which I observe another to be placed; his experience moves in my mind, changes it to accord with its own nature, and represents in my thought how *he* would act. Upon the common judgment of mankind about other men's existence and activity — a judgment framed out of the dead letter of empty formulas — no reliance can, indeed, be placed. . . . But if — as must be the case where *life* is really present — an inner activity accompanies the play of the imagination, and the judgment is an explicit consciousness of this inner activity — then that which is apprehended as external to the mind of the beholder gives form to his mind, as if it were really his own, as if he had himself performed the outward action which he contemplates. Thus, in the future as in the past, by the power of this inner activity I shall take possession of the whole

world, and shall make better use of it all in quiet contemplation than if I
had to accompany each quickly changing image with some outward action.[38]

Such a grim determination, as Emerson said of Margaret Fuller, to *eat* this huge universe!

But the other interpretation of the diversitarian ideal is not
less — on the whole, it is rather more — ardently insisted
upon by Schleiermacher; he presents it in the *Monologen* as the
chief outcome of the course of reflection through which he had
arrived at a new ethics.

> So there came to me what is now my highest insight. It became clear
> to me that every man should exemplify humanity in his own way, in a unique
> mixture of elements, so that humanity may be manifested in *all* ways and
> everything become actual which in the fullness of infinity can proceed from
> its womb. . . . Yet only slowly and with difficulty does a man attain full con-
> sciousness of his uniqueness. Often does he lack courage to look upon it,
> turning his gaze rather upon that which is the common possession of mankind,
> to which he so fondly and gratefully holds fast; often he is in doubt whether
> he should set himself apart, as a distinctive being, from that common
> character. . . . The most characteristic urge of Nature often goes unnoted,
> and even where her outlines show themselves most clearly, man's eye all
> too easily passes over their sharp-cut edges, and fixes itself firmly only upon
> the universal.[39]

By "individuals," Schleiermacher elsewhere explains, he
does not mean solely persons; there are also collective individuals, such as races, nations, families, and sexes; each of these,
also, may and should have its distinctive character. And in the
*Reden* — applying both of the two interpretations of diversitarianism — he reverses the fundamental assumption common
to the Church and to the deists, and declares that variety even
in religious beliefs is desirable and essential:

> The different manifestations of religion cannot be mere subdivisions, dif-
> fering only in numbers and size, and forming, when united, a uniform
> whole. In that case every one by a natural progress would come to be like
> his neighbor. . . . I therefore find the multiplicity of religions to be
> grounded in the nature of religion. . . . This multiplicity is necessary
> for the complete manifestation of religion. It must seek for distinctive
> character, not only in the individual but in society.

He admonishes with especial severity those who seek for a
universal creed expressing the uniform reason of man. "You
must," he says to the deists:

You must abandon the vain and foolish wish that there should be only one religion; you must lay aside all repugnance to its multiplicity; as candidly as possible, you must approach everything that has ever, in the changing forms of humanity, been developed in its advancing career from the ever fruitful bosom of the spiritual life. . . . You are wrong, therefore, with your universal religion that is supposed to be natural to all; for no one will have his own true and right religion if it is the same for all. As long as we each of us occupy a separate place, there must be in these relations of man to the universe a nearer and a farther, which will determine such feeling differently in every life. . . . *Nur in der Totalität aller solcher möglichen Formen kann die ganze Religion wirklich gegeben werden.*[40]

Christianity is, indeed, for Schleiermacher, the highest of the positive religions; but its superiority lies only in its freedom from exclusiveness. It does not claim "to be universal and to rule alone over mankind as the sole religion. It scorns such autocracy. . . . Not only would it produce within itself variety to infinity, but it would willingly see realized even outside of itself all that it is unable to produce *from* itself. . . . As nothing is more irreligious than to demand general uniformity in mankind, so nothing is more unchristian than to seek uniformity in religion." [41] Any man, in short, Schleiermacher concludes, may, and it is well that every man should, have a religion of his own — one, that is, which has *something* unique in it which corresponds to what is unique in his own personality and to his unduplicated position in the universe.

If we should attempt, in the light of subsequent history, an appraisal of these two strains in the Romantic ideal, most of us would perhaps agree that both contributed to bring about some happy and some unhappy consequences in the next dozen decades. The first strain was the promulgation and the prophecy of an immense increase in the range — though not always in the excellence — of most of the arts, and of an unprecedented widening of men's gusto in the recognition and the enjoyment of what Akenside had called "the fair variety of things." The program of the early Romantic school *was* to be the deliberate program of the drama, much of the non-dramatic poetry, the novel, music, and painting in the nineteenth century; and it is mere blindness not to see in this a vast enrichment of the sources of delight in life. And this was not merely an aesthetic gain. It tended — in so far as it was not offset by an opposing tendency — to nothing less than an enlargement of human nature itself — to an increase of men's, and nations', understanding and appreciation of one another, not as a multitude of samples of an identical model, but as representatives of a legitimate and welcome diversity of cultures and of individual reactions to the world which we have in common. Yet all this had its dangers. The *Stofftrieb* — one comes back to Schiller's dualism — has tended to overwhelm the *Formtrieb*. The revolt against the standardization of life easily becomes a revolt against the whole conception of standards. The God whose attribute of reasonableness was expressed in the principle of plenitude was not selective; he gave reality to all the essences. But there is in man a reason which demands selection, preference, and negation, in conduct and in art. To say 'Yes' to everything and everybody is manifestly to have no character at all. The delicate and difficult art of life is to find, in each new turn of experience, the *via media* between two extremes: to be catholic *without* being characterless; to have and apply standards, and yet to be on guard against their desensitizing and stupefying influence, their tendency to blind us to the diversities of concrete situations and to previously unrecognized values; to know when to tolerate, when to embrace, and when to fight. And in that art, since no fixed and comprehensive rule can be laid down for it, we shall doubtless never attain perfection. All this has now, no doubt, become a truism; but it is also a paradox, since it demands a synthesis of opposites. And to Schiller and some of the Romanticists its paradoxical aspect made it seem not less but more evidently true.

A similar bifurcation of tendencies may be seen in the other of the two elements in the Romantic ideal, as an influence in the subsequent century. It served to promote, in individuals and in peoples, a resistance to those forces, resultant largely from the spread of democracy and from technological progress, which tend to obliterate the differences that make men, and groups of men, interesting and therefore valuable to one another. It was the perpetual enemy of *das Gemeine*. But it has also (being in this precisely opposite to the other Romantic tendency) promoted a great deal of sickly and sterile introversion in literature — a tiresome exhibition of the eccentricities of the individual Ego, these eccentricities being often, as is now notorious, merely conventions painfully turned inside out, since a man cannot by taking thought become more original or 'unique' than Nature has made him.  It has lent itself all too easily to the service of man's egotism, and especially — in the political and social sphere — of the kind of collective vanity which is nationalism or racialism.  The belief in the sanctity of one's idiosyncrasy — especially if it be a group idiosyncrasy, and therefore sustained and intensified by mutual flattery — is rapidly converted into a belief in its superiority.  More than one great people, in the course of the past century and a half, having first made a god of its own peculiarities, good or bad or both, presently began to suspect that there was no other god. A type of national culture valued at first because it was one's own, and because the conservation of differentness was recognized as a good for humanity as a whole, came in time to be conceived of as a thing which one had a mission to impose upon others, or to diffuse over as large a part of the surface of the planet as possible.  Thus the wheel came full circle; what may be called a particularistic uniformitarianism, a tendency to seek to universalize things originally valued because they were not universal, found expression in poetry, in a sort of philosophy, in the policies of great states and the enthusiasms of their populations. The tragic outcome has been seen, and experienced, by all of us in our own time.

But — *corruptio optimi pessima*.  The discovery of the intrinsic worth of diversity was, in both of its aspects, and with all of the perils latent in it, one of the great discoveries of the human mind; and the fact that it, like so many other of his discoveries, has been turned by man to ruinous uses, is no evidence that it is in itself without value.  In so far as it was historically due to the age-long influence, culminating in the eighteenth century, of the principle of plenitude, we may set it down among the most important and potentially the most benign of the manifold consequences of that influence.  I cannot forbear to add that there is perhaps a certain appositeness in this theme, at least, to the memory of the man whose name this lectureship bears. William James, whatever the verdict of the future upon some of his more technical philosophic theses, was in himself an embodiment, in a just and sane balance, of the two elements in the ideal of which I have been speaking.  In him were united, as in few men of our time, or perhaps of any time, distinctiveness of mind, the gift of seeing familiar facts and old problems in fresh and highly personal ways, and a rare degree of the sort of universality of mind which the Romantics, in their more happily inspired utterances, praised.  Temperamentally incapable of holding his own convictions lightly or of any easy eclecticism, he nevertheless took delight in the rich diversity of the characters, the mental processes, and — within limits — of the opinions of others.  This was no superficial toleration arising, as most toleration arises, from indifference.  He had — what is one of the least common of qualities — a constant sense that other people have, as he put it, "insides of their own," often quite different from his; and he had an eager desire and an extraordinary power to get outside of what was peculiar to himself and to understand, "from the centre outwards," what was peculiar to any of his fellows.  To intolerance, conventionality, and pedantry this imaginative sympathy did not, indeed, extend.  But any spark, or even seeming spark, of originality or uniqueness in his students, or in any man or writing, however little regarded by most of the professional philosophers, aroused his instant interest, his sometimes too generous admiration, and a hope that there might be here the disclosure of one of the many aspects of a happily very various universe which an adequate philosophy could not neglect.

# XI

## THE OUTCOME OF THE HISTORY AND ITS MORAL

WE BEGAN our history with the formation of those conceptions of metaphysical theology which were to remain dominant — though not without rivals — in Western thought for two millennia: the conceptions which first clearly manifest themselves in the *Republic* and the *Timaeus* of Plato and were developed and systematized by the Neoplatonists. And with a phase of the history of metaphysical theology we may conclude. The most noteworthy consequence of the persistent influence of Platonism was, we have seen, that throughout the greater part of its history Western religion, in its more philosophic forms, has had two Gods (as, in its less philosophic forms, it has had more than two). The two were, indeed, identified as one being with two aspects. But the ideas corresponding to the 'aspects' were ideas of two antithetic kinds of being. The one was the Absolute of otherworldliness — self-sufficient, out of time, alien to the categories of ordinary human thought and experience, needing no world of lesser beings to supplement or enhance his own eternal self-contained perfection. The other was a God who emphatically was not self-sufficient nor, in any philosophical sense, 'absolute': one whose essential nature required the existence of other beings, and not of one kind of these only, but of all kinds which could find a place in the descending scale of the possibilities of reality — a God whose prime attribute was generativeness, whose manifestation was to be found in the diversity of creatures and therefore in the temporal order and the manifold spectacle of nature's processes. The device which, for centuries, served to mask the incongruity of the two conceptions was the simple dictum of Plato in the *Timaeus*, elaborated into the fundamental axiom of emanationism — that a "good" being must be free from "envy," that that which is more perfect necessarily engenders, or overflows into, that which is less perfect, and cannot "remain within itself."

The device, though it served its purpose, did not in fact over-come the contradiction of the two ideas; but its effectiveness was increased by its seeming congruence with an assumption about the causal relation which, however gratuitous, seems natural to the human mind — that the 'lower' must be deriva-tive from the 'higher,' the cause be, at the least, not less than its effects. With this theological dualism — since the idea of God was taken to be also the definition of the highest good — there ran, as we have likewise seen, a dualism of values, the one otherworldly (though often in a half-hearted way), the other this-worldly. If the good for man was the contemplation or the imitation of God, this required, on the one hand, a transcend-ence and suppression of the merely 'natural' interests and de-sires, a withdrawal of the soul from 'the world' the better to prepare it for the beatific vision of the divine perfection; and it required, on the other hand, a piety towards the God of things as they are, an adoring delight in the sensible universe in all its variety, an endeavor on man's part to know and understand it ever more fully, and a conscious participation in the divine activity of creation.

Of the breaking apart of the two elements of this dualism we have already observed some examples in the eighteenth cen-tury. The logic of the principle of plenitude itself seemed to entail the conclusion that the imitation of an otherworldly God, even assuming such a God, could not be the good for man, or for any creature, since the reason or the goodness of God demanded that each grade of imperfect being should exist after its distinctive kind. And meanwhile the idea of God was itself becoming predominantly this-worldly, tending to-wards a fusion with the conception of 'Nature' infinitely vari-ous in its manifestations and endlessly active in the production of differing kinds of beings. Our present concern is with the culmination of this latter tendency. When the Chain of Being — in other words, the entire created universe — came to be explicitly conceived, no longer as complete once for all and everlastingly the same in the kinds of its components, but as gradually evolving from a less to a greater degree of fullness and excellence, the question inevitably arose whether a God eternally complete and immutable could be supposed to be manifested in such a universe. The question was not always, or at first, answered in the negative; there were numerous eighteenth-century attempts, some of which we have noted, to combine the belief in a Creator who, being always the same and always acting in accordance with the same necessities of absolute reason, could not generate a creation different at one time from what it is at another, with the conviction that the world, being expansive and progressive, *is* essentially different at one time from what it is at another, and that the general order of events in time is not a negligible feature of finite existence, irrelevant to those eternal aspects of things with which metaphysics has to do, but is an aspect of reality of profound significance for philosophy. So long as the two beliefs were held together, the seeming axiom to which I have referred — that the antecedent in a causal process cannot contain less than the consequent, or a higher type of being come from a lower — could still be precariously maintained. But with the end of that century and the opening decades of the nineteenth these assumptions of the traditional theology and metaphysics began to be reversed. God himself was temporalized — was, indeed, identified with the process by which the whole creation slowly and painfully ascends the scale of possibility; or, if the name is to be reserved for the summit of the scale, God was conceived as the not yet realized final term of the process. Thus for emanationism and creationism came to be substituted what may best be called radical or absolute evolutionism — the typically Romantic evolutionism of which Bergson's *L'Évolution créatrice* is in great part a re-editing. The lower precedes the higher, not merely in the history of organic forms and functions, but universally; there is more in the effect than was contained, except as an abstract unrealized potentiality, in the cause.

This development can best be seen in Schelling. In much of his philosophizing between 1800 and 1812, it is true, he has still two Gods and therefore two religions — the religion of a time-transcending and eternally complete Absolute, an "Identity of Identities," the One of Neoplatonism — and the religion of a struggling, temporally limited, gradually self-realizing World-Spirit or Life-Force. The latter is the aspect under which the former manifests itself to us. In its manifestation the principles of plenitude and continuity rule. The temporal order is, as it were, a projection, a spread-out image, of the Absolute Intelligence, and its concrete content consists of the succession of organisms and their states. And any such succession *must*, says Schelling, constitute a progressive graded series, for the following reason:

> Succession itself is gradual, i. e., it cannot in any single moment be given in its entirety. But the farther succession proceeds, the more fully the universe is unfolded. Consequently, the organic world also, in proportion as succession advances, will attain to a fuller extension and represent a greater part of the universe. . . . And on the other hand the farther we go back in the world of organisms, the smaller becomes the part of the universe which the organism embraces within itself. The plant-world is the most limited of all, since in it a great number of natural processes are lacking altogether.[1]

But the new conception is set forth still more boldly and clearly in the treatise *Ueber das Wesen der menschlichen Freiheit* (1809). Even here vestiges of the Neoplatonic Absolute remain; but Schelling dwells with predilection upon the thesis that God never is, but is only coming to be, through nature and history.

> Has creation a final goal? And if so, why was it not reached at once? Why was the consummation not realized from the beginning? To these questions there is but one answer: Because God is *Life*, and not merely being. All life has a *fate*, and is subject to suffering and to becoming. To this, then, God has of his own free will subjected himself. . . . Being is *sensible* only in becoming. In being as such, it is true, there is no becoming; in the latter, rather, it is itself posited as eternity. But in the actualization (of being) through opposition there is necessarily a becoming. Without the conception of a humanly suffering God — a conception common to all the mysteries and spiritual religions of the past — history remains wholly unintelligible.[2]

Yet the principle of plenitude, with some qualification, and with it the cosmical determinism of Abelard, Bruno, and Spinoza, is once more affirmed by Schelling. It is, says Schelling — still using the phrases of Dionysius and the Schoolmen — because "the act of self-revelation in God is related to his Goodness and Love" that it is necessary. But none the less, or rather, all the more, "the proposition is absolutely undeniable that from the divine nature everything follows with absolute necessity, that everything which is possible by means of it must also be actual, and what is not actual must also be morally impossible. The error of Spinozism did not at all consist in the assertion of such an inexorable necessity in God, but only in conceiving of this necessity as something lifeless and impersonal." It recognizes only "a blind and mechanical necessity." But "if God is essentially Love and Goodness, then that which is morally necessary in him follows with a truly metaphysical necessity." Leibniz, on the other hand, was wholly wrong in attributing to God a choice between possible worlds, a sort of "consultation of God with himself" at the conclusion of which he decided upon the actualization of only one among a multitude of possibilities.[3] To assume such a free choice would be to imply "that God has chosen a less perfect world than, when all conditions are taken into account, was possible, and — as some, in fact, assert, since there is no absurdity which does not find some spokesmen — that God could, if he had wished, have created a world better than this one." (This, it will be remembered, had long since been declared by Abelard to be an absurdity.) There thus is not, and never was, a plurality of possible worlds. True, at the beginning of the world-process there was a chaotic condition, constituting the first movement of the Primal Ground (*Grund*), as "a matter still unformed, but capable of receiving all forms"; and there was therefore then "an infinity of possibilities" not yet realized. "But this Primal Ground is not to be assimilated to God; and God, given his perfection, could will only one thing." "There is only one possible world, because there is only one God."[4] But this one possible world cannot contain less than all that was really possible.

The "God" even of this passage, it will be seen, still retains some otherworldly attributes, and the necessity of the production of all possible creatures is still deduced by arguments which are closely akin to the dialectic of emanationism. God is not the *Urgrund*, nor is he the final consummation of the process in which the *Urgrund* gives rise to increasingly various forms and eventually to self-consciousness in man; he remains, here, a perfection prior to the world and yet generative of it as a necessary logical consequence of his essential nature. Yet the generation is a gradual and successive one; and if Schelling meant seriously his emphatic thesis that God is "a life" and therefore "subject to suffering and becoming," he could not consistently hold to this conception of a transcendent Absolute who does not genuinely participate in the world-process in which his self-revelation consists. The two theologies still subsist side by side; but one of them is a survival, the other is an innovating idea which is on the point of destroying the former.

Schelling's friend and disciple, the naturalist Oken, simultaneously set forth much the same conceptions, with some additions and variations, in his *Lehrbuch der Naturphilosophie*, 1810. "The philosophy of Nature is the science of the eternal transformation of God into the world."

It has the task of showing the phases of the world's evolution from the primal nothingness: how the heavenly bodies and the elements arose, how these advanced to higher forms, how finally organisms appeared and in man attained to reason. These phases constitute the history of the generation of the universe. . . . The philosophy of nature is in the most comprehensive sense cosmogony, or, as Moses called it, *Genesis*.[5]

Oken, it will be observed, here speaks of a God in some sense antecedent to the world, of an Absolute which metamorphoses itself into a universe. There are, in fact, in his metaphysical terminology also, residual traces of the language of emanationism. But in Oken they are even more recessive than in Schelling. For this antecedent Absolute is described in the most unequivocally negative terms. Except as self-evolving in time, says Oken, God = zero, or pure nothingness. All numbers may, no doubt, be said to be contained in zero, since they may all be described as determinations of zero; and so all beings may be said to pre-exist in God. But they so exist, "not in a real but only in an ideal manner, not *actu* but only *potentia*." [6] The *realization* (*Realwerden*) of God, then, takes place only gradually, through the history of the cosmos. Its primary manifestation and universal condition is time. "Time is nothing but the Absolute itself." "The Absolute is not in time, nor before time, but *is* time." Again, "time is simply the active thinking of God." It is "the universal that includes all particulars, hence all particular things are in time, and created Time and creation are one." [7] This temporal *Realwerdung* of the Absolute reaches its highest point in man, a being capable of self-consciousness. "Man is the creation in which God fully becomes an object to himself. Man is God represented *by* God. God is a man representing God in self-consciousness. . . . Man is God wholly manifested, *der ganz erschienene Gott.*" [8]

These early manifestations of an approximation to radical evolutionism in theology were not permitted to pass unchallenged. And the challenge came from the man who, two decades before, had been regarded with special admiration and piety by nearly all the young leaders of the German Romantic movement. F. H. Jacobi published in 1812 an essay, *Von den göttlichen Dingen und ihrer Offenbarung*, which was chiefly devoted to a vehement and (as Schelling afterwards described it) tearful attack upon this new way of thinking. In the issue which Schelling had raised, Jacobi saw the deepest-reaching antithesis in the entire philosophy of religion. "There can," he wrote, "be only two principal classes of philosophers: those who regard the more perfect (*Vollkommnere*) as derived from, as gradually developed out of, the less perfect, and those who affirm that the most perfect being was first, and that all things have their source in him; that the first principle of all things was a moral being, an intelligence willing and acting with wisdom — a Creator — God." Jacobi's reply is rambling and dogmatic; but he takes his stand finally upon what he regards as a self-evident and fundamental axiom of metaphysics: that something cannot "come from nothing" nor the superior be "produced by" the inferior. Such a philosophy as Schelling's, in fact, is, Jacobi asserts, a direct contradiction of a law of formal logic. For, as he observes — the observation is a commonplace of Platonistic theology — the relation of God to the world may, among other things, be conceived as the relation of a logical *prius*, a *Beweisgrund* or reason, to its consequences, the implications deducible from it. But "always and necessarily a *Beweisgrund* must be *above* that which is to be proved by means of it, and must subsume the latter under it; it is from the *Beweisgrund* that truth and certitude are imparted to those things which are demonstrated by means of it; from it they borrow their reality."

To this attack Schelling replied in a piece of controversial writing celebrated for its ferocity and for the damage which it did, at least in the eyes of his contemporaries, to the philosophical reputation of his critic.[9] What is pertinent here is the fact that the attack caused Schelling, not to tone down his theological evolutionism, but to give it more radical and more nearly unqualified expression than before. He might conceivably have met the criticism by pointing out the passages in his previous writings in which the infinity, timelessness, and self-sufficiency of the Absolute Identity had been recognized. So far is he from doing this that he now almost unequivocally repudiates such a conception, and quite expressly denies that such an Absolute can be the God of religion. From Jacobi's formulation of the issue, and his estimate of its philosophical significance, Schelling does not dissent; nor does he repudiate his critic's account of the essentials of his doctrine. It is, indeed, Schelling observes, needful to make some distinctions, if the meaning of the doctrine is properly to be understood. Those who held it did not, for example, maintain that the "more perfect sprang from a less perfect being *independent of* and different from itself," but simply that "the more perfect has risen from its own less perfect condition." Nor, accordingly, did they deny that, in a sense, "the all-perfect being — that which has the perfections of all other things in itself — must be *before* all things." But they did deny that it thus pre-existed as perfect *actu* and not merely *potentia*. "To believe that it did," says Schelling, "is difficult for many reasons, but first of all for the very simple one that, if it were in actual possession of the highest perfection [or completeness], it would have had no reason (*Grund*) for the creation and production of so many other things, through which it — being incapable of attaining a higher degree of perfection — could only fall to a lower one."[10] Here the central contradiction inherent in the logic of emanationism — but for so many centuries persistently disregarded — was pointed out with the utmost sharpness. The promise and potency, then, of all that evolution should unfold might, if one cared to insist on this, be said to pre-exist from the beginning; but it was a promise unfulfilled and a potency unrealized:

I posit God [says Schelling] as the first and the last, as the Alpha and the Omega; but as Alpha he is not what he is as Omega, and in so far as he is only the one — God 'in an eminent sense' — he can not be the other God, in the same sense, or, in strictness, be called God. For in that case, let it be expressly said, the unevolved (*unentfaltete*) God, *Deus implicitus*, would already be what, as Omega, the *Deus explicitus* is.[11]

Upon what grounds, in the face of Jacobi's objections, does Schelling justify this evolutionary theology? First of all on the ground that it accords with the actual character of the world of our experience, as that character is disclosed to our everyday observation and to the more comprehensive vision of natural science. On the face of it, the world is, precisely, a system in which the higher habitually develops out of the lower, fuller existence out of emptier. The child grows into a man, the ignorant become learned; "not to mention that nature itself, as all know who have the requisite acquaintance with the subject, has gradually risen from the production of more meagre and inchoate creatures to the production of more perfect and more finely formed ones."[12] A process which is constantly going on before our eyes can hardly be the inconceivability which Jacobi had made it out to be. The new philosophy had simply interpreted the general or 'ultimate' nature of things, and their order in being, in the light of the known nature and sequences of all particular things with which we are acquainted. The "ordinary theism," defended by Jacobi, had, on the contrary, given us "a God who is alien to nature and a nature that is devoid of God — *ein unnatürlicher Gott und eine gottlose Natur*."[13]

Again, Schelling observes, the fact of evil, the imperfection of the world, is irreconcilable with the belief that the universe proceeds from a being perfect and intelligent *ab initio*. Those who hold this belief "have no answer when they are asked how, from an intelligence so clear and lucid, a whole so singularly confused (even when brought into *some* order) as the world can have arisen." In every way, then, Schelling finds the picture of reality which accords with the facts is that of a more or less confused and troubled ascent towards fuller and higher life; and the only admissible conception of God is that which is in harmony with this picture. Nor has the contrary view, he declares, the religiously edifying and consoling character to which it pretends. For it "derives the not-good from the Good, and makes God, not the source and potentiality of the good, but the source and potentiality of the not-good." Conceived — as in the theology of absolute becoming it is conceived — as a good in the making, *als ein ins Gute Verwandelbares*, evil or imperfection itself is not the hopeless and senseless piece of reality which it must be if conceived as good in the *un*making, as a lapse from a perfection already realized. The God of all the older theology, moreover, had been a God eternally complete, "ready-made once for all," as Schelling puts it. But no conception could be more barren and unprofitable than this; for it is really the conception of "a dead God," not of the God that lives and strives in nature and in man. It is inconceivable, Jacobi had declared, that life should arise out of death, being out of non-being, higher existences out of lower. Is it, then, asked Schelling, easier to conceive that death should arise out of life? "What could move the God who is not a God of the dead but of the living, to produce death. Infinitely more conceivable is it that out of death — which cannot be an absolute death, but only the death which has life concealed within it — life should arise, than that life should pass over into, should lose itself in, death." [14]

Jacobi's error, however — Schelling observes — is a natural consequence of the logical doctrine of the older philosophy from which he never fully emancipated himself; it is, indeed, the crowning example of the pernicious results in metaphysics of the acceptance of the Wolffian theory of knowledge, which based everything upon the logical Principle of Identity, and regarded all certain judgments as "analytical." According to this view, says Schelling — not with entire historical accuracy — "all demonstration is merely a progression in identical propositions, there is no advance from one truth to a different one, but only from the same to ,the same. The tree of knowledge never comes to bloom or to fruitage; there is nowhere any *development*." But true philosophy and truly objective science are not a chanting of tautologies. Their object is always a concrete and living thing; and *their* progress and evolution is a progress and evolution of the object itself. "The right method of philosophy is an ascending, not a descending, one"; and its true axiom is precisely opposite to that pseudo-axiom which Jacobi had enunciated:

Always and necessarily that from which development proceeds (*der Entwicklungsgrund*) is lower than that which is developed; the former raises the latter above itself and subjects itself to it, inasmuch as it serves as the matter, the organ, the condition, for the other's development.

It is — as has too little been noted by historians — in this introduction of a radical evolutionism into metaphysics and theology, and in the attempt to revise even the principles of logic to make them harmonize with an evolutional conception of reality, that the historical significance of Schelling chiefly consists. The question at issue in his controversy with Jacobi is, indeed, as he clearly recognized and emphatically declared, one of the most fundamental and momentous of all philosophical questions, both by its relation to many other theoretical problems, and also by its consequences for the religious consciousness. Schelling's thesis meant not only the discarding of a venerable and almost universally accepted axiom of rational theology and metaphysics, but also the emergence of a new mood and temper of religious feeling.

For Schelling himself, however, the implication of this doctrine of a God-in-the-making could not be simply a blandly cheerful evolutionary meliorism. The progress of the world, the gradual manifestation or self-realization of God, is a struggle against opposition; since the full possibilities of being were not realized all at once, and are not yet realized, there must in the original nature of things be some impediment, some principle of retardation, destined to be triumphed over, indeed, but not without suffering and temporary defeats. The Life-Force advances — as Robinet had said — fumblingly, by trial and error. There is a tragic element in cosmic and in human history; the world-process is *ein Wechselspiel von Hemmen und von Streben*. This conception Schelling had already expressed in his youthful poem *Das epikureische Glaubensbekenntnis Heinz Wiederporstens*, well known through the felicitous translation of part of it by Royce in *The Spirit of Modern Philosophy*.[15]

Thus, at last, the Platonistic scheme of the universe is turned upside down. Not only had the originally complete and immutable Chain of Being been converted into a Becoming, in which all genuine possibles are, indeed, destined to realization grade after grade, yet only through a vast, slow unfolding in time; but now God himself is placed in, or identified with, this Becoming. The World of Ideas which defines the range of diversity of possible existence has definitely been transformed into a realm of mere possibility awaiting actualization, empty and without value until it attains it; and even the Idea of Ideas is no longer exempted from this status. The world-generating process starts not at the top but at the bottom, in those *ultime potenze* (in Dante's phrase) in which the infinite productive power had been supposed to reach the limit of its capacity. There is no longer a 'way down,' but there is still a 'way up.' But the inversion of the Platonistic scheme of things, and especially of the genetic order assumed in the *Timaeus* and by Plotinus, while it converts the Scale of Being into an abstract ideal schema, does not alter its essential character. The elements of the ancient complex of ideas whose history we have reviewed remain potent in Schelling's evolutionistic metaphysics. The insatiable generativeness, the tendency to produce diversity, the necessity of the realization of the greatest possible 'fullness' of being — these attributes of the Platonistic world are still the attributes of the world of the Romantic philosopher. But the generativeness is now that of an insufficiency striving unconsciously for richer and more various being; and the fullness is not the permanent character but the flying goal of the whole of things.

This historic outcome of the long series of 'footnotes to Plato' which we have been observing was also, so far as it went, the logically inevitable outcome. Whatever else be said of Schelling's reasoning in this phase of his philosophy, he at least showed the ineluctability of a choice between the two strains in Platonism, by making explicit their essential incompatibility. He put before the metaphysics of the succeeding century a forced option — though many of his successors have failed to recognize it or have ingeniously sought to evade it. The two Gods of Plato and of Plotinus cannot both be believed in; and the two schemes of values associated with these theological conceptions cannot be reconciled, either in theory or in practice. The otherworldly Idea of the Good must be the idea of a spurious good, if the existence of this world of temporal and imperfect creatures be assumed to be itself a genuine good; and an Absolute which is self-sufficient and forever perfect and complete cannot be identified with a God related to and manifested in a world of temporal becoming and alteration and creative advance. These propositions will seem to some in our own day evident and perhaps truistic, to others paradoxical and groundless. The reasons for their acceptance have not, assuredly, been completely set forth in these lectures, though some of them have repeatedly suggested themselves in our analysis of the phases of the history of thought which we have passed in review. But with these historical intimations of the argument I must here be content; one philosophic moral of the story which I have been relating is, I think, plainly suggested by the very course of the tale.

It is not, however, the only moral suggested by our history of the fortunes of an idea. There is another which should not be left wholly unexpressed. The principles of plenitude and continuity, as that history has shown, usually rested at bottom upon a faith, implicit or explicit, that the universe is a rational order, in the sense that there is nothing arbitrary, fortuitous, haphazard in its constitution. The first of these principles (to restate it once more and finally) presupposed that, not only for the existence of this world, but for every one of its characteristics, for every kind of beings which it contains — in strictness, indeed, for each particular being — there must be an ultimate reason, self-explanatory and 'sufficient.' And the second principle followed from the first and was like unto it: there are no sudden "leaps" in nature; infinitely various as things are, they form an absolutely smooth sequence, in which no break appears, to baffle the craving of our reason for continuity everywhere. Plato's question 'Why?' could, then, be legitimately asked and be satisfactorily answered; for though our intelligence is doubtless too limited to give a specific answer to it with respect to every detail of existence, it is capable of recognizing the broad principles essential to any consistent answer. By this sort of faith in the rationality of the world we live in, a great part —

probably, in spite of the recurrent and powerful opposing tendencies, the greater part — of Western philosophy and science was, for a score of centuries, animated and guided, though the implications of such a faith were seldom fully apprehended and came only slowly to general recognition. The culmination of it we have observed in the two great rationalistic ontologies of the seventeenth century and, in a more popular form, in the usual eighteenth-century argument for optimism. A rigorously rational world, as these made clear, must be, in William James's term, a "block-world" in the strictest sense, a scheme of things determined throughout and once for all by 'necessary truths'; in final analysis there are no contingent facts, there are not and never have been any open options; everything is so rigorously tied up with the existence of the necessarily existent Being, and that Being, in turn, is so rigorously implicative of the existence of everything else, that the whole admits of no conceivable additions or omissions or alterations.

In so far as the world was conceived in this fashion, it seemed a coherent, luminous, intellectually secure and dependable world, in which the mind of man could go about its business of seeking an understanding of things in full confidence; and empirical science, since it was acquainted in advance with the fundamental principles with which the facts must, in the end, accord, and was provided with a sort of diagram of the general pattern of the universe, could know in outline what to expect, and even anticipate particular disclosures of actual observation. And with no less sweeping hypothesis could a belief in the complete rationality of what is have been reconciled. The principles of plenitude and continuity were legitimate consequences of that belief. If, of two kinds of creature which were logically equally possible, and possible together, one had been left out, or if the spatial and numerical extent of nature was fixed at some one finite magnitude or number, then there clearly was some arbitrary and fortuitous factor in the ultimate constitution of being — even though this factor were described as the will of God, since such a will would be one, as Leibniz said, not completely controlled by reason. And if it were admitted to be not completely so controlled, the extent of such arbitrariness and contingency was unpredictable.

Doubtless some existences are in some sense of more worth than others, as the principle of gradation implied; but, below the level of the one perfect being, a stoppage of the series at one point rather than another would be an act of caprice. And the same is true of the *continuum formarum*; if nature "made leaps," they must be groundless leaps; if there were gaps, or *really* missing links, in a sequence of existing forms, such that, for example, one kind of animal existed, but was separated from its most nearly similar actual species by a blank stretch of unrealized possibilities of intermediate kinds, the cosmos must be admitted to be lacking in orderliness, to be characterized by a kind of incoherency and whimsicality.

But the history of the idea of the Chain of Being — in so far as that idea presupposed such a complete rational intelligibility of the world — is the history of a failure; more precisely and more justly, it is the record of an experiment in thought carried on for many centuries by many great and lesser minds, which can now be seen to have had an instructive negative outcome. The experiment, taken as a whole, constitutes one of the most grandiose enterprises of the human intellect. But as the consequences of this most persistent and most comprehensive of hypotheses became more and more explicit, the more apparent became its difficulties; and when they are fully drawn out, they show the hypothesis of the absolute rationality of the cosmos to be unbelievable. It conflicts, in the first place, with one immense fact, besides many particular facts, in the natural order — the fact that existence as we experience it is temporal. A world of time and change — this, at least, our history has shown — is a world which can neither be deduced from nor reconciled with the postulate that existence is the expression and consequence of a system of 'eternal' and 'necessary' truths inherent in the very logic of being. Since such a system could manifest itself only in a static and constant world, and since empirical reality is not static and constant, the 'image' (as Plato called it) does not correspond with the supposed 'model' and cannot be explained by it. *Any* change whereby nature at one time contains other things or more things than it contains at another time is fatal to the principle of sufficient reason, in the sense which we have seen it to have had for those philosophers who understood it best and believed in it most devoutly. A temporal succession, moreover, has a beginning or it has no beginning. If the process be supposed to have had a beginning, the date of its beginning and its temporal span *a parte ante* are arbitrary facts; there could be no conceivable rational ground for the world's having popped into existence — in however rudimentary a form — at one instant rather than at an earlier one, or for its having one durational magnitude rather than another. In its theological form, this was the difficulty wrestled with by Augustine, and many another metaphysician and divine: if it is God's nature or essence to be generative, to create a world, such an eternal essence could not *begin* to be, by commencing to create on a certain day in time — whether the date were 4004 B.C. or vastly more remote. Even if that essence could be supposed to express itself in a temporal succession at all, only an infinite succession could be its temporal counterpart. The struggles of the more rationalistic philosophers and theologians who were committed, for dogmatic or other reasons, to the doctrine of a beginning of the creation, to deal with this problem provide extraordinary examples of the ingenuity of the human mind; but they were struggles to reconcile two patently irreconcilable propositions. Perhaps the world *may* suddenly have burst into being one fine day; but if so, it is a world which just as logically might not have been, and it is in that sense a colossal accident, with no necessity of reason behind it. If the alternative, Aristotelian doctrine of the 'eternity of the world,' i. e., of the infinity of the past temporal process, was adopted, difficulties of another sort arose: the paradox of a completed and told-off infinite sequence of events, and either the supposition — plainly contrary to experience — of an infinity of moments in which nothing ever changes, or else of an infinite number of changes through which no commensurate realization of values seems to have been attained. The latter difficulty was precisely and wittily expressed in a parable by Royce many years since: "If you found a man shoveling sand on the sea-shore, and wheeling it away to make an embankment, and if you began to admire his industry, seeing how considerable a mass of sand he had wheeled away, . . . you might still check yourself to ask him: 'how long, O friend, hast thou been at work?' And if he answered that he had been wheeling away there from all eternity, and was in fact an essential feature of the universe, you would not only inwardly marvel at his mendacity, but you would be moved to say: 'So be it, O friend, but thou must then have been from all eternity an infinitely lazy fellow.'" [16] Those whom we have seen expressly temporalizing the conception of the Chain of Being and converting it into a program of cosmic progress through the gradual increase of the fullness and diversity of being, thus have naturally — being doubtless more or less mindful of this difficulty — assumed, as a rule, an absolute beginning of the world's history. By doing so they could conceive of that history as having another sort of reasonableness, since reality could then be supposed to be struggling, and to have already in an appreciable degree moved, *towards* a rational goal, to make for an enrichment of the total excellence or value of existence. But they at the same time tacitly denied its essential logicality in the sense in which it had so long been supposed to possess that attribute. Its getting started only a certain number of centuries or of millions of millennia ago, and the direction which its march was assumed to have taken, were by implication chance-happenings, even though the chance be considered a fortunate one.

Yet this is only half of the second moral which our history suggests. The other half is that rationality, when conceived as complete, as excluding all arbitrariness, becomes itself a kind of irrationality. For, since it means the complete realization of all the possibles, in so far as they are compossible, it excludes any limiting and selective principle. The realm of possibles is infinite; and the principle of plenitude, as the implicate of the principle of sufficient reason, when *its* implications were thought through, ran on, in every province in which it was applied, into infinities — infinite space, infinite time, infinite worlds, an infinity of existent species, an infinity of individual existences, an infinity of kinds of beings between any two kinds of beings, however similar. When its consequences were thus fully drawn, it confronted the reason of man with a world by which it was not merely baffled but negated; for it was a world of impossible contradictions. Thus — to give only a single illustration — the assumption of the continuity of forms, implicit though it was in the rationalistic premises, was at variance with itself. Aside from the paradoxes of the concept of the mathematical continuum, which contemporary mathematics purports (unconvincingly, as I can't but think) to have resolved, a qualitative continuum, at all events, is a contradiction in terms. Wherever, in any series, there appears a new *quale*, a different *kind* of thing, and not merely a different magnitude and degree of something common to the whole series, there is *eo ipso* a breach of continuity. And it follows that the principles of plenitude and continuity — though the latter was supposed to be implied by the former — were also at variance with one another. A universe that is "full," in the sense of exhibiting the maximal diversity of kinds, must be chiefly full of "leaps." There is at every point an abrupt passage to something different, and there is no purely logical principle determining — out of all the infinitely various "possible" kinds of differentness — which shall come next.

The world of concrete existence, then, is no impartial transcript of the realm of essence; and it is no translation of pure logic into temporal terms — such terms being themselves, indeed, the negation of pure logic. It has the character and the range of content and of diversity which it happens to have. No rational ground predetermined from all eternity of what sort it should be or how much of the world of possibility should be included in it. It *is*, in short, a contingent world; [17] its magnitude, its pattern, its habits, which we call laws, have something arbitrary and idiosyncratic about them. But if this were not the case, it would be a world without a character, without power of preference or choice among the infinity of possibles. If we may employ the traditional anthropomorphic language of the theologians, we may say that in it Will is prior to Intellect. On this issue the late-medieval opponents of the strict rationalists in theology, the seventeenth- and eighteenth-century adversaries of Leibniz and Spinoza, and Voltaire and Dr. Johnson in their polemic against the whole conception of the Chain of Being, must be admitted to have had the better of the argument. It is to this conclusion that the history of the principles of plenitude and continuity, as metaphysical theorems, and of the principle of sufficient reason from which they derived much of their persuasiveness, leads. In the course of the century of reflection since the period at which our historical survey has ended, that conclusion has become increasingly current, explicitly or tacitly — so much so that the sense of the significance of the issue, and of the historic rôle and motivations of the contrary assumption, has been in great degree lost. One aspect of the outcome is well illustrated in a passage of Professor Whitehead's, which would, no doubt, have horrified Plotinus and Bruno and Spinoza and even Leibniz, since it gives the name of God, not to the Infinite Fecundity of emanationism, but to the "principle of limitation." "An element in the metaphysical situation," Mr. Whitehead writes, "is that such a principle is required." "Some particular *how* is necessary, and some particularization in the *what* of matter of fact is necessary"; otherwise the "apparent irrational limitation" of the actual world can only be taken as a proof of its pure illusoriness. "If we reject this alternative, . . . we must provide a ground for the limitation which stands among the attributes of the substantial activity. This attribute provides the limitation for which no reason can be given, for all reason flows from it. God is the ultimate limitation, and His existence is the ultimate irrationality." [18] In its contrast with, and yet its unintended confirmation of, such an assertion of the primacy of the non-rational, the history of the complex of ideas with which we have been occupied has at once its most pathetic interest, as a manifestation of a certain persistent craving of the philosophic mind, and its permanent instructiveness for the philosophical reflection of our own and later times.

Yet — as many historic examples show — the utility of a belief and its validity are independent variables; and erroneous hypotheses are often avenues to truth. I may, therefore, perhaps best bring these lectures to a close by a reminder that the idea of the Chain of Being, with its presuppositions and implications, has had many curiously happy consequences in the history of Western thought. This at least, I hope, is sufficiently evident from our long, yet inadequate, review of the part it has played in that history.

# NOTES

## NOTES TO LECTURE I

1. Cf. the writer's papers on "The Chinese Origin of a Romanticism," *Journal of English and Germanic Philology* (1933), 1–20, and "The First Gothic Revival and the Return to Nature," *Modern Language Notes* (1932), 419–446.
2. *Science and the Modern World* (1926), 106.
3. *Ueber das Studium der griechischen Poesie* (Minor, Fr. Schlegel, *1792–1804*, I, 95).
4. Preface to *The English Works of George Herbert* (1905), xii.

## NOTES TO LECTURE II

1. *Kerngedanken der platonischen Philosophie* (1931), 8: "Already in the *Cratylus* and *Meno* there is to be found much positive content which, as no one doubts, goes beyond the conclusions of Socrates; and this is in increasing measure true of the *Phaedo* and the *Republic* and also of the *Phaedrus*." Cf. the same writer's *Platon*, II (1923), 293 (on the *Phaedo*): "That the philosophical considerations of the dialogue are foreign to the historical Socrates, that they are therefore essentially Platonic — on this there exists hardly any difference of opinion."
2. Burnet, *Platonism* (1928), 115.
3. Taylor, *Commentary on the Timaeus of Plato*, 11.
4. *Ibid.*, 11.
5. *Ibid.*, 10. This contention is, however, in other passages considerably qualified by Taylor; we may, after all, "expect to find a broad general agreement between [Timaeus's] doctrine and things which are taught in the dialogues, or even things which we know Plato to have maintained from statements of Aristotle about his teaching" (*ibid.*, 133).
6. Cf. *Metaphysics*, I, 987b 1 f., XIII, 107b 27 ff.
7. It is impossible here, and it is perhaps no longer necessary, to present at length the reasons for accepting the authenticity of this Epistle. The case has been well presented by Souilhé, *Platon, Oeuvres complètes*, t. XIII, 1re partie (1926), xl–lviii, and by Harward, *The Platonic Epistles* (1932), 59–78, 188–192, 213. Cf. also Taylor: *Plato, the Man and his Work*, 2d ed. (1927), 15–16, and *Philosophical Studies* (1934), 192–223; P. Friedländer, *Plato* (1928), *passim*. One of the oddest things in recent Plato-interpretation is the tendency of scholars who do not reject the Seventh Epistle to present accounts of the Platonic doctrines which are utterly irreconcilable with it.
8. Ep. VII, 341c–344d. Against the thesis that the Theory of Ideas is abandoned or minimized even in the latest dialogues, the principal objection is well put by Shorey: "The challenge to find the ideas in dialogues later than the *Parmenides* is easily met. Nothing can be more ex-

plicit than the *Timaeus*. The alternative is explicitly put: are the objects of sense the only realities, and is the supposition of ideas mere talk? (51c) And it is affirmed that their reality is as certain as the distinction between opinion and science. . . . They are characterized in terms applicable only to pure Being, and the familiar terminology is freely employed (52a, 27d, 29b, 30, 37b)" (*The Unity of Plato's Thought*, 1904, p. 37). And of the assertion that "souls take the place of ideas in Plato's later period," Shorey observes (equally justly, I think) that "this is a complete misconception of Plato's thought and style. It is quite true that he did not confine the predicates of true and absolute Being to the ideas; God is, of course, true Being, and in religious and metaphysical passages need not always be distinguished from the ideas taken collectively." But "that the ideas still take precedence of souls appears distinctly" in several of the later dialogues, e. g., the *Statesman, Timaeus*, and *Philebus* (*ibid.*, 39). Cf. Ritter, *Kerngedanken*, 174: "While the original Theory of Ideas passes gradually quite into the background, we may nevertheless affirm that not a single proposition is ever formally retracted or even tacitly abandoned." That the exegesis of Plato is far from an exact science is further illustrated by the fact that Sir J. G. Frazer — in an early work recently republished — defends the view that Plato in his early writings *did* hold the Theory of Ideas, admitting, however, ideal subsisting counterparts only of "good" things; but that later in life he abandoned the theory probably because "he saw that logic compelled him to make an Idea of every common notion, and hence of bad things as well as good." (*Growth of Plato's Ideal Theory*, 51.)

9.  *The Platonic Tradition in English Religious Thought* (1926), 9.
10. *Kerngedanken der platonischen Philosophie*, 77.
11. *Ibid.*, 91: "die Lehre vom dem jenseitigen Ideenreich" is not held by Plato, at least as a "festes Dogma."
12. *Ibid.*, 82.
13. *Ibid.*, 89.
14. *Ibid.*, 83.
15. *Phaedo*, 76e, 92a–e.
16. From Shorey's review of Ritter's *Neue Untersuchungen über Platon*, in *Classical Philology*, 1910, 391.
17. *Unity of Plato's Thought*, 28.
18. *Die Kerngedanken der platonischen Philosophie*, 56–57.
19. *Republic*, 507b.
20. *Ibid.*, 518c.
21. *Ibid.*, 509b.
22. *Ibid.*, 517d.
23. *Ibid.*, 516d.
24. E. g., in *Philebus*, 22, it is at one point intimated that "the divine mind is identical with the Good." Yet even in this dialogue "the most divine of all lives" is beyond "either joy or sorrow" (*ibid.*, 33).
25. *Philebus*, 60c.

26. *Ibid.*, 67a. This is qualified by the above-mentioned intimation that the "divine mind" *is* the good. It manifestly follows that that mind possesses the attribute of self-sufficiency in an absolute sense.

27. *Eth. Eudem.*, VII, 1244b–1245b. That there are other passages in Aristotle which conflict with this is true, e. g., *Magna Moralia*, II, 1213a. The authenticity of the *Eudemian Ethics* must now be regarded as established by the studies of Mühlls (1909), Kapp (1912), and especially of W. Jaeger (1923). Cf. also the Pseudo-Aristotelian *De Mundo*, 399b ff.

28. *On the End in Creation*, I, 1.

29. *Philosophical Aspects of Modern Science* (1932), 331–332.

30. *Republic*, 509b.

31. On the reputation and influence of the *Timaeus*, cf. Christ, *Griechische Literaturgeschichte* (1912), I, 701. It was translated into Latin by Cicero, but was known to the Middle Ages chiefly through the fourth-century Latin version of Chalcidius. Over forty ancient or medieval commentaries on it are known. It is the *Timaeus* that Plato holds in his hand in Raphael's "School of Athens." In the eighteenth century the ideas it contained exercised influence, not only through the text of Plato, but also through the vogue of the supposed treatise *De anima mundi*, believed to be an older writing of the Pythagorean Timaeus himself which was utilized and "embellished" by Plato. It is in fact a poor abridgment or *précis* of part of the dialogue, of much later date. There were at least three seventeenth-century editions of it; and editions with French translations by d'Argens (1763) and by Batteux (1768) show the interest still taken in this dull rehash of Plato's argument.

32. *Prolegomena to Ethics*, § 82.

33. *Timaeus*, 29, 30.

34. *Timaeus*, 33d.

35. *Ibid.*, 30c, 6: καθ' ἓν καὶ κατὰ γένη μόρια. The former interpretation was, as Taylor has noted, "definitely held by some Neoplatonists (Amelius, Theodorus of Asine)." That it offers some difficulties cannot be denied; and the second way of construing these words is therefore, perhaps correctly, preferred by Taylor, i. e., that "καθ' ἓν refers to *infimae species*, such as horse, man, κατὰ γένη to larger groups, such as mammals, quadrupeds, and the like" (*Commentary on Plato's Timaeus*, 82). Aristotle testifies that Plato and his followers asserted the numerical equivalence of the Ideas and the kinds of things that are their sensible counterparts: "those who assumed the Ideas as causes . . . introduced the notion of a Second Class of entities equally numerous with them" (*Metaph.*, 990b 2). For further expressions of the thesis that all the Forms must be realized in the cosmos, cf. *Timaeus*, 39e, 42e, 51a, 92c. Though clearly fundamental in Plato's reasoning here, the principle received full development only from his successors. Of the rôle of "Place" as the receptacle and therefore the "Mother" of the embodied Forms I have not spoken, since I am not attempting a general exposition of Plato's cosmology.

36. Mr. Bertrand Russell in his early work on Leibniz, 73, refers to it, fol-

lowing an occasional usage of Leibniz himself, as the "principle of perfection," but the designation is not happily chosen, since "perfection"
and "fullness" are primarily antithetic rather than equivalent terms.
It is only by a logical *tour de force* that the latter is derived from the
former. The principle of plenitude is rather the principle of the necessity of imperfection in all its possible degrees.

37. This is substantially true, in spite of a very few not altogether clear
*obiter dicta* of Aristotle's in which he seems to ascribe efficient causality
to the deity. The question has been carefully examined, in the light of
all the pertinent passages, by Eisler in his monograph (1893); cf. also
W. D. Ross, *Aristotle's Metaphysics* (1924), Introd., cli.

38. *Metaphysics*, II, 1003a 2, and XI, 1071b 13. Book IX, 1047b 3, ff. seems
at first to contradict this: "it cannot be true to say that this thing is
possible, and yet will not be." But the context here shows that there is
no conflict between the two passages. Aristotle is simply remarking that
if a thing is not logically incapable of existing, i. e., does not involve contradiction, we are not entitled to *assert* that it will never exist in fact.
For if it were possible to assert this, the distinction between that which
is and that which is not capable of existing would disappear. To be
exempt from logical impossibility is to be a potential existent; only of
that which *is* logically impossible can we know that it will never exist in
fact. But the passage does not say that whatever is logically possible
*must* at some time exist in fact. Nevertheless, it has been construed by
some medieval and modern writers as an expression of the principle of
plenitude; cf., e. g., Wolfson, *Crescas' Critique of Aristotle*, 249 and 551,
and Monboddo, *Origin and Progress of Language*, 2d ed., I (1772), 269.

39. *Metaphysics*, X, 1069a 5. On the infinite divisibility of the continuum,
cf. *Phys.*, VI, 231a 24.

40. *De Categoriis*, 4b 20–5a 5.

41. *De animalibus historia*, VIII, 1, 588b; cf. *De partibus animalium*, IV, 5,
681a. The passage was accessible to writers from about 1230 A.D. in
the Arabic-Latin version of Michael Scott. A version directly from the
Greek by William of Moerbeke was apparently completed in 1260. Cf.
also *Metaphysics*, XI, 1075a 10: "We must consider in what way the
nature of the universe is related to the good and the most excellent:
whether things exist separately, each by itself, or whether they constitute an ordered arrangement, or whether they have both characteristics,
like an army. . . . All things are arranged in order in a certain manner,
but not in the same manner — birds and beasts and plants. They are
not disposed in such a way that there is nothing which relates one to
another." Cf. also *De gen. an.*, 761a 15.

42. *De partibus animalium*, IV, 13, 697b; cf. *De animalibus historia*, II, 8 and 9,
502a.

43. Aristotle: *Selections*; Introduction, x.

44. *De generatione animalium*, 732a 25–733b 16; cf. Ross, *Aristotle*, 116–117,
and Aubert and Wimmer's edition of *Historia animalium*, Einleitung, 59.

45. *De anima*, 414a 29–415a 13.

46. W. D. Ross, *Aristotle*, 178. On 'privation' cf. *Metaphysics*, IV, 1022b 22 and VIII, 1046a 21. Pure privation is 'matter' in one of its Aristotelian senses, that of στέρησις or negation (*Phys.* I, 190b 27, 191b 13). Thus matter, as "in itself non-being" defines the lower limit of the scale of being.

47. "Providence," ll. 133–136: in *The English Works of George Herbert*, ed. by G. H. Palmer (1905), III, 93. The example of continuity to which the last line refers is obscure; "perhaps there is allusion to the popular fancy that minerals grow" (Palmer, *op. cit.*, p. 92).

48. H. Daudin, *De Linné à Jussieu* (1926), 81, 91–93.

49. *Enneads*, V, 2, 1, Volkmann ed. (1884), II, 176.

50. *Enn.*, V, 4, 1; Volkmann, II, 203; cf. V, 1, 6, *ib.* 168–169. On the historical importance of the characteristic simile of emanationism which appears in these passages, cf. B. A. G. Fuller, *The Problem of Evil in Plotinus*, 1912, 69 ff.

51. *Enn.*, IV, 8, 6; Volkmann, II, 150. Translation in part that of S. Mackenna.

52. *Enn.*, V, 2, 1–2; Volkmann, II, 176–178.

53. *Comment. in Somnium Scipionis*, I, 14, 15. This, of course, was *not* "Homer's golden chain."

54. *Enn.*, III, 3, 3; Volkmann, I, 253.

55. *Enn.*, II, 9, 13; Volkmann, I, 202. For a comprehensive and illuminating analysis of the Plotinian theodicy, see especially Fuller, *op. cit.*

56. *Enn.*, III, 3, 7; Volkmann, I, 259.

57. *Enn.*, III, 2, 11; Volkmann, I, 239.

58. *Enn.*, III, 2, 14; Volkmann, I, 242.

59. *Enn.*, III, 2, 15; Volkmann, I, 243.

60. *Enn.*, III, 2, 16; Volkmann, I, 247.

61. *Enn.*, VI, 6, 17–18; Volkmann, II, 420–424.

## NOTES TO LECTURE III

1. *Comment. de div. nom.*, 9; cited by Busnelli, *Cosmogonia e Antropogenesi secondo Dante . . . e le sue fonte*, 1922, 14. The argument is taken from *De div. nom.*, IV, 10 (Migne, *Patr. graeca*, III, col. 708).

2. *De div. nom.*, IV, 1; *ib.*, col. 695.

3. *Paradiso*, VII, 64–66; in Longfellow's version:
   Goodness divine, which from itself doth spurn
   All envy, burning in itself so sparkles
   That the eternal beauties it unfolds.

4. *Paradiso*, XXIX, 130–145; Longfellow's tr. "Power" is, of course, an inadequate rendering of *valor*: the term in such a context contains also the idea of "excellence" or "that which is of supreme value."

5. *Ibid.*, XIII, 56, 58–63, but reading *nuove* for *nove* in 59. *Atto* in l. 62 means the actualization of possibles.

6. *Introd. ad Theologiam.*, III; in Migne, vol. 178, cols. 1093–1101.

7. The Spinozism of Abelard has, it appears, been pointed out by Fessler, whose work I have not seen. Cf. Erdmann, *Hist. of Philos.*, I, 322. Leibniz refers to Abelard's argument in *Théodicée*, 171, and endeavors earnestly but unconvincingly to differentiate his own theory of "inclining reason" from Abelard's "necessity."

8. *Epitome Theologiae Christianae*, in Migne, *Patr. Lat.*, vol. 178, col. 1726–1727.

9. *Capitula haeresum Petri Abelardi*: Bernard's *Opera* in Migne, vol. 182, col. 1052.

10. *Sententiarum libri quatuor*, I, dist. 44, 2. Cf. William of Ockham's criticism of the rationalistic and optimistic arguments, in his commentary *Super IV lib. sent.*, Lib. I, dist. 43 in Migne, *Patr. Lat.*, vol. 192, col. 640.

11. *Summa contra Gentiles*, I, 75.

12. Rickaby, *Of God and his Creatures*, 57.

13. *Summa Theol.*, I, q. 19, a.4; the last three words probably refer chiefly to Abelard.

14. *Summa contra Gentiles*, I, 81; tr. Rickaby, *op. cit.*

15. *Summa contra Gentiles*, II, 45; tr. Rickaby.

16. *Summa contra Gentiles*, III, 71; and I *Sent.*, dist. XLIV, q. 1, a.2, in *Opera omnia*, Pavia, V (1855), 355. *Cf. Summa Theol.*, I, q. 47, a. 1, 2, and q. 65, a.2.

17. Gilson, *Le Thomisme*, 126. Gilson does not, of course, fail to indicate elsewhere the other, or emanationist, side of the Thomist doctrine.

18. *Summa Theol.*, I, q. 25, a.6; cf. also *De Potentia*, I, 5. The same contradiction is common in later writers: cf., e. g., Nicolaus Cusanus, *De ludo globi*, I: *perfectiorem mundum potuit facere Deus; licet factus sit ita perfectus sicut esse potuit. Hoc enim est factus quod fieri potest.*

19. *De animalibus*, Lib. II; cited by K. Ufermann, *Untersuchungen über das Gesetz der Kontinuität bei Leibniz* (1927), 8.

20. *Summa contra Gentiles*, II, 68.

21. Nicolaus Cusanus, *De docta ignorantia*, III, 1.

22. Cf. Gilson, *Le Thomisme*, 128.

23. *Night Thoughts*, VI. For the same argument, cf. Locke, *Essay*, III, ch. 6, 12; Addison, *Spectator*, 519.

24. *Les Contemplations*, II, Liv. VI, 26.

25. *Metaphysics*, tr. Horten, p. 200.

26. Boethius, *De Consolatione*, IV, 6; in H. R. James's translation:
    Towards the Good do all things tend,
    Many paths, but one the end,
    For naught lasts unless it turns
    Backwards in its course, and yearns
    To that source to flow again
    Whence its being first was ta'en.

    For a seventeenth-century poetic paraphrase, *v.* John Norris's poem "Beauty" in *A Collection of Pieces*, etc. (1706).

27. Sencourt, *Outflying Philosophy*, 303.

28. *De diversis quaestionibus* LXXXIII, in Migne, *Patrol. Lat.*, vol. 40.

29. *Inferno*, XI, 104.

30. Bruno, *Spaccio*, II.

31. *Summa contra Gentiles*, II, 45.

32. *A Collection of Pieces, etc.* (1706), 257–259 and 69; all this is more lengthily set forth in prose by Norris in *The Theory of the Ideal World*, 1701, I, pp. 255–263.

33. *A Collection*, etc., p. 247.

34. An interesting and rather elaborate example of this conception is to be seen in the *Theologia Naturalis* or *Liber creaturarum* (? 1480) of Raymond Sebond, which Montaigne translated, especially p. 3 ff. of the 1605 ed. of this translation.

35. *Op. cit.*, 27.

36. Cf. e. g. *Enneads*, V, 7, 41: The One "is nothing to itself. . . . It is the Good, not for itself but for others. It does not behold itself; for from such beholding, something would exist and come into being for it. All such things it left to the inferior beings, and nothing that exists in them belongs to it, not even being." — Augustine, *De Trinitate*, V, 1, 2: (Deum esse) sine qualitate bonum, sine quantitate magnum, sine indigentia creatorem, sine situ praesidentem, sine habitu omnia continentem, sine loco ubique totum, sine tempore sempiternum, sine ulla sui mutatione mutabilia facientem, nihilque patientem. — *Dionysius Areop.*, *De div. nom.*, VI, 3: "He is neither conceived nor expressed nor named. And he is not any of existing things, nor is he known in any one of existing things. And he is all in all, and nothing in none. And he is known to all from all, and to nothing from none." — *Joh. Scotus Erig.*, III, 19: God as "nothing." — Thomas Aquinas, *Summa Theol.*, I, q.13, a.12. Thomas endeavors, it is true, to show that positive affirmations which we can make about God can be true, but it can only be *sensu eminentiori*; the predicates which we use have for us only the meaning whereby they are applicable to creatures; but no predicate can be applied univocally to God and any other subject of discourse, since all the "perfections which in created things are distinct and multiple pre-exist in God indivisibly and simply." No distinctions between predicates are really pertinent to such a subject; though Thomas elsewhere seeks to reconcile this with the proposition that the divine attributes are not all synonymous. The notion that terms may, without ceasing to have any meaning, be employed in a *sensus eminentior*, and the whole device of reasoning by a deliberate attribution to God of contradictory predicates, whose contradictions are masked by that notion, still (as is usually overlooked) survives in Spinoza; cf. *Eth.*, I, 17, sch.: *Intellectus et voluntas, qui Dei essentiam constituerent, a nostro intellectu et voluntate toto coelo differre deberent, nec in ulla re, praeterquam in nomine, convenire possent; non aliter scilicet quam inter se conveniunt canis, signum coeleste, et canis, animal latrans.* Cf. also *Cogitata Metaphysica*, Cap. V.

37. *Mosaicall Philosophy* (1659), 53–54. The two principles Fludd most frequently terms the "volunty" and "nolunty" of God.

38. Fludd, *op. cit.*, p. 143.

39. In the end Fludd is, of course, compelled by his premises to assert that

the two attributes are one, since the divine essence is indivisible, and that both are good; in other words, he is still involved in the contradictions inherent in all philosophy of this general type.

40. *Mosaicall Philosophy*, 52.

41. John Norris, "The Prospect," in *A Collection*, etc. (1706), 97.

42. Cf. *Summa Theol.*, II, 1, q. 2, a. 8. "Impossibile est beatitudinem hominis esse in aliquo bono creato. . . . Objectum voluntatis, quae est appetitus hominis, est universale bonum, sicut objectum intellectus est universale verum. Ex quo patet quod nihil potest quietare voluntatem hominis nisi bonum universale; quod non invenitur in aliquo creato, sed solum in Deo." So far as concerns Neoplatonism the same conflict of ideas has been pointed out with admirable penetration and lucidity by B. A. G. Fuller, *The Problem of Evil in Plotinus*, pp. 89–102. I have treated the point the more briefly because Mr. Fuller has left so little to say about it.

43. Cf. the Buddhist formula of the Ten *Avyâkatâni* or "points not discussed."

44. I use the term pessimism here in the only sense in which it has much historical applicability. Absolute pessimism, the teaching that this world is wholly evil but that there is no alternative, is a rare phenomenon; actual pessimism is usually merely the negative side of some religious system that offers a completely "other" — which is only accidentally a future — world as an alternative.

## NOTES TO LECTURE IV

1. *Op. cit.*, Bk. III, chap. 14.

2. *Opus Majus*, ed. Bridges, I, 181; cf. also Dreyer, *Planetary Systems*, 234.

3. Sylvester's *The First Weeke*, 1605 ed., Third Day.

4. Cf. Burtt, *The Metaphysical Foundations of Modern Physical Science*, 4–6.

5. While not literally or physically tenanted, the other planets were, of course, the symbolical or, so to say, official seats of various grades of the blessed, and were ruled by differing angelic Intelligences, though the actual place of all of these was in the Empyrean. Thus these bodies did not, as has sometimes been said, "exist solely for man's enjoyment, instruction or use."

6. *Apologie de Raimond Sebond; Essais*, II, 12. Montaigne added that there was no reason to suppose that life and thought are to be found on the earth alone. By this he did not mean that the other stars were inhabited by man-like creatures; he protests against the notion that the moon is a mere suburb of the earth with similar denizens. But the heavenly orbs themselves might legitimately be believed to be animated with reasonable souls, "as much greater and nobler than man's as those globes themselves surpass earth." For the argument of Aristotle that "the most important and precious part of the world" is not, as some had maintained, the centre, but rather the "limit" or periphery, v. De Caelo, II, 293a–b; cf. also Cicero, *De nat. deorum*, II, 6.

7. *Discovery of a New Planet*, in *Philosophical and Mathematical Works* (1802), I, 190.

8. *De revolutionibus orbium* (1873 ed.), I, 28. Copernicus, however, did not definitely pronounce against the infinity of the world, but left that "to the discussion of philosophers," *disputationi physiologorum* (*ibid.*, 21–22).

9. William of Ockham and Buridan had also opposed this theory.

10. The passage is cited in full in Burtt, *op. cit.*, 47–49, where further illustrations of Kepler's "sun-worship" are given.

11. On the other hand Kepler still adhered to Platonic and Aristotelian principles in arguing that the universe as a whole must be a sphere. He admits that there are no strictly "astronomical" reasons for holding this view; but there are two good "metaphysical" reasons for it. The first is that the sphere is "the most capacious" of all figures, and therefore the most suitable shape for the whole of things sensible; second, that the archetype of the physical world is God himself, to whom, if any such comparison may be made, no shape is more like than the surface of a sphere (*Epitome*, I, ii; *Op. omnia*, VI, 140) — i. e., the traditional "perfect" figure, emblem of self-sufficiency:

> En la forme ronde
> Gît la perfection qui toute en soi abonde,

in the words of Ronsard.

12. *Epitome astronomiae Copernicanae*; *Op. omnia*, VI, 110, 122, 143, 310.

13. *Mysterium cosmographicum*, 1596; *Op. omnia*, I, 106; cf. 123.

14. *De revolutionibus orbium*, I. Kepler similarly insists upon the indispensability of the immobile envelope to render the motion of other things conceivable: *fixarum regio praestat mobilibus locum et basin quandam, cui velut innitantur mobilia et cuius per se immobilis comparatione motus intelligatur fieri* (*Epitome*, 311). The sphere of the fixed stars had in the astronomy of the Copernicans one of the rôles sustained by the ether in immediately pre-Einsteinian physics.

15. *Age of Reason*, ch. 13.

16. *Discovery of a New World*, ed. cit., I, 102.

17. *Descriptio globi intellectualis*, in *Philosophical Works*, Ellis and Spedding ed. (1905), 683.

18. *Ibid.*, 685.

19. *Anatomy of Melancholy*, Boston (1859), II, 147.

20. Cf. Newcomb, *The Stars* (1902), 140 f.; and D. L. Edwards in *Science Progress* (1925), 604.

21. *Crescas' Critique of Aristotle: Problems of Aristotle's Physics in Jewish and Arabic Philosophy* (1929), Introd., 217, 117.

22. *De doct. ignor.*, II, ch. 11, 12.

23. *De venatione sapientiae* (1463), ch. 28.

24. *De Beryllo* (1458), ch. 29.

25. *De doct. ignor.*, II, ch. 12.

26. *Zodiacus Vitae, ca.* 1531, Bk. VII; 1557 ed. (Basle), 160. Cf. also *id.*, pp. 156–157:

*Nam nisi fecisset meliora et nobiliora
Quam mortale genus, fabricator maximus ille,
Nempe videretur non magno dignus honore,
Nempe imperfectum imperium atque ignobile haberet.*

27. *Ibid.*, Bk. XI, p. 294. Whether the living beings in the rest of the world (below the Empyrean) are incorporeal or have bodily members like our own, Palingenius is uncertain; but he inclines to, and argues for, the latter view.

28. *A Perfit Description of the Caelestiall Orbes*, . . . , 1576, appended to his edition of the *Prognostication Everlasting* . . . of his father, Leonard Digges. This, perhaps the most important sixteenth-century English defence of Copernicanism, which had been "almost completely neglected by all writers on the history of science in the Elizabethan period," was recently rediscovered in the Huntington Library by Francis R. Johnson and Sanford V. Larkey and has been published by them in *The Huntington Library Bulletin*, No. 5, April, 1934, with a study of its background and influence; it was unknown to me when the present lecture was orally delivered.   That Digges expressed the theories of the infinity of worlds and the diffusion of the stars throughout infinite space in English before Bruno had propounded them (in Italian and Latin) Johnson and Larkey conclusively show, but, as we have seen, this was not without pre-Copernican precedents; the novelty lay in its combination with Copernicanism.   Digges's discoverers declare that, unlike the generality of sixteenth-century astronomers, "in approaching this problem, he consistently kept to the scientific point of view"; but there is no evidence in Digges's text to show this.   While he is "scientific" enough in his defence of the heliocentric theory, the only ground which he actually suggests — that cited above — for affirming the numerical and spatial infinity of the celestial system is of the usual *a priori* type.   That "the infinity of the universe was an ever recurring subject of metaphysical discussion throughout the Middle Ages and the Renaissance" is remarked by Johnson and Larkey, with further illustrations (104–105).

29. *Ibid.*

30. *De Immenso*, I, 9 (*Op. lat.*, I, 1, 242 f.) and *De l'infinito universo e mondi*, III (*Op. italiane*, ed. Lagarde, 360).

31. *De l'infinito universo e mondi*: Lagarde, I, 314.

32. *Ibid.*, 312.

33. *De Immenso*, II, ch. 13.

34. *De l'infinito, etc.*: Lagarde, I, 316. Bruno was, however, not a perfectly "hard determinist"; he goes on to assert that this universal necessity is entirely compatible with individual freedom, though without attempting to explain how, or in what sense.

35. *De la Causa*, V: Lagarde, I, 277–279. I have previously cited this in a paper on "The Dialectic of Bruno and Spinoza," *University of California Publications in Philosophy*, I (1904), 141 ff., where a fuller analysis of the

parts of Bruno's system not especially pertinent to the present study is presented.

36. *De la Causa*, V, *passim*.

37. This view seems also to have been definitely defended at least as early as 1585 by the astronomer G. B. Benedetti in *Diversarum speculationum mathematicarum et physicarum liber*, which I have not seen; cf. Dreyer, *Planetary Systems*, 350.

38. *Op.*, I, 399. Still more emphatically Galileo writes in a letter to Ingoli, 1624: "No man in the world knows or humanly can know what the shape of the firmament is, or that it has any shape" (II, 73).

39. *Dialogue, etc.*, III.

40. *Op.*, I, 114. Kepler's belief in the existence of living beings in the moon is expressed in four passages in his writings (cf. *Op. omnia*, II, 497), especially in his *Somnium, seu opus posthumum de astronomia lunari*, 1634 (*ib.*, VIII, Pt. 1, 33 ff.). He perhaps did not hold it very seriously, since he says that in these writings *in [hac] materia mihi post Pythagoram et Plutarchum ludere placuit* (*ib.*, VIII, 497).

41. Cf. the preface of 1664 to *Le Monde, ou Traité de la lumière*, by D. R.: "L'auteur savait que, si quelque part on défendait de parler du système de Copernic comme d'une vérité, ou encore comme d'une hypothèse, on ne défendait pas d'en parler comme d'une fable. Mais c'est une fable qui, non plus que les autres apologues, ou profanes ou sacrés, ne répugne pas aux choses qui sont par effet" (*Oeuvres*, ed. Adam et Tannery, XI; cf. *Principia*, III, 15–17).

42. Letter to Chanut; *Ep.*, I, 36; *ed.* Cousin, X, 46.

43. *Principia*, III, 29.

44. *Principia*, III, 1.

45. *Principia*, III, 3.

46. *Oeuvres*, IV, 292.

47. From the English translation of the oration, appended to the 1728 edition of *A Week's Conversation on the Plurality of Worlds*, an English version of Fontenelle, on which see below. For an earlier English ascription of the credit for this widening of the world to Descartes, cf. H. Power, *Experimental Philosophy* . . . , 1664, Preface.

48. *Democritus Platonissans* (1647), 47, 50, 51. In a later writing More speaks of "that vastness of the universe which is more consonant to the sacred attributes of God, his Power and Goodness, if we consider the world as the effect of so omnipotent a cause," as a distinctive merit of Cartesianism (*The Apology of Dr. Henry More, in a Modest Inquiry into the Mystery of Iniquity* (1664), 486). More's opinions on the question of the conceivability of the infinite were, however, subject to waverings, which there is not space to follow here.

49. *Lux Orientalis* (1682), 72.

50. Letter to Père Noël, cited by Brunschvicg in his edition of the *Pensées*, II, 131.

51. *Pensées*, 72 (I, 70). In the phrase, "le vaste tour que décrit cet astre," "this star" means, it would appear, the sun, not the earth; i. e., Pascal

is assuming the Ptolemaic system. He seems to conceive of the sphere of the fixed stars as also revolving, while for Copernicus and Kepler it was stationary.

52. *Pensées*, 420.

53. *Ibid.*, 793, 348.

54. *Ibid.*, 365.

55. *Ibid.*, 72.

56. In all this the affinity between Pascal and Cusanus is close, and one may, I think, see in the *De docta ignorantia* one probable source, direct or indirect, of the sceptical side of the *Pensées*. It will be observed that in one passage cited Pascal virtually quotes the famous phrase of Cusanus, applying it as did the latter to the infinity of the physical world. The fifteenth-century philosopher had also made much of the argument that "there is no proportionality between the finite and the infinite" in his contention that all our knowledge reduces to a deeper assurance of our ignorance: *quanto in hac ignorantia profundius docti fuerimus, tanto magis ad ipsam accedimus veritatem.* Cusanus also (as Long has expressed it) found "not merely a definite number of antinomies, such as Kant was to set up, but as many of them as there were things that exist." The conception of the nature of every part of the universe as organically involved in the nature of every other part (*quodlibet in quolibet*), so that none can be truly known unless all are known, was especially characteristic of the philosophy of the Cusan. Pascal's use of it in the interest of a similar devout agnosticism is indicated above.

57. The earliest translation was by Mrs. Aphra Behn (1688, other editions, 1700, 1715), the second by the Platonist Glanvill (1688, 1695, third ed. by 1702). That published in the name of W. Gardiner (1715, 1728, 1757, and numerous other editions) is a palpable plagiarism of Glanvill's. The book "was read with unexampled avidity, and was speedily circulated through every part of Europe. It was translated into all the languages of the Continent, and was honored by annotations from the pen of the celebrated astronomer Lalande, and of M. Gottsched, one of its German editors" (Sir D. Brewster, *More Worlds than One*, 3). For an example of the influence of Fontenelle's (and similar) arguments, cf. W. Molyneux, *Dioptrica Nova* (1692), 278–279.

58. *Entr.*, V.

59. Addison found this a convincing argument. "The author of the *Plurality of Worlds* draws a very good argument from this consideration, for the peopling of every planet; as indeed, it seems very probable from the analogy of reason, that if no part of matter we are acquainted with be waste and useless those great bodies which are at such a distance from us should not be waste and useless, but rather that they should be furnished with beings adapted to their respective stations" (*Spectator*, 519).

60. *Entr.*, VI.

61. *Op. cit.*, Preliminary Discourse, xxxviii–xlii.

62. *Ibid.*, 237.

63. *Ibid.*, 246.

64. *Op. cit.*, Bk. II.
65. *Ibid.*, Bk. III.
66. *Cosmologische Briefe* (1761), 63, 106.
67. *Allgemeine Naturgeschichte und Theorie des Himmels* (1755), in Kant's *Populäre Schriften*, ed. P. Mesiger (1911), 7.
68. *Ibid.*, 28. Kant, however, thinks that it can with more assurance be conjectured "that celestial bodies which are not yet inhabited will be hereafter, when their development (*Bildung*) has reached a later stage."

## NOTES TO LECTURE V

1. This was published in 1753 by Koenig in the course of the celebrated controversy with Maupertuis in which Voltaire took the most conspicuous part. The authenticity of the letter was denied by Maupertuis and by the Berlin Academy, of which he was President, but its genuineness is sufficiently established by both external and internal evidence, and is not questioned by contemporary Leibniz specialists. The letter was quoted at length by Flourens in his *Analyse raisonnée des travaux de Cuvier*, 1841. The text may be found in Buchenau and Cassirer's *Leibniz: Hauptschriften zur Grundlegung der Philosophie*, II, 556–559.
2. For the derivation of the principle of continuity from that of plenitude, cf. *Principes de la nature et de la grâce* (1718), 3: "Tout est plein dans la nature, ... et à cause de la plénitude du monde, tout est lié."
3. *Philosophy of Leibniz*, 34.
4. For a typical expression of this, cf. Fénelon, *De l'existence de Dieu* (1718): "Mes idées sont supérieures à mon esprit, puisqu'elles le redressent et le corrigent. Elles ont le caractère de la Divinité, car elles sont universelles et immuables, comme Dieu. ... Si ce qui est changeant, passager et emprunté existe véritablement, à plus forte raison ce qui ne peut changer et qui est nécessaire." (Pt. II, ch. iv).
5. The conception of the essences of things as contained in the mind of God goes back at least to Philo, and had been imposed upon most medieval thought by the influence of Augustine; hence the transition from the Platonic to the modern sense of the term "idea." Cf. Webb, *Studies in the History of Natural Theology*, 247.
6. So Leibniz speaks of *ille transitus ab uno contingente ad aliud contingens prius aut simplicius qui exitum habere non potest* (*ut etiam revera unum contingens non est causa alterius, etsi nobis videatur*): *Opuscules et fragments*, ed. Couturat (1903), 19. Cf. also *Philos. Schriften*, ed. Gerhardt, VII, 303 ff. "The reasons of the world lie in something extramundane, different from the chain of states or series of things, of which the aggregate constitutes the world. We must then pass from physical or hypothetical necessity, which determines posterior states of the world by prior, to something which is of absolute or metaphysical necessity, the reason for which cannot be given."
7. I have put the conception in these two alternative ways because there is

much wavering in Leibniz and his contemporaries on the question whether necessary judgments are ultimately "analytic" or "synthetic." Usually Leibniz himself called them analytic; but he certainly did not mean by this that they were mere tautologies. Such a judgment, as he somewhere says, is not a *coccysmus inutilis*. It does not fall within the purpose of the present historical study to discuss the fundamental logical questions involved in this distinction. For further comment upon it, see the writer's "Kant's Antithesis of Dogmatism and Criticism," *Mind*, N. S., 1906.

8. J. Jackson, *The Existence and Unity of God* (1734), 39.

9. *Philos. Schriften*, ed. Gerhardt, III, 637.

10. Clarke's *Demonstration*, etc. (1706), 22–26. Eight editions of this work, usually with Clarke's Boyle Lectures of 1705 added, were published by 1717. For further expressions of the same argument, see J. Clarke, *Defence*, etc. (1722), Jackson, *op. cit.*

11. S. Clarke, *op. cit.*, 27.

12. J. Jackson, *op. cit.* (1734), 31.

13. Among those who expressly took this extreme position were E. Law (in King, *Origin of Evil*, 1732 ed., I, 52–56) and Thomas Knowles, *The Existence and Attributes of God* (1746). Yet even such opponents of the "*a priori* theology" were unable to avoid occasional admissions of the proposition they elsewhere denied; e. g., Knowles (*op. cit.*, 48–49). It is to be noted that Law treats all the reasoning about God's necessary existence as "built upon the principle of sufficient reason" (*op. cit.*, 77).

14. *Ethics*, I, Prop. 8.

15. *Ibid.*, I, Prop. 11.

16. *Ibid.*, I, Prop. 17, Scholium.

17. *Ibid.*, I, Prop. 35.

18. *Ibid.*, I, Prop. 16; cf. Tschirnhausen's comment on this proposition, Spinoza's *Opera* (1895), II, 428.

19. *Ibid.*, I, Prop. 11.

20. *Ibid.*, I, Prop. 17, Scholium.

21. *Ibid.* The dialectic of the principle of plenitude, in its most rigorous sense, is still more fully developed in the *Short Treatise*, I, chaps. 2 (14–16), 6.

22. *De rerum principio*, q. 4; cf. also *Opus Oxoniense*, I, d. 1, q. 2, n. 10. So Cusanus wrote that if you add the creation to God, you have added nothing, *Creatura non habet etiam entitatis sicut accidens, sed est penitus nihil* (*De doct. ignor.*, I).

23. The fusion was, of course, made easier by the presence in Platonism, from the outset, of the last as well as the first of these conceptions.

24. *De civ. Dei*, XII, 14–17; iv; *De Genesi contra Manichaeos*, I, 2. With the paradoxes of this doctrine Augustine in the former passage struggles painfully, ending in an amazing tangle of formal contradictions.

25. *De diversis quaestionibus* LXXXIII, 22.

26. *Rép. aux sixièmes objections*, par. 12. For another example of the same conjunction of ideas, cf. Malebranche, *Entretiens*, VI, 5: "La volonté de

créer des corps n'est point nécessairement renfermée dans le notion de
l'être infiniment parfait, de l'être qui suffit pleinement à lui-même.
Bien loin de cela, cette notion semble exclure de Dieu une telle volonté."

27.  Descartes, *loc. cit.*
28.  *Op. cit.*, 1659 ed., 110; italics mine.
29.  *Hymne de l'Eternité: Oeuvres*, ed. Marty-Laveaux (1891), IV, 159–163. For
the reference to the "goddess Eternity" Ronsard had good theological
authority; cf. Nicolaus Cusanus, *De ludo globi*, I: "Aeternitas Mundi
creatrix Deus est."
30.  *An Hymne to the Fairest Faire: Poetical Works*, ed. Kastner, II, 40; spelling
modernized. The passage may have been also partly inspired by the
similar lines in Du Bartas's *Première Sepmaine*; cf. Sylvester tr. (1598), 3.
31.  Dante, for example, could not refrain from seeking an explanation of
this mystery from Beatrice; the answer, though in accord with tradition,
was scarcely illuminating, nor very well in accord with itself:

> Non per avere a sè di bene acquisto,
> ch'esser non può, ma perchè suo splendore
> potesse, risplendendo, dir 'Subsisto.'  (Par. XXIX, 13–15.)

32.  John Norris, *A Divine Hymn on the Creation* (1706).
33.  *Tr. of Chr. Doctr.*, Sumner's tr., ch. III, 35.
34.  *P. L.*, VII, 171–172.
35.  *Tr. of Chr. Doctr.*, ch. V, 85. To the Arian Milton the Son was only the
greatest of created beings.
36.  *P. L.*, VIII, 415 f., 427 ff.; cf. IV, 417–419.
37.  The passage may be described as a summary of the chapter of the
Eudemian Ethics already cited in Lecture II (VI, 12).
38.  Yet it is in the thought of the divine self-sufficiency — with some weak-
ening of its meaning and a happily confused logic — that Milton finds
religious comfort, and the theme for some famous though in part rather
feeble lines, in the sonnet "When I consider how my light is spent." It
is because "God doth not need either man's work or his own gifts" that
all service is equal, and "they also serve who only stand and wait."
The notion of self-sufficiency, which properly implied the complete impassibility and indifference of deity, naturally tended to be transformed
into the essentially different but religiously much more satisfying notion
of the disinterestedness of the divine activity. Thus (1) Henry More
argues that, since God could not conceivably be benefited by anything
that man is, does, or suffers, he must be supposed to aim only at man's
good; this, of course, tended to destroy the conception, still potent in
popular religion, of the jealous celestial autocrat, insistent upon subservience and compliments from his creatures.

> All what he doth is for the creature's gain,
> Nought seeking from us for his own content:
> What is a drop unto the Ocean's main? (*Psychathanasia*, III, iv, 22.)

This made for a sort of ethical utilitarianism upon theological grounds.
The same argument occurs in Bruno's *Spaccio*, II. (2) For the same
reason another Platonist, Norris of Bemerton, points out that religious

exercises are for man's benefit, not to afford any gratification to the object of worship. (*A Collection of Miscellanies*, 211.) (3) Henry More finds a curious argument for immortality in the idea of a self-sufficient God. If the eternal spectator of human life could be supposed to derive any satisfaction from beholding that moving scene, there would be (to use the phrase of a philosopher of our own time) a certain conservation of the values of each life, and the extinction of the individual would not be an absolute loss.

"But alas! What doth the perpetual repetition of the same life or deiform-image throughout all ages add unto him that is at once infinitely himself, *viz:* good and happy? So that there is nothing considerable in the creation, if the rational creature be mortal. For neither is God at all profited by it, nor man considerably." (*Complete Poems*, ed. Grosart, 165.)

It should be borne in mind that More and Norris (with some inconsistency) denied that the creation was arbitrary, while asserting it to be motiveless.

39. *Par. Lost*, IV, 748–749; VIII, 422–426.

40. *Tr. de l'existence de Dieu*, II, v.

41. *Ibid.*, cf. King, *Origin of Evil*, 1732 ed., 295: "If God was moved by the goodness of things to create the world, he would be a necessary agent."

42. Clarke, *Demonstration*, etc. (1706), 7th ed., 65 ff. Clarke, it is true, speaks of a "necessity of fitness," which means that "things could not have been otherwise than they are without diminishing the beauty, order, and well-being of the whole — which would have been impossible, since it is impossible for a wise being to resolve to act foolishly." Clarke here seems to approximate Leibniz's position, but in the later controversy between them he is a long way from it.

43. *P. L.*, V, 472–479.

44. *P. L.*, V, 482–487.

45. *Tr. of Chr. Doctr.*, 184.

46. *Summa Theol.*, I, q. 61, a.3; *Paradiso*, 29, 37. Of course Milton could hardly have made an epic out of a theodicy if he had not adopted this theory; there would have been no stirring tale of the wars in heaven to relate. But it is difficult to believe that John Milton framed his theological creed to suit the exigencies of his literary ambitions.

47. We have, however, noted elsewhere some slight trace of the influence of the principle of plenitude upon Milton, when he is dealing with certain questions of cosmography.

48. *Creation*, Bk. V; the lines appear to be a versification of a passage of S. Clarke's, cited in part above.

49. *Principes de la nature et de la grâce* (1714), §§ 7–8; in *Philos. Schriften*, VI, 599–602; the same connection of ideas in Wolff (1731). At this point, it will be seen, the principle of sufficient reason and Leibniz's other "great principle," that of contradiction, come to the same result. A necessary being must exist because there would otherwise be no *sufficient* reason for anything; but also, a necessary being must exist because its essence in-

volves existence, so that to conceive of it as non-existent would be self-contradictory; and again, unless the opposite were thus self-contradictory, it would not meet the requirements of a sufficient reason. The second proposition is simply the ontological argument. Some writers on Leibniz have made too much of his criticism of that argument. He accepts it absolutely, but adds that, as usually stated, it omits a needful logical precaution. The "possibility" of the idea of God — i. e., its non-contradictoriness, should be shown before the necessity of existence is, through the principle of contradiction, inferred from it. Leibniz, however, had in fact no doubts about the "possibility" of the idea of God; so that the distinction does not affect his conclusions in any way, and remains only a logical refinement upon the Anselmic reasoning. Cf. *Philos. Schriften*, IV, 294, 296, 359, 424.

50. *Réf. inédite*, etc. (1854), 50.

51. *Philos. Schriften*, VII, 390.

52. *Théodicée*, in *Philos. Schriften*, VI, 386.

53. *Philosophical Poems*, ed. Grosart, 1878; *Psychathanasia*, Bk. III, Canto 4, stanzas 19–21, p. 85.

54. *Philos. Schriften*, VI, 401.

55. *Philos. Schriften*, II, 420. As such a psychological generalization, Leibniz in substance points out, the principle of sufficient reason is equivalent to the proposition "accepted by everybody except some doctors too much wrapped up in their own subtleties," and approved by the greatest of the Schoolmen, that all volition is *sub specie boni*, a choice of what either is, or is by the chooser believed to be, a good. (*Philos. Schriften*, VI, 412–413.)

56. Leibniz on occasion puts the case even for the principle of contradiction on pragmatic grounds — for those who will accept none other. Reasoning with a correspondent who had evinced a leaning towards "the scepticism of the Academics," he points out that that principle can be sufficiently justified on the ground of its needfulness if we are to reason at all. "Without assuming it we should be obliged to give up all hope of demonstrations. One ought not to demand the impossible; to do so would be to give evidence that one was not seriously seeking for truth. I, therefore, shall boldly assume (*supposerai*) that two contradictories cannot be true." (*Philos. Schriften*, I, 382.)

57. *Philos. Schriften*, VII, 372.

58. *Philos. Schriften*, V, 286.

59. Cf. *Opuscules*, etc. (ed. Couturat, 1903), 522.

60. Russell, *Philos. of Leibniz* (1901), 66; the interpretation is based chiefly upon *Philos. Schriften*, II, 51.

61. Spinoza did not include self-contradictory notions, or what were called "chimaeras," among the essences. A round square is merely an *ens verbale* — it cannot even be imagined, still less, of course, subsist in the order of Ideas. Cf. Spinoza, *Opera*, II, 468. Any incompossible *world* would have been for Spinoza merely one of the chimaeras.

62. *Philos. Schriften*, VI, 218, 318, 413, 126; VII, 389.

63. *Philos. Schriften*, VI, 386.

64. *Philos. Schriften*, VI, 423 (from the criticism of King's *De Origine Mali*).
Cf. also VI, 219; and VII, 311: *Ratio veritatum latet in rerum ideis quae ipsi divinae essentiae involvuntur*; it is for this reason that it is an error to suppose *rerum bonitatem a divina voluntate pendere*. This would be similar to saying that "the truth of the divine existence depends upon the divine will."

65. *Philos. Schriften*, VII, 305.

66. *Philos. Schriften*, II, 56; cf. also VII, 200, 309, 311; and in Couturat's collection of *Opuscules et fragments* (1903), 518 f. and 1–3. I cite part of the last: "Veritas est, inesse praedicatum subjecto. Ostenditur reddendo rationem per analysin terminorum in communes utrique notiones. Haec analysis vel finita est, vel infinita. . . . Series infinita a Deo perfecte cognoscitur," etc. In this passage, however, Leibniz, presumably to avert the charge of determinism, gives an unusual meaning to "necessary," making it equivalent to "demonstrative," i. e., capable of reduction to an intuited necessity *by us*. That it is an intuited necessity to the perfect understanding, however, the passage plainly affirms.

67. *Ibid.*, II, 62 (from a letter to Arnauld, 1686).

68. This has been recognized and well expressed by Couturat (*Logique de Leibniz*, 1901, p. 214). Russell, on the other hand, has denied that Leibniz held the view "that the difference between the necessary and the contingent has an essential reference to our human limitations, and does not subsist for God." "Everything that is characteristic of Leibniz depended upon the ultimately irreducible nature of the opposition between existential and necessary propositions" (*op. cit.*, 1901, 61–62). Leibniz, however, as will be seen, enunciated categorically and repeatedly the opinion which Russell thinks he cannot have held. It is true that he often said things which sound, and taken literally are, inconsistent with it; and these are more "characteristic" in one sense, namely, that they make his system look more different from that of Spinoza. But he had obvious non-philosophical reasons for employing such expressions; and they are capable of being construed in a Pickwickian sense which would harmonize them with the thesis cited above. The latter, on the contrary, Leibniz had no conceivable motive for asserting unless he believed it; it is, in fact, plain that he thought it both true and fundamental; and his expression of it cannot possibly be given any sense which would admit the "ultimately irreducible nature of the opposition between existential and necessary propositions." Russell is also in error, I think, in asserting an ultimate distinction in Leibniz between the necessary and the *a priori* (*op. cit.*, 231). Cf. *Opuscules*, etc. (1903), 518.

69. *Modesta disquisitio*, 27–67. Cf. also the Latin essays of D. Straehler (1727) and Chr. Langhansen (1727), both of which criticize Leibniz and Wolff as "pseudo-defensores contingentiae." That the principle of sufficient reason itself meant for Leibniz that every true proposition is, and by a perfect intelligence is apprehended as, reducible to "primitive" or "identical" truths, is noted by Straehler (p. 37).

70. Art. *Leibnitzianisme.*
71. Art. "Suffisante raison," *passim.*
72. *Philos. Schriften*, VII, 303, 305, 310.
73. For a denial of the idea that finite essences have of themselves a tendency to existence, cf. Spinoza's *Tractatus Politicus*, II, sec. 2.
74. An earlier seventeenth-century writer, Matthew Barker, had, indeed, reversed the usual reasoning, deducing the existence of God from the necessity of a full Chain of Being, rather than the Chain of Being from the necessary existence of God: "These degrees in nature are by learned men called the Scale of Nature; and we must come to some top in the Scale or Ladder, and not ascend *ad infinitum*, though we must into infinity, which is the Infinite God . . . where there are degrees of perfection, there must needs be some greatest perfection, and what can that be but God, who is *Optimus et Maximus*, who is the most Excellent Being and the first Perfection" (*Natural Theology* (1674), 27). Substantially the same argument has recently been independently advanced by Professor W. H. Sheldon, *Philos. Rev.* (1923), 355 ff.
75. *Philos. Schriften*, VII, 304; cf. 303: "It is most evident that, out of the infinite combinations of possibles and the infinite number of series, that one exists *per quam plurimum essentiae seu possibilitatis producitur ad existendum.*" Cf. also Couturat, *op. cit.* (1901), 226.
76. *Philos. Schriften*, VII, 290; cf. also 304, and Couturat, *op. cit.*, 224–225.
77. *Monadology*, 54; *Philos. Schriften*, VI, 616.
78. *Philos. Schriften*, VII, 195.
79. *Philos. Schriften*, VII, 290–291.
80. *Ibid.*, III, 573.
81. *Ibid.*, I, 331. Cf. VII, 289: "Dici potest omne possibile existiturire, prout scilicet fundatur in Ente necessario."
82. *Ibid.*, VII, 304.
83. An extreme example is the *Tentamen Anagogicum* (*Philos. Schriften*, VII, 270 ff.).
84. Russell seems curiously to miss the point when he writes: "Why Leibniz holds that substances form a continuous series it is difficult to say. He never, so far as I know, offers the shadow of a reason, except that such a world seems to him pleasanter than one with gaps." (1901, p. 65.) The reason, as indicated above, is the same as the reason for believing that there *is* a reason for anything — namely, that the alternative would be a world of chance. Leibniz's aversion from the latter supposition is, no doubt, as I have suggested, at bottom pragmatic, but it is not unintelligible nor merely whimsical. Let a single gap be supposed in the Chain of Being, and, according to his logic, the universe would by that alone be shown to be non-rational, and therefore utterly untrustworthy.
85. In his comment upon King's book Leibniz expressly approves this argument. (*Philos. Schriften*, VI, 172–173.)
86. One of the arguments against real space is itself derived from the principle of sufficient reason; *v.* Leibniz's third letter to Clarke (*Philos. Schriften*, VII, 364).

87. He also argues against the vacuum on the ground of the identity of indiscernibles. Between two regions of empty space there would be no difference whatever, and therefore they would *not* be distinct regions. They are supposed (by vacuists) to differ " *solo numero,* which is absurd." (*Opuscules,* etc., ed. Couturat, 1903, p. 522.)

88. *Cf. Philos. Schriften,* IV, 368; VII, 363; and *A Collection of Papers,* 103.

89. *Math. Schriften,* ed. Gerhardt, III, 565; tr. by Latta in *The Monadology,* etc. (1925), 257.

90. *Opuscules,* etc. (1903), 522.

91. *Nouveaux Essais,* III, 6, 12.

## NOTES TO LECTURE VI

1. *Essay concerning Human Understanding,* III, chap. vi, § 12. Locke, unlike Leibniz, does not insist upon the *a priori* necessity of the plenitude and continuity of the chain; the theory is merely "probable" (*ibid.*).

2. Addison quotes "Mr. Lock" in support of this.

3. Law's edition of King's *Essay on the Origin of Evil* (1732), 143 n.

4. *Libri sententiarum,* II, 1, 8.

5. *De sapientia veterum* in *Works,* Ellis and Spedding ed., VI, 747.

6. Abbadie, *Traité de la vérité de la religion chrétienne,* pub. 1684; 7th ed. (1729), I, 95.

7. " *On ne trouverait plus d'animaux féroces, que dans les forêts reculées, et on les réserverait pour exercer la hardiesse, la force et l'adresse du genre humain, par un jeu qui représenterait la guerre, sans qu'on eût jamais besoin de guerre véritable entre les nations.*" *Traité de l'existence de Dieu,* I, 2.

8. Cited in Mornet, *Les Sciences de la nature en France au 18e siècle* (1911), 149 ff., where numerous well-chosen examples of these fatuities may be found.

9. *Dialogo di due massimi systemi,* III, 400.

10. *Antidote against Atheism,* II, ch. 9, 8.

11. *Principia,* III, 3.

12. Leibniz, *Philos. Schriften,* I, 150.

13. *Fragments,* etc., in *Works* (1809), VIII, 169.

14. *Ibid.,* 232. Cf. also *Fragments,* LVI, *ibid.,* 288–289: "If the divine attributes had required that there should be no such thing as physical and moral evil, man would have been visibly the final cause of a world made solely for his use, and to be the scene of his happiness. This world would have been visibly the final cause of the universe. All the planets would have rolled in subserviency to ours, and the fixed stars themselves would have served no other purpose, than to twinkle by night, and to adorn our canopy." The passage is amplified and versified by Pope, *Essay on Man,* I, ll. 131–140. The wittiest attack upon anthropocentric teleology in the eighteenth century is in the Sixth Discourse of Voltaire's *Essai sur l'homme* (1738).

15. Cf. also the poem by John Hawkesworth, "The Death of Arachne," in

Pearch's *Supplement* to Dodsley's *Collection of Poems*, 4 vols., 1783, vol. III, 183.

16. Locke, *loc. cit.*

17. Addison, *Spectator*, *loc. cit.* Cf. also Bolingbroke, *Fragments* in *Works* (1809), VIII, Fragment 44, 186.

18. *The Petty Papers*, ed. by the Marquis of Lansdowne (1927), II, 24, 32. Petty's principal excursion into pure philosophy was a sketch of an essay on "The Scale of Creatures," which he left unpublished. He believed himself to have hit upon the idea independently, which is extremely unlikely.

19. *Essays upon Several Subjects in Prose and Verse Written by the Lady Chudleigh* (1710) 123.

20. *Spectator*, No. 621, Nov. 17, 1714.

21. *Philosophical Miscellanies*, English tr. (1759), 107 ff.

22. *Fragments*, etc.; *Works*, vol. VIII, 173; cf. *id.*, 279. For the same idea in Young, *v.* above, p. 139. As has been noted in Lect. IV, this speculation had been anticipated by Cusanus.

23. *Essay on Man*, Ep. II, ll. 31-34.

24. *Allgemeine Naturgeschichte und Theorie des Himmels* (1755), 133. It is not improbable that the suggestion of this theory actually came to Kant from Bolingbroke through Pope, whom he quotes with admiration on the same page, and from whom he takes the mottoes prefixed to each of the three Parts of his disquisition on cosmology. It would be hardly excessive to say that much of Kant's cosmology is a prose amplification and extension of the "philosophy" of the First Epistle of the *Essay on Man*.

25. *Ibid.*

26. *Ibid.*, 129-133.

27. *Ibid.*, 134. Kant also thought it probable that "the same cause," i. e., the superiority of their physical constitution, gives to the inhabitants of these planets a much longer life-span than man's; *ibid.*, 136-137.

28. *Contemplation de la Nature*, 2d ed. (1769), I, 23-24. Beyond even the highest of the planetary worlds, Bonnet adds, there rise "the celestial hierarchies." *Ibid.*, p. 84.

29. *Fragments, or Minutes of Essays* in *Works* (1809), VIII, 168-169. Cf. 346: "When we look down on other animals, we discern a distance, but a very measurable distance, between us and them."

30. *Fragments*, etc.; *Works*, VIII, 231.

31. *Essay on Man*, I, ll. 207-210, 221-232.

32. *Ibid.*, III, ll. 151-156.

33. Soame Jenyns, *Disquisitions on Several Subjects*, I, "On the Chain of Universal Being," in *Works*, 1790 ed., 179-185.

34. *Ibid.*

35. *Essay on Man*, Ep. II, ll. 3-10, 13-18.

36. *Gedanken über Vernunft, Aberglauben und Unglauben.*

37. *Ueber den Ursprung des Uebels*, III.

38. *Essay on Man*, I, ll. 189-192.

39. For further illustrations of this cf. the writer's "Pride in Eighteenth Cen-

tury Thought," *Mod. Lang. Notes* (1921), 31 ff. Montaigne had written in the *Apologie de Raimond Sebond*: "La présomption est notre maladie naturelle et originelle. La plus calamiteuse et fragile de toutes les créatures, c'est l'homme, . . . et la plus orgueilleuse." The theme had been a favorite one of La Bruyère and La Rochefoucauld, though they had dwelt chiefly upon the ubiquity of individual rather than racial pride; and the numerous series of seventeenth- and eighteenth-century "satires against man" find in the pride of man his crowning absurdity.

40. *Nature and Origin of Evil* (1757), 124–126.
41. *Ibid.*, 137.
42. *Ibid.*, 165–167. The argument is criticized by Dr. Johnson in his review of Jenyns's book, 1757.
43. R. Shepherd, *Letters to Soame Jenyns, Esq.* (1768), 14.
44. *Essay on Man*, IV, ll. 49 ff.
45. *Théodicée*, 246.
46. Note to King's *Origin of Evil*, 1732 ed., 156.
47. *A Free Inquiry into the Nature and Origin of Evil* (1757).
48. Richardson's *Pamela;* Everyman's Library ed., I, 235. Whether Richardson composed or quoted the lines is not clear.

## NOTES TO LECTURE VII

1. See, for an example, the writer's paper "Rousseau's Pessimist," *Mod. Lang. Notes*, XXXVIII (1923), 449; and for an earlier one, Prior's *Solomon* (1718), a poetical elaboration of the thesis that "the pleasures of life do not compensate our miseries; age steals upon us unawares; and death, as the only cure of our ills, ought to be expected, not feared."
2. *A Free Inquiry into the Nature and Origin of Evil* (1757), 60–62. Jenyns for the most part merely puts into clear and concise form the arguments of King, Leibniz, and Pope; but he differs from these in unequivocally and emphatically rejecting the freedomist solution of the problem of moral evil. His book had a considerable vogue, went into numerous editions, and was translated into French.
3. *Ibid.*, 104, where the curious reader may, if he will, find why this option was "necessary," and how "Infinite Wisdom" made the best of it.
4. Voltaire, however, is arguing in the poem against two distinct and essentially opposed types of theodicy: the philosophical and necessitarian type, which endeavored to explain such a thing as the Lisbon earthquake as
l'effet des éternelles lois
Qui d'un Dieu libre et bon nécessitent le choix,
and the theological and indeterminist type, which saw in such catastrophes special interpositions of deity in punishment of men's free choice of moral evil. The reasonings aimed at these two opposite objectives Voltaire confusingly runs together.
5. *Ethics*, V, Prop. 6.
6. *An Essay on the Origin of Evil by Dr. William King, translated from the Latin*

*with Notes and a Dissertation concerning the Principle and Criterion of Virtue and the Origin of the Passions; By Edmund Law, M.A., Fellow of Christ College in Cambridge.* I quote from the second edition, Lond., 1732, here referred to as "Essay."

7. The dates are 1731, 1732, 1739, 1758, 1781.

8. Stephen, *English Thought in the 18th Century*, II, 121.

9. Bolingbroke in the *Fragments* quotes King frequently and with respect. I can see no sufficient reason for doubting that in the *Fragments* as printed we have, as Bolingbroke asserted, in a somewhat expanded form "the notes which were communicated to Mr. Pope in scraps, as they were written," and utilized by the latter in writing the *Essay on Man*; the numerous and exact verbal parallels between passages in the *Fragments* and the *Essay* are not susceptible of any other probable explanation (see Bolingbroke's *Works*, 1809 ed., VII, 278, and VIII, 356). Law wrote in the preface to the 1781 edition of the *Essay on the Origin of Evil*: "I had the satisfaction of seeing that those very principles which had been maintained by Archbishop King were adopted by Mr. Pope in the *Essay on Man*." When this was challenged by a brother-bishop, Pope's truculent theological champion Warburton, Law replied by referring to the testimony of Lord Bathurst, "who saw the very same system in Lord Bolingbroke's own hand, lying before Mr. Pope while he composed his *Essay*"; and added: "The point may also be cleared effectually whenever any reader shall think it worth his while to compare the two pieces together, and observe how exactly they tally with one another" (*op. cit.*, p. xvii). Such a comparison seems to me to give reason to believe that Pope made use of King's work directly, as well as of Bolingbroke's adaptation of a part of it. Since it was in 1730 that Pope and Bolingbroke were "deep in metaphysics," and since by 1731 the first three Epistles seem to have been completed (cf. Courthope, V, 242), it must have been from the Latin original, not Law's translation, that the poet and his philosophic mentor drew. Thus essentially the same theodicy appeared almost simultaneously in Law's English prose rendering and in Pope's verse. On the relation of King's work to Haller's *Ueber den Ursprung des Uebels* (1734) cf. L. M. Price in *Publications of the Modern Language Assoc. of America*, XLI (1926), 945–948.

10. *Essay*, I, 208.

11. *Ibid.*, 109–113.

12. *Ibid.*, xix. This argument remained as the usual starting point of a numerous series of subsequent theodicies, some of which have a place in literature: e. g., Victor Hugo still thought it needful to devote a number of lines to the exposition of it in *Les Contemplations* ("Ce que dit la Bouche d'Ombre," 1905 ed., 417 ff.).

13. See the patristic authorities cited by Sumner in his tr. of Milton's *Christian Doctrine*, 187, n. 4. The view adopted by Milton, however, was of dubious orthodoxy. It had been rejected by Thomas Aquinas, *Summa Theol.*, I, q. 61, a.3; and by Dante, *Paradiso*, XXIX, 37.

14. King, *op. cit.*, I, 116 f. For the same conception of the Scale of Being and

its necessary completeness in a well-ordered universe, cf. Bolingbroke, *Fragments* (*Works*, 1809, VIII, 173, 183, 186, 192, 218 f., 232, 363, 364–365).

15. *Op. cit.*, 137 f., 129–131 f., 156. Both King and Law fell into curious waverings, and in the end into self-contradiction, when the question was raised whether the number of degrees in the scale of being is actually infinite. Into this it is unnecessary to enter here.

16. *Essay*, I, 131. The argument may already be found in Plotinus, *Enn.*, III, 2, 11.

17. *Op. cit.*, 137.

18. For the same argument in Bolingbroke, see *Fragments* (*Works*, 1809, VIII, 233, 287, 363, 364–365).

19. *Essay on Man*, Ep. I, ll. 48, 193–194, 241–244. For an example of the diffusion of this argument into writings dealing with the most various subjects, cf. George Turnbull's *A Treatise on Ancient Painting* (London, 1740), xiii: "If any one thinks meanly of our Frame and Rank, let him seriously consider the Riches and Fullness that appears in Nature as far as we can extend our Enquiries; and how every Being in the Scale of Life within our Observation rises in due degree: Let him then consider how necessary the Existence of such a Species as Man is to the ascending Plenitude of Nature; to its *Fullness and Coherence*; and let him impartially examine our Constitution, and the Provision made for our Happiness; the Excellence to which our natural Powers and Dispositions may be improved and raised by good Education and proper Diligence; or the Dignity and Felicity to which we may attain by the Study of Wisdom and Virtue, especially in well-regulated Society; for he will plainly see, that though there be good reason to think that there are various Orders of rational Beings in the Scale of Existence, the lowest of which is superiour to Man, yet he is crowned with Glory and Honour, is well placed, and hath a very considerable Dominion allotted to him."

20. *Essay*, I, 147–149; cf. *Essay on Man*, I, ll. 169–170
   But all subsists by elemental strife,
   And passions are the elements of life.

21. *Essay*, I, 134.

22. *Ibid.*, I, 176. The argument for the necessity of natural evils based upon the principle of plenitude is supplemented by that drawn from the indispensability of uniform general laws; e. g., I, 150–153, 196–197; cf. *Essay on Man*, I, ll. 145 ff.

23. *Essay*, I, 183–185.

24. J. Clarke, *Discourse concerning Natural Evil* (1719); the same argument in Plotinus, *Enn.*, III, 2, 15. Goldsmith, among others, was still repeating it later in the eighteenth century; *v.* his *Essays* (1767), 132, and an essay of 1760 reprinted in Crane's *New Essays by Oliver Goldsmith*, 34. The most elaborate exposition of it with which I am acquainted is *A Philosophical Survey of the Animal Creation, wherein The general Devastation and Carnage that reign among the different Classes of Animals are considered in a new Point of View; and the vast Increase of Life and Enjoyment derived to the Whole*

*from this Institution of Nature is clearly demonstrated    Translated from the French*, Dublin, 1770.

25. It is only fair to add that King is equally ready to view as "necessary," and consequently to approve and justify, specific evils less remote from archiepiscopal experience, such as "gout, one of the most tormenting diseases that attend us" — by which, in fact, this resolute optimist was cruelly harassed for nearly half a century, and from an attack of which, according to his biographer, he died (see Sir C. S. King's life of William King, 1906, 14 and *passim*). Gout, the archbishop observes, in a sportsmanlike if not wholly edifying vein, has compensations which, on the whole, outweigh its pains: "Who would not rather endure it than lose the pleasure of feeling? Most men are sensible that eating certain meats, and indulging ourselves in the use of several drinks, will bring it; and yet we see this doth not deter us from them, and we think it more tolerable to endure the gout, than lose the pleasure that plentiful eating and drinking yields us" (I, 177). Why it was "necessary" *a priori* that these pleasures should be purchasable only at that price remains, in the end, somewhat obscure.

26. *Essay*, I, 176; cf. also 148–149. Soame Jenyns struggles with the same difficulty in the preface to *A Free Inquiry*, etc., in *Works* (1790), II, 6: against the argument "but one material objection has been urged; which is this, that, in order to make room for this necessity of evil, the real existence of a paradisaical state is represented as at all times impossible; and consequently the Mosaic account of that state is utterly exploded." Jenyns's reply consists, first, in intimating some doubt whether "a literal belief in that account is essential to the true faith of a Christian"; and, second, in maintaining that the Mosaic history does not offer a description of a "primitive state of absolute perfection, void of all evil," since "the parent of all evil is one of the principal characters of that history." Jenyns elsewhere rejects the whole primitivistic assumption on the ground that it is inconsistent with the doctrine of the eternal necessity of all the evils we know. "That man came perfect, that is, endued with all possible perfections, out of the hands of his Creator, is a false notion," possible only to men who were ignorant of the origin of evil, i. e., who did not understand that "in the scale of beings there must be," at all times, "such a creature as man, with all his infirmities about him" (*ibid.*, p. 71).

27. *Fragments or Minutes of Essays*, § XVI.

28. *Ethics*, I, *ad. fin.*

29. There is no question of any influence of King upon Leibniz or of Leibniz upon King. Though the *Théodicée* was not published until 1710, eight years after the *De origine mali*, the greater part of it was written between 1697 and the beginning of 1705; and the ideas it contains had long been familiar to Leibniz. Cf. Gerhardt's preface to Leibniz's *Philosophische Schriften*, VI, 3–10.

30. "Remarques sur le livre sur l'origine du mal publié depuis peu en Angleterre," appended to the *Théodicée*, *Philos. Schriften*, VI, 400 ff.

Leibniz observes that he is in agreement with King "only in respect to half of the subject"; the disagreement relates chiefly to King's chapter on liberty and necessity, which (quite inconsistently with the implications of his argument for optimism) asserts that God exercised a *liberum arbitrium indifferentiae* in creating the world.

3      *Théodicée*, § 124.

32. *Ibid.*, § 118; cf. the remark of Thomas Aquinas, quoted in Lecture III, about the value of two angels as compared with that of one angel and one stone. Kant was still enunciating the same principle, varying only the illustration, in 1755: lice "may in our eyes be as worthless as you like, nevertheless it is of more consequence to Nature to conserve this species as a whole than to conserve a small number of members of a superior species" (*Allg. Naturgesch.*, 127).

33. *Théodicée*, §§ 120, 10, 124; cf. also § 213.

34. For this sequel, see Lect. X.

## NOTES TO LECTURE VIII

1. Several of the topics of this and the following lecture have been interestingly dealt with in an article by A. Thienemann, "Die Stufenfolge der Dinge, der Versuch eines natürlichen Systems der Naturkörper aus dem achtzehnten Jahrhundert," in *Zoologische Annalen*, III (1910), 185–275. It includes the text of a previously unpublished and anonymous German writing of 1780, "Entwurf einer nach der mutmasslichen Stufen-Folge eingerichteten allgemeinen Naturgeschichte," in which the mineralogy, botany, zoology, and theology of the period are employed in the construction of a detailed Scale of Nature from the "element earth" to the Trinity.

2. *Op. cit.*, III, Ch. 6, §§ 3, 6. "By this real essence I mean that real constitution of any thing, which is the foundation of all those properties that are combined in, and are constantly found to coexist with, the nominal essence; and that particular constitution which everything has within itself, without any relation to anything without it. . . . As to the real essences of substances, we only suppose their being, without precisely knowing what they are; but that which annexes them still to the species, is the nominal essence, of which they are the supposed foundation and cause" (§ 6). The passage is one of those which bring out the fact about Locke which the historians of philosophy have in great part missed — that in his epistemology he was essentially a Platonist. In the case of material things, however, Locke confuses the logical distinction between the necessary and the merely contingent coinherence of attributes with the metaphysical distinction of primary and secondary qualities and the physical distinction of perceptible gross matter and the insensible minute components of matter (*Ibid.*, § 2).

3. *Ibid.*, § 20.

4. *Ibid.*, §§ 38, 27.

5. *Ibid.*, § 27.
6. *Ibid.*, § 36.
7. *Histoire naturelle*, I (1749), 12, 13, 20, 38.
8. *Ibid.*, XIII (1765), 1.
9. Of the sterility of hybrids Buffon now writes: "This point is the most fixed which we possess in natural history. All the other resemblances and differences which we can observe in comparing beings with one another are neither so real nor so certain; these intervals, therefore, are the only lines of demarcation which will be found in our work." *Hist. nat.*, XIII, *loc. cit.*
10. *Contemplation de la Nature* (2d ed., 1769), I, 28.
11. From Goldsmith's review of R. Brookes, *A New and Accurate System of Natural History*, in *The Monthly Review*, XXIX (October, 1763), 283–284.
12. Thomas Sprat, *The History of the Royal Society* (1667), 110.
13. *Encyclopédie*, art. "Cosmologie."
14. Sander, *Ueber Natur und Religion* (1779), II, 193, cited in Thienemann, *op. cit.*, 235.
15. Günther, *Die Wissenschaft vom Menschen im achtzehnten Jahrhundert*, 30.
16. Published by Lönnberg in his *Carl von Linnée und die Lehre von der Wirbeltieren*, 1909. For my acquaintance with this I am indebted to Thienemann, *op. cit.*, 227. The use of the expression "relations of man" cannot with certainty be taken as an assertion of identity of descent, but that is the most natural meaning of Linnaeus's language.
17. *The Lay Monastery*, by Blackmore and Hughes (2d ed. of *The Lay Monk*) (1714), 28. Cf. the remark of Sir John Ovington, *Voyage to Surat* (1696), cited by R. W. Frantz in *Modern Philology* (1931), 55–57: the Hottentots are "the very Reverse of Human kind, . . . so that if there's any medium between a Rational Animal and a Beast, the Hottentot lays the fairest claim to that species." Sir William Petty had still earlier remarked, in treating of the "Scale of Creatures," that "of man itself there seems to bee severall species," and refers to the "Negros who live about the Cape of Good Hope as the most beastlike of all the Sorts of Men with whom our travellers are well acquainted" (*The Petty Papers*, 1927, II, 31). Soame Jenyns in the middle of the century also cites, among the evidences of the continuity of the chain of beings, the way in which the attribute of reason "in the dog, the monkey and the chimpanzè unites so closely with the lowest degree of that quality in man" — exemplified here also by "the brutal Hottentot" — "that they cannot easily be distinguished one from another."
18. Cf. the writer's "The Supposed Primitivism of Rousseau's Discourse on Inequality," *Modern Philology* (1923), and "Monboddo and Rousseau," *ibid.* (1933); Rousseau, *Second Disc.*, note j; Monboddo, *Origin and Progress of Language*, 2d ed., I (1774), 269 ff.
19. *Contemplation de la Nature*, III, ch. 30. As the passage was added as a footnote to the edition of 1781, Bonnet may have been reading Rousseau or Monboddo; the latter had ascribed similar mental and moral qualities to the orang-outang.

20. Écouchard-Le Brun, *De la Nature, chant troisième*. The *homme des bois* was, of course, the orang-outang, this being the accepted translation of his Malayan name. Fusil in his *La poésie scientifique* sees in these lines an expression of "the great law of change and evolution"; here "for the first time poetry attempts to sing the epic of life as modern science conceives it." But, as is so often the case in writings of the period, it is impossible to be sure whether the poet is speaking of a temporal sequence of stages of evolution or merely of the consecutive "steps," i. e., grades, in the Scale of Beings; the latter seems here the more probable. Even if the French poet be credited with the former conception, he had been anticipated by Akenside (*v.* below, Lect. IX).

21. M. R. Werner, *Barnum* (1923), 59.

22. Cf. Dobell, *Antony van Leeuwenhoek and his 'Little Animals'* (1932); P. de Kruif, *The Microbe Hunters* (1926); S. Wood, "Leeuwenhoek and his 'Little Beasties,'" *Quarterly Rev.* (1933).

23. *Experimental Philosophy, in Three Books. . . .* By Henry Power, D. of Physick. London, 1664. I am indebted for this passage to Dr. Marjorie Nicolson of Smith College, whose comprehensive study of this phase of the history of science and of its repercussions in literature will, it is to be hoped, soon become available to all students of these subjects. An earlier foreshadowing of microscopic discoveries not yet made, in all the "three kingdoms of the universal spirit (the Vegetable, Animal and Mineral)," is to be found in T. Mayerne's preface to *The Theater of Insects or Lesser Living Creatures* by Thos. Moufett, 1634. The creatures not visible to the naked eye "all testifie the infinite Power of the Supreme Creator of all things." Cf. also Pascal on the infinitely little, *Pensées*, 72.

24. *Troisième soir*. The argument was repeated by King, *Origin of Evil*, I, 157.

25. It is, of course, beyond the scope of this history to deal with the relation of all this to the modern beginning, or renewal, and development of the germ-theory of disease. (It had been suggested in antiquity as an explanation of malaria by Varro, *De re rustica*, I, 12, 2.) But it is of some relevance to note that the theory was propounded by Sir William Petty in 1677 to explain the manner of diffusion of the plague: "There is no better hypothesis whereby to make out the destructions of so many thousand men in a season by the disease called the plague, than by imagining the same to be done by Millions of invisible Animals, that travell from Country to Country, even out of Africa into England" (*The Petty Papers*, II, 29). To such a hypothesis Petty was naturally predisposed by his belief in the fullness of the "chain of creatures."

26. *Loc. cit.*

27. A number of other passages in the same strain may be found in later eighteenth-century writings: e. g., Henry Baker, *The Microscope Made Easy . . .* (1742), pp. 306–309 (partly borrowed from Addison and Locke) and his *Employment for the Microscope* (1753); *An Account of Some New Microscopical Discoveries . . .* (1745) (? by John Turberville Needham); George Adams, *Micrographia Illustrata . . .*, 2d ed. (1747); John

Hill, *Essays in Natural History and Philosophy. Containing a Series of Discoveries by the Assistance of Microscopes* (1752); and *Essays on the Microscope* (1798), by the younger George Adams. To these also my attention has been called by Dr. Nicolson.

28. *The Seasons: Summer* (1727).
29. *Kr. d. r. V.*, A. 654–668.


## NOTES TO LECTURE IX

1. John Clarke, *A Defence of Dr.* [Samuel] *Clarke's Demonstration of the Being and Attributes of God* (1722), 56.
2. Joseph Clarke, *A Further Examination of Dr. Clarke's Notions of Space*, etc. (1734), 166.
3. Pluche, *Histoire du Ciel* (1759 ed.), II, 391–392.
4. *Three Physico-Theological Discourses* (3d ed., 1713), 149. Ray adds that this philosophical opinion is supported by Scripture: "That it is so, appears, in that it (Providence) was so careful to lodge all Land-Animals in the Ark at the Time of the General Deluge."
5. *The Universal Beauty*, III, 98 ff.
6. *The Immortality of the Soul*, II, chap. 17, 7; cf. also III, chap. 1, 3, 5.
7. *Spectator*, No. 111, July 7, 1711.
8. *Philosophische Schriften*, ed. Gerhardt, VI, 606.
9. *An Essay on the Origin of Evil* (1732 ed.), 121–122. On the same conception in Law's later *Considerations on the State of the World*, etc. (1745), cf. R. S. Crane's "Anglican Apologetics and the Idea of Progress," *Mod. Philology*, XXI (1934), 349 ff.
10. The English is that of the 1713 version of Toland.
11. *Philos. Schriften*, VII, 309. Cf. also the passages of Law's last cited.
12. *In einem unauflöslichen unendlich feinen Bande.*
13. *Versuch über das erste Prinzipium der Moral* (1772).
14. *Dict. philos.*, 1st ed. (1764), art. *Chaîne des êtres créés.*
15. Voltaire raises the same objections more briefly in a note to his *Poem on the Lisbon Disaster*, 1755, in which he partly confuses — as Pope had done before him — the conception of the chain of causality (*chaîne des évènements*) with the chain of beings. But with respect to the latter he observes, in his note of 1756:
    "The chain is not an absolute plenum. It is demonstrated that the heavenly bodies perform their revolutions in a non-resistant space. Not all space is filled. There is not, therefore, a series (*suite*) of bodies from an atom to the most remote of the stars; there can therefore be immense intervals between sensible beings, as well as between insensible ones. We cannot, then, be sure that man is necessarily placed in one of the links which are attached one to another in an unbroken sequence."
16. *Il faut prendre un parti*, ch. IV.
17. *A Review of a Free Inquiry into the Nature and Origin of Evil* (i. e., of Soame Jenyns's book), 1757. The review originally appeared in *The Literary*

*Magazine*, and was reprinted in pamphlet form, n.p., n.d. Johnson was apparently ignorant of the history of the conception of the Chain of Being; he refers to it as "The Arabian Scale of Existence."

18. *Ibid.*

19. *Nouveaux Essais*, III, vi, § 12: "Qu'il y ait des créatures mitoyennes entre celles qui sont éloignées, c'est quelque chose de conforme à cette même harmonie, quoyque ce ne soit pas tousjours dans un même globe ou système." *Philos. Schriften*, V, 286.

20. *Oeuvres de Maupertuis*, I (1752), 35–36.

21. The adoption by Leibniz of transformism "in a rudimentary form" is recognized by E. Rádl, *Geschichte der biologischen Theorien seit dem Ende des 17ten Jahrhunderts*, I, 72, by Buchenau and Cassirer, *Leibniz: Hauptschriften zur Grundlegung der Philosophie*, II (1906), 26, and by Thienemann, *Zool. Annalen*, III, 187.

22. *Op. cit.*, 1749 ed., p. 41: "credibile est per magnas illas mutationes etiam animalium species plurimum immutatas."

23. Cited by Rádl, *Geschichte der biologischen Theorien*, I, 71. Here, however, Leibniz still admits the possibility of "natural species," but insists that our determination of them can be "only provisional and in correspondence with our [limited] knowledge." Nevertheless, the number of such species was obviously vastly reduced, and the descent of most forms commonly regarded as of different species from common ancestors differing very greatly from most of their descendants is implied.

24. *Miscellanea Berolinensia*, I, 1710, 111–112.

25. Letter to Bourget (1715), *Philos. Schriften*, III, 593.

26. *Ibid.*, III, 582.

27. *De rerum originatione radicali* (1697), in *Philos. Schriften*, VII, 308.

"In cumulum etiam pulchritudinis perfectionisque universalis operum divinorum, progressus quidam perpetuus liberrimusque totius Universi est agnoscendus, ita ut ad majorem semper cultum procedat, quemadmodum nunc magna pars terrae nostrae cultum recepit et recipiet magis magisque. . . . Et quod objici posset: ita oportere ut Mundus dudum factus fuerit Paradisus, responsio praesto est: etsi multae jam substantiae ad magnam perfectionem pervenerint, ob divisibilitatem continui in infinitum, semper in abysso rerum superesse partes sopitas adhuc excitandas et ad majus meliusque et, ut verbo dicam, ad meliorem cultum provehendas. Nec proinde unquam ad terminum progressus perveniri."

This had already been more briefly said by Leibniz in a letter to the Electress Sophia (Nov. 4, 1696): "Since there is nothing outside the universe which could prevent it from doing so, it must necessarily be the case that the universe develops and advances continually" (*Werke*, ed. Kopp, 1873, VIII, 16). It must be added that there are other passages in Leibniz which it is difficult, if not impossible, to reconcile with these, and that his views on the matter were probably not unwavering. Cf. *Philos. Schriften*, IV, 344, and *Nouveaux Essais*, III, iv. For recent discussions of the evolutionism of Leibniz cf. L. Davilé, *Leibniz historien*

(1909); K. Ufermann, *Untersuchungen über das Gesetz der Kontinutät bei Leibniz* (1927), 75–92; A. Fischer, '*Sein*' *und* '*Geschehen*' *bei Leibniz* (1929), 132 ff.

28. Draft of letter to Arnauld of Nov. 28–Dec. 8, 1686, *Philos. Schriften*, II, 75; tr. in Montgomery, *Leibniz: Disc. on Metaphysics*, etc., 155.

29. *Philos. Schriften*, III, 579.

30. *Monadology*, § 74.

31. *Ibid.*, 75.

32. *Philos. Schriften*, VI, 152.

33. *Werke*, ed. Kopp, VIII, 15–16.

34. Cf. Letter to Arnauld, Apr. 30, 1687, *Philos. Schriften*, II, 99 f.; tr. in Montgomery, *op. cit.*, 195.

35. *Werke*, ed. Kopp, *op. cit.*

36. From a previously unpublished fragment cited by J. Baruzzi, *Leibniz* (1909), 296.

37. A somewhat analogous temporalizing of Spinoza's metaphysics — which, as we have seen, is, with respect to the principles of sufficient reason and plenitude, not essentially different from that of Leibniz — has recently been attempted by S. Alexander in his *Spinoza and Time*. But this is admittedly a reconstruction of Spinoza's doctrine, whereas Leibniz reconstructed his own.

38. *Night Thoughts*: Night the Ninth.

39. R. D. Havens, *The Influence of Milton in the English Poetry of the Eighteenth Century*, 386.

40. *Pleasures of Imagination*, 1st ed., Bk. I, 1744.

41. *Ibid.*, Bk. II.

42. Akenside's approximation to evolutionism has already been pointed out by G. R. Potter, "Mark Akenside, Prophet of Evolution," *Modern Philology*, XXIV (1926), 55–64.

43. *Pleasures of the Imagination*, 2d ed., Bk. II, 1765.

44. *Allgemeine Naturgeschichte*, 1755, 4th ed., 7.

45. *Ibid.*, 87.

46. *Ibid.*, 23.

47. *Ibid.*, 82.

48. *Ibid.*, 84.

49. *Ibid.*, 87–88.

50. *Ibid.*, 90–91. Kant in one passage (p. 91) seems inconsistently to suggest that this law of alternate cycles of evolution and dissolution applies also to the entire cosmical system: "the time will finally come when even the great system of which the fixed stars are the members will similarly, through the cessation of its motions, collapse into chaos." But it is probable that he is referring to the fixed stars that already exist and are visible to us; before the systems which these compose reach their term, at the further limits of the creation, in the region occupied by unformed matter, "Nature with a continuous advance proceeds to extend further the plan of the revelation of deity and to fill eternity, as well as all space, with its wonders" (*ibid.*).

51. On these cf. the writer's "Some Eighteenth Century Evolutionists," *Popular Science Monthly*, 1904, 238 ff. and 323 ff.

52. *Op. cit.*, Pt. I, ch. 6. For a similar passage, cf. Delisle de Sales, *Philosophie de la Nature*, 3d ed., 1777, I, 215: it is reasonable to suppose that nature has *parcouru successivement tous les degrés de la grande échelle*.

53. Of the *De la Nature*, vol. I appeared in 1761; II in 1763; III and IV in 1766 with new editions of the first two volumes. A fifth volume was added in 1768, more generally cited by its sub-title: *Vue philosophique de la gradation naturelle des formes de l'être, Les Essais de la Nature qui apprend à faire l'homme*. A slight work, *Parallèle de la condition et des facultés de l'homme avec la condition et les facultés des autres animaux*, was published in 1770 as a translation from the English; if it has an English original, I am unacquainted with it.

54. *De la Nature*, III, 182.

55. *Ibid.*, 183.

56. *Ibid.*, 183–184.

57. *Essay concerning Human Understanding*, III, ch. 6, § 12. The first great modern book of descriptive natural history, Gesner's *Historia animalium* (1551–1587), in its fourth volume (in the German tr., *Fischbuch* (1598), 104 ff.) had included *homo marinus* among the recognized denizens of the deep, upon the testimony of trustworthy observers, and had presented woodcuts of these creatures, including an *episcopus marinus*; and the belief in them, supported as it seemed to be both by the principle of plenitude and the supposed testimony of many witnesses, could claim a certain respectability down to the late eighteenth century. Cf. De Maillet, *Telliamed*, 1748, Eng. tr., 1750, 230–244; Delisle de Sales, *Philos. de la Nature*, 3d ed., 1777, I.

58. *Origin and Progress of Language*, 2d ed., I, 269. This, as we have seen, was a misinterpretation of Aristotle.

59. *Op. cit.*, I, 25.

60. *Ibid.*

61. *Ibid.*

62. *Ibid.* It will be observed that for Robinet "perfectibility" does not entail solely improvement. He held at this time the doctrine, which much of his first volume is devoted to expounding, that every good is attended by its complementary evil, and that the sum of goods and of evils is therefore equal and constant.

63. *De la Nature*, III, 142–143.

64. *Pensées sur l'interprétation de la Nature*, § LVIII.

65. *De la Nature*, V, 148.

66. *Ibid.*, IV, 1–2.

67. *Ibid.*, 4–5.

68. I proposed this term, which seems to be a needed addition to the philosophical vocabulary, at the *Sixth International Congress of Philosophy*; see *Journal of Philosophical Studies*, II (1927).

69. *Ibid.*, IV, 11–12. In this, and again "in including among the animals the fossils, the semi-metals, air, fire," etc., Robinet has, he grants (or

boasts) "ventured farther than any naturalist who has preceded" him; but he reiterates, quite justly, that in doing so he is but following out the same principles as the others. "Ils ont établi les premisses dont j'ai tiré la conséquence qui semble si surprenante; et de quoi pourrait-on me blâmer, si elle est légitimement déduite?" (*ibid.*, IV, 211).

70. *Ibid.*, IV, 17.

71. Cf., e. g., IV, 78–79.

72. *Pensées sur l'interprétation de la Nature*, § XII.

73. *De la Nature*, IV, 17–18.

74. *Ibid.*, V, 6.

75. *Ideen zu einer Philosophie der Geschichte der Menschheit*, 1784–1791, Bk. V, chap. 1. Herder, however, finds the identity of fundamental form only in the animal kingdom. The same chapter is full of the idea of the Chain of Being as an "ascending series of forms."

76. From the poem Αθροισμος (1819). For Goethe's elaboration of the conception cf. his *Versuch über die Gestalt der Tiere* (1790) and *Erster Entwurf einer allgemeinen Einleitung in die vergleichende Anatomie* (1795). In the latter work, for example, Goethe insists upon the all-importance for the zoologist of recognizing "eine allgemeine Bilde, worin die Gestalten sämtlicher Tiere, die Möglichkeit nach, enthalten wären, und wonach man jedes Tier in einer gewissen Ordnung beschriebe . . . Schon aus der allgemeinen Idee eines Typus folgt, dass kein einzelnes Tier, als ein solcher Vergleichungsform ausgestellt werden könne: kein Einzelnes kann Muster des Ganzen sein . . . Betrachten wir nach jenem, erst im allgemeinsten aufgestellten Typus die verschiedenen Teile der vollkommensten, die wir Säugetiere nennen, so finden wir, dass der Bildungskreis der Natur zwar eingeschränkt ist dabei, jedoch, wegen der Menge der Teile und wegen der vielfachen Modificabilität, die Veränderungen der Gestalt in's Unendliche möglich werden." Goethe's excitement over the discovery of this idea, during his Italian journey, may be seen in his letter to Frau von Stein, July 10, 1786: he wishes that he could "impart to everyone" his "vision" and his joy, but it is impossible. And it is no dream, no phantasy. "It is a discovery of the essential form with which Nature always plays, and in playing brings forth all the manifoldness of life. Had I time in the short span of a single life, I would devote myself to extending it to all the kingdoms of Nature — to her entire domain." Cf. Elisabeth Rotten, *Goethes Urphänomen und die Platonische Idee*, 1913.

77. This conception of the "fumbling" advance of nature is probably also derivative from Diderot's *Pensées sur l'interprétation de la Nature*, §§ XII, XXXVII.

78. *Op. cit.*, V (1768).

79. E. g., vol. IV, Planche iv.

80. Cf. the writer's *Bergson and Romantic Evolutionism*, 1914.

81. *Vue philosophique de la gradation naturelle des formes de l'être* (1768), 8–10.

82. *Ibid.*, 12. Elsewhere Robinet slightly amplifies this last intimation: "Enfin elle [la force active] se dématérialiserait entièrement, si j'ose ainsi m'ex-

*primer, et pour dernière métamorphose elle se transformerait en pure intelligence.*"
However, he adds, this is but "a bold conjecture, which he gives only
for what it is worth." This idea was adopted by Lord Monboddo in his
*Antient Metaphysics* (1779–99), and it is not altogether without parallel
in the philosophy of Bergson; cf. the conclusion of chap. III of *L'Évolution créatrice.*

83. *Palingénésie*, I, 22.
84. *Ibid.*, I, 212.
85. *Ibid.*, I, 89.
86. *Ibid.*, I, 216.
87. *Ibid.*, I, 158.
88. *Ibid.*, I, 174. Bonnet thinks it possible that there is no limit to the "perfectibility" of any animal whatever: "it may be that there will be a continual, more or less slow progress of all species towards a higher perfection; so that all the grades of the scale will be continuously variable in a determinate and constant ratio: I mean that the *mutability* of each grade will always have its reason in the grade which immediately precedes it" (*ibid.*).

## NOTES TO LECTURE X

1. *Éléments de la Phil. de Newton*, I, ch. 6.
2. *Tusc. Disp.*, I, 30: "omni in re consensio omnium gentium lex naturae putanda est."
3. *Justiniani Institutiones*, I, 2, 11. Cf. *id.*, § 1: "Quod naturalis ratio inter omnes homines constituit, id apud omnes populos peraeque custoditur, vocatur jus gentium, quasi *quo jure omnes gentes utuntur.*" In the same article *jus gentium* and the *human* "law of nature" are expressly used as synonyms.
4. *Fragments, or Minutes of Essays*, xvi, in *Works*, 1809, VII, 468.
5. *De Sublimitate*, § VII; tr. by W. Smith, 1770. I have thought it more pertinent here to cite an eighteenth-century version, but add Professor Rhys Roberts' more literal rendering of the last sentence: "When men of different pursuits, lives, ambitions, ages, languages, hold identical views on one and the same subject, then that verdict which results, so to speak, from a concert of discordant elements makes our faith in the object of admiration strong and unassailable" (*Longinus on the Sublime*, 1899, p. 57). Longinus, says a typical (because commonplace) writer of the middle of the century, "might with equal justice have extended the same criterion to all the inferior excellencies of elegant composition." W. Melmoth, the younger, *Fitzosborne's Letters* (1746), 130.
6. Mr. Saintsbury has, I think, stopped just short of the main point, when, *à propos* of the *Essay on Criticism*, he writes: "What [Pope] meant by 'following nature' and what *we* mean by it, are two quite different things. He, usually at least, means 'stick to the usual, the ordinary, the commonplace'" (*Hist. of Criticism*, II (1902), 456). This is true; but Pope

enjoins "sticking to the usual" only because the poet cannot otherwise expect to reach all mankind.

7. *Lives of the Poets*: Life of Dryden; ed. G. B. Hill, I, 433.

8. "The poet does not number the streaks of the tulip, or describe the different shades in the verdure of the forest; he is to exhibit in his portraits of nature such prominent and striking features as recall the original to every mind; and must neglect the minuter discriminations, which one may have remarked and another have neglected, for those characteristics which are alike obvious to vigilance and carelessness."

9. W. Melmoth, *Fitzosborne's Letters*, 130.

10. Lucas de la Haye, *La vie de M. Benoît de Spinoza*; cited by Brunschvicg, *Spinoza et ses contemporains*, 333.

11. A part of Milton's *Areopagitica* is the most remarkable seventeenth-century exception to this universalism.

12. For numerous examples of this, cf. R. Bray, *La Formation de la doctrine classique en France*, 1927, Pt. II, chapters iv–vi.

13. Formey, "Essay on the Scale of Beings" in *Philosophical Miscellanies*, 1757, the English translation of his *Mélanges philosophiques*, 1754.

14. *Disc. sur la métaphysique*, IX.

15. *Monadology*, §§ 57–58; *Philos. Schriften*, VI, 616.

16. *Spectator*, 519, Oct. 25, 1712. I repeat the citation here because of its close similarity even in expression to that of Schiller given below (n. 19).

17. From the unfinished Fourth Part of *The Pleasures of Imagination*, 1770.

18. P. Reiff in *Euphorion* (1912), 591 ff. In a letter to F. Schlegel in 1798 Novalis wrote: "I do not know if I have already spoken to you of my beloved Plotinus. Through Tiedemann I have been initiated into this philosopher, born expressly for me, and I have been almost frightened by his resemblance to Kant and Fichte. He pleases me more than either of them" (cited in Spenlé, *Novalis*, 188 ff., where the nature of the Plotinian influence upon that writer is analyzed).

19. *Op. cit.*, Cotta ed., XII, 189, 188. The *Letters* were first published in 1786 and (the last) 1789; but the *Theosophie des Julius*, from which most of the citations here are taken, was certainly in part, and probably as a whole, written in 1781 or 1782. On the dates and probable sources of the *Philosophische Briefe*, cf. Ueberweg, *Schiller als Historiker und als Philosoph* (1884), 72–96; and on the significance of this early work for the understanding of Schiller's philosophical biography, *v.* J. Goebel in *Jour. of English and Germanic Philology*, XXIII (1924), 161–172. That Schiller was at this time acquainted with the works of Leibniz at first hand appears improbable; but, as a pupil in the Karlsschule, he had early become familiar with the general principles of the Leibnitio-Wolffian system. On this cf. W. Iffert, *Der junge Schiller* (1926), 34–57.

20. *Philosophische Briefe*, last letter; *ibid.*, 193.

21. Cf. Ueberweg, *op. cit.*, 88.

22. *Briefe über die aesthetische Erziehung*, Letter XI.

23. Letter XV.

24. Letter XIII; italics mine.

25. Letter XVIII.
26. Letter XVI.
27. *Gespräch über die Poesie*, 1800.
28. A. E. Lussky, *Tieck's Romantic Irony* (1932), 78, 68–69.
29. *Ueber die Philosophie: an Dorothea*; in *Athenaeum*, II, 1, 15–16.
30. *Herzensergiessungen*, 1797.
31. *Vorlesungen über dramatische Kunst und Literatur*, 1809; in *Sämmtl. Werke*, V, 5, 15–16.
32. *Fragmente* (1798), in *Athenaeum*, I, 2, 36.
33. *Athenaeum*, III, 15.
34. Schriften (1837), II, 224–225.
35. *Reden*, II.
36. *Ibid.*
37. *Monologen*, ed. Schiele, 1914, pp. 72–74; some phrases of the translation have been taken from the English edition of H. L. Friess, *Schleiermacher's Soliloquies* (1926), 76–78.
38. *Op. cit.*, ed. Schiele, 77–78.
39. *Monologen*, ed. Schiele, 30–31. Of any incongruity, logical or practical, between the cultivation of catholicity and uniqueness Schleiermacher seems to have been unaware; they were for him two aspects of the same program.
40. *Reden*, V.
41. *Ibid.*

## NOTES TO LECTURE XI

1. *System of Transcendental Idealism* (1800), *SW*, I, Abt. 3, 492; cf. also such formulations of the *Identitätssystem* as the dialogue *Bruno* and the *Further Expositions*, both of 1802. Even in these the distinctive emphasis is upon the second conception.
2. *Op. cit.*, in *Schellings Werke*, herausg. von A. Weiss (1907), III, 499.
3. We have already seen that this was not Leibniz's real position, in spite of passages which seem to justify Schelling's interpretation.
4. *Op. cit.*, in *Schellings Werke*, ed. Weiss, III, 493–494.
5. That the metaphysical evolutionism of Oken implied for him the theory of the transformation of species through natural descent is not clear.
6. *Lehrbuch der Naturphilosophie*, I, 4.
7. *Ibid.*, 22. Here, no doubt, is the original of the Bergsonian *temps-créateur*. I do not, of course, mean by this to imply that M. Bergson directly derived the conception from Oken.
8. *Ibid.*, 26.
9. *Denkmal der Schrift von den göttlichen Dingen*, 1812.
10. *Op. cit.*, *SW*, I, Abt. 8, 64.
11. *Op. cit.*, 81.
12. *Ibid.*, 63.
13. *Ibid.*, *SW*, I, Abt. 8, 70.
14. *Ibid.*, 77.

15. *Op. cit.* (1899), 187–189.
16. *The Religious Aspect of Philosophy* (1885), 248–249.
17. I use the word 'contingent' in its absolute sense, defined by Spinoza: *Res singulares voco contingentes, quatenus, dum ad earum solam essentiam attendimus, nihil invenimus, quod earum existentiam necessario ponat* (*Eth.*, IV, Def. 3).
18. *Science and the Modern World*, 249. There is, it should be observed, a somewhat obscure intimation of the same conception in Schelling's *Denkmal der Schrift von den göttlichen Dingen, ed. cit.*, 65.

# INDEX

# INDEX OF NAMES AND SUBJECTS

(Footnotes which merely give references for statements or quotations in the text are not separately indexed.)